This book has been one of the biggest catalysts in my spi
– Sue LeShien

This book explains in detail how the Creator communicates with me through spirits, angels, animals, nature, and everyday objects and events. On my spiritual path I always wanted to hear God. This book is the best tool I have ever had to help me understand messages from the Creator.
– Donald Paul

Spirit Talk is required reading for anyone seeking to make the most of their life journey. The wealth of information, worksheets, and a symbols dictionary are essential for trying to make sense of it all. When you find a tool like this, you want to share it with the world!
– France Blair

This book is phenomenal. It gives an excellent overview of understanding your dreams and messages from spirit.
– Marjory MacMartin

Thanks to this book, I now understand that I'm not just a body detached from everyone and everything — I am a constantly growing soul connected to all. Understanding and living this truth brings meaning into my life and supports me through life's ups and downs.
– Tina Pane

I now understand nearly all the messages that I receive at night, and I am well on my way to better understanding the symbols, feelings and situations that I experience during the day.
– Dorothy Reynolds

This book is about much more than interpreting dream symbols — it's an essential tool for anyone on their spiritual path.
– Tanja Kisslinger

Spirit Talk has made me more alert to the messages from my unconscious and my spirit guides, and to my deepest needs. The comprehensive glossary is extremely helpful in figuring out how the symbolic messages I receive from daily events, apparent coincidences, and nighttime dreams relate to my current life.
– Kathy Shotten

I can't believe I've been missing so much! I never realized that spirit was communicating to me every day through symbolism. This is turning my world upside down — but all for the better.
– Pat Peterson

Spirit Talk

❁

Understanding Spirits' Messages

Spirit Talk

❁

Understanding Spirits' Messages

by
Kerry Palframan

Balboa Press books may be ordered through booksellers or by contacting:

Balboa Press
A Division of Hay House
1663 Liberty Drive
Bloomington, IN 47403
www.balboapress.com
1-(877) 407-4847

Because of the dynamic nature of the Internet, any web addresses or links contained in this book may have changed since publication and may no longer be valid. The views expressed in this work are solely those of the author and do not necessarily reflect the views of the publisher, and the publisher hereby disclaims any responsibility for them.

The author of this book does not dispense medical advice or prescribe the use of any technique as a form of treatment for physical, emotional, or medical problems without the advice of a physician, either directly or indirectly. The intent of the author is only to offer information of a general nature to help you in your quest for emotional and spiritual well-being. In the event you use any of the information in this book for yourself, which is your constitutional right, the author and the publisher assume no responsibility for your actions.

Any people depicted in stock imagery provided by Thinkstock are models, and such images are being used for illustrative purposes only.
Certain stock imagery © Thinkstock.

ISBN: 978-1-4525-2971-4 (sc)
ISBN: 978-1-4525-2972-1 (e)

Printed in the United States of America

Balboa Press rev. date: 3/16/2011

Edited by: Linda Jenkins, Red Pen Services
Book design and production by: Mary Hunter

For
Franci

Preface to the Second Edition

It has been a decade since I wrote the first edition of this book, *Healing Into Wholeness Through Dreams: A Guide To Self-Mastery*. Since then, my awareness has shifted and changed dramatically.

I began my dream studies in the early 1990s. The most startling revelation that came to me during my early dream studies was that the symbolic information I was receiving in dreams was also being shown to me through signals, signs, coincidences and seeing repetitive objects and numbers throughout the day. This was the awesome beginning of my own expansion of awareness and realization that Creator and spirit helpers surround me all day — as well as at night — with their support, love and guidance.

However, I presented the first edition of this book in the context of dream interpretation because our rational minds already accept that we dream in symbols and it was the only way I could think of to explain the symbolic nature of the messages we receive from Spirit during the day. It has taken me many years to realize that this book is for everyone — not just those who can remember their dreams – because Spirit talks to each of us throughout the day as well as in the dream time.

Over the years, I also realized that to many people the word *symbol* is an intimidating one — they assume that interpreting symbols is very difficult and complicated. Nothing could be further from the truth. Understanding symbols, signals, signs, coincidences, omens and repetitive objects or numbers is especially easy in our North American culture because we are surrounded by marketing symbols and logos. The transition from thinking in literal terms to thinking in symbolic terms is an easy one — everyone in our culture does it all day without even being aware of it. This book will show you how easy it is to translate your messages from Spirit.

Also, the dream interpretation methods outlined in this book will help you gain clarity and understanding of the deeper meaning of events that happen in your life during the day. Similarly, the dictionary section is not just for interpreting symbols in your dreams — use it to help you understand your everyday signs, symbols, coincidences, repetitive objects and numbers, and *anything else* that gets your attention while you're awake. Do not limit the use of this book to the dream time — use it as a reference book for your life and for your journey to enlightenment and self-mastery.

Many Blessings
Kerry Palframan 2010

Contents

Figures

※

Introduction

Dreaming My Way Back to Health

Dreams and dreaming have always been a part of my life. The magic and wonder of dream interpretation found me when my health problems came to a climax at the age of thirty. The story of how my nightly dreams saved my life and brought me back to health is a fascinating journey that I share with you now.

My health began to decline when I was only eight years old, and life continued its slow descent until 1979, when at eighteen I was diagnosed with a brain tumour. At the time I was quite content with the diagnosis and the possibility of my own death because my father had just passed away after a lengthy illness and I expected to follow him.

My father had a very rare immune system disorder and was told by doctors that he had two to five months to live. I was only seven years old at the time and he was forty years old with four children under the age of nine. I was extremely close to my father and not particularly fond of my mother and siblings. My father was my world and when I was told he was going to die it felt as though my whole world fell apart — the proverbial rug was pulled out from under me. I refused to talk or listen to my parents and would run from the room screaming with my hands clamped tightly over my ears anytime they tried to mention his impending death to me. Ironically, I soon developed problems with hearing that required surgery to correct. I clearly did not want to hear the truth of my situation. I was to be left alone in the world by the one person who I felt truly loved and supported me.

My father spent a great deal of time in the hospital. My mother returned to work when he was diagnosed and we (my siblings and I) spent our after-school time in a large downtown Toronto hospital or were dropped off at a nearby park to play while my mother visited — we were not allowed in the ICU. This was my life and my experience for ten years. My father suffered greatly with his illness, but surprised his doctors and surpassed all their expectations. In retrospect, his quality of life could not have been great — but he was alive.

Meanwhile, I became a withdrawn child, and by the age of twelve I noticed I was different from the other children. It is now hard to pinpoint exactly what made me different, but I was very aware of how the other girls were beginning to show signs of puberty and I was not. I remember clearly not wanting to grow up and wanting to remain "daddy's little girl" forever. I did not want breasts or a menstrual period and much preferred being a tom-boy. I later learned that these strong thoughts and beliefs played a role in my underdeveloped body. I never did grow breasts and I never did start my period. By age fourteen I was apathetic and tired all the time. I slept for long periods of time and had headaches constantly. I carried a jumbo bottle of pain tablets in my purse and would eat them dry in my high school classes. I also had dizzy spells and little enthusiasm for life. I began to smoke hashish and marijuana, drink alcohol and generally withdraw from social and school life.

Mercifully, my father passed away a month before my eighteenth birthday. The family had been through hell with his illness and the relief of his death was felt by all. I closed the door on my father's memory that day. I refused to open it or remember him for many years to come. I felt abandoned and alone in the world.

On my eighteenth birthday my mother asked me if I had begun my period yet. Mortified and ashamed beyond bearing, I answered no. Thus began my own health journey — in the very hospital my father had just died in. It started with visits to the gynecologist and within months I had surgery to investigate my reproductive system. It was a humiliating and degrading experience that caused me to further isolate myself from others and from my true feelings. Six months after my father's death I ended up as a patient on the neurosurgical floor of this very familiar hospital — I had been roaming its corridors for the last ten years.

I was diagnosed with a benign brain tumour on my pituitary gland. I had never heard of the thing and really didn't care if the tumour killed me. I had no idea how sick I was. I thought the way I felt was normal for everyone. I thought that everyone felt exhausted all day long and suffered from headaches and dizzy spells. The tests I endured were nasty and I allowed all this poking and prodding of my body to continue while my mind simply wasn't present. I was too ill to be operated on right away and had to wait several months to rebuild my body and blood system. I dropped out of grade thirteen and spent several months at home taking medication and smoking pot with a friend. I was in denial about my illness and that was fine with me.

Surgery was performed and the tumour was removed. Because the tumour had invaded the entire pituitary gland and the area in which it sits, my entire pituitary gland had to be removed. Little did I understand the enormity of this little gland's function at the time, and I was put on a lifetime regime of hormonal replacement medications. My whole life changed with the removal of this "master gland," and although my energy levels improved somewhat, I was soon to start on a descent that would consume my every waking and sleeping moment.

I learned that the pituitary gland is about the size of a pea and sits in the middle of the head. It is an endocrine gland and called the master gland because it controls all the other glands in the body (thyroid, ovary, adrenal). It also plays a role in a host of functions including *all* hormonal and metabolic function in the body. Even after the doctors explained it to me, I wasn't sure what hormones or metabolic functions were, and it took years for me to understand the magnitude of the loss of this gland. The pituitary is associated with the body's sleep cycles, temperature, rate of fuel consumption, water regulation, reproduction, growth, muscle and nerve function, production of energy, thirst, hunger, blood sugar levels, libido, the ability to respond to stress, how minerals are used in the body, and so much more! It pretty much has a role in all bodily functions. Since you cannot live without a pituitary gland, I was placed on a regime of drugs for life.

These heavy-duty drugs caused plenty of side effects, which played a role in my health's continuing decline. Because of my age, ignorance and lack of enthusiasm for life, I just did what the doctors told me to do and shrugged off the thought of worrying about my health.

In the month following my surgery the drugs caused a huge change in my body. I went from a 99-pound skinny, flat-chested kid to a 130-pound large-busted, bloated-faced woman in *one* month's time. I was horrified by these changes and could not take all this in. I withdrew from my reality even more. I hated this new body and the image it projected. I was consumed with self-loathing and self-hatred.

Unsure of what I wanted to do with my life, I did temporary office work for two years before deciding I wanted to be a nurse. I had spent my childhood in the hospital setting and had spent more hours at home nursing my father than I spent socializing with friends. It seemed like a reasonable thing to pursue and I truly did want to help sick people feel better. I later recognized that I was a people pleaser and had "good girl" syndrome (always trying to be good or nice and putting others before me), and nursing simply allowed me to continue in these roles.

My physicians advised against a career in nursing because of the stress and heavy work load associated with the profession. I did not really understand that my body could *not* deal with *any* type of stress — physical, emotional or mental. I simply did not make any anti-stress hormones and had no fight-or-flight boost of energy available to me. It took me about twenty years to actually accept this and surrender to it. I just kept fighting my way through every day of my life. Every day was a battle zone to make it through my exhaustion and then into bed. I was in total denial that I had anything wrong with me and told no one otherwise. I tried to act as though I were normal — trying in vain to fool others and myself.

I stubbornly refused to hear the doctors' advice and pursued a career in nursing. Ironically, I specialized in neurosurgical intensive care nursing and subsequently learned a great deal about the pituitary gland and its functioning. It was a very stressful job and I slept on my breaks and would go home and sleep to try to recover from my twelve-hour swing shifts. I started to use sleeping pills, prescription drugs, and alcohol regularly, or anything to numb me from my reality, which was becoming increasingly hard to cope with. I was also a smoker and ate junk food consistently. Oddly enough I also exercised as much as possible at health clubs, swam, biked and took vitamins: a real dichotomy.

Coughing up blood and excruciating gut pain eventually motivated me to quit some of my substance abuses, but it always had to get ugly before I would quit. My mind was determined I was going to live a "normal" life (which, in my mind, included smoking and drinking). But my health continued to deteriorate throughout my twenties, and eventually I was confronted with the undeniable fact that I was unable to continue with my nursing career. I was not yet thirty years old.

Shortly after I married at age twenty-seven I began to lose the use of my arms and legs. I couldn't stand in one place and had difficulty walking. I had zero energy and was a walking dead person. I felt doomed to die a slow painful death.

I was still in denial even after I left my hospital job. I stubbornly continued to work as a registered nurse doing paramedical exams on a contractual basis. My husband drove me to my job assignments because I could no longer drive. He filled out my forms because it was excruciating to write. He helped me dress and prepare food. I doggedly refused to admit I could not do things for myself. When I could no longer lift my arms to take a blood sample from my patients, I finally admitted defeat and applied for long-term disability. Now I had to face the reality of my health problems. I was completely devastated by having to go on disability benefits — it meant the end of *everything* as I knew it, and the unknown was as frightening to me as my overwhelming health crisis.

The extent of my illness was such that conventional medicine was unable to give me a diagnosis. My main concern was an unprecedented muscle- and fat-wasting condtion that left my arms hanging useless at my sides and my legs wobbling dangerously. This was excruciating in itself, but my problems mounted to include difficuties with my bowel, liver, pancreas, kidneys, lungs, gallbladder — all of my bodily systems were functioning poorly. In addition, my endocrine glands had been redered inactive by the removal of my pituitary gland. Soon I was to discover I also had chronic fatigue, candida, environmental sensitivities, food sensitivities and fibromyalgia. I basically had sick-all-over syndrome compounding my already compromised system.

Being very conventional, I continued to seek out diagnosticians in Ontario. Too ill to watch television or read, I simply lay on the couch waiting to die. I was not quite thirty years old and believed I would soon be dead (I now humorously note what this strong belief system was doing for me at the time). The conventional doctors were concentrating on diagnosing my extensive muscle-wasting problem, but I was experiencing fat wasting and fat redistribution in addition to the musculoskeletal problems.

In desperation I went to the Mayo Clinic in the United States. There, they repeated all the same testing to which I had already been subjected, but at least they had a diagnosis. They informed me that my illness was all in my head and I needed to see a psychiatrist.

I came back home totally despondent and in shock. At this time I began having night dreams that quite literally saved my life. I had always been a vivid dreamer but did not know what the dreams meant and I made little effort to understand them. But these dreams were different — they portrayed me sitting in front of a practitioner listening to health advice that I had never heard of before, such as trying naturopathic medicines, colour-light therapy and acupuncture. Later, the actual names of remedies, food supplements and specific trigger points were revealed to me through my dreams. Remarkably, I found myself beginning a voyage into the dream time that I believe saved my life and continues to lead me to toward my destiny.

Within a day or two of my first lucid dream, a new acquaintance told me of a naturopathic doctor she had been seeing. I sat up and listened. Prior to these dreams I had never even heard of natural medicine. Since my dreams had just made reference to naturopathy, I decided to check it out.

After so much poking and prodding by conventional medicine I was skeptical about this foreign type of medicine (of which I knew nothing). My convictions and suspicions were heightened when the practitioner declared, after a mere ten minutes of seeing me, that my inability to move my arms or walk with any coordination was caused by infected wisdom teeth. Imagine my exasperation at hearing such a silly diagnosis.

Since I believed I was dying and felt totally desperate, I decided I had nothing to lose and so I went to a dental surgeon. After x-rays, the surgeon pronounced that all my wisdom teeth were infected; I elected to have the teeth removed right away. I awoke from the surgery and could immediately raise my arms, albeit weakly, and felt an overwhelming sense of euphoria for the next four full days (not the usual response to this type of surgery, I am told).

I later discovered that the meridian (invisible energetic pathway) that runs through the wisdom teeth supplies energy to the ligaments. My shoulder, arm and leg ligaments were not being energetically fed because of the tooth infections. Thus my muscles wasted secondarily to my ligaments not functioning.

I thought that if such miracles were possible by listening to my dreams, then perhaps I could set an even bigger dream goal. A year or two prior to this experience I had been seeing a chiropractic student for adjustments. He was very enthusiastic about my healing process and suggested I grow back my lost pituitary gland by connecting to my etheric blueprint. I had never heard of an etheric blueprint and I thought he was crazy. But the seed had been planted and the idea of pituitary gland regeneration never left my mind.

It became a dream of mine to regrow my pituitary gland, get off all my medications and have a vital, living body again (something I had only experienced as a small child). A huge goal perhaps, but one I was willing to pursue. I had just discovered that my dreams were offering me messages and advice. I had nothing to lose by trying. I began spending three to five hours a day studying my dreams (I could remember up to fourteen dreams in a night). Focussing on my dream information and growing back my pituitary gland became my full-time job. I maintained this extreme focus on dream study for several years, reading and studying dream interpretation methods for hours every day. Slowly but surely I was guided in the right direction and my health began to improve. The methods in this book were formulated over those years of dream study, and they are the methods that helped me the most. I also became engrossed in a wide variety of other studies and modalities, and devoted all my time and energy to healing my body, mind, emotions and spirit. *Every single dream* I had contained vital information about my perceptions in life and how they affected my health.

My dreams led me to study nutrition, alternative medicines, energy work, metaphysical subjects, esoteric subjects and anything related to holistic or alternative interventions. At first my focus was mainly about the physical aspects of my illness, but my dreams eventually led me to explore my emotional, psychological and divine parts of self in great depth. My dreams showed me how these parts of self were affecting my physical health.

Meditation became a big part of my life and I spent an hour or two every day tuning-in to my body and its vibration. Because I was acquiring knowledge of symbolism by doing dream study, I was able to begin translating the symbolic material that was being held in the tissues of my body. I discovered that I was extremely sensitive to vibration at a molecular level and began picking up information that was being held in the vibrations of my subtle bodies (auric or energy field). My dreams kept revealing that these parts of my self could help me understand myself and the world around me.

I gradually became more aware of and attuned to my dream guides and guardians, and began to formulate methods for teaching others how to fulfill their goals through dream study. I discovered that any goal, from finding a lost piece of jewellery to opening the doors to one's ultimate destiny, is quite possible with dream study. In 1997, my dreams guided me to begin teaching others how to interpret their dreams.

As I taught others I realized we are all given the same gift in dream time — the opportunity to know our true self or our soul self. These pieces of our self are shown to us in every dream. All this information seemed miraculous to me given the North American culture/paradigm that I grew up in, which all but ignores the dream time as useless and irrelevant.

I was even more surprised to discover that attention-getting events occurring during my waking hours, such as seeing the same objects or numbers over and over again, coincidences, and signs, could be translated *exactly* the same way as my dream symbols. I could even apply my dream interpretation methodology to daytime events that confused me or that I wanted to understand at a deeper level. This was so eye-opening and life changing that it turned my world upside down. I had never imagined there could be so much more to life, that messages and guidance could surround me throughout my waking hours, or that we — as a society — were so unaware of this guidance.

For those wishing to know themselves better and improve the quality of their health and happiness, I feel there is no greater gift given to us than our dreams, daydreams, and those everyday attention-getting events.

What is even more remarkable about dreams is that they are easier to understand than most people think. Once you learn how to turn on your "symbolic" ears and turn off your literal ones the process is quite simple. I have developed easy-to-use methods of interpreting dreams and waking-hour events that even non-believing novices can implement. Using the methods in this book will help you gain greater clarity and a deeper understanding of anything you experience, day or night.

Dream work and attention-getting waking-hour events both offer you *free* guidance at all times. It is up to you to regulate how much or how little you uncover about yourself. You are "in choice" about your own future when you take the time to know your self. Understanding symbolism will change your life when you begin to realize and recognize that the Creator is constantly sending you messages all through the day and all through the night.

The best outcome of dream work for me has been the achievement of some of the health goals I set. Although it has taken twenty challenging years, some of my pituitary networking and functioning has returned. I have started to produce some of my own hormones for the first time in my life. I continue to work toward freeing myself from the medications I am taking.

I have been very blessed with the gifts and talents of comprehending the dream time, and I want to share the benefits of dream analysis and the Mystery School Teachings of Egypt with you through this book. Go at your own pace, follow your heart and know that Knowing Yourself and Knowing Your Symbols is a life-long endeavour. There is no hurry if you realize and remember that your God is setting the stage for you and that everything is Divine timing.

I wish you all the best on your magical journey of self-discovery.

Part 1

The Power of Dreams

Chapter I

The Significance of Dreams

Dreams are a road map to your soul. During this life-long journey, your dreams provide a window into the deeper meaning of your purpose on Earth and the world around you. Dreams are a way to get to know all parts of your self, including your body, your inner reality — your mind and emotions, which no one else can experience — and your spirit or divine self. This book cannot teach you about yourself directly, but it shows you how to use your dreams to explore all aspects and levels of your self.

The language of the Universe is not English or any other spoken language. It is the world of vibration, symbols, images and feelings. Your dreams are part of the language of the Universe and in this way you are in direct contact with your God in the dream time.

Dreams are designed to help you remember Who You Are (your spirit or whole self), and most of what you learn through dream interpretation can also be applied to your waking hours (that is, you can interpret everyday events, signs, coincidences and synchronicity using the dream interpretation methods). You do not have to have a night dream in order to apply this information or the interpretation techniques. In fact, I encourage you to recognize that all of life is a waking dream and that you can use the symbolic messages that are presented to you at all times — while you are dreaming and while you are awake.

This book is based on the teachings of the four levels of the Ancient Mystery School of Egypt. These ancient levels or perspectives, which are discussed in detail in Part 2, offer an approach that will help simplify the language of your dreams. In fact, they are a tool for living your everyday life in a more balanced, harmonious and sacred way.

Understanding the "dream basics" is as essential to dream work as is laying a foundation to a house. Understanding dreaming is complex, and yet it can be readily appreciated with a little exploration.

"Recognize that all of life is a waking dream."

Schools today do not educate us in dream work, whereas in ancient cultures this was considered a necessity of life and dream interpretation was taught to children from a very young age. If you are just beginning to explore the meaning of dreams, you will probably feel as though you are in kindergarten — and this is how it should feel. Our culture does not embrace "process" in general, and it is often a culture of wanting all the answers up front without taking the necessary baby steps toward the fulfilment of a goal. Dream work, like any new endeavour, requires practice, patience and a good sense of humour for success. You will quickly learn that your dreams can be very pun-ny (full of puns) and that they can bring much enjoyment and a sense of togetherness when you relate them to family and friends. Indulge and delight in this new adventure.

Readers who are learning about the Egyptian Ancient Mystery School approach for the first time will find *Healing Into Wholeness Through Dreams* an accessible introduction to the subject. At the same time, this book is a valuable resource for advanced students of dream interpretation because it offers a new approach.

What Is a Dream?

According to mainstream Western thinking, the word "dream" has three meanings — the nighttime phenomenon of mental activity that creates miniature movies in our mental landscape while we sleep; the realistic goals that we set for ourselves in our waking-time reality; and, sometimes, less practical aspirations that are probably unattainable except in our imagination.

But dreams are so much more: they are quite simply, and literally, sources of information that are usually delivered in a symbolic or picture format. This is true of day dreams, night dreams and your waking-hour goals or aspirations. Dreams offer you individual and personal guidance for everyday living — whether you choose to acknowledge your dream information is your personal choice.

Dreams provide you with an endless supply of knowledge about who you are and how you view the world around you. This information is available to you every night and is conveyed through your higher self (that wise part of you that connects to a greater Source). Dreams are *designed* to bring information that is below the surface (or below your everyday waking-hour awareness) into your everyday awareness.

Where to Begin Dream Study?

Learning dream work is a process, which means it is done in little bits and pieces and baby steps. Process is not something readily embraced by most North Americans, and in general it is not well supported or practised here. For this reason you may find the baby step approach challenging. This book is therefore written in easy to read chunks to help facilitate an extended, paced learning process. Dreams are an avenue to personal happiness and inner peace, but learning this material is not a pill you can swallow to make everything better overnight. The pill approach is North American thinking; you will require patience and compassion for *yourself* as you progress with this type of study.

Dreams will *always* tell you the inherent truth of your self. Self refers to the whole of who you are as a human being and a spiritual being here on the planet. The Egyptian Ancient Mystery School approach to dream study will further clarify what self or wholeness means. The dream approach in this book focusses on the study of self, and you will quickly learn that everything in your dreams (and waking life) is a mirror of your soul self or whole self.

In this book, the definition of "self" is broken down into categories similar to the four Egyptian levels in order to facilitate the learning and integration process. Determining exactly where to begin with this approach to dream interpretation differs from one interpreter to another. At first you may choose to begin dream study by interpreting your friends' dreams or even by observing the symbolism in your everyday waking experiences (this is explained in Chapter 3). You will notice that making observations about another person's dreams is far easier than unravelling your own. This is because you do not feel the other person's emotions as you listen to their dream — you are detached from their internal experience. In contrast, when you start interpreting your own dreams you will likely feel your emotions, which will influence how clearly you are able to see your dreams' meaning.

How much time you have spent on self study and personal growth is also a factor in determining where to begin your dream study. Perhaps recognizing what emotions you are feeling will be a good starting place, or maybe becoming familiar with your own thought processes is where you need to start. As you read through the material on the four perspectives (in Chapters 6 through 9), make a note about which levels you can easily identify within yourself. Your own dreams will guide you in understanding where to start in this exploration of self.

"Dreams are an avenue to personal happiness and inner peace."

Identifying parts of self that you are less familiar with (such as emotions, mind chatter, beliefs, attitudes) and then *familiarizing* yourself with these parts is what dream work is all about — Knowing Your Self and all its components (this is the first level of the Ancient Mystery School perspectives). Because *all* of life is a process, I suggest that you learn to slow down and savour this self-discovery process — it is a lifetime endeavour.

If you begin to feel overwhelmed with the information you read in this book, please do yourself the great honour of recognizing this (that you are in overwhelm) and put the material aside for now. Give yourself time to process or digest what you have just learned. This is essential to dream work and self study. In general, North Americans have been taught to cram in as much information as possible while studying. Start practising Knowing Your Self by recognizing when you are full and need to take a break. Practise digesting new material; it will make the journey so much easier.

Many North Americans want everything now and in a holy second (because that is what society has taught us), but it cannot possibly happen that way. "Life" is a holy second in the eyes of Spirit. So if you can manage to grasp some of this information in a lifetime, then you are doing it in a holy second.

❁

Scientific Proof – Rapid Eye Movement

A 1953 scientific experiment at the University of Chicago proved that we all dream, even blind people. This is when rapid eye movement (REM) was discovered. REM occurs four to five times every night and each interval of REM can last up to ninety minutes. Even if you do the bare minimum of dreaming each night, you will spend a total of six years of your life dreaming — a considerable amount of time to leave unrecognized and/or underutilized. The REM discovery proved that we are not brain dead when we sleep. These dreamtime studies verified that some part of us is active and alert when we are asleep.

The University of Chicago studies also proved that dreaming plays an important role in the health of our central nervous system and that people deprived of their

REM became highly agitated. Now that we have established a scientific explanation for dreaming, what else can we derive from our dreams?

🔯

A Source of Guidance

Dreams today are little understood by society in general and are often considered to be irrelevant, nonsense and just plain silly (in fact, the silly ones often contain the most information). In ancient societies and cultures, dreams were considered to be relevant and useful and a part of everyday life. Today we tend to view the Internet as our most practical source of information. In fact, ignoring our dreams is to ignore the most viable source of information and *guidance* available to us — that of the divine storehouse of knowledge and inexhaustible wisdom.

This abundant supply of dreamtime information is relayed to you from a very reliable source, commonly known as your higher self, which is sometimes described as the part of self that is connected to the Divine. The four parts of self are often referred to as your body, emotions, mind and spirit. They can be more clearly understood as the physical body and its health; emotions and feelings; the mind and its thoughts, attitudes, opinions and beliefs; and the higher self, which connects you to your soul and to your concept of divinity.

All these parts speak to you *every* night in *every* dream. It is when you are asleep and in the dream state that your parts of self are clearly visible and when you remember the whole of yourself. (It is important to note that these parts also speak to you when you are awake, but you are usually much less aware of them). Dreams are therefore intended to be your guidance system in life. If you can understand the different parts of your self with greater clarity and insight, it becomes possible to feel happier and more fulfilled in your day-to-day life and to experience less stress. To achieve a greater sense of happiness and fulfilment, it is essential to Know Your Self. To know your self is to know your body, your mind, your emotions and your spirit. Every night dream, every day dream, and the symbolism that you encounter in your waking life will show you *all* these levels of self.

🔯

Ancient History

Members of ancient civilizations had a much broader perspective of life and its mysteries than we do. In North America today, we perceive our physical reality as being the focus of life, whereas they knew that life was about more than just the physical. They honoured the magic of the dream time and understood that phenomena happen with every dream and accepted this as a fact of life. They understood that there is a force or energy in the Universe much more vast than our own human perceptions. We are all constantly aware of these perceptions on some level, albeit not a conscious one — they become more realized in the dream state. Dream time is beyond a doubt one of the greatest sources of information available to us; our ancestors understood this and used the dream time to aid them in their everyday life.

> *"Members of ancient civilizations had a much broader perspective of life and its mysteries than we do."*

Our modern hospitals are actually fashioned after Greek health-care facilities, which are considered to be the first hospitals. People would travel great distances (often by foot) in order to find healing and help at a hospital. Much like in hospitals today, anyone with a health problem or other weighty problem would be assigned a bed and spend the night, being attended to by a practitioner. There was, however, a fundamental difference between today's health-care system and ancient health-care practice. Before patients went to sleep at night, they were asked to write down a dream request (further explained in Chapter 2). They literally asked their dreams to help diagnose, explain and offer advice on their problem. In the morning the practitioner would help patients interpret their dream and then base their care and therapies on the dream content. These practitioners were highly skilled in dream interpretation and understood the concept of holism (that human beings consist of many aspects beyond just the physical body). These ancient Greek hospitals were more commonly known as dream temples and the practitioners were considered priests and priestesses of the Ancient Mystery School knowledge.

These ancient practitioners understood that a lot of knowledge about our health and well-being could be obtained from a single dream. They also understood that symbolism not only applied to our dreams, but also to our waking hours (this is discussed further in Chapter 3). These ancient Greek doctors helped patients interpret their dreams and based their treatment upon the information received.

Civilizations such as the Mayans, Incas, Native American Indians, Sumerians, Lemurians, Australian and New Zealand aboriginals, Celts and Egyptians all used the power of dreams to reach a better understanding of who they were as individuals and how they related to the world around them.

❁

Modern History

Over the past century, many well-known people have used the creative power of their dreams to express themselves. Reference books on dreams are abundant and the pages are filled with examples of dreamtime creations. Many popular songs, including Jingle Bells, have been written from dreams. Both Michael Jackson and Paul McCartney claim to have heard a song while dreaming and written it down upon waking. Many books have been written from dreams, including *Dr. Jekyll and Mr. Hyde*. In fact, in his autobiography, Robert Louis Stevenson wrote that he got many of his writing ideas from dreams.

Albert Einstein was known to follow and observe his nightly dreams, and the now well-known concept of the DNA strand was introduced to its discoverer, Dr. Francis Crick, in a dream. Many, many inventions have been formulated by following a dream idea. Thomas Edison was so keen on getting ideas from his dreams that he actually kept a cot in his work room. This was so he could have an afternoon nap and literally dream up new inventions; he had hundreds of patents.

Even the modern sewing machine came from a dream idea. The inventor, Elias Howe, had an amusing dream that he often shared. He had been frustrated with his new invention the sewing machine, and didn't know how to work it with the bobbin and thread together. He asked for an idea to come to him in the night while he dreamt. He dreamt of being held hostage by an African tribe and they pointed spears at him. He was told that he would not be set free until he came up with a solution to his problem. As he stared at the spears, he noticed something different about them – they had holes at the end of them. That's when Elias Howe came up with the idea of putting the eye of the needle at the bottom, and threading both the needle and the bobbin through it. This helped him to realize his dream!

❁

Religion and Dreams

All major religions share a common denominator about dreaming. They all believe that our dreams accomplish something, although their viewpoints vary.

The Christian bible has over one hundred and forty references to dreams as being the bearers of messages, with the story of Jacob's ladder being perhaps the best known. In Judaism, dreams are thought to be a direct connection to God, and the Hebrew word for "dream" means "to make whole or healthy." Islam's holy book,

9

the Koran, is said to have been written by Mohammed from a dream, and to this day Muslims tend to revere their dream interpreters as great leaders.

Across the Cultures

It is important to take note of cultural symbolism because every culture has its own lore about dreams and the meaning of symbols. It is important for students of dreams to know the cultural symbols of their ancestors in order to grasp the meaning of their own dream symbols. For example, I discovered that Italians often recognize the symbol of excrement or feces in their dreams as a symbol of money coming into their hands. This also seems to pertain to some South American cultures. I have also heard that a bird flying into the house portends a death. Many examples of symbols that mean bad luck and superstitious lore, such as opening an umbrella in the house or having a black cat cross your path, are common in society today. Be aware of and honour your cultural beliefs and background when learning to interpret your dreams. You can use your awareness of these beliefs to help interpret your dream symbols.

Now that you know some dream basics, the next step is learning how to remember and interpret your dreams, which will help you Know Your Self better. This is the first level of the Egyptian Ancient Mystery School teachings.

Preparing to Learn From Your Dreams

How to Remember Your Dreams

Poor or no dream recall is common and is often related to stress, exhaustion, alcohol or drugs. However, it is more frequently due to early childhood conditioning. The simple steps outlined below will usually trigger dream recall right away. Keep using these steps until you are successful.

1) Show intent – This is the most powerful tool for remembering your dreams. To show intent, simply put a pen and paper at your bedside. This shows that you intend to remember your dreams.

2) Use an affirmation – A simple affirmation such as "I remember my dreams" is an effective tool in helping remember your dreams. If you think of yourself as a giant computer, you can see how early childhood programming may be interfering with your ability to remember your dreams. If you were ever told to "forget it, it's only a dream" as a child, then every time you dream, you will "pull up" this "program" (to forget it) and you will do just that — you will forget the dream. Saying the simple affirmation "I remember my dreams" will help reprogram your hard drive. Say this in your head or out loud just before sleep *and* whenever you can during the day.

3) Stay in bed and replay the dream – It is very important to remember to stay in bed for a minute or two when you awaken and replay the dream content. Take note of any feelings you had in the dream. Replay the dream as if it's a movie. Jumping out of bed immediately upon waking while you are learning to remember your dreams leads to non-remembering.

4) *Jot down a few words upon waking* – Take a moment to write down a few keywords and feelings before you leave the bedside, even if you're just going to the bathroom. Most people forget their dream before returning to bed. Writing down a few keywords will help jostle your memory. It does not take long to build new pathways for remembering your dreams.

> *"The essential oil of lavender has been used for centuries as a dream stimulant."*

5) *Drink water or tea before bed* – This will get you up in the night to use the bathroom, creating an opportune time to remember your dreams. The dream stage of sleep lasts for up to ninety minutes per sleep cycle, and we experience four or five complete cycles a night. Creating an opportunity to wake up in the night is a great way of "catching" a dream.

6) *Use lavender* – The essential oil of lavender has been used for centuries as a dream stimulant. Place a few drops in a seashell or other small container at your bedside. The smell *will* help you to remember your dreams. Dream pillows can be purchased as well, and these contain dried lavender.

7) *Hang up a dreamcatcher* – Surprisingly, people report that these do help them with dream recall. Hang one in your bedroom or near where you sleep.

8) *Avoid loud clock-radio alarms* – Awake to softer music or just program yourself to wake up at a certain time (five minutes before your alarm goes off).

❈

Making a Dream Request

Dream requests are a wonderful tool for self-exploration and personal development. You can ask *any* question you like about *yourself.* Keep in mind that the question must be pertinent to what is going on in your life at the time you ask the question. For example, if you are currently in the process of a heated divorce and ask the question, "What is my biggest blockage to self-mastery?" you will most likely *not* get the answer. That question is not *essential* to your well-being at this time. Asking a question about how the divorce is affecting you or how best to deal with a certain aspect of the divorce would be appropriate and therefore would be answered.

Remember that *any* question *ever* asked, either consciously or unconsciously, will at some point be answered either in a dream or while awake! Every time you ask a question (whether out loud or in your mind), a filament of energy is sent out from your body and off into the universe (see Figure 1). This filament continues until it intersects with the answer, which exists energetically in the vast network of the Universe. The answer is sent back to you in the language of the Universe, which you experience as vibration, feelings and symbolic messages. You receive your answers as soon as you ask them, but are you aware enough or skilled enough to understand the Creator's message? With continued dream interpretation practice you will become skilled in understanding the language of the Universe, and this will make interpreting the Creator's messages much easier.

Accept *all* dreams that you experience that night as answers to the dream request you made before going to sleep. It is common not to see the answer immediately and to think you did not get your answer. If your question is about yourself and pertinent to your life, you will *always* get an answer. This cannot be emphasized enough. You will get your answer. If you do not remember a dream the night you ask your question, ask again for several nights until you remember a dream. But be very aware of possible signs and symbols in your waking hours. Dream requests are often answered while we are awake, so stay alert.

This method of dream request works best if you write the question out *in detail* and then repeat it in your head as you fall asleep. Writing a detailed question is very important. For example, you may make a dream request such as "When will I be moving?" The intent behind such a question seems apparent. You may mean moving to a new house or apartment, but your subconscious mind will interpret this simple question on all levels. So your subconscious mind may answer you by telling you when you will be moving ahead in your emotional life, or in your beliefs or attitudes. Or it may tell you when you will be moving along on your spiritual quests/paths. The question could be rephrased to be more specific: "When will I be physically moving from my current house?" So be *specific* in asking your questions. Many people assume they will remember their question in the morning, but this is seldom true. Remember to write it down and leave the pen and paper at your bedside.

Another way to help you receive a clearer answer is to review some of your daytime events prior to sleep. Make a conscious effort to be aware of your daytime feelings, make connections between your words or actions and their consequences, and review whether you "spoke your truth" or were true to yourself during the day. This is called clearing up the day's events prior to sleep, and it will open the doorway for your request to be answered. Since your dreams are designed to bring information into your waking-time awareness, doing a little foot work before bed will free your higher self from having to use your valuable dream time bringing the day's events into your waking-time awareness.

13

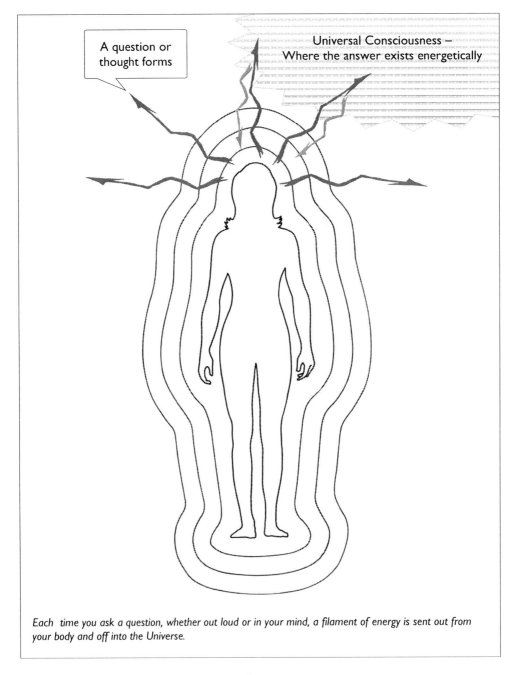

Each time you ask a question, whether out loud or in your mind, a filament of energy is sent out from your body and off into the Universe.

Figure 1. Your thoughts send energy out to the Universe

A little preparation before dream time will save you time and give clarity to the interpretation process. This can most easily be accomplished by jotting down the most relevant events of that day. Writing down these significant events will bring the maximum amount of clarity. Your journaling need not be long and overly detailed. Simply highlight the day's events in list form. It is important to note how you were *thinking* and *feeling* with each event or experience of the day — again, if you don't make these connections while awake, you will waste precious dream time on information that you could have seen by simply journaling and getting the insight that way.

"Any question ever asked will at some point be answered either in a dream or while awake!"

Sample Questions

1) *I am currently working on [project] and need some inspiration to continue with my goals. I request an idea to assist me at this time.* (Be as detailed as possible about the project you have in mind and what your desired outcome is.)

2) *What is my biggest blockage to self-mastery?* (To master your self is to know your self and know that you are fully "in choice" but never in control. Self-mastery is self-love, self-compassion, self-everything. When you are living a balanced inner life without strife because you realize that all is well in the Universe and within your self, you have mastered your self in all its levels. The concept of self-mastery is similar to what Buddhists call enlightenment or psychologists call self-actualization.)

3) *What is the source of my [illness]* (be specific), *and what can I do to help myself heal?* (Expect to get information about the physical, emotional, mental and spiritual causes, unless you specify which kind of cause you are most interested in.)

4) *What lessons are there for me to learn about my health concerns at this time?* (be specific about your health concerns)

5) *What would it behoove me to work on most in my spiritual endeavours at this time?*

6) *What career course would I most benefit from following at this time?*

7) *What would be in my best and highest good at this time in regards to [situation or concern]?* (Be specific about the situation or concern you require information about.)

15

Remember you can ask any question you like, as long as it is about you and your own life.

Be sure to remember to keep a pen and paper at your bedside to write accounts of your dreams.

Create a Personal Symbol Dictionary

Part 3 of this book is the Dream Symbol Dictionary. Knowing your personal symbolism is essential, but you also have to know a bit about universal symbolism in order to gather more in-depth information. Part 3 can help you learn universal and cultural symbolism. Take some time to familiarize yourself with the content and it will help you interpret the symbols in your dreams. In the meantime, creating your own symbol dictionary will be your most valuable ally/asset in interpreting your dreams. Use a loose-leaf notebook or the space provided in Appendix A.

As you work with your own dream symbols, write each one down with a description of how each symbol relates to your life experiences. In this way you will create the most useful dream dictionary possible. Once a symbol is established, it usually has the same meaning every time it occurs in a dream and in your waking hours. However, symbolic meanings can and do change as you change — as your perceptions, attitudes and opinions shift into new awarenesses, your personal symbolism may also change to reflect the new you.

This dictionary will come in handy if you have previously recorded dreams and have yet to interpret them. Reference your personal dream dictionary often, for it will provide you with the most accurate meaning of your dream symbols.

Be mindful of your thoughts throughout the day. They most often reveal the symbolism behind the dream images. For example, I dreamt of a pig one night and this was not a symbol I had come across before. Reading about pig symbolism in a book did not help me understand the meaning. Later in the day I heard my own thoughts saying, "I am pigging out so much lately." Bingo! That was the meaning behind my dream pig. If you are creative in the waking hours, you can bet your dreams will be more creative in the symbols they use to get your attention.

Chapter 3

Types of Dreams

Day Dreams

Have you ever been driving a car when you suddenly realize you have not been paying attention to the road, yet have miraculously arrived at your destination? One part of your brain was in the alpha state, which is the same level of consciousness (as measured by brain waves) at which you have nightly dreams. You were having a day dream — one of those watery times of drifting that we often experience while doing a hobby, driving, gardening, or engaged in any routine or mundane chore, such as cleaning or showering. It is during these drifting moments that you learn important clues about your self.

Day dreams are small snippets of time during the waking hours when information from your higher self is coming through to your waking-hour consciousness. Your mind drifts from its current task and creates imaginative scenarios in which you try out different stances or emotional states, much like a dress rehearsal. These imaginative portrayals give you a chance to role-play with yourself in your head. You can either recall an actual situation that happened to you and then mentally role-play different things that you could have done or said in that situation, or you can imagine future (or hypothetical) situations and mentally rehearse what you might do or say.

Day dreams are invaluable sources of information about your self and your perceptions. They are meant as tools for guidance and are richly available every day. We often get new ideas during alpha states; they are a time that allows for inspirational thought.

Your waking dreams are as rich and full of information as your nightly dreams. They contain information about your self just as night dreams do, and they can be interpreted in the same way.

When you catch yourself day dreaming, be aware! The trick is to realize that you are day dreaming, and to remember the content of the day dream. Later you can write your day dream down and interpret the meaning using the dream interpretation methods outlined in Chapters 4 and 10. The interpretation methods also work well on "visions" or other quick images that flash through your mind throughout the day — everything has meaning.

It's also useful to become aware of what triggers your day dreams, and to make a mental note that you'd like to remember your day dreams. You will gradually become more aware of your day dream information, and will be able to use this information for your self-growth and as a source of guidance. It really is that easy. Once you start practising tuning in to your day dreams, you won't be disappointed at the amazing amount of information they reveal to you.

🔯

Waking-Hour Symbolism

Your everyday waking-hour events, relationships and experiences have symbolic meaning, just as your nighttime and daytime dreams do. Everything that occurs during your waking hours is rich with meaning — it is only a matter of acknowledging this. Once you do, you will begin to see the magic in every moment of your life.

These waking-hour symbols often hold similar messages to the ones that your night dreams are already trying to relay to you. These seemingly coincidental experiences are not coincidental at all. The Universe sends you endless messages during your waking hours as well as in the dream time.

For example, you may dream of bumping your head and then wake up and actually bump your head. Or you may dream of your wristwatch falling off and the next morning your wristwatch actually falls off. If these types of incidents aren't catching your attention, they should be. For it is no mistake that your dream content and your waking-hour events are similar in nature. Watch for it — dreamtime characters and symbolism are presented to you all the time during your waking hours.

See "Symbolism and the Waking Time" in Chapter 7 for further details on this phenomenon.

Sample Day Dream: The Great Hero

I am driving along the highway when I begin to day dream that there is a horrific accident ahead. I imagine myself leaping from my car and heroically rescuing someone involved in the accident. I see reporters arriving and I am made hero of the day.

Most Significant Feeling Accomplishment	**Most Significant Symbol** Myself as the hero
Meaning of Symbol A hero is someone who is brave, courageous and admirable. Heroes commit acts that deserve acknowledgement, acclaim and recognition.	**Waking-Hour Connection** I realize I have a high need for recognition. I need and I'm seeking acceptance and approval from outside of myself. This day dream helps me see this about myself. But I know that true acceptance, approval and recognition can only come from within. I can now try to work on shifting away from this desire for external validation to recognizing my own inner merits.

Precognitive Dreams

Precognitive dreams, which are also called ESP dreams, are dreams that come true — you "see" something prior to it taking place in the waking hours. For example, you dream of a disastrous plane crash and you awake to hear that this has actually occurred. Only a small percentage of the population experiences ESP and precognitive dreams, and people who are prone to prediction dreams are often very aware of a special quality or feeling in the dream that is different from the quality of a regular dream. They describe it as a "knowing" feeling and they recognize it as such immediately.

To determine whether a particular dream is predicting something, consider your past experiences with ESP-type dreams. Are you prone to these types of dreams? Have you ever had one? If the answer to these questions is no, then chances are that this is not an ESP dream. Similarly, ask yourself whether you had that special knowing feeling in the dream; the feeling is usually all-encompassing in a true precognitive dream. But this is not to say that you should entirely rule out the possibility that this was an ESP dream. Remember that it is always wise to consider all possibilities and act on what you believe you need to rather than ignore the possible warning in the dream.

> *"In lucid dreams, you experience yourself in a more awakened state."*

Other minor ESP incidents may happen with more frequency in your dreams. For example, you dream of receiving a speeding ticket and actually get one within a day or two of the dream. This type of mini-ESP dream is common and is a type of warning dream. We create our own future every day with our thoughts, words and actions (or inaction). A speeding ticket in the dream time is a warning that you are speeding through some everyday situation without giving it enough thought. Perhaps you are not grounded and rushing around so much that you are not picking up on important inner signals. This dream is very common among people with hectic lifestyles and simply warns them to slow down. You create the "speeding ticket" dream with the feverish pace you are keeping. An actual speeding ticket received in the waking time is presenting you with the same message to slow down — you are going too fast and in danger of hurting yourself or others. This is the same message your dream speeding may have for you. This seemingly coincidental type of experience is not coincidental at all. The Universe sends us endless messages during our waking hours as well as in the dream time. See the discussion on waking-hour symbolism above for further details on this phenomenon.

✤

Lucid Dreams

In lucid dreams, you experience yourself in a more awakened state. This may sound dualistic or contradictory, but that is the sensation of a lucid dream state. In fact, you feel so awake in some lucid dreams that it's hard to believe your physical body is asleep. Some part of you is wide awake, lucid and experiencing the dream state with great clarity. The scenery is brighter and sharper, your vision is more acute and your senses are extraordinarily heightened. It's a very exciting feeling but sometimes disorienting because of its realness.

There are varying degrees of wakefulness in a lucid dream. Sometimes you are just aware you are dreaming while the dream is going on. At other times you may experience such intense alertness that you are confused about where you are and how you got there. But it is only your senses that are awake, not your physical body — which, of course, is sleeping. Lucid dreaming is a common and natural state of being and actually feels wonderful. Once you accept that you are conscious on some level, you are able to control the flow of the dream state, creating whatever you wish, merely by thinking about it. In fact, you will be creating even as you come to grips with the fact that you are "awake" and able to control the dream.

If you ever have a lucid dream you will know it, because these dreams have a certain quality that is hard to describe — a quality of being more awake and alert than in your normal waking hours. How is it possible to be more awake than you are in normal waking hours? Because in normal waking consciousness you are actually in touch with very little of who you are. In the dream time you are in touch with, or remembering, a far greater portion of your self. Therefore, if you "wake up" in the dream, you have an expanded view, awareness or consciousness of yourself that you are not likely to have experienced in your waking hours.

The following example, which was my first full-blown lucid dream, may help clarify the degree to which these dreams can be experienced.

Lucid Dream Example: "Am I Drunk?"

In actual reality I am asleep beside my partner in our home in the suburbs of our town (I'll call it Hometown). In the lucid dream I awake in a bed in another country 3,500 miles from Hometown. I am confused and sit up in the bed blinking and rubbing my eyes. My mind is awhirl in chaos as I try to figure out how I went to bed in Hometown and got to this place so far away. My only rational explanation is that I must have drunk so much that I passed out and someone kidnapped me. My partner is asleep in the upper bunk of a bed beside the bed I'm in, so I reason that he must have brought me here when I passed out. Then I remember that I don't drink, so this explanation isn't even feasible.

I'm still blinking my eyes and only seconds have passed since I awoke. I can feel the bed, I can see my partner, and I am awake and feeling rational. So what is going on? I'm more confused than scared. Then musicians with violins start shuffling into the room dragging their chairs on the floor. I can hear the chairs and I can hear them start to tune their violins. Then my partner's alarm clock goes off and he hops out of the bunk bed and starts to walk around the bed I'm sitting in. I am incredulous and yell to him, "Do you see them? What are we doing here? How did we get here? Isn't this amazing?" He looks at me as though I'm crazy and he says, "See what?" My jaw drops in disbelief. At the same time, a man walks over to the bed and telepathically says to me, "He doesn't see them (referring to the musicians)." I'm stunned and repeat, "He doesn't see them?" The man telepathically answers no.

21

When he says this, I instantly wake up in my bed in Hometown with my partner walking around my bed and shaking his head at me. I am sitting bolt upright in bed as I had been just a second ago in the lucid dream and I now excitedly ask him what is going on. "Did you see that? Holy cow! That was amazing. How did we get there so fast and back? What's going on?" He just stops and stares at me and asks me what I'm talking about. He has not had the same experience I have and he thinks I'm a bit crazy.

> *"If you 'wake up' in the dream, you have an expanded view, awareness or consciousness"*

Since that first lucid dream many years ago, I have been blessed with many more. There are varying degrees of wakefulness, and the example above is what I'd call a full-blown lucid experience. I have since learned that you can easily control the content of your dream experience by the thoughts you have in the dream time. For example, if you dream of standing outside in a field but begin to think of a cosy bed, you will find yourself instantly dreaming of being in a bed. If you think of a loved one, that person will instantly appear beside you. Other types of lucid dreaming include out of body experiences (OOBEs), astral travel, remote viewing and simple moments of insight and intuition that trigger a déjà vu sense that grabs your attention. In an OOBE you are free of your physical body but you're thinking clearly. Often you see your body asleep in the bed or viewed from above. Astral travel is often experienced as flying about in the air while feeling awake. Once again you are free of your physical body and usually experiencing the astral plane or dimension. Remote viewing is when you see something or someone that is not in your physical environment — you see them from above or from afar as though you were actually present (a "fly on the wall" type of experience). All lucid dreams are attention getters and usually quite pleasant.

I have been fortunate to have lucid dreams that set me on my path to healing. Many times in lucid dreams I have found myself sitting across from a practitioner and being told what to do — go see a natural doctor; juice wheat grass; do green colour-light therapy; seek out acupuncture; try this remedy or vitamin (actual names were given to me); use a loofah brush on your neck to help with lymphatic drainage. I have been shown maps of my body that indicate where energy is blocked and advised how to assist in its healing. I have met guides, teachers and angels bringing information and guidance. My degree of wakefulness in these dreams varies.

Lucid dreams are an exciting testament to the expansiveness of who you are and a great time to experience your self without the confines of a physical body. Because you are awake in the dream, you can go anywhere and do anything you desire — and all with a simple thought. As you think, so will you create. This principle holds true for the waking hours too, but with a time delay. Not so in lucid dream time. You move and create with your thoughts and can therefore create to your heart's delight. Perhaps you would like to travel to the moon, or Rome or anywhere your imagination can create — you will go there instantly. Perhaps you would like to help a friend heal or visit them. You can do healing work or prayers while in their presence (this does not mean they will remember the encounter, but the effects are just as powerful as if you were standing before them in the waking hours). Contacting other realities is also possible. There is really no end to what can be accomplished in a lucid dream.

Inducing and Maintaining Lucidity

If you want to experience lucid dreams, make sure to specify that in your before-bed dream request and use your dream request to create a dreamtime trigger. For example, you could ask that when you "find your hand" in the dream time, your dream will become a lucid one. You may dream of seeing your hand several times before this trigger works, but it will work eventually. Once you see your hand in your dream and remember your request, you will "wake" up. Decide in advance (while you're awake) on a plan of action (do you want to go to Rome? pray for a friend? meet a famous person?) so you'll be ready to act as soon as your dream becomes a lucid one.

Maintaining the lucid dream state can be tricky. Because the dream scenery changes with your thoughts, it is extremely easy to get pulled back into a regular dream state (an unconscious dream state like you normally experience). The key is to practise focussing on a stable object (in our example, your hand) while in the lucid state. This is often a good reminder that you are "awake" and need to maintain focus in order to stay awake.

We all leave our bodies via our crown (seventh) chakra in order to sleep. But you are always attached to your physical body by a silver cord or thread (somewhat like a life line) and can therefore always return to your physical body in a fraction of a second. This is important to remember while you are lucid dreaming, because novice lucid dreamers may be frightened by the feeling that they are not in their physical body.

If you find yourself in an unpleasant or frightening lucid dream, simply think yourself back to your body or back to your bedroom and you will either wake up or go into a regular dream state in a split second. You are totally at choice at all times (dreaming or awake!).

And remember to interpret your lucid dreams like a regular dream using one of the dream interpretation methods. For example, if in a drowning dream you are able to "think" yourself swimming safely to shore, refer to the Swimming entry in Part 3, the Dream Symbol Dictionary, to understand the symbolic meaning of this occurrence.

❁

Nightmares

Nightmares are dreams that are so frightening that they wake you up in the middle of the night, often sweating and terrified. They can feel so real that they make you put the light on and stay awake for some time. Children are especially prone to not wanting to go back to sleep for fear of experiencing the same dream.

Nightmares reflect confusion of the mind and try to tell you that there is a situation in your current life that needs immediate attention. Something is upsetting your balance and sense of what is right and wrong for you personally. Often you have a feeling of impending threat or danger at a deeper level of your awareness, and your higher self (wisdom) or inner voice is trying to draw your attention to that threat. Since you are not hearing or getting the message while you are awake, the information comes through at night when you are very relaxed and therefore much more receptive. Nightmares *are* trying to get your attention (and they usually do) and they *are* trying to get you to "put the light on"; i.e., to see the situation that is creating such concern.

Nightmares are common in children because often they don't feel in control of their lives or their actions. Parents, society and school all influence children and tell them what to do, think and feel. This kind of well-meaning advice often runs against the child's true nature and therefore causes significant distress that the child is unable to express.

At a deep, unconscious level, adults often feel that their lives are not aligned with their true selves or their fundamental goals and desires. But because they are not in touch with what their true self is, they need nightmares to tell them that their true nature is feeling threatened.

There are a few simple techniques to help you get the message that the nightmare is trying to bring into your waking-hour awareness. These techniques work well for both adults and children. Once you get the message or meaning of the dream, the nightmares will stop.

How to Get Your Nightmare's Message

Step One – Turn on the light and acknowledge that this was a frightening experience. Telling yourself or a child to "forget it, it was only a dream" not only perpetrates the problem, but leads to poor dream recall. Reassuring yourself and/or your child is a healthy first step in abating nightmares.

Step Two – Ask the child to recount the dream to you in detail and comfort them as needed. Adults should write the nightmare out in detail, noting the feelings and the main symbol of the dream. This simple step in itself will do a lot to reassure the child or yourself that it was a real experience and that their/your feelings are valid.

Step Three – Ask the child to recount the dream again, but this time to change the ending or scary part to something that is more appealing or more positive. Being chased by monsters is the most common type of nightmare among children. In the newly created "dream," they can replay the scene to have themselves remove the monster from the sequence, have help arrive, or talk to the monster to find out why it is chasing them. Children are often very creative and can easily think of new endings for their nightmares. Anything they create that helps them deal with their monster will help them go back to sleep and/or end the frightening dreams. Simply asking the monster why it's chasing them may give you clues as to the issue bothering the child.

The same technique applies for adults. Either replay the dream in your mind with an ending you like, or rewrite one that suits your sense of what's more appropriate. If applicable, ask your monster why it is after you. Pretending what the monster would say back to you is an invaluable technique that will lead to insight. If your rational mind tells you that doing this is just making things up, that's all right. In fact, your make-believe scenario will be very close to the "truth." Pretending an answer is almost always valid and relevant and leads to greater insight and understanding. Listening to that first response in your head will often lead you in the right direction. Even if you still don't have a clue what the nightmare symbolizes about your life, talking to the monster will create a new avenue at deeper levels to replay a positive outcome in your new version of the nightmare. Later, when you have more time, you can use one of the interpretation methods in Chapters 4 and 10 to help you understand the nightmare's meaning.

It is interesting to note that studies conducted on the visual cortex of the human brain reveal that the brain response is *exactly* the same to what you see with your eyes and what you imagine in your mind. That part of the brain *cannot* distinguish between what is real and what is imagined — seeing or visualizing are perceived as being the same. This is why replaying your dream content is so helpful — it actually does change the outcome!

> *"Nightmares will lessen every time you take the time to acknowledge and honour the feelings that the experience brought up."*

Step Four – Taking measures to reassure the child, such as checking under the bed or in the closets for monsters, leaving a light on, or allowing them to sleep with a stuffed animal, will help the child go back to sleep. In the morning, offer to talk about the nightmare with the child. Honouring a child's fears gives them a great sense of security, and this alone will help abate the nightmares to a certain degree.

This counsel goes to adults too. Honour your own feelings of fear after a nightmare. Acknowledging your feelings and acting without judgement will assist you greatly in lessening the frequency of nightmares. Telling yourself that you are silly or stupid for wanting some comfort measures after a traumatic nightmare does not acknowledge the nightmare or your own feelings. Leave the light on if necessary and check under your own bed if you want. In the morning talk about the nightmare with a friend. All this talking will help integrate and validate the message into your waking-time awareness, even if you haven't yet gained full insight into the nightmare's meaning.

Nightmares will lessen every time you take the time to acknowledge and honour the feelings that the experience brought up. Continue to search for ways to comfort yourself and child after a nightmare and use the visualization techniques suggested. You will be pleasantly surprised at how readily you can decrease the frequency and intensity of nightmares just by recognizing and honouring them as real.

🏵

Recurring Dreams and Symbols

Recurring dreams and symbols are common and indicate a conflict that has gone unresolved. A message is trying to get through to your waking-hour awareness; if you are still having the same dream or if a particular symbol keeps showing up in your dreams, then you haven't got the message yet. This conflict may be an internal one or an external problem. For example, a recurring dream of your mother-in-law driving your car could represent your feelings about your mother-in-law driving you crazy, or perhaps taking too much control in your life. A recurring dream from childhood may indicate an internal conflict with your self (mind, body or spirit) that has followed you into adulthood and is still unresolved. This could be any issue, pattern, habit or belief that no longer serves you well. The recurring dream is trying to get your attention about it, in order to restore balance for your internal reality.

Think of your recurring dreams and symbols like a benign bill collector. It keeps sending you invoice after invoice, patiently waiting for you to pay your bill. In a recurring dream, "paying the bill" is simply "becoming consciously aware." As soon as you get the message, your recurring dream will stop. But if the conflict remains unresolved, the recurring dream or symbol may turn into a nightmare.

Try using the dream interpretation methods in Chapters 4 and 10 to help you interpret your recurring dreams and symbols.

Chapter 4

Dream Interpretation: The Fundamental Methods

Presented here are three different models of dream interpretation. The first, the Seer's Path Method, is an in-depth, eight-step method that offers a profound look into a dream's meaning. The second, the Magical Path Method, is a three-step mini interpretation that offers a glimpse into a dream's meaning. The third, the Intuitive Method, is a quick verbal method that can be used by anyone, but it may be of special interest to therapists, counsellors, teachers and healers. For ardent dream interpreters, the Seer's and Magical Path methods can be expanded to include the four Egyptian Ancient Mystery School perspectives, which are discussed in detail in Part 2. These modifications are outlined in Chapter 10.

The fundamental interpretation methods are presented as a series of steps for you to work through. Because the dream is about you and your dream content, only you can provide the necessary information; you were the one who experienced the dream content. No one can interpret the meaning of your dream but you. My intent as a dream interpreter, and as the author of this book, is to assist you in understanding the content of your dream based on your life experiences. Since no one else has ever walked in your shoes, you are the expert on your life and your experience.

Remember that these interpretation methods can be used for night dreams, day dreams and waking-time events.

꙰

The Seer's Path Method

Overview of Steps

1 – Feelings
2 – Background or Setting
3 – Most Significant Symbol
4 – Theme
5 – Symbols' Meaning
6 – Dream's Meaning
7 – Title and Summary
8 – Decision and Application

How to Fill in the Answers

Write out the dream in full prior to attempting the dream interpretation steps. Writing out your dream will reveal greater depth than just recalling it in your mind. Writing taps directly into your subconscious and unconscious mind and can therefore reveal much more than merely thinking. Note the date of the dream, which is relevant for understanding what triggered the dream material in the first place.

Step 1: Feelings

Identify and write out which emotions you and other characters (people and animals) were feeling in the dream. Note the most significant feeling first and then list the others in the order in which they appeared in the dream. If you felt any strong emotions when you woke up, list them as well.

If identifying your dream feelings is new to you, take a look at the Identifying Your Feelings exercise in Chapter 8.

> ▸ What was I thinking?

> ▸ Was I comfortable or uncomfortable?

> ▸ Was I experiencing anything or was I numb, void, empty or detached?
> If you are unable to identify any feelings, this is a strong indication of hidden or repressed emotions.

▸ Did I experience any physical sensations such as pleasure or pain?

▸ Did I have any intuitive sense or gut sensations?

Go through your written account of your dream carefully and be aware of statements that begin with "I am," since this phrase sometimes highlights a feeling.

Seer's Path Method Example 1: Wild Horses

I am happily walking down a beautiful road with my friend Dave. We see some wild horses running freely across the countryside.

        Feelings — Happy, free

Step 2: Background or Setting

Write down where the dream takes place. This will reveal your area of mental awareness or consciousness and is an important ingredient in understanding the purpose of the dream. For example, dreams that take place in the kitchen are often referring to "food for thought" or how you are taking in, processing and digesting a certain waking-hour situation, relationship or event.

If the setting changes during the dream, describe each scene in order of appearance.

Make note of the following: Are you inside or outside? What specific type of building or room are you in? Is the location familiar or unfamiliar? These will further assist you in pinpointing what area of awareness you were in. For example, a dream where you find yourself in a foreign country is likely telling you about a part of your self that you are unfamiliar with or unaware of — in other words, a part of your self that is foreign to you.

Identify whether it is dark or light in the dream (see the discussion on Daylight vs. Darkness in the Backgrounds and Settings section of the dictionary in Part 3 for further discussion on this). This immediately tells you how much daytime or waking-time awareness you have of the dream's meaning. If the dream takes place in a well-lit environment, you can be assured that you will be familiar with the information that is being presented. If it is a dark dream or in blackness, then you may not have as much waking-time insight about the material being presented. It is always wiser to begin interpreting your dreams by looking at the ones that take place in the light, since they are easier to comprehend. With practice the content of your darker dreams will become clearer.

Seer's Path Method Example 1: Wild Horses

I am happily walking down a beautiful road with my friend Dave. We see some wild horses running freely across the countryside.

Background or Setting — Countryside

Step 3: Main or Most Significant Symbol

Write down the main or most prominent dream symbol: this will point out the most important message of the dream. There may be more than one symbol that stands out, but list the most prominent or memorable one first and then others in the order in which they appear. If it is a long dream and the background changes a lot, write down the most significant symbol for each of the settings.

Symbols can be other people, animals or objects. Look for nouns to help you pinpoint a symbol; go through your dream notes and *circle* the nouns (symbols) that stand out for you. (Note that in the examples we use boldface text rather than circles to identify the symbols.) You will have either a sense of the main symbol or it will be emphasized or highlighted in some manner. For example, you look down at your hands and notice that you have extra-large fingers, or you meet a person whose nose is bigger than their whole head. Anything that stands out or catches your attention is of importance and will have a significant message for you.

Seer's Path Method Example 1: Wild Horses

*I am happily walking down a beautiful road with my friend Dave. We see some wild **horses** running freely across the countryside.*

Most Significant Symbol — Horses

Step 4: Theme

In this step, write down the overall theme or pattern of the dream. Like a movie, your dream has a plot, and the theme will create a blueprint of your present daytime situation (or what took place in the waking time one or two days prior to having the dream).

Begin by *underlining* all the verbs or action words in your dream account. Then go back and circle all the nouns (people, objects or animals) that you didn't circle in the previous step.

Now rewrite the dream, line by line, based on the action words. As you rewrite each sentence, leave out the actual nouns (circled words) and instead insert the words "something," "somewhere," or "someone." Leave out all adjectives or descriptive words as you write. You are creating new sentences with only the action words and the replaced nouns (something, someone, somewhere).

After each "someone" or "something," write the actual noun in parentheses. These bracketed words are the symbols you will want to explore the meaning of in the next step.

Seer's Path Method Example 1: Wild Horses

I am happily <u>walking</u> *down a beautiful road with my friend* **Dave.** *We see some wild* **horses** <u>running</u> *freely across the* **countryside.**

Theme

▸ I am walking somewhere (road) with someone (Dave).

▸ Something (horses) is running somewhere (countryside).

The theme is an important ingredient in the dream interpretation process, but it may seem like a redundant step at first. However, the theme nicely paints a picture of the waking hours and is extremely helpful in understanding the meaning behind the dream. The next step will help clarify the meaning of the theme.

Step 5: Meaning of the Symbols

Begin interpreting your symbols, starting with the setting word and then working on each noun that you put in parentheses in Step 4. Do them in order.

For each symbol noted, write down the first thing you think of when you say or write the word. Ask yourself, What personal experience have I had of this animal, person or object? Usually your first impression (in your mind) is the correct symbolic answer for you.

For example, if your symbol is a shoe, what are your first thoughts about that particular type of shoe? Was it a pair of beach thongs, perhaps the very kind you hate and would never wear? Or was it a pair of comfortable sneakers you wear every day? This type of first impression will ultimately point you in the direction of the symbol's meaning. So always note your initial thoughts and opinions about your dream symbol and write them down. Remember not to censor any of your thoughts about the symbol; after all, it's your thoughts that your dream is trying to draw to your attention.

Understanding the meaning of your symbol can be somewhat like a guessing game, and you keep guessing until you come up with an answer that resonates with you. This can be seen as an answer that rings a bell with you, vibrates with you, gives you the "ah-ha" sensation, or feels like a light bulb goes on. We all have a built-in radar that will signal when we hit the truth; discovering what yours is will be revealed with practice.

The meaning of your dream symbols is *always* there within you — finding it is a matter of asking yourself some probing questions and being aware of the first response or thought that you have for each question. It is pivotal to take your very first thoughts and record them as part of the answer.

Many symbols have a deeper universal meaning, and it is here that the Dream Symbol Dictionary (see Part 3) can be most helpful.

People who are new to dream interpretation may find it helpful to categorize their dream symbols as human, animal, or object. Here are some suggestions for how to do this.

Human Symbols

Remember: almost all the people in your dreams represent a part of your self. Write down three characteristics or personality traits you associate with that person. Even if you don't know the dream character personally, you will likely have a sense about them. Try to list at least three characteristics and realize that these reflect your own traits. You may have judgements about these traits, but realize also that they are your judgements and not those of your higher self or the Creator. Judgements are strictly those of the ego/personality, which can sometimes add resistance to accepting the dream information. Just carry on with your analysis steps and let the final dream meaning be brought together in the last step.

Review the discussion at the beginning of the People section in Part 3 to help clarify the meaning further. This is especially helpful if you do not know your dream character or if the symbol is a universal word like "mother" or "father."

Animal Symbols

As with the human symbols, ask yourself what three characteristics or traits you personally associate with the dream animal. These three attributes will likely tell you which aspects of your self that are being revealed to you. Many animals, however, also have a universal symbolic meaning, so after you've listed your three personal associations with this animal, check the Animals section in Part 3 for more possible answers. Watch for that "ah-ha" feeling when you come across the right meaning for you.

Object Symbols

Try asking yourself some of the following questions about your symbol. Remember that the symbol is trying to tell you something about your self, so watch for the "light bulb" response to know when you've found the right answer for you. After you have answered the questions, check the dictionary for further assistance.

> ‣ Have I ever had any experience of this symbol? If so, when? Is this something I am in contact with every day or only once in my life?
> ‣ If I have had an experience of this symbol, why or how was I involved with it?
> ‣ If the symbol has any use, how is it used?
> ‣ What connections or memories does this object bring up?

Describe the object, including its look and function, as though you were describing it to an alien who has never encountered this object before.

Write down your description if possible, and really listen to your thoughts for symbolism and double meanings.

Now you're ready to look at the symbols or keywords in your dream's content. For a long involved dream, try to pick out the most significant symbol from each paragraph or dream segment. Analysis of every symbol is challenging and often leads to information overload (which beginners especially want to avoid).

Ninety percent of the symbols in your dream represent some aspect of you, so write your symbolic meanings in the fashion shown below.

Seer's Path Method Example 1: Wild Horses

I am happily walking down a beautiful **road** with my friend **Dave**. We see some wild **horses** running freely across the **countryside**.

Meaning of Symbols

1) **Road** — my pathway in life (my spiritual pathway)
2) **Dave** — masculine aspect of self that is witty, courageous and daring
3) **Horses** — aspect of self that is powerful, strong, bold
4) **Countryside** — my awareness of freedom and peace

To learn how to identify and interpret your dream symbols, see Chapter 5. Note that this is also discussed in detail in Chapter 7.

Step 6: Meaning of the Dream

If you made a dream request prior to having this dream, rewrite it now before starting this step.

Look back to the feelings in the dream and write out the statement, "One to two days prior to this dream I was experiencing . . . (write dream feelings here)." This will tell you the *true* feelings you were experiencing when you were awake and what prompted the dream when you were asleep.

The next step is to rewrite the theme, this time removing the "somethings" and "someones" and replacing them with the symbolic descriptions you wrote down in Step 5.

After you have rewritten the theme, think back to the day or two prior to the dream and see if you can connect which experiences felt similar to the dream feelings and which events were similar to the theme's actions.

Seer's Path Method Example 1: Wild Horses

I am happily walking down a beautiful road with my friend Dave. We see some wild horses running freely across the countryside.

Dream Meaning

In the last twenty-four hours I was feeling happy and free (in my waking hours).

> Rewritten theme with symbolic descriptions inserted will read as follows.
>
> ▸ I am walking my spiritual path (road) and I am aware that this is the daring and courageous aspect/marble of my self (Dave).
> ▸ My power, strength and boldness (horses) are running or functioning with freedom and peace.

The dreamer had to think back to the last day or two prior to the dream and remember when and why she felt happy. She also had to note when and why she may have felt daring, courageous, bold, strong, free and peaceful. These keywords from the dream helped her identify the waking-hour situation (event or relationship) that triggered the dream.

In this dream example, the dreamer recalls having felt very *happy* and *free* the previous day when she boldly drew some much needed boundaries in a new relationship. Having faced this waking-hour challenge, she felt *stronger, freer* and more at *peace*.

This step can take patience and practice to accomplish. You may want to speak the dream out loud to someone (even if they know nothing about dream work) as part of this step. They will often make the connection for you. Listen carefully to your thoughts and words when thinking back to previous days' events. You will often think or speak words that were used in the dream (in this example, the words in italics in the previous paragraph).

Step 7: Title and Summary

Summarize what the dream means to *you* by restating the entire meaning in just a few lines.

Give the dream interpretation a brief title. List all your dream interpretation titles and short summaries of the dreams on a separate sheet and review them at the end of the week, month or year to help remind you of the progress you are making. This is a great self-confidence booster and reviewing a year's worth of dream titles makes a great New Year's resolution.

Seer's Path Method Example 1: Wild Horses

I am happily walking down a beautiful road with my friend Dave. We see some wild horses running freely across the countryside.

Title and Summary

Running Free Like a Horse: setting new boundaries is a courageous step on my spiritual path. I feel stronger and more peaceful about myself.

Step 8: Decision and Application

Decision: What would you like to do with this information? Be brief. One word will do, or you may choose to do nothing. It is up to you.

Application: List three ways in which you can implement your decision. These need to be realistic and practical — something that you can start accomplishing right away. Personal growth is a *process* that requires baby steps. Be gentle to your emerging self!

Seer's Path Method Example 1: Wild Horses

I am happily walking down a beautiful road with my friend Dave. We see some wild horses running freely across the countryside.

Decision and Application

1) I plan to enjoy my new-found freedom and do something special just for me.
2) I will make a list of three things I've always wanted to do, but haven't done, and set out to do them. I will create a spa day just for me at home: I will turn off the phone and pamper myself with a bath, pedicure, manicure, mud mask and a glass of wine.

To help you visualize this information, here it is formatted into a chart. You'll find a blank copy of this chart in Appendix B.

Feelings Happy, free	Background or Setting Countryside	Theme ▸ I am walking somewhere (road) with someone (Dave). ▸ Something (horses) is running somewhere (countryside).
Most Significant Symbol Horses	Meaning of Symbols ▸ Road – my pathway in life (my spiritual pathway) ▸ Dave – masculine aspect of self that is witty, courageous and daring ▸ Horses – aspect of self that is powerful, strong, bold ▸ Countryside – my awareness of freedom and peace	Dream's Meaning In the last 24 hours I was feeling happy and free (in my waking hours). I am walking my spiritual path and I am aware that this is the daring and courageous aspect/marble of my self. My power, strength and boldness are running or functioning with freedom and peace.
Title: Running Free Like a Horse **Summary:** I'm setting new boundaries is a courageous step on my spiritual path. I feel stronger and more peaceful about myself.		
Decision and Application 1) I plan to enjoy my new-found freedom and do something special just for me. 2) I will make a list of three things I've always wanted to do, but haven't done, and set out to do them. I will create a spa day just for me at home: I will turn off the phone and pamper myself with a bath, pedicure, manicure, mud mask and a glass of wine.		

Seer's Path Method Example 2: Turbulent Waters

This dream was recorded by 38-year-old woman.

*"I am <u>looking</u> at two deep muddy **rivers** that are flowing rapidly. I <u>know</u> I have been here before: in the <u>past</u> I just got into the **water** and allowed the turbulent water to take me wherever it wanted to go and I had no control. The water is so deep and rapid that I <u>don't think</u> I'd like to have this happen again. Suddenly the water just stops <u>flowing</u> as if a **dam** has closed off the flow to a trickle. I have never seen this happen before but I <u>accept</u> it easily and with relief. Now I <u>won't have</u> to be swept away without control again."*

Feelings Relief	Background or Setting Outdoors by water	Theme
		▶ I am looking at something (water). ▶ I know something (I've been here before). ▶ In the past I allowed something (being uncontrollably swept away by turbulent flow) to happen. ▶ I don't want this to happen again. ▶ Suddenly something (water) stops. ▶ I accept something (water stoppage) with relief. ▶ I won't have to allow something (being swept away without control) to happen again.
Most Significant Symbol Deep, rapid flow muddy of water	**Meaning of Symbols** Water – Universally, water is symbolic of dreamer's emotional life and feelings (commonly expressed in such ways as "I feel as if I am drowning"). ▶ muddy water describes emotions that are not easily seen or clearly identified ▶ turbulent water indicates tumultuous and chaotic feelings ▶ deep water signifies feelings that are overwhelming	**Dream's Meaning** ▶ In the two days prior to this dream, I felt relief about something. ▶ I am looking at my emotions (water). ▶ I know I have been here before (looking at my turbulent emotions). ▶ In the past I have allowed my turbulent emotions (deep, muddy, turbulent water) to sweep me away uncontrollably. ▶ I don't want this to happen again. ▶ Suddenly I see the turbulent feelings stop.

Most Significant Symbol	Meaning of Symbols	Dream's Meaning
	▸ deep, muddy, turbulent water represents dreamer's chaotic, overwhelming emotional state that she is not able to see clearly	▸ I accept this with relief. ▸ I won't have to be swept away uncontrollably by my emotions again.

Title: Facing My Fears
Summary: I have faced my fearful feelings and am now learning not to let them control my life and the direction in which I flow.

Decision and Application

I will practise being aware of my emotional states by
1) checking in on how I feel several times a day and journal at the end of each day,
2) continuing with dream work to help me recognize the truth of my emotional state, and
3) recognizing when emotions are pulling me off my intended goals – I will keep focussed on goals.

Dreamer's Comments on Meaning

This 38-year-old woman immediately understood the implications of the dream's message. She had been experiencing some strong emotions (fear) for some time. For her, the dream was a clear indication that she had finally been able to "dam" or stem the flow of fearful emotions that had been overwhelming her. In the past she would have allowed her emotions to carry her away, which was not at all helpful. She felt great relief at having finally accepted and faced her fears.

Seer's Path Method Example 3: Making a Dream Request

Wolves in the Night

This dream was recorded by 32-year-old woman.

Her dream request (question) asked prior to sleep was, "What am to learn with my partner/boyfriend at this time?"

"It is very dark in the dream and there are two wolves sitting back to back or rump to rump. One is grey and one is black. One of the wolves barks and this startles me. I feel love for, and from, the wolves, but I also fear them."

Feelings	Background or Setting	Theme
Protected, startled, love, fear	Darkness or black	‣ I see something (wolves) that I both love and fear. ‣ Something (wolves) is sitting somehow (back to back) that makes me feel protected. ‣ Something (barking) startles me.
Most Significant Symbol Wolves	**Meaning of Symbols** 1) Black – represents the void, mystery and a place of growth 2) Wolves – represent an act by instincts. Wolves are teachers; they run in families and are protective of each other. I believe the wolves represent my boyfriend and me. 3) Barking – animals' expression or way of communicating 4) Back to back – standing firm, mirror images, protecting each other's back 5) Grey – grey matter or head. My boyfriend lives in his grey matter	**Dream's Meaning** Dream Request question: "What am I to learn with my partner/boyfriend at this time?" In the last day or two of my waking hours I have been feeling fear and love. ‣ What I see is my relationship with my boyfriend (two wolves, one black and one grey). ‣ My boyfriend and I (wolves) are protecting each other and mirroring each other (sitting back to back). ‣ My boyfriend communicates (barks/speaks) his love for me and this startles me.

Most Significant Symbol	Meaning of Symbols	Dream's Meaning
	(mind) whereas I live more in my intuition and am interested in the mysteries of life, which to me are represented by the colour black.	

Title: Wolves in the Night
Summary: What can I learn from my relationship? It is a tool for my self-growth and has much to teach me. I am safe and protected in this union and can speak my truth.

Decision and Application
Accept and digest dream information. Application will include
1) sharing this information with my boyfriend,
2) beginning to learn more about my self by applying principles of mirroring in this relationship, and
3) just enjoy this union and the protection it offers me.

Dreamer's Comments on Meaning

"I realize that when my boyfriend told me yesterday that he loved me, it startled me and aroused confusing feelings of both love and fear. I realize now that I am to see that this relationship is an excellent tool for learning more about myself (a period of fertilization and growth) because my boyfriend is mirroring me. I am also beginning to learn that he offers me a sense of protection and safety which I have never felt in a relationship before."

Seer's Path Method Example 4: Applying the Method to a Waking-Time Event

My Engine Groans

Submitted by a 50-year-old man.

"I am experiencing car problems. The engine is groaning and straining when I drive on the highway and I wonder if this has some symbolic or deeper meaning in my life."

Feelings	Background or Setting	Theme
Acceptance	On highway	▸ I am driving something (car) somewhere (highway). ▸ Something (engine strain) happens. ▸ I am resigned to this happening and accept it without upset (as if I know it will all turn out ok anyway).
Most Significant Symbol ▸ Car ▸ Engine ▸ Highway	**Meaning of Symbols** 1) Car – Represents my lifestyle or the way in which I "drive myself." Can also represent my physical body. 2) Engine – The engine gives me the power to drive, to be and to go in life. It is the vitality of the car and therefore my vitality. 3) Highway – The faster way to travel in life, or indicates I am in the fast lane and moving quickly at this time — perhaps even hurriedly.	**Event's Meaning** ▸ My lifestyle is currently fast-paced and moving quickly. ▸ My vitality is strained/stressed (from going too fast, doing too much, overloading myself with work). ▸ I am resigned and accepting of this situation.

Title: My Engine Groans

Summary: I realize how hard I have been pushing my body and myself. My body is stressed and in need of some slow-down time.

Decision and Application

This event reflected to me, reminded me and warned me to slow down and stop pushing myself so hard before more serious problems set in. I accept the consequences of my behaviour and realize that all will be well if I heed the messages inherent in the car's current problems. I will also get the car checked out and maintained by a mechanic.

※

The Magical Path Method

Overview of Steps

1 – Feelings
2 – Most Significant Symbol and Its Meaning
3 – Waking-Hour Connection

The Magical Path Method is a three-step interpretation method designed to speed-up the time it takes to interpret your dreams and waking-hour events. For those who have mastered the eight-step Seer's Path Method, the Magical Path Method provides the simplest and quickest way to understand the deeper meaning in your dreams and waking events. If you are choosing to start your interpretation practice with the Magical Path Method, understand that it is *not* as in-depth as the Seer's Path Method and will therefore reveal less information initially. With practice it can reveal depth just as well as the Seer's Path Method. Just follow the three steps outlined here and answer the questions based on the content of your dream and your personal experiences. A worksheet for this method is provided in Appendix C.

Remember: only you can interpret your dreams and all the answers are within yourself. This is meant only as an aid or guide in revealing your answers to you.

Step 1: Feelings

Choose the main feeling from the dream. This could be anger, happiness, sadness, fear, joy, anxiety, or a sense of control — whatever stands out the most for you. If identifying your feelings is new to you, or if you are unable to recognize what the dream's feelings are, then review the information in the Seer's Path Method (specifically, step 1) or try the Identifying Your Feelings exercise in Chapter 8.

Step 2: Most Significant Symbol and Its Meaning

Choose the most prominent symbol from your dream: a scene, object, animal, person or even something you were thinking or saying in the dream — whatever stood out the most. To help identify the meaning of the symbol you have chosen, write down your answers to the following questions.

46

▸ What has been my experience of this person, place or thing?

▸ What does the word mean to me?

▸ What is it used for?

▸ Why is it used?

▸ How is it used specifically, and when is it used?

▸ If the symbol is a person, what three words describe that person's characteristics and/or personality?

▸ What are my personal beliefs regarding this symbol?

▸ Do I have any gut feelings about what it means?

Review Step 3 of the Seer's Path Method for more assistance in identifying your symbol's meaning.

Step 3: Waking-Hour Connection

Look at the feeling you have identified from the dream. Can you remember when you felt this way in your waking-hours in the last day or two? If so, what incident, event or situation are the feelings linked to?

Look at the meaning of the symbol you have chosen. Can you link the meaning to a daytime event, situation or relationship, or can you identify this as being one of your marbles (an aspect of your self; see Chapter 7)?

Can you link the feeling and symbol's meaning to one particular daytime situation, or to an aspect of self?

Refer to your journal (if you keep one) to help pinpoint what triggered the dream. Also, asking family and friends to help is advisable in the beginning, since they may remember an incident you have forgotten. Dreams often try to remind you of events, parts of self or feelings that may have been swept under the carpet or gone unrecognized by you.

The following examples will help you make the connection between dream feelings, dream symbols and a waking-hour event.

Magical Path Method Example 1: The Exploding House

Recorded by a 36-year-old woman.

"I dream of being on a hillside and seeing a little white bungalow. As I look at the house it explodes. I know my sister is inside, yet I do nothing to rescue her. I feel very detached from what is going on and I don't even try to move toward the house."

Most Significant Feeling Detachment (cut off from feeling anything)	**Most Significant Symbol** Sister
Meaning of Symbol Dreamer's comments on the sister symbol: ▶ The sister in my dream is my real sister, who died many years ago when we were teenagers. ▶ We were walking home from school one day when I was sixteen and she was thirteen. I was supposed to be watching over her, but she ran ahead of me and was hit by a car and killed. ▶ My life changed very dramatically because my parents held me responsible for her death. ▶ I have carried a heavy burden of responsibility for twenty years now. I try not to speak about her and I even avoid thinking about her. I always push thoughts of her from my mind.	**Waking-Hour Connection** The dreamer realizes that she feels detached from (the symbol of) her sister: ▶ In the past I have been very detached from the explosive feelings (represented by exploding house) that have been going on inside me, and I have done nothing about them. ▶ Lately, many things have triggered memories of my sister and I can now relate the dream to the feelings I have buried inside about her death. ▶ I never before recognized how much of an impact her death had on me. ▶ This is a huge relief for me to recognize and release the burden that was placed on my shoulders twenty years ago.

Magical Path Method Example 2: Construction Zone

This dream was recorded by a 25-year-old woman.

"I was driving along at night on a road under major construction. There was so much construction that traffic was at a snail's pace and I even had to detour onto the sidewalk at points. The turns and manoeuvring were so tight and intricate that it took much skill to navigate the narrow strip of road that was free from construction. For one particularly difficult manoeuvre on the sidewalk, I needed to back up and try several times before I could make the tight corner. But I made it and I am proud of my ability to manoeuvre through all the construction. I continue on along this road, hoping to find the entrance to the highway."

Most Significant Feeling	Most Significant Symbols
Pride	▸ Darkness ▸ Road and road under construction ▸ Construction
Meaning of Symbols ▸ Darkness – the unknown or "being in the dark" about something that is occurring in my life ▸ Road and road under construction – my spiritual path ▸ Construction – change, development and improvement of road conditions. Therefore, a road under construction in the dark is the improvement and development of my spiritual path, even though I am not aware of the progress I've been making.	**Waking-Hour Connection** The dreamer was able to connect the dream symbol of "dark road under construction" to the immense changes in her spiritual path. She did not think she was doing the right things in her life at this time — she thought she wasn't manoeuvring properly in her spiritual endeavours. However, the dream clearly points out her remarkable skill at progressing through such major construction (changes). Now she realizes the dream is pointing out the part of her that feels proud about her spiritual progress. The dream further encourages her to continue on her developing spiritual path despite the darkness (unknown). She expresses relief and gratitude for these realizations. She says it makes the daily challenges easier and she can now connect with her feelings of pride.

Magical Path Method Example 3: My Angry Father

Submitted by a man in his 40s.

"I have only a snippet of a dream that I remember. It involves my father, who died thirty years ago, and I know I was angry in the dream. But I recall nothing else."

Most Significant Feeling Anger	**Most Significant Symbol** Father
Meaning of Symbol ▸ His father died thirty years ago and he does not think of him often, since he was only ten when his father died. ▸ He goes on to say he doesn't even really have any memories of him. The dream does not feel like a visit from beyond.	**Waking-Hour Connection** The dreamer remains baffled about the connection to the waking hours until he is asked some questions about feeling angry recently. He ponders this and tells the story of his trip to a movie theatre the night before. He was waiting in a line-up in the men's washroom when a man pushed to the front of the line. "This made me really angry," he says. Then he says, "ah-ha," as if a light bulb has been turned on. He now remembers an incident that involved his father and him when he was a very young boy. He recalls standing in a men's washroom line-up and a similar incident occurred. A man butted in front of the line and he now remembers how his father reacted with anger. He sees that his response of anger is something he learned from his father's behaviour. This dream inspires him to further investigate the roots of his anger.

Magical Path Method Example 4: Spinning Out of Control

Submitted by 29-year-old man.

"I was driving my car and when I went to use the brakes they failed. The car started to spin out of control, doing doughnuts. Later I inspected the brakes and found that a small bracket had come off."

Most Significant Feeling Fear	Most Significant Symbol Brakes
Meaning of Symbol Brakes represent a part of me that has the ability or power to stop.	**Waking-Hour Connection** When asked to connect the feeling (fear) and the desire to stop something (put the brakes on) in his waking time, the man said, "I have been having a week from hell at work. I have been working a ton of overtime because I needed money. However, this is creating insanity in my life and I said to myself the day before this dream that all this (overtime) *has to stop.*" He now realizes that he wants to stop creating so much instability in his life (spinning out of control) and that the excessive overtime hours are not serving him well. The fear revealed in his dream is a belief that if he doesn't work the overtime hours, he won't have enough money to meet his financial obligations. He reached the conclusion that some new thought needs to be given to his work situation in order to restore his sense of balance and peace of mind. This can be accomplished by reviewing his workload and overtime strategy.

Magical Path Method Example 5: Applying the Method to a Waking-Time Event

Embarrassing Diarrhea

Submitted by 20-year-old woman

Event

"Every time I am around certain people (especially authority figures like doctors) I get cramping in my gut, usually followed by diarrhea. I wonder why this happens and what is the deeper meaning."

Most Significant Feeling Unease, distress	**Most Significant Symbol** Gut cramps, diarrhea
Meaning of Symbol ▸ Gut – The gut is the home of gut feelings and, according to the chakra system (second chakra), it is the seat of the emotions. It can also represent gut-wrenching experiences. ▸ Diarrhea – Represents letting go of something too quickly without processing it, or that whatever is occurring is "indigestible." Often connected to emotional (second chakra) issues, such as being over-whelmed by emotions and feelings. May indicate feelings of loss of control over emotions.	**Conscious Connection** I realize that certain people trigger my feelings of inadequacy, which I often feel as distress. The diarrhea is my body's way of telling me I am emotionally uncomfortable with certain authority figures (medical doctors or highly intellectual men). Making this connection will help me be more aware of my feelings and what triggers them in the future.

❂
The Intuitive Method:
Quick Verbal Interpretation

This simple approach is great for healers and practitioners of all kinds who need to learn to ask simple questions and make the connection between their client's dream and their waking hours. This comes with the practice of doing dream interpretation on yourself! As you become familiar with and advanced in applying the Magical Path Method, you can apply the dream interpretation principles verbally.

The key ingredient to the verbal approach is to listen to the dreamer's story, not just their dream information. Especially listen to their waking-hour experience because herein lies the answer to the dream's message. Your clients have all the answers — it's a matter of tuning in to the hidden message, which is much easier than you think. Clients will unconsciously talk about the underlying issues/meaning with little or no prompting.

For example, anyone who does hands-on work like massage or energy work may have already noticed how a client responds when touched in certain areas. Thoughts and emotions are energetically stored in the physical tissue and can therefore be released or realized by physical touch, manipulations or increased energy flow. Simply asking a client to focus on a particular body part or location will lead the client's unconscious thought flow right to the heart of the matter. This is a powerful tool to use in helping your clients relieve restrictions or blockages in their energy field and thereby improve their physical health. See the Body section of the dictionary (Part 3) and Chapter 6: The Literal Perspective for more details.

When a client recounts a dream, listen to the "sayings" they use and action words. For example, a dream may be explained as, "I am running away from the monster and can't face it for fear." When listening to the dreamer talk about their recent waking-hour experiences, listen for the words "running" and "can't face." Most likely they will use these exact words to describe a waking-hour situation.

Intuitive Method Example 1: Hanging Snakes

"I see snakes hanging on sticks from the rafters. Thousands of snakes just hanging there. It's scary."

Listen for the word "hanging" to be mentioned by the client in relation to their recent waking-hour experiences. In this case, the client spoke of hanging around with a certain group of people lately. The snakes were the people she was hanging around with and her unconscious was trying to get her attention that this association was causing her fear at a deeper level.

It is important to listen for clues and focus on action words being repeated when clients are speaking about their waking hours. In fact, you will find the dream's meaning faster and more easily by making connections between action words and waking-hour events. Watch for descriptive words too; they often point to the waking-hour situation that is triggering the dream. For example, colours are descriptive words often used in dream accounts and then spoken of to describe something seemingly unrelated. For example, "I am wearing a red shirt and I have red hair in the dream." Later the dreamer describes "seeing red" over an issue with her husband. In this example, the red is speaking about angry emotions the dreamer had.

Clients will often tell you the dream answer before they tell you the dream. This happens all the time, because the information is already on their mind and they will unknowingly share this information with all who will tune in and listen. Listen carefully for similarities between the dream account and what was discussed prior to your client describing the dream.

Put on your "symbolic ears" and learn to listen in a new way. You will soon realize that interpreting dreams is as easy as really hearing someone else tell their waking-hour stories.

Intuitive Method Example 2: Radio Realization

Submitted by 45-year-old man.

"I am in a restaurant and listening to radio station 99.9 FM. I suddenly realize something that I had not before, although I'm now foggy about what that realization was."

Ask your client four questions:

> 1) What was the main feeling in the dream?
>   *Answer:* realization
>
> 2) What was the most significant symbol in the dream?
>   *Answer:* radio station 99.9
>
> 3) What does radio mean to you, or does the number nine have
>   special meaning?
>   *Answer:* Radio stations broadcast information. The number nine
>   in numerology represents the idea of completion, termination
>   or the end of something.

4) Can you make the connection between these symbols and feelings and recent waking-hour events?
Answer: "Just the day before I had been out for the entire day with my wife, who I have recently separated from. I had thought that there was hope for the relationship. But I realized that the relationship truly was terminated and finished (represented by the number nine). This realization was being 'broadcast' loud and clear by yesterday's encounter."

Chapter 5

Interpreting Symbols

Silly Symbols

Silly, outrageous and nonsensical symbols are attention getters, but they are often disregarded as being meaningless because of their absurdity. In fact, these gems are usually the most meaningful on a personal level and were creatively designed just for you based on your personal symbolism. It is your creativity and cunning that is producing these often elaborate symbols for your viewing pleasure. This type of symbol is simply an opportunity for personal growth (as are all symbols), but they indicate just how ingenious and imaginative you really are. Silly symbols offer more in-depth information about your self. Enjoy your silly symbols and work with your own past and current associations in order to comprehend their meaning fully.

Example

"I dream of a grasshopper with springy coils instead of legs and it is lovingly attached to a blade of grass."

Look at each part of this silly symbol separately. Interpret grasshopper, coils and grass as individual symbols and then put them together like a jigsaw puzzle. Remember, you will have a personal association for each symbol. For example,

> **grasshopper:** ability to leap
> **coils:** something that entwines
> **grass:** something that grows

To further interpret these symbols it is important to take note of the feelings in the dream, which in this case was "lovingly." Then connect all the components to a waking-time experience. In this case the three symbols added up to represent the dreamer's recent ability to hold herself lovingly as she grew by leaps and bounds. It represented to the dreamer that her long-term goal of self-love was becoming more apparent, and she was enjoying it.

When you are able to make the connection between a dream symbol and a waking-time event, it will immediately lift your feelings and bring you one step closer to your goals. It takes waking-hour awareness to bring your goals to fruition and dreams help bring your goals closer with every symbol you interpret.

❁

Symbols that Change

When scenery changes from one room or situation to another, it can seem confusing. Remember, this is a mini movie about your life that is painting a picture of your daily perspectives. Just as you can walk from one room or environment to another in waking time, so too will your dreams lead you toward realization by showing you how your inner processes work — how you think, feel, speak and act. You change constantly throughout the day within these various capacities, so it is normal for dreams to follow your footsteps.

Example

"I dream I am in the kitchen and suddenly I find myself on the moon and then in a neighbour's house. How can I follow this seemingly nonsensical pattern?"

Look at each setting as an individual symbol, translate it into a personal meaning, and then piece them together in order to understand how you have been recently perceiving something in your waking time.

The dreamer's personal symbolic meaning of the dream's symbols were

> **kitchen:** place where I prepare, take in, digest or process food (and, since food is a symbol for thoughts, this represents how I process my thoughts)
>
> **moon:** totally foreign place
>
> **neighbour's house:** something that is right beside me or next to me

This dream is trying to indicate the dreamer's thoughts or thinking processes (kitchen). Some current way of thinking felt totally foreign (moon) to the dreamer. She was able to connect the dream's feeling (bewilderment) to an event that happened the previous day, when she was presented with a new perspective on an old problem. This seemed to be a totally new and unfamiliar viewpoint even though the perspective or solution had been right next to her (neighbour's house) all along.

This type of dream is helpful in showing you how you walk through a problem or situation in your life. Such dreams will help you to see whether your current processes are working for you. Dreams will show you when your actions are not working well for you, so watch for this type of guidance in these seemingly perplexing dream movies. The questions and answers are almost always presented within the same dream.

❁

Enlarged or Emphasized Symbols

Symbols that are enlarged or emphasized, such as wearing shoes that are twelve feet long, are trying to get your attention. These types of glaringly disproportionate dream symbols are often taken as a matter of course ("oh well, it's just a silly dream"). Such symbols may seem obvious but they are often overlooked because of the sheer amount of detail and symbolism in a single dream. Overemphasized or disproportionate symbols (small or large) can be considered a main symbol and are important to note when interpreting a dream.

When symbols are emphasized in a dream, they are simply a bold statement that whatever this symbol represents for you is compelling, and it would behoove you to explore it. Sometimes the fact that something is missing or totally irrational is an attention getter, such as a person without a head or a horse with fish gills. Just make note of these dream oddities and use them for your benefit by examining them as your most significant symbol (this is explained in Step 3 of the Seer's Path Method in Chapter 4).

❁

Names and Words Spoken Out Loud

Dream communication is almost always telepathically relayed, so if you have spoken words in your dreams it is very important to write them down. These statements are direct messages, and this type of communication is your higher self trying to get you to recognize something that is occurring in your waking hours. Write down the words spoken in the dream and then read them as though someone else were relaying this communiqué to you. Spoken words can often bring powerful insights, and even warnings. Other forms of relaying a message may come via any written word, such as a street sign, name badge, or text in a book or newspaper.

> *"Spoken words can often bring powerful insights."*

Be aware of spoken names as well: often they will have a special, personalized meaning to you. Search your memory banks for the connection. If it is the name of someone you know or once knew, then choose three words to describe that person's personality or characteristics and write them down. Recognize that these traits are mirrors of your own personality that are striving to be shown to you. Dreams show you your traits in the hopes that you will recognize or own them, helping to create greater inner stability and wholeness. Revealed personality traits, regardless of whether you deem them good or bad, are opportunities for self-growth and self-improvement. Every dream presents an opportunity to know your self better by mirroring you in other people, animals or objects.

Example: Names

In a dream you are walking down the street and meet Mr. Green. This particular name may refer to a friend or acquaintance of yours named Green. To interpret this symbol you will have to recall whether you have known or currently know a person named Green. If you do, then choose three words to describe Mr. Green's personality or characteristics. The words you choose will help you understand what traits the dream character is mirroring for you. Or, meeting Mr. Green may be trying to highlight the colour green for you. Search your memory for an association to the colour green. Do you like the colour green or are you repelled by it? Does it mean growth and healing to you, or envy? Connect the meaning with a current situation, relationship or feeling in your life and you will have a better understanding of the dream's meaning.

Names of people can also indicate a feeling you've been having or an attitude you've been holding. Names in dreams can be varied and creative. You may encounter a dream person named Mrs. Moody, a pet named Grumpy, or a book titled *Extreme Defence*, or you may find yourself on a street named Resistance Road. These types of names in dreams indicate something about your personality, character or nature. Notice whether you can make the connection between these names and any parts of your self and ask yourself, "How well is this part serving me?"

Recurring Symbols

Recurring symbols are people, objects or animals that keep popping up in dream after dream. This can go on for days, months or even years before you recognize it is an important message that is trying to get through. Keep working with your recurring symbol until the meaning is uncovered. Often asking another person to listen to your dream, as you listen yourself, is a helpful way of uncovering the meaning. Pretend your listener is an alien and describe the symbol in as much detail as possible and then ask for their feedback.

Recurring symbols often point out a current conflict in your life. Conflict is a common part of everyday living and occurs both internally and externally. You may hold conflicting feelings or opinions about a circumstance or person in your life. Quarrelling with another may seem like an obvious type of conflict and these types of external quarrels have an impact at a deeper level of your being. Over time this can do harm to the physical body, which is partly why it is shown to you again and again: to get your attention so you will change the situation or take a new look at it. Once a symbol is understood in the waking time, it will stop occurring in your dreams.

Part 2
The Wisdom of the
Egyptian Ancient Mystery School

What Are the Perspectives?

All of life's events and happenings can be viewed from four very different levels or viewpoints. These four perspectives are based on Egyptian Ancient Mystery School teachings and the four levels of temple life that an individual passed through in order to become enlightened. These are the same Mystery School teachings that Christ used. A rudimentary look at the four levels is offered here as a tool for dream interpretation.

Dream perspectives are simply categories. They help break down the huge amount of dreamtime information into sections that are easier to digest. Each perspective is a distinct point of view, and each is designed to teach you something about yourself and the world around you.

The four dream perspectives presented in this section offer students a unique approach to understanding the dream time and, consequently, the self (physical, emotional, mental and spiritual aspects of self). Each perspective offers different information about your self and every dream can be viewed from *one or all* of the perspectives. This approach to dream work allows you to simply scratch the surface of your dream's meaning or to reach to the greatest depth of information about you and your soul's journey. You are truly in control of how much information you wish to obtain.

In ancient Egypt, all members of society were considered students of life and were required to attend temple or school for their education. Simplified, there were four levels or grades to Egyptian schooling. Each level taught a distinct way to view everyday life and assisted individuals to live a fulfilling and reverent lifestyle geared toward their individual make-up.

The four levels or grades were given names, and every member of society attended at least the first grade. Continuing with higher education was optional. The first level was called the literal level, the second the symbolic level, the third was the irrational level and the fourth was the Creator level. Each level took a minimum of seven years to complete (if not longer) and if you were one of the few who chose to continue through the higher grades, you would be considered a wise one, initiate or adept. The few who actually completed the fourth level were called priests and priestesses, and they were considered the enlightened ones or teachers of society.

Each perspective given here offers you a simplified look into each temple level. The perspectives demonstrate that dreams are designed to assist you in understanding and expanding your knowledge of self. Each perspective can be found in *every* dream, including day dreams, as well as in the symbolism that is all around you in your waking hours (see Chapters 3 and 7).

The Four Dream Perspectives	The Essence of Teaching
Literal	Know Your Self
Symbolic	Know Your Symbols
Irrational	Know Who You Are Not
Creator	Know Your Creator

All of life is a reflection of your inner reality, and the four perspectives are designed to help you get to know your inner world so you can then create and recreate your reality as you would like it to be. This powerful and ingenious tool can benefit all who choose to seek to understand it.

Chapter 6

The Literal Perspective

The literal perspective offers you an opportunity to Know Your Self by showing or reflecting the literal world in which we live. We live in a three-dimensional world that is comprised of elements (air, water, earth, fire), plants, animals and humans. This may seem obvious, but the energetic complexity and interaction of these components of life is not always apparent. In order to understand how your dreams offer you factual information about yourself, it is imperative that you understand a bit about energy and how it flows.

Einstein proved long ago that all matter is comprised of vibrating particles of energy. This includes all the components of life here on Earth — water, air, fire, earth, plant life, animals, humans and even inanimate human-made objects. Each of us is affected vibrationally by the energy that is all around us, everywhere, at all times, so in a sense the particles from these sources around you play a role in forming your self. And since all dream information is a reflection of your self, your dreams reflect these elements, plant life and animal life and how you are part of the larger ecosystem of life. It is important to integrate this into your learning because when you dream at night your awareness expands to include these often unseen vibrations of energy.

Therefore, we'll start our exploration of the literal perspective with some fundamental information about the human energy field.

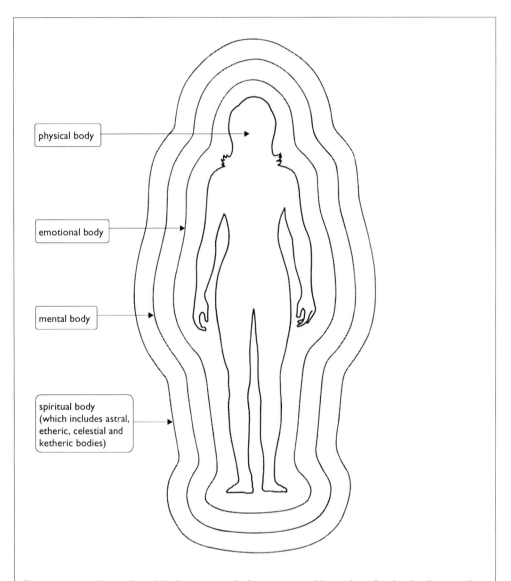

physical body

emotional body

mental body

spiritual body
(which includes astral,
etheric, celestial and
ketheric bodies)

The space around your physical body is comprised of an immeasurable number of molecules that are vibrating so fast that they are invisible to the human eye. This energy field (or auric field) around your body houses your six subtle bodies: emotional, mental, astral, etheric, celestial and ketheric. The subtle bodies in your auric field also correspond to your seven major chakras, with the first chakra representing your physical body and chakras two through seven corresponding to your six subtle bodies.

Figure 2. An energy field made up of an immeasurable number of molecules surrounds your physical body

✵
The Human Energy Field

Einstein said, "Energy can neither be created nor destroyed." If we and the Universe are nothing but pure energy — which we are — then this statement leads to the questions, "What happens when we die?" and "How were we created in the first place?"

To understand the human energy field it is practical to first have an understanding of the nature of reality.

The world in which we live appears to be full of solid matter, and it is. But if viewed at a quantum level (under an extremely powerful microscope), the matter would appear as swirling particles and molecules of energy — and much empty space. That which appears solid has been proven not to be.

Furthermore, you are not just a body occupying space here on the planet. You are a dynamic interplay of multiple layers of energy. Your physical body, which appears solid, is comprised of quadrillions of vibrating molecules. The space around you houses even more molecules that are vibrating so fast that the human eye cannot detect them. This space around your physical body is your energy field or auric field, and it can be said to house your subtle bodies (see Figure 2).

The subtle bodies have been named as follows: emotional body, mental body, astral body, etheric body, celestial body and ketheric body. They correspond to six of the seven major chakras (the first corresponds to your physical body). Chakras are energy centres and are a reflection of your soul energy. Just as a prism refracts light into the seven colours of the rainbow, so too does your soul light refract into seven major colours (wavelengths) when embodied (chakras are explained in more detail in Part 3, the Dream Symbol Dictionary). These levels of being are what is referred to as the self throughout this book. So the self is comprised of your physical body and its functioning; the emotional body and your feelings; the mental body and its thoughts, attitudes and beliefs; and the spiritual body and all its insights, visions and connections to All That Is. It is these parts of self that are shown to you in every dream.

Besides being a human being, you are also a multi-bodied, multi-systemed, multi-dimensional being of pure, vibrating energy. The physical body is seen by the human eye because its vibration is very slow in the scope of the Universal energies. Because you are pure light, your physical body could be called "light trapped in gravitation."

The fact that energy cannot be created or destroyed points to the concept that we all stem from one source of energy. This Source is often referred to as God (or any of the other names that have been chosen by cultures all over the world). The point is that all humans, animals, plants and elemental life are fragments of the one source of energy. If we took a gigantic mirror and let it shatter over Earth, each one of the resulting shards would still be part of, and reflect, the whole. But now they would appear as separate pieces.

> *"You are a dynamic interplay of multiple layers of energy."*

To understand the first level of the Ancient Mystery School teachings it is helpful to understand some of these energetic truths and principles.

You are a fragment of the Whole, One, Source, or whatever name you ascribe to your God. It can be no other way if Einstein's statement is correct — which it has been proven to be. You have a unique energetic pattern that designates you much like your fingerprint does.

During normal waking-hour consciousness many people are only aware of their physical bodies. This level of awareness is rapidly changing in society as we begin to realize and remember that there is much more to being human than just having a body.

When you dream at night your consciousness (awareness) changes, in fact expands, to encompass *all* of these subtle bodies and *all* the information they contain. When you are in the dream state you experience your whole self with crystal clarity and truth that far exceeds your waking-hour consciousness. When you dream, you become whole or "holy," and humans who have accomplished wholeness are experiencing all their parts/bodies with that same dreamtime clarity, but while awake. This level of awareness or consciousness are what the Christ and Buddha experienced while incarnated as human beings. This same level of consciousness is accessible in the dream time and *every* dream contains vital information about your self that will guide and enhance your everyday life and can lead you to enlightenment.

In order to Know Your Self, you must know all of your parts in all their depth and truth. The literal perspective begins this process by revealing the nature of all your bodies (physical, emotional, mental, and spiritual). These parts or bodies contain information about the truth of your feelings, thoughts, attitudes, beliefs, ideas, judgements, opinions and your divinity or God-self. This is the information revealed in the literal perspective of the Egyptian Ancient Mystery School teachings.

Dreams, then, are mirrors or windows into the very matrix or spirit of who you are as a human being and spiritual being. The literal perspective shows you who you are by allowing you to examine these subtle bodies in detail. Each dream contains information about your physical body, your emotional body, your mental body and your spiritual body.

If the paradigm of your self as a multi-dimensional being is new to you, you may want to spend some waking-hour time becoming aware of the fact that you have feelings, intuition and mental talk or chatter. Studies suggest that humans have between 50,000 and 90,000 thoughts a day. How many of those thoughts are you aware of? In the dream time, feelings, thoughts and "knowing" are revealed with clarity. Beginning to recognize these aspects of self in your everyday waking life is an excellent tool for building dream interpretation skills. The application will be clarified and further explained in Chapter 10 when we examine using the Ancient Egyptian Mystery School perspectives in the dream interpretation process. We begin with a discussion of the different levels of information available from the literal perspective.

🜨

The Physical Level

The physical level or body is the densest and slowest-vibrating of the four bodies, and it comprises all the organs, glands and systems. Because the dream time allows you access to endless information about your self, dream interpretation becomes the perfect avenue to use to help heal a physical condition. For example, if you have kidney pain or disease and wish to return the organ to health, you could use any of the four perspectives to promote healing. Simply becoming aware of the energetic meaning behind your illness will begin the healing process, and this is what the dream time offers you — an opportunity to understand and expand your knowledge of self.

Although this viewpoint may seem like the easiest to understand, and most beginners to dream work will, in fact, translate all their dream material quite literally, it is vital that the beginner recognize that night dreams are rarely literal. Dreams do not often give us a verbatim, literal account of our physical condition/health. This is, in fact, the rarest way for dream information to be given. However, it is possible to receive literal information with practice and in the lucid dream states (discussed in Chapter 3). Dreams do reveal a great amount of information about the physical body, but it often delivered symbolically.

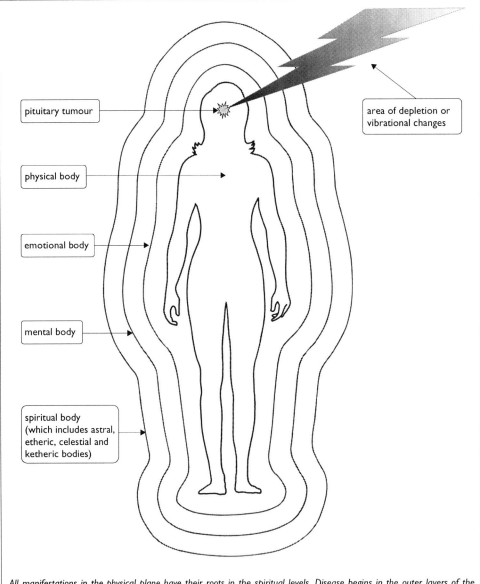

pituitary tumour

area of depletion or vibrational changes

physical body

emotional body

mental body

spiritual body
(which includes astral, etheric, celestial and ketheric bodies)

All manifestations in the physical plane have their roots in the spiritual levels. Disease begins in the outer layers of the auric field when a part of the field weakens, becomes disrupted, and begins to vibrate at a different rate in the outer layers first. This weakened area of the energy field causes disease, illness or injury to occur in the associated area of the body. In this example, a brain (pituitary) tumour was created when a section of the auric field around the head became disrupted. Note that Figure 10 looks at this example in more detail.

Figure 3. Disease manifests on the physical plane only after depleting the energy fields on the other levels of your being

When energy is not moving well through the emotional, mental or spiritual body, it has the potential to create disease in the physical body. This type of information is often revealed in dream time, and it is quite possible to see where future physical problems will spring up based on dream content. The literal perspective is a useful tool for prevention as well as an avenue to address current problems (see the dream requests section in Chapter 2 for a discussion on how to gather information about your health concerns).

In order for disease to manifest in your physical body, the energetic vibrations are first and always affected in the other levels of your being (i.e., your emotional, mental and spiritual bodies). Disease does not begin in the physical body, but rather in the spiritual body (see Figure 3). All disease in the physical body can be seen as a spiritual crisis in the happening. Complete healing and restoration of physical functioning will happen when you become aware of the underlying issues that have occurred on the emotional, mental and spiritual levels. Once awareness is brought into the waking time about the underlying issues, old energy patterns are energetically released from your auric field and this allows room for new healing energy to enter this space. This new energy is the energy of the Divine and it promotes complete restorative healing. This process of clearing energy patterns held in the auric field is as simple to do as learning to recognize and honour what the self is trying to tell you in the dream time (day dreams and waking-hour symbolism apply as well).

To keep this literal perspective simplified, it will be sufficient at this point to understand that you are a complex energetic system and that your personal experience of health, wealth, happiness and fulfilment in everyday life is dependant on how much or how little you know of your self — physically, emotionally, mentally and spiritually.

❀

The Emotional Level

Dreams reveal your emotions or feelings in great abundance. In order to interpret your dreams you must be able to identify the feelings revealed. To assist you in understanding the emotional aspect of the literal perspective, it is important to acknowledge that you have emotions or feelings during your waking hours and to recognize what they are. This may seem obvious to most, but it is very common within our society to feel nothing (numb) or to feel only one or two different feelings. If working with your feelings is new to you or if you need help in identifying your feelings, then try the Identifying Your Feelings exercise in Chapter 8.

71

Dreams not only reflect what is going on in your everyday life, they also show you the true feelings of your heart. Since many people have forgotten that they have feelings or have been unable to connect to them, they may not realize how they truly feel at a deeper level of their being. Dreams are a very useful tool for practitioners who are addressing their clients' emotional concerns. The dream will *always* indicate the true feeling at the core of an issue, even if the waking-time feeling is different.

> *" Learning to identify your dream feelings is an excellent tool for self-growth and healing."*

Dream feelings are our true feelings and they do not lie. Identifying your dream feelings is the simplest and quickest way to get to the heart or essence of your truth. Even if you have been aware of your everyday waking feelings for some time, your dream feelings will often show you deeper and further-reaching levels of truth about yourself. For example, suppose that your waking-time feeling is one of depression and your dream displays angry emotions (this may be portrayed in the dream through you or another character). Your dream is trying to tell you the underlying truth of your feelings. In this example it is anger, not depression, that your true being is experiencing, and this anger will affect the vibration or health of your whole being (your mind, body and spirit). This has far-reaching implications and therefore simply learning to identify your dream feelings is an excellent tool for self-growth and healing.

Remember, your emotions or feelings are actually a vibration that surrounds your physical body. The emotional body is vibrating faster than the physical body, and it is usually not detected by the average person's eye. This level of vibration is often seen by a clairvoyant's vision because these people are able to detect a larger band of vibrational frequencies and can therefore see auras or colours in your energy field. They can see the actual manifestation of feelings in your emotional body. Our language reflects this clairvoyant sight with such expressions as red with anger, green with envy, feeling blue and tickled pink. Unexpressed or unrecognized emotions eventually affect the physical vibration and cause loss of vitality and health in the area affected.

Begin to see your emotions as part of your guidance system in life. They will always point you in the direction that is best for you and show you how to take the next step. Learning to allow your feelings full expression without judgement will lead to restoration of the physical body. It will also broaden the avenues to your spiritual growth.

✿

The Mental Level

The mental body is the part of us that houses our thoughts, attitudes, beliefs, ideas, opinions and judgements. With respect to the literal point of view, it is important to note that these aspects of self exist and will be shown in every dream. It is sufficient to understand at this point that all of your thoughts, attitudes, beliefs and opinions are part of the whole of yourself and affect the other levels. It is human to have thoughts, attitudes and beliefs, and dream information will tell you how well they serve you and your overall health. The biggest imbalance and therefore the largest amount of information about the mental part of yourself is seen in the irrational perspective and will be discussed in greater depth in Chapter 8.

Remember that this body or level is a vibration of swirling particles of energy just as your physical and emotional bodies are, but this one is vibrating even faster. People who are clairaudient (clear hearing or hearing thought forms) or telepathic are able to hear this level of vibration.

Just as the emotions you experience affect your physical body, so too does your mental body (thoughts, attitudes, and beliefs) affect the health of your physical body. As you begin to recognize and understand different parts of your mental body (revealed in every dream), you can alter the vibration flow here to allow for greater healing of the body and make room for peace of mind.

Meditation and the Mental Level

If connecting to your waking-hour thoughts is new to you, some simple meditation practices can assist you in becoming familiar with your own "mental chatter." Most Eastern and Western teachings about meditation suggest quieting the mind as part of the meditation protocol. I suggest the opposite as outlined below.

Turn off telephones, pagers, television and radio to make your chosen meditation spot as quiet and free from distraction as possible. You will need only a few minutes to begin with and may increase the amount of time spent in meditation as you feel necessary. Sit comfortably, becoming aware of how your body feels in its current position. Adjust your body until it's comfortable, then begin to observe your breathing pattern without changing it. Then take a deep breath, inhaling and spreading your ribs, and notice how this deeper breathing pattern changes your physiology. Now listen to your thoughts. Don't try to block them out or quiet them — listen intently to them and note what they are about. Try to become the witness or observer of your own thought processes, even if your thoughts are seemingly insignificant, such as "this exercise is silly" or "this isn't working — I can't hear any thoughts." These are thoughts and they are trying to get your attention. If your mind wanders to worry, or to making lists of things that need to be done, then this too is the thought process in motion. Allow all voices to be heard; simply oversee the mental chatter process. In this way you will slowly get to know the mental level of your being.

> *"Try to become the witness or observer of your own thought process."*

If you are always pushing your thoughts away or trying to quiet them, then you cannot learn from them. It is your thoughts that bring you extensive information about your self, and your dreams reveal this level of self in great detail. Many people find it challenging to listen to their own mental chatter, but that is often because their thoughts are self-judging and self-berating. The difficulty stems from the quality of their thoughts, not the act of listening itself.

You will find the very matrix of who you are at this level of self. Simply tuning in to your daily thought patterns can lead you to your greatest growth and knowledge of self. So do not push away your thoughts. Really listen to them and see what they are telling you. Most often they will point to the area of greatest stress and worry in your life. This is great information to know. Once you know what is causing your worry, you can begin to take steps to ease the burdens of your mind.

A simple tool for meditative practice is to sit quietly and imagine or pretend that a three-way conversation is taking place in your head. One will be the asker, one the experiencer and the third is the observer. The observer is the role I suggest you focus on as your centre, for it is this part that has no comments or judgements about the conversation taking place between the asker and the experiencer. This may seem silly, but you will quickly discover you do indeed have what seems to be a constant conversation going on in your mind. This is normal and an extremely helpful tool for doing dream work. This inner dialogue or conversation will be revealed to you in the dream time. Becoming aware of this conversation in the waking-time will really help you excel at dream interpretation.

Meditation does not mean sitting like a yogi for great lengths of time. The type of simple practice outlined above can be done while standing in a bank line-up or anywhere you find yourself waiting or pausing. If fact, you can begin to train yourself to observe your thoughts by creating a stimulus for remembering. An example of this would be to say to yourself that every time you are in the shower you will take deep breaths and focus on your thoughts for five breaths. It is that simple to begin to tap into the mental level of your self.

A great practice to get into is responding to your mental chatter. So if you hear your inner critic judging something you've just done or said, respond to it by saying something like, "I hear you have some criticism of the way I handled that situation." You may be very surprised by "its" response to your acknowledgement. In fact, most often these inner voices will clam right up with surprise. This is the beginning of relating to your self in a new way.

Begin to pay attention to your mind — it is one of your greatest gifts and the most powerful tool for self-growth, awareness and creativity you have been blessed with.

❁

The Spiritual Level

The spiritual level of the literal perspective is a very personal level and often means different things to different people. The spiritual level is your personal connection with and experience of the Creator or God or whatever it is you believe in.

To help you understand what *spiritual* means to you, ask yourself what person or image resonates with you as a spiritual teacher or model. This may mean Christ, Buddha, Mohammed, the Dalai Lama, Mother Mary, Mother Teresa, Kuan Yin or whoever sets an example for spiritual living. Now write down three characteristics or traits that you feel that person possesses. The traits you choose will give you an idea of what your spiritual nature means to you. Often such traits as unconditional love, compassion, grace, wisdom, patience, humility or honour may be associated with spiritual assets. The spiritual level of the literal perspective is what connects you to the Divine or your own divinity.

The spiritual, on a more universal level, comprises other qualities as well, such as creativity, courage, strength, willingness, gentleness, flexibility, peace, passion, clarity, acceptance, openness, trust, joy, faith, hope, unity, consciousness and honest expression. As you may glean, these are all human traits that everyone possesses and has the potential to express if they choose. You are a spiritual being having a human experience and you embody all these spiritual traits by the mere fact that you exist. Your spirit will naturally pull you toward these traits and reveal them to you in your dream time.

Practising these traits in your relationship with your self is what self-love is all about. This means treating yourself with unconditional love, compassion and gentlenes . . . at all times. Recognizing that you have these traits and learning to apply them to yourself is what your dreams will show you at this spiritual level of the literal perspective.

"You are a spiritual being having a human experience."

Dreams will inevitably show you that you possess these spiritual qualities and guide you toward them as food for your spiritual growth. We are all inherently wise, patient and loving, and every dream will show you your wisdom by the mere fact that you are dreaming and attempting to guide yourself. Learning about these beautiful glowing parts of self is a real treat and a wonderful reward for doing dream work. There are days when we all feel off-centre in today's fast-paced, ego-centred lifestyle. Dreams are just a lovely reminder that you are far more than simply a body, emotions and a mind — so much more.

Beyond all these wonderful traits listed as part of your spiritual make-up is a whole world of spiritual pleasures that are beyond the human mind's comprehension. Doors to other realities and universes await the ardent dreamer, and lucid dreaming (discussed in Chapter 3) is one of those pleasures. These unearthly delights will start to be revealed as you continue to open doors to your spiritual growth.

Opening your personal door to spiritual growth will be a unique experience different from anyone else's experience. But know that whatever you dream of (imagine) can be manifested through the use of your dream time. Your spirit will guide you while you are asleep, and while you are awake, toward your greatest potential.

Chapter 7

The Symbolic Perspective

The essence of the teaching of the symbolic perspective is to assist you in Knowing Your Symbols. Knowing your symbolism will take you to greater depths of who you are and is the most widely known and studied level of dream work. As you begin to understand and apply symbolism in your daily life you will encounter a deeper connection to yourself, others and the world around you. Symbolism study helps you to understand that everything has a vibration, everything has a meaning, everything has a purpose, and everything has context. Applying symbolism helps to decrease daily worry and struggle, and deepens your ability to accept your current burdens in a healthy way.

Although symbolism can take up to seven years to understand and master, you can begin to apply it immediately in your dream work and to your waking-life experiences.

What Is a Symbol?

A dream symbol is simply a representation in picture form. People, animals and objects in the dream are all symbols that represent something about *your self*. The symbol may represent *anything* about your self, including your *current* thoughts, beliefs, attitudes, perceptions, spirit, illnesses, burdens, issues or feelings. Dreams are designed to bring this information about the self from your unconscious (below your waking-time awareness) into your conscious awareness. Other people in your dreams are also symbols and representative in nature. You are not here on Earth to solve other people's problems, and your dreams simply use the image of other people (often ones you know) as a representation or reflection of a part of your self.

It's an ingenious tool for self-reflection and should not be mistaken for information about another person's path. This guideline (of other people in your dreams representing a piece of your self) applies ninety percent of the time.

Symbols can be found not only in day dreams and night dreams but also in everyday waking life (usually described as a sign, omen, coincidence or synchronistic event). When you are able to recognize and understand your symbolic messages (of all types), you will begin to feel more connected to yourself, to others, and to the world around you. This connection can lead to a decrease in inner chaos and an increase in your sense of clarity and fulfilment. Symbolism is empowering and powerful, fulfilling and rewarding to your whole sense of self. Symbolism can bring magic into the ordinary, mundane acts of everyday living.

You can learn to access and use your dreamtime and waking-time messages to assist you in reaching almost any personal goal. Symbolism work can assist you to clear up old or current issues, identify and heal health concerns, and improve relationships with yourself and others.

Dream symbols, then, are representations of *your* experience. Because everyone has different experiences and perspectives, it is normal that most of your dreams will be comprised of your personal symbolism. A dream of gardening, for example, will bear a different meaning for you than for someone else, because your experience of gardening is unique to you and only you. Learning the language of dreams now becomes a matter of looking at your symbols from a different angle — more specifically, your angle.

Why Do We Dream in Symbols?

Why do dreams seem so complicated? Why do we dream in symbols instead of just seeing the words in writing? This is easy to understand if you are aware that as a human you actually think in symbols. Symbols are easier to grasp than you may think. Our society is inundated with symbols, which is readily apparent when you consider advertising slogans. If you have ever watched television with the volume turned off and recognized the advertisement from the pictures alone, then you have understood symbolism. For example, if you see an ad with a little pink bunny strolling along hitting a drum, you may think "batteries"! You have understood the theme with just one symbol. Advertisements of all types have us well trained with their chosen symbolism (this includes radio, billboards and magazines). In a similar way your dreams advertise a message to you in picture form. They even include a soundtrack that will help greatly in your understanding.

❖

Understanding Your Personal Symbolism

Learning your own symbolism is easier than it sounds. Simply describing the dream symbol (object, person or animal in the dream) will often lead to clues and insights as to its symbolic meaning. It takes some practice to start thinking in a different way, so an exercise is offered here. Answering these questions will assist you in learning to recognize your inner mental images and associations (the answer to the symbol's meaning).

Exercise 1:

When you hear the word "pyramid," what is the first impression you have? Say it to yourself now. Did you have an image or sensation of seeing a pyramid or did you see the actual word written in your mind? (Note that some people do see the word, but this is rare.)

If you were asked to describe your living room, would you see it in your mind first and then describe it, or would you see words describing the setting? Note your own response and describe your living room out loud as if to another person.

At the mention of the word "cat," what image comes to mind? Is it large or small, black or white, long-haired or short-haired, hissing or friendly? Notice that a single word can produce hundreds of possibilities.

Only your personal observation and/or description is necessary in order to discover your personal symbolism. Your answer is the only correct one.

Now you can recognize that you think almost exclusively in pictures and symbols, not words, and your dreams are therefore in pictures as well (remember, the mind is one of the "parts" that speaks to us in the dream state). The truth of the saying "a picture paints a thousand words" is apparent when you start looking at the tremendous amount of information a *single* symbol may contain.

The next exercise can be carried out alone, with a friend or in a group. Speaking your answers out loud is beneficial at this stage of learning; it allows you to listen to your own response. *Fifty percent of dream work is learning to listen!* Really listen to the answers in a new way and from a slightly different angle, the angle of symbolic versus literal.

Exercise 2:

The following are simple everyday words to help you recognize your personal symbolism. This is great fun when played with a group. Give a one-word answer — just one descriptive word — to describe what each of the words below means to you. Note if you see anything with your mind's eye at the same time. You may write the word down, but it is helpful to speak it out loud first.

> ▸ *dog*
>
> ▸ *camping*
>
> ▸ *marriage*
>
> ▸ *wedding*

Let's look at your responses. As you can imagine there are dozens of one-word answers that could apply to each word, but each response is based on *that individual's experience* of the symbol. For example, if you've ever been bitten by a dog your one-word description may be fear or menace. Others may choose such descriptive words as companion, love, or joy — completely different perspectives for the same word. This clearly demonstrates that most dream-symbol books cannot possibly describe your personal impressions of most symbols. (Universal symbolism and national symbolism are exceptions, and these will be discussed later.)

"Camping" often elicits responses ranging from bugs, uncomfortable and hard work to relaxation, fresh air and satisfaction. Again, these responses are based on the individual's experience of camping. Most people get some type of visual imagery just by saying the word. Often an impression of a past experience is instantaneous; it is these impressions that you want to be aware of, for they will lead you to a quick understanding of the meaning of the dream symbol.

The word "marriage" is a good one to ask in large groups because it can rouse some interesting responses. If you know anyone who has recently been through an unpleasant divorce you can imagine what impressions this word can provoke. The response to this one word is as varied as the number of people answering the question.

I found a book on dream symbolism that suggested that the symbolic meaning of "wedding" is death. How many people have you met who attended a wedding, had the experience of someone dying, and then connected these two events together in their mind? That symbol book's example appears to be based on folklore and will be practically useless in helping you understand the meaning of your dream symbol. If you were raised with that particular folklore (that attending a wedding will create death) and it is now part of your belief system, then this type of symbolism may apply. Otherwise, you will need to ask yourself what "wedding" means to you personally in order to understand the symbol's meaning.

Always look to your own experience of a symbol first before you check a symbol book. If the suggested meaning in the book does not ring a bell, resonate or produce an "ah-ha" moment for you, then that suggested meaning does not apply to you. Most people's symbolic understanding of wedding will likely be the union of two things. In a dream, it can literally represent two persons coming together, or it may represent the union of two ideas, thoughts, beliefs or just about anything, depending on what is going on in the dreamer's life at the time of the dream.

Universal Symbolism

The above examples will help you understand your personal symbolism. Universal symbolism is still a representation through pictures, but this time the meaning is usually understood globally. Therefore a person in China, Canada or Africa would have a similar understanding of a word. The sun, for example, usually represents a source of warmth, energy or light to everyone on the globe.

Marriage, as we have already observed, is another universally understood symbol for the coming together of two different parts or things. Other universal symbols include mother and father. Globally, a mother is often seen as the nurturer and the father as provider. Note that these symbols have a personal meaning based on your experience of your actual mother and father as well as the deeper universal meaning.

Universal symbolism is shared meaning embraced by a great number of people. Water is another example of a universal symbol. It is often representative of feelings that can include the way you feel inside (happy, sad, glad, mad), what you feel for others (love, hate, anger, envy), or how you sense the world around you at a deeper level (picking up vibes). Next time you hear someone say, "I feel like I'm drowning," ask them what they are drowning in. The response is usually that they are drowning in their emotions. If you hear that someone is "in the flow," you may understand this to mean in the flow of life or, more specifically, in the flow of their emotions or spirit.

Some symbolism books may aid you in understanding universal symbolism, but *remember to always look to your own experience of the symbols first* and a book second. If the meaning in the book does not resonate with you or no light bulbs go off, then that meaning is inappropriate for you at this time. The initial thought you have about a symbol is almost always the correct meaning.

❂

National Symbolism

National symbolism is specific to a nation or country. Here is an exercise to help you understand national symbolism.

Exercise 3:

With each of the words listed below, see what image or country pops into your mind first.

> ▶ *pyramids*
>
> ▶ *Statue of Liberty*
>
> ▶ *kangaroo*

If you thought of Egypt, the United States and Australia, then you understand the national symbolic representation of these objects. Understanding your dream symbolism is very similar and as easy as doing this exercise. Choose the most significant symbol and be aware of the first image or association that pops into your mind upon writing or thinking of the chosen word. Little thinking is required here: your mind will conjure up an impression immediately, just as it did with the above exercise.

Other examples of national symbolism include representations particular to a culture or religion. To many Italians, the symbol of faeces or excrement means that money will soon be coming to them. This is particular to European folklore and has been passed down through the generations.

Americans may see the symbol of an eagle as their national symbol representing freedom in the United States. Even families create their own symbolism. Uncovering your symbol's meaning can be a creative adventure into the self.

❁

Plays on Words

Plays on words or figures of speech are a great source of information when learning to switch from a literal meaning to a symbolic meaning. We tend to have a very literal approach to life in North America and yet our lives are inundated with symbolism every day. Consider the following list of metaphors and similes.

 ▸ *I've been stabbed in the back.*

 ▸ *I'm bending over backwards.*

 ▸ *It's like pulling teeth.*

 ▸ *He's driving me up the wall.*

Most people have used one of these phrases once or twice in their life. But did they mean them literally? Do people actually mean they have been stabbed in the back, or is this expression more of a metaphor for feeling betrayed? Does bending over backwards tell you that person actually was contorting his body backwards, or does it mean that he is overextending himself in a particular situation?

Therefore, if you dream of someone pulling your teeth out with a pair of pliers, you can bet this is not telling you that you literally had or will have any teeth removed this way. Most likely it suggests that pulling *words* out of your mouth is currently the challenge in your life. Perhaps you have been having a tough time expressing yourself with words lately, or maybe someone you spoke with recently was painfully poor at communication. But note that dreams can and do give us legitimate advice about our physical health at times, so this dream may be telling you to see a dentist. It is your job to consider all angles and options given you.

If you had a dream about a car driving up a wall, I would ask you if something or someone was annoying you recently, not whether you had recently had a car accident involving a wall or whether you had literally driven up any walls lately. These common, everyday phases are symbolic in meaning, not literal, and they are the foundation upon which your dream symbolism is built. So start becoming more aware of your everyday language and you will see these words and phrases in your dream content. It is very common to hear and use these plays on words every day, and they are a wonderful way to recognize symbolism both in your dreams and in your everyday life.

We tend to live in a very literal world, yet we switch to symbolic meanings constantly in our day-to-day lives. Usually we do this without even realizing it (i.e., without being consciously aware of it). The next exercise is designed to help you perceive how readily you switch from literal to symbolic thinking and speaking without even realizing it.

Exercise 4:

Here are some mini dream symbol examples to begin with. Remember that all dreams reflect something that is going on in *your current waking hours*. If you have a dream with these particular symbols, you have to relate it back to your personal life to understand the deeper meaning, but these mini examples will help your mind make the switch from literal meaning to symbolic meaning.

Practise flexing your new muscle by looking at these mini dream examples and seeing if you can guess what they are trying to represent. Symbols are simply mental images that are trying to paint a picture for you of an event, experience, perception, feeling, attitude or belief that you are currently experiencing. The symbols are trying to tell you something about your self ninety percent of the time. Even if the

Dream Examples	Symbolic Meaning
You are stabbed in the back.	You are currently feeling betrayed in some area of your life.
Someone is being killed.	A part of you feels like it is dying or you are trying to get rid of (kill off) an aspect of self (this is often done through self-berating or beating yourself up inside).
Someone's neck hurts.	You are currently sticking your neck out in a situation or relationship.
You can't stand up and keep falling down.	There is something, someone or some situation you are having challenges standing up to or facing in your life.
You hit a brick wall.	You don't feel you can go any further with a certain situation.

symbolic event is happening to another person, animal or object in the dream, it is still trying to tell you about an aspect or piece of your self.

Start listening for simple turns of phrase in your everyday life and work and you'll be surprised at just how much symbolism you already know. Listening for symbolism in everyday conversations is an excellent way to improve your listening skills and start recognizing dream symbolism.

Another easy way to begin recognizing symbolism in everyday language is to note how often adults can easily switch their perspectives from a literal angle to a symbolic sexual angle with certain spoken phrases. For example, in an office setting you may hear the phrase "let's do it on my laptop." The word "it" is often used to denote a sexual situation in our language if viewed from that angle. Notice whether you have ever recognized a sexual symbolic phrase from a different point of view.

Names in dreams can represent a play on words and can help point out something that you may have missed or not recognized about yourself during the day. If you dream of meeting a Mr. Moody on the street, try to connect this name with the fact that you may have been moody or gloomy in the last day or two. Remember our dreams are telling us something about ourselves and rarely about someone else. Recognizing these ignored or judged aspects of self can help you to grow and expand your awareness of self and decrease feelings of stress. "Know yourself and you will know the Universe" is a well-known phrase/concept within spiritual and Mystery School teachings.

Try to associate dream names with someone you know. If you dream of a street sign with the name Smith on it, try connecting it with someone you know named Smith. Just one word to describe the Smith you know will often point out something you have missed within yourself.

Have fun with your waking-time and dreamtime metaphors and plays on words.

More on Personal Symbols

The largest amount of symbolism in your dreams is personal symbolism, and this simply means that the representations or the symbols' meaning are yours alone and unique to your perspectives in life. These types of dream reflections are based on your past and present attitudes, beliefs, habits, relationships and life experience in general. Since we have all had different experiences, our symbolism is also different. How different depends on many social, cultural and familial conditions. All these reflections or parts of your self speak to you in every dream.

Uncovering the meaning of your personal symbols is as simple as learning to listen to your own thoughts. Remember, all of life is a reflection of your inner world and its dynamics. So the more you *know yourself* and the more familiar you are with your inner reality, the easier dream symbol interpretation will become. As with the symbol games above, your initial image, feeling or sense of a symbol is most often the correct one. Connecting the symbol's meaning to your everyday life is the next step in dream interpretation. Practise listening to your thoughts. It is one of the most helpful tools you will learn to use for dream interpretation. All the answers are inside of you and flow through your everyday thoughts and thinking processes. This is why meditation is such a useful skill to practise. Listening to your thoughts while sitting quietly will point directly to what weighs most heavily on you. Problem areas are very often related to us through our dreams and especially through nightmares. Give yourself the gift of five minutes a day to listen to your internal voice. Daily meditation practise has been presented to us repeatedly throughout the years by every master who has walked on Earth. Meditation (or sitting quietly in focussed awareness) is an indispensable means for living a healthier and more fulfilled life.

> ───────
> *"All the answers are inside of you and flow through your everyday thoughts and thinking processes."*
> ───────

Not only is learning to listen to your own thoughts pivotal for dream work, but your spoken words are an even greater tool in helping you understand your symbolism. Make a conscious effort to listen to what you are speaking out loud and creating in your life. Make it a one-day or one-hour goal to pay attention to the words you speak. Words help you create your experience (as do your thoughts and actions) and you will begin to see this connection as you begin to connect symbolism to waking-time events.

It is important to be aware that your unconscious mind will take everything you say quite literally. If you are familiar with muscle testing you can demonstrate this phenomenon easily. Have someone stand and extend their right arm straight out to the side of their body. Now apply a downward pressure to their arm while asking them to resist. This will give you an idea of how strong their muscle is at this time. Then ask the volunteer to close his eyes and repeat out loud ten times, "I am weak and unworthy." When they are done, have them open their eyes and once again test the strength of their arm while you apply pressure and they resist. Almost always there is a significant decrease in their ability to resist your applied pressure. In fact, the arm is often affected to such a degree that the person cannot resist at all and the arm drops easily to their side. Never leave your volunteer in a weakened state. Ask them to close their eyes and say out loud, "I am strong and worthy" ten times and then retest muscle strength. This will restrengthen and even improve muscle strength in the arm. This demonstrates how quickly our thoughts and words affect the physiology of the body.

Think back to what you may have been told repetitively as a child. Did you make this your truth? How has it affected your body and health today? For example, I have often heard parents tell their child they are stupid, dumb or clumsy without them realizing the powerful effect this will have on their child's inner reality. The mind takes everything in as real and will then portray these messages in a symbolic format in the dream time.

Watch for people who say their job is killing them and note whether they seem to be continually stressed about their job. Make an observation about someone who repeatedly says, "I haven't a leg to stand on," and note whether they have hip, leg or foot problems. Start making these kinds of connections to help you understand your personal symbolism and what you are creating with your words.

If you are not working on your dreams with another person or in a group, then writing down your first impressions of a symbol will be of benefit. It is important to write down your first impressions and not edit it with a lot of thinking. To begin with, you will find it much easier to help someone interpret their dream than to do your own. This is because we often wear rose-coloured glasses and judge ourselves while interpreting our own dreams. Our emotions may ride high and block out the necessary connection. It is helpful to describe a symbol as though you were describing it to an alien. If you don't have a first impression, just try describing it in as much detail as possible.

✺

Symbolic Mirroring

It is important to remember that almost everything in your dreams (animals, people and objects) is a reflection of some aspect of your self, a reflection of your inner world. This guideline applies ninety percent of the time. Remember, you are dreaming to gain knowledge about yourself, not about other people. This cannot be emphasized enough, because you will tend to *not* want to own some of the aspects of self that your dreams show you. If you dream of a neighbour or friend, that person probably represents an aspect of your self. This is called mirroring or reflection

87

and it applies not only to the dream time but the waking time as well. This is symbolic mirroring; irrational mirroring will be discussed in Chapter 8.

Defining a dream character's personality and characteristics in three words will help pinpoint what aspect of your self is being reflected. For example, if you dream of your neighbour and then describe her character as nosy, gossipy and bothersome, you can bet the dream is trying to reflect the nosy, gossipy aspect of you. To understand how this dream information was triggered, look back to the last twenty-four to forty-eight hours of your life and see if you can identify when you may have been gossipy or nosy. Your mind chose a symbol (the neighbour) that it already deemed nosy and gossipy and then used it (the neighbour) in the dream to help you see this side of yourself.

> *"Dreams always show or reflect your traits, habits and behaviours in the hopes that you will own them."*

Dreams always show or reflect your traits, habits and behaviours in the hopes that you will own them. Personality traits, regardless of whether you deem them good or bad, are revealed as an opportunity for self-growth and enlightenment. Every dream will present this opportunity (of knowing your self better) by mirroring other people, animals or objects. It is wise to learn not to judge your own traits, which can often be a challenging step but an extremely helpful tool for dream work and daily life.

Mirroring is a great tool for self-growth, whether you choose to pay attention to it in your dreams or your waking time. Every person you meet reflects something about your self. It is simply a matter of being aware of what your thoughts (often in the form of judgements or admiration of characteristics) are with regard to another person. Are you attracted or repelled by their behaviour? Do you mentally note their negative or positive qualities? This will often point out aspects of your self that you accept and admire or perhaps disdain and reject. Choose a word or two to describe your dream person and you can be assured that you possess the same character trait.

❁
Inner Marbles

Have you ever heard the phrase, "I think I'm losing my marbles"? The person was speaking symbolically, not literally. Most likely they meant they were feeling overwhelmed and not able to think clearly. Imagine the human being as a container full

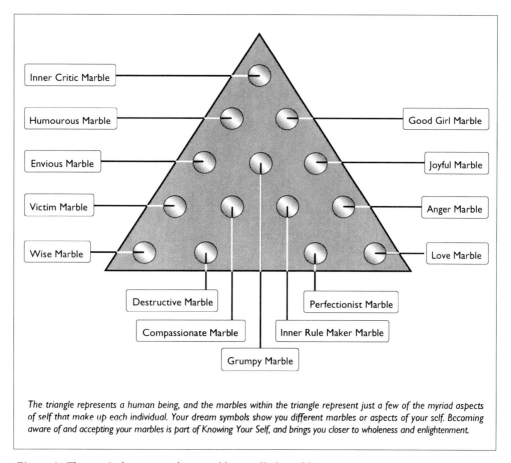

The triangle represents a human being, and the marbles within the triangle represent just a few of the myriad aspects of self that make up each individual. Your dream symbols show you different marbles or aspects of your self. Becoming aware of and accepting your marbles is part of Knowing Your Self, and brings you closer to wholeness and enlightenment.

Figure 4. The myriad aspects of your self are called marbles

of marbles. It would take thousands of marbles to fill up a human body. Now imagine that each one of these marbles can be given a name or a label representing just one aspect or part of self. Such traits might be joy, pride, arrogance, anger, inner critic, perfectionist, creativity, inspiration, victimization, hopelessness, and so on. This will give you a better perspective on the countless aspects of self you actually have. The term "marbles" is simply an easy way to denote aspects of self. It will help give clarity and perspective to the various mirrored aspects of your self presented in the dream time.

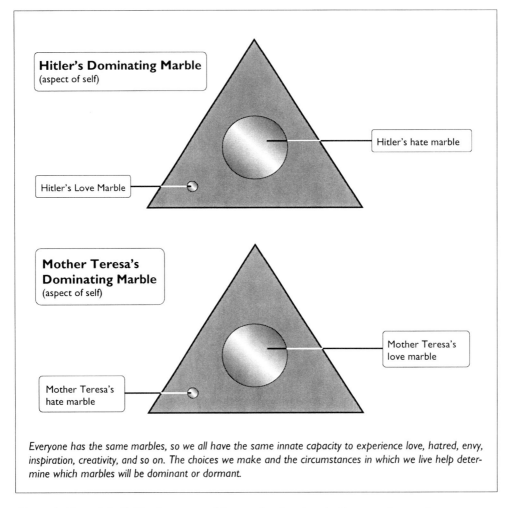

Hitler's Dominating Marble
(aspect of self)

Hitler's hate marble

Hitler's Love Marble

Mother Teresa's Dominating Marble
(aspect of self)

Mother Teresa's love marble

Mother Teresa's hate marble

Everyone has the same marbles, so we all have the same innate capacity to experience love, hatred, envy, inspiration, creativity, and so on. The choices we make and the circumstances in which we live help determine which marbles will be dominant or dormant.

Figure 5. In each individual, some marbles are dominant and others are dormant

As a human being you have all the same marbles inside you as the next person does. It is how you choose to express and relate to your marbles that is unique and makes you an individual. As individuals we tend to judge our marbles as good or bad, and want to get rid of some and not acknowledge others. Getting to know your marbles is a quick avenue for becoming whole or self-realized. When you learn to stop judging aspects of self, your dreams will show you the way to enlightenment.

To help you understand marbles further, let's look at two well-known figures in history and discern what marbles they had and how they may have used them (see Figure 5). Mother Teresa, for example, may be said to have had a large compassion marble, whereas Hitler may be said to have had a large hate marble. Both had the compassion and hate marbles within. Perhaps they did not express them in the same way or as openly as the other did, but the capacity to have compassion or to hate is within us all. It is the choices we make and the circumstances in which we live that help determine which marbles will be dominant or dormant. Every dream you have brings one or more marbles to the surface for examination. After you recognize a marble, the next step is acceptance of its existence and, hopefully, the beginnings of a new relationship with this part of your self. These are some of the steps toward liking, and then loving, your self.

❦

Symbolism and the Waking Time

A great benefit to understanding dream symbolism is that all of these guidelines can also be applied to your everyday waking experiences! You can write out a recent waking-time event or experience and then use the guidelines to interpret the meaning behind the event's most significant symbols. This also applies to signs you may receive during the day and to synchronistic events. For example, if an animal darts out in front of your car, you may take this as a symbol or a message to you. You can apply the interpretation process to any event, situation, relationship, problem or issue you are experiencing in your everyday life. Ask yourself why you notice what you notice or what grabs your attention throughout the day. Hopefully it doesn't take a heart attack or a car accident to get your attention.

The Divine, God, Goddess, Great Spirit, Source — whatever you choose to call your personal concept of the Creator — is constantly sending you signals, messages, inspiration and guidance during the daytime. Learning to understand your daytime messages will be easier when you apply the dream symbol interpretation process. After all, everyday life is a waking dream and the wisdom and grace of the Divine is only a thought away from you every second of the day and night.

If you find yourself in a difficult or seemingly unsolvable situation, write out the situation as if it were a night dream. Following the suggested interpretation process will help you gather more insight into the meaning of a challenging situation and offer you ideas for resolution.

Interpreting a Waking-Time Event: Example 1

You are currently in crisis about losing your job and are already in a financial crunch. Write out your story just as you would a dream. Look at the main symbol from your story and use the same principles you would for interpreting a dream symbol. This added bit of information will give you a different perspective and may very well offer you the answer to your perplexing waking-hour situation.

There is always a positive side to every situation no matter how negative it seems. Trust in this process to assist you in gaining insight and you will be pleasantly surprised at the Creator's wisdom that helped generate these challenges in your life.

For example, if you have just lost your job, the Creator's message may be that you lost your current job in order to open the door for a better job, and your financial strife may be just what your spirit required to help you find your inner strength. It is tough to see the higher point of view when in crisis or in a difficult situation, but the dream interpretation process will assuredly offer some insight.

Remember, all of life is offering and sending you constant signals that can be symbolically interpreted. It can add new dimensions of fun and hope to hear, see, feel and experience the Creator's hand in your everyday life. Miracles are abundant if you know how to interpret the Creator's symbolic messages.

Interpreting a Waking-Time Event: Example 2

You feel depressed and look up to the sky and see a hawk circling. If you knew the symbolic meaning behind hawk, then you may feel supported and cared for by the benevolent Universe. The hawk will have a personal meaning for you (what personal experience or thoughts do you have about soaring birds?), but all animals also have a more universal symbolism associated with them. In doing dream work, you will look at these deeper meanings beyond your personal meaning. In this case the hawk is the messenger of spirit and is always telling you to be on the alert for guidance and messages from Great Spirit.

Interpreting a Waking-Time Event: Example 3

You ask for a "sign" when confronted with a decision. The answer will always present itself in some manner, and most likely in the manner you were least expecting. You may overhear two people talking in a line-up and hear them speak the answer to your problem, or the answer may come through on the radio, the television, or a book you're reading. The Divine speaks to us in as many ways as we can be creative about receiving the answer. It may come in the shape of a cloud that reminds you of something or a movie that triggers exactly the emotion you were needing to experience. Really pay attention when you ask for a sign; keep your eyes, ears and senses open for anything. Miracles happen every day. And remember: be careful what you ask for because you *will* get your answer.

Chapter 8

The Irrational Perspective

This perspective is the body of knowledge that the ancient Egyptians called the irrational. This is a challenging level for many North Americans because it is the level that does not follow reason. In fact, it is irrational and illogical to the intellectual mind. For example, you do not fall in love based on reason — it may be based on smell, emotions, a gesture, or your soul saying, "Hey, this is the one." Falling in love has nothing to doing with intellect or reason.

The irrational perspective causes us to change. It teaches us lessons so we will change and understand that we are not on Earth by ourselves — we are with Earth and not separate from it.

This perspective is challenging because as a Westerner you try to do everything with reason. The more you try to follow your heart or your spirit, the more you will be misunderstood by others because you will seem irrational to them. They cannot feel your heart or the passions that drive you forward in your life. This is the irrationality of the world we live in. On the Earth plane, we experience the dynamic tension caused by our feelings (heart) and our thinking (mind).

Much of daily life can be irrational and it is helpful to take note of what you perceive to be irrational or illogical in your own life. For example, the ancient oriental exercise called tai chi seems trivial in its action, but can have great effect on your well-being. This is illogical to the human mind. A woman lifting a car off her child who is trapped underneath may seem to be another irrational happening. But illogical events such as these happen daily in our lives, and the dream time is no exception. Learning to trust the processes of life to guide you toward a greater level of self is part of what the irrational perspective can teach you.

The irrational perspective is known as the divine dichotomy and the everyday world you live in is a world of opposites. Everything has an opposite: up/down, left/right, yin/yang, black/white, negative/positive, female/male . . . on goes the list endlessly. These polar opposites create unity and wholeness when in balance with each other.

> *"The irrational perspective causes us to change."*

The irrational perspective teaches you about the dualistic nature of living on planet Earth by revealing the world of opposites and the divine dichotomy in our three-dimensional existence. This may sound like something out of *Star Trek*, but it is our reality here as human beings. We live in a world driven by opposites, polarities and dynamic tension. In the irrational we confront the very belief systems that compose us as individuals, as part of the human race and as spiritual beings.

It is also about healings and miracles happening through other channels, such as when you do tai chi and your arthritis ceases to bother you. Like the Eastern viewpoint of yin and yang energies, our body, mind and spirit will always strive for balance, and this need for balance is reflected in almost every dream.

When you are born into this physical reality, the energies of the Divine are split into polar opposite frequencies or energies. These may be referred to as masculine and feminine energies or yang and yin. These are energies that oppose one another in nature, yet create wholeness when together. (Note how irrational that sounds, yet it is the nature of our reality and the foundation upon which the irrational perspective is built.)

Giving your energy to what makes change easier for you is wiser than giving energy to what makes change hard for you. One of the things that makes change easier is having enough energy, both physically and metaphorically. The irrational perspective offers you an opportunity to see both sides of yourself. That is to say, you can view what you perceive to be right about you and what you perceive to be wrong about you. Focussing on the positive aspects of self revealed in your dream work will create energy that can be used to move you forward in life. Focussing on what you judge to be negative aspects of your self will drain you of energy. The irrational level offers this great opportunity to create change by focussing in the "right" direction. This level is revealed in every dream you have, and can also be detected in your waking hours.

The easiest way to apply this level of the Ancient Mystery School teachings in your dream work is to watch for male and female characters in your dreams. These characters represent your male (yang) and feminine (yin) flows of energy. They are the most common and prevalent representations I have seen in dream work, and they are a great way to help you see where you are out of balance and how to get back to a more equalized state.

" Knowing Who You Are Not is what the irrational perspective will teach you."

The contradictory nature of this level is difficult to understand, but it is very rewarding and a pivotal part of self-growth. Knowing Who You Are Not is what the irrational perspective will teach you, and this viewpoint will help you to find and maintain your centre or balance within. It is a gift of freedom to be in balance in this chaotic world. Every dream you have will offer you information about this level and help you reconnect to your true self.

You are perfected at the level of your soul self or spirit, and your dreaming self remembers this. It will try to guide you back toward that perfection of your spirit through the irrational viewpoint. The irrational perspective continually tries to stabilize your waking self by pointing out areas where you are currently out of balance.

To function wholly and smoothly in the physical, you must have some state of balance between these two energies of which you are comprised. If one is too dominant and the other too passive, you can bet your life will be somewhat chaotic.

Your body, mind, emotions and spirit are in a constant dynamic tension to maintain balance in an otherwise irrational space. Because of the opposing tensions it is quite common to live in an all-or-nothing consciousness. Many people tend to view things in extremes of rigidity in order to maintain some reason and control in this ongoing, seemingly irrational struggle. This is not a realm of reason, and it is a trying concept for the intellect to grasp because it is the very nature of the intellect or ego to rationalize one's existence in order to experience inner peace.

The irrational perspective, being the realm of opposites, exists perpetually, and it creates a constant dynamic pressure inside you on a daily basis. Because you will tend to try to find reason and meaning in most things, your belief system will often get stuck in one extreme of these polar opposites. Another way of understanding this is by the metaphor that refers to our thinking as "all or nothing" or as "all black or all white." Be aware of dreams that are presented in black and white colours only; they may be telling you that your thinking is too all or nothing/black and white, and that you have been unable to see the dichotomy of the irrational perspective. (Note: lack of colour in a dream may also represent lack of feeling because colour in the dream time denotes emotional states.)

In the dream time this constant dynamic tension we experience is often portrayed as a battle. Your body, mind and emotions constantly attempt to restore balance, and your dream indicates exactly where and when you are straying too far from that centre. Your whole being can be likened to a scale that is constantly seeking balance by applying the same weight on both sides. This is most often seen in the dream as a struggle between characters (usually your masculine and feminine energies, which are often portrayed by male and female characters). Learning a bit about belief systems at this point will demonstrate how your masculine and feminine energies function within your waking time and dream time.

❁

Core Beliefs

The basis or foundation of your personal belief system (core beliefs) was loaded into your system, starting at birth (or even in the womb). These beliefs motivate and determine your every move and decision in life (albeit mostly unconsciously), similar to the way your computer's hard drive contains the information that drives it. And, just as in a computer hard drive, you cannot change the information recorded in your core beliefs unless you know what the information is. You need to be consciously aware of what information is driving you.

Different aspects of your core beliefs are shown to you in every dream, so your core beliefs are an essential part of dream work.

Every parent, teacher, organization, church, school, institution, television commercial — everything you have ever heard — is information you took in and chose either to believe or disbelieve and then store somewhere in your belief system (your personal hard drive).

Once a belief is stored on your hard drive, it remains there, influencing *every* thought, attitude, word and action. You live *all* your life experiences based on these core beliefs stored inside you. Your beliefs have a tremendous influence on your decisions and life experiences. Your dreams constantly point out your personal (as well as societal) belief systems. Often these beliefs have been carried from childhood and no longer serve you well. This is because you have outgrown the need for certain beliefs. Your dreams will point you in the right direction by indicating just what your outmoded views are.

If you want to change something in your life, you need to get to your core beliefs first. Every change you ever make has to start with awareness before you can take the next step. The core belief will stay on your hard drive until you make a deliberate (conscious) decision to change it. You can't change it until you know what it is.

Working on the next exercise will help you understand some of your own beliefs. Remember, beliefs are based on life experiences and will differ from person to person, just like a fingerprint. The acronym for "my experience" is M.E. You will discover you have a core belief about absolutely everything. Just work on the ones that have meaning for you now.

Core Belief Exercise

For each of the sample words, compile a written list of your core beliefs about that word — what that word means to you.

For example, if you are looking at your core beliefs about money, ask yourself, "What does money mean to me? Do I believe it 'grows on trees' or is the 'root of all evil'?" Search your memory banks to see what associations you make with money and what your parents, grandparents or society has taught you.

List at least five one-word descriptions for each of the categories below. These first impressions are often your core beliefs. Remember that these are just generalities, so some of your descriptive words will apply to more than one of these categories. There are no right or wrong answers, so just list the first words that pop into your mind. Remember, once you have a clearer understanding at what motivates you in each category, then — and only then — can you take steps to change it. These lists come in handy when doing dream work and trying to identify dream information.

Here are some concepts you may choose to look at:

sex	God	society
old age	religion	government
mothers/fathers	parenting	death
sisters/brothers	teacher/learning	values/morals
fun/humour	spirituality	my physical body
my creative abilities	work/employment	my home
emotions	authority figures	children

Cont'd on page 100

Cont'd from page 99

attitudes and beliefs	sexuality	intimacy
different cultures	relationships	health
touch/affection	money	responsibility
love	husbands/wives	

Core Beliefs about Masculine and Feminine Self

You are energetically made up of fifty percent feminine energy and fifty percent masculine energy regardless of what sex you actually are. Masculine energy is action oriented, whereas feminine energy is receptive in nature. Fifty percent of you is able to be receptive and fifty percent of you is able to take action. However, in practice your use of these capabilities is rarely perfectly balanced, and you may lean toward using one more often than the other.

Since beliefs about your masculine and feminine nature are revealed in almost every dream, I suggest that you spend a few minutes taking note of your own beliefs about masculine and feminine (i.e., men and women). List as many items as come to mind regarding your beliefs about what it means to be a man in our society today and what it means to be a woman. Just let whatever information comes to mind be written down (usually your first impressions are the strongest beliefs you have).

Try thinking back to the roles men and women have played over the years in your life when making your list, especially early childhood role models such as your parents or grandparents. Try to list at least five qualities under each heading. These are your core beliefs. Do not be concerned if some traits cross over into both categories, and remember that these are just generalities. There are no right answers — only your answers, based on your experiences.

Universal or archetypal symbols for masculine include action oriented, determined, intellectual, intense and assertive. Feminine universal symbols include receptive, soft, yielding, creative and intuitive. These universal symbolic traits are present in you; however, you may not have been taught how to recognize them or activate them. In order to experience inner harmony, you have to begin to recognize and use both the masculine and feminine parts of your self. This is how you restore inner balance. But first you have to be aware of where you are out of balance. This is why understanding what is at the core of your belief system is so important.

Sample Masculine and Feminine List

(an actual list made by a student)

Masculine	Feminine
hard	angry
unyielding	mean
angry	threatening
hatred	sensitive
rigid	numb
emotionally crippled	fearful

This list portrays a person who is out of balance in their "inner marriage" of masculine and feminine energy for two reasons: neither list includes any of the universal symbols or deeper traits one can actually possess, and both lists have more negative traits than positive ones. Your inner relationship with your self depends on a healthy relationship between these two (masculine and feminine, yang and yin) internal dynamic energies. Getting to know, accept and eventually love these inharmonious parts of self will heal and restore balance inside of you. Pay attention to your masculine and feminine dream characters. Recognize where you are out of balance. Accept these aspects of self and move on to loving them just as they are — this is how you practise unconditional love for your marbles. Practising unconditional love for your dream characters and for your waking-time self will quickly lead to balance, harmony and inner peace.

Just like a marriage, learning to negotiate peace between your inner masculine and feminine parts is a healthy step toward having a happy and harmonious inner life. Negotiating can only come after you have learned to recognize, accept and own your own traits. It is well worth the effort to do a bit of inner research about your masculine and feminine parts.

More on Masculine and Feminine Energies

If you could feel the flow of your masculine and feminine energies, they would feel much like a gentle wave that flows in through the top of your head and out through your solar plexus (note that the second, fourth and sixth chakras are intake oriented and the first, third and fifth chakras are output chakras; see the Chakra section in

101

Part 3 for more information on the chakras). The feminine "in" flow is designed to allow you to be receptive and bring in new ideas, feelings and experiences in a gentle way. Your masculine energy is designed to take the information you have received (from the feminine aspect of self) and act on it. This is a simplistic illustration, but it demonstrates how so much of our dream content focusses on the constant challenge before many us to bring our basic core energies of masculine and feminine into balance. Much of our North American society is based on action and many people are on output most of the time. Take a moment to observe your own nature — do you tend to be a "doer" and always doing something? If so, you are likely in need of some "being" or sitting in a quiet, receptive, non-chaotic state of mind to balance your life out.

Most of our world has lived in a patriarchal society for the last two thousand years. This has created a society where the focus has been on activity, intellect and striving/pushing. Great shifts in this old paradigm have been underway for many years now, and as the feminine energies enter our planet's energy field (and our own), we can notice great shifts in the waking time and, especially, the dream time. Dreams show your masculine and feminine energies' attempts at balance by portraying male and female characters in the dream time. Watch for these inner relationship issues to pop up in many dreams. They reflect your inner marriage and how well it is functioning. This information is simply an opportunity to learn where you are out of balance and how to restore harmony.

The irrational paradigm can be difficult to grasp because society has often taught us rigid rules and codes of behaviour. For example, it is quite possible to hold two opposing feelings at one time. You may love someone and hate them at the same time, and this is "normal" within the irrational perspective. We have the capacity to feel any emotion at any time. Great actors do this readily and we may forget that everyday life is a stage upon which we choose how to react (and how to feel) in any given situation. It is also possible to hold two opposing beliefs about a subject at any given time. You may believe that

"The feminine 'in' flow allows you to be receptive and bring in new ideas, feelings and experiences in a gentle way."

Your masculine energy takes the information you have received (from the feminine aspect of self) and acts on it."

money is the source of all evil, yet believe it would be a blessing to be rich. Such opposites are normal in the make-up of a human being and are very readily revealed to you in *every* dream. This type of opposing information is the irrational perspective, and learning to accept this as part of your path (and not fight it) will lead to greater ease and flow in everyday life.

Being out of balance can lead to chaos in the waking hours. It is quite possible not to feel or notice the chaos on a tangible or concrete level. But the finer, subtler energies of our bodies will nonetheless continue to exert this dynamic tension on our bodies. This leads to disease and illness in the physical body if it goes unrecognized or unacknowledged.

Keep your masculine and feminine list handy when doing dream work. When a male character (symbol) is portrayed in a dream, use your list to see if any of the traits on your list can be attributed to this character. Likewise, if a female character is being examined as a dream symbol check your list and note any characteristics that fit at this time for this particular symbol. You may add to your list over time, and different traits will be highlighted in different dreams depending on which trait is most out of balance at the time of the dream.

❈

Feelings and Dreams

Recognizing your feelings and emotions is also pivotal to doing dream work. Your dream feelings are the truth of how your inner self feels and these feelings are presented as an opportunity for growth. Your feelings will actually lead you toward your own enlightenment.

The first step is to simply recognize your feelings. The next step is to own them (they don't own you; hence, they do not control you, but guide you). Step three is to accept your feelings without judgement, belittlement or hatred for yourself because you have them. Feelings are normal. They are an ingenious tool designed by the Creator to lead you on your Earth walk. Much of North American thought has been to ignore feelings and judge them as either good or bad. Good and bad are not feelings — they are judgements *about* your feelings. Ignoring your feelings creates conflict within. Denying your feelings only serves to disregard and reject a huge part of self.

Take heart if you are unable to identify what you are feeling (happy, sad, glad, mad . . .). This simply means you are numb and *that* is a feeling. Everyone feels something, even if it is numb, frozen or dead.

103

Take a moment to see if you can identify what you are feeling right now.

If you answered, "I am feeling good" or "I am feeling bad," be aware that these are not feelings but rather opinions about your feelings.

Your dreams are filled with feelings and emotions. If you are *unable* to identify what you are feeling right now, then you may have trouble recognizing feelings and emotions in your dreams. If this is the case, then try the Identifying Your Feelings exercise below to get you started. Identifying your feelings in the waking time will greatly enhance your ability do dream work, because recognizing your dream feelings is the first step in the dream interpretation processes presented in this book.

Identifying Your Feelings Exercise

In this list, a few feelings are shown with an opposite feeling. This is the duality of our nature and the irrational perspective, and reviewing this list of contrasts will help you identify what feeling you may be having. See if you are able to recognize how you are feeling by reading through the list. Note which ones resonate, ring a bell or give you an "ah-ha" impression. Especially note the ones you find distasteful or that you judge as not good or bad to have. These will often point to feelings you have but have not yet accepted or owned. (You may be surprised that loving is shown as the opposite of fearful. This is correct — love is the main vibration in the Universe, as well as the matrix upon which the Universe is constructed. The polar opposite of this vibration is fear.)

adequate	inadequate	defensive	open
happy	sad	lovable	unloved
fearful	loving	secure	insecure
full	empty	free	trapped
positive	negative	powerful	powerless
abundant	deprived	successful	failure
connected	disconnected	accepted	rejected
weak	strong	joy	despair
trusting	suspicious	hopeful	hopeless
worthy	unworthy	vulnerable	safe
capable	inept	committed	ambivalent

Remember, this is just a sample of the many types of feelings that exist. You can use this list to help identify your dream feelings.

> " 'Shadow self'
> simply
> refers to
> those parts
> of self that
> you (or society)
> have judged
> as not
> good, bad or
> too scary to
> reveal."

Because you have the capacity to feel anything, opposing feelings are normal. Remember that we are all composed of the same marbles, but each of us experiences them differently. These opposing feelings show you how the irrational realm operates, so accepting that you can and will have opposing feelings in the dream time and waking time is easier and more realistic than living with an all black or all white mindset.

As you begin to recognize your dream feelings and waking-time feelings you will notice that they can shift and change constantly. Getting to know your waking-hour feelings will be a tremendous advantage when doing dream work. Keep in mind that the first step to dream interpretation (discussed in Chapter 4) is to identify the dream feelings. Connecting the dream feeling with a waking-hour feeling is part of the dream interpretation process. Start now by developing an awareness of your daily feelings and how they change from situation to situation. Note what triggers a high or low moment for you and whether you are a prisoner to the way you feel (i.e., whether your feelings own and control you rather than guiding you).

Also, pay attention to which feelings are easier to allow and which ones are challenging. Judging feelings is something you have been taught (often by parents, teachers and society in general). None is better than another and *all* feelings are designed to assist you on your personal journey. Honour whatever you feel and accept your feelings as part of your path, as a gift to you. Then you'll be able to start loving them (even the scary ones). Challenge yourself to name the scarier ones and understand that these judged feelings are leading you to examine your shadow self.

"Shadow self" simply refers to those parts of self that you (or society) have judged as not good, bad or too scary to reveal. You have therefore buried them in your subconscious — the very matrix of what your dreams reveal. But remember that you have also buried your treasures and gifts as well as these shadow traits. All manner of characteristics and dispositions are revealed in your dreams. Your shadow parts of self and disowned feelings are *not* negative. In fact, you will discover some very favourable and delicious feelings as you travel through your dream material.

※
Accepting Your Irrational Marbles

After much self-study, when you have learned Who You Are (the literal level) and What Your Symbols Are (the symbolic level), you will be ready to learn Who You Are Not (the irrational level). Notice that this statement is dualistic; at the irrational level it makes perfect sense that you can hold contrasting and seemingly contradictory points of view at the same time.

To learn Who You Are Not, you must meet your irrational marbles and experience mirroring from the irrational perspective. At this level, you begin to step outside of the Illusion (of the earthly third-dimensional experience) and recognize that you are a unique spiritual being who is comprised of all the marbles you see in others as well as in yourself.

As discussed in Chapter 7, mirroring is an ingenious tool for self-growth that was designed by a benevolent Universe. At the symbolic level, others mirror or represent some aspect of you. For example, if you speak with your neighbour and consciously note how defensive they are, symbolic mirroring allows you to see the defensive part of you. But at the irrational level your neighbour's behaviour reveals something about *them* rather than about you, such as, for example, that they may have been hurt in the past and are acting this way in order to protect themselves. In a way, this irrational mirroring does show something about you — you have learned benevolence, insight and compassion.

What's perplexing is that both the irrational and symbolic perspectives are "correct." As with the above example, you are both mirrored and *not* mirrored. You have the capacity to be defensive (as all humans do) and at the irrational level you have the capacity to recognize that you are *not* defensive but empathetic. This type of irrational thought can be confusing to your intellect (third chakra), but humorous to your spiritual being (which understands the third-dimensional perspective and the irrational level).

For many people, learning to recognize and fully accept the irrational can take years. It is part of the Great Mystery of life, and is not readily understood by the intellect. Knowing that it is part of your genetic make-up as a human being can give you a sense of freedom. Accepting your irrational dream thoughts and feelings and your waking-time experiences will lead you to feel more centred, grounded and free from worry. This acceptance gives you permission to "play" once again, by allowing you to return to a time free of self-judgement, worries and concerns.

Once you accept your irrational marbles, you will begin to experience the freedom to explore human behaviour without becoming immersed in right and wrong. You can own and live in all the marbles that comprise you at the deepest level of your being (that is, your spirit). In fact, you will begin to recognize your spiritual self in the waking time, and to live and walk your spiritual self. At this point, symbolic mirroring will no longer apply in the same way and irrational mirroring will begin to apply most of the time.

Chapter 9

The Creator Perspective

This level of the four perspectives is the most difficult to understand because it attempts to reveal the Divine's will. Although glimpses are possible, it is impossible to comprehend all the workings of the Great Mystery of life. This is the level of the Holiest of Holies and it is a level that is easily misunderstood. In order to begin to comprehend this level, your belief system has to include that a Creator exists and whatever the Creator is, It is ineffable, beyond your comprehension, and you will not be able to fully understand It.

God's view of your life will present itself as a fairly detached point of view — one of a sacred witness or observer. This is a challenging perspective for most people to see in their own life. It is the role of examiner who views without judgement or conditions. Through the dream time you are honoured with a glimpse of your Creator perspective in every dream. Becoming attuned to this level takes practice, patience, and loving kindness toward your self.

Trying to explain the Creator perspective would be like trying to explain the workings of the Universe and of life itself. It is impossible for our human minds to comprehend — or is it? This perspective is revealed in your dreams (and waking time) and offers you a peek at the Divine's viewpoint. It is an awesome tool for self-growth and allows you to Know Your Creator. Understand that from your God's perspective everything is in perfect order, and that all events contain opportunity and a gift for you personally. *Everything* that happens is an opportunity for your self-growth no matter how devastating, how perverse or how painful it may seem to you. There is always a message and always a meaning — we just don't often get to understand this perspective until months or years (or even lifetimes) later. But know that this level of reality exists and is all-pervasive in your everyday activities, during your highest highs and your lowest lows. The Creator perspective can stretch you and nurture you at the same time.

"Practising detachment from outcome is part of practising your trust in your God."

In every dream there is a Creator's viewpoint or perspective through which you can access even greater knowledge about your self and the world around you. This viewpoint is based on the knowledge that all circumstances in life happen for a reason and for the greater good of your self and the whole of humanity. It is here, in this perspective, that the interconnectedness and oneness of life is revealed. Just as the ripples from a pebble thrown into the pond affect every droplet of water contained therein, so too will every thought, word and action of every human being affect the workings of the Whole.

Part of incorporating this perspective into your life is beginning to surrender to Divine will and stop being attached to outcome. This shows that you Trust Your God to bring life to you according to the Divine plan/will and not your personality's will (which may be familiar to you as the controlling ego aspect). Practising detachment from outcome is part of practising your trust in your God. Remember, the language of the Universe is *not* English (or any other language spoken here on Earth) but rather a combination of vibration, sound, feelings, thoughts and symbolic representations. Get to know how your Creator is talking to you. Trust your feelings, senses and the mental pictures that flash in your mind. Be aware of what catches your attention and the myriad possibilities that exist for your Creator to grab your awareness. The Creator perspective informs you that the benevolent Universe is always at work for your best and highest good and it can be *no other way*.

This perspective reminds you that you are always at choice on this planet of free will called Earth. You are creating your reality, or rather co-creating it with the Divine, with every word you choose to speak, every thought you have in your mind (conscious or unconscious) and every action you take in your daily life. It is an awesome responsibility to realize that you are ultimately in charge of what you experience in your life.

This spiritual viewpoint encompasses all the spiritual laws and principles (listed later in this chapter) plus many more. We humans can never conceive of knowing all the mysteries of the Universe and therefore the full scope of why things happen as they do. But knowing and understanding some of the principles that guide the Earth plane and accepting that we live in a benevolent Universe certainly helps in accepting seeming tragedies in our lives. The consequences of your thoughts, words and actions are outcomes of these unbreakable laws of the Universe, and the Creator perspective will help you see how your past actions have helped create your current reality.

Things always happen for a reason, and it is this Creator perspective that helps you understand some of the higher perspectives for these events. The Creator's viewpoint gives your life deeper meaning, purpose and context. It reminds you that there is a God watching over your every move with love and compassion. But it is important to remember that your God "doesn't care" what choices you make, in the sense that He has given you free will. So the Creator is both loving and detached.

The Creator perspective helps you see the patterns and consequences of your life choices and helps to remind you that you are *always* at choice. Your soul drives you in this life and this part of your self can be revealed by studying your dreams from the Creator perspective. Getting to know your soul self and beginning to see yourself and the world around you through the eyes of Spirit is part of what will be revealed to you through the Creator perspective.

Karma

To begin to understand some of what this perspective can teach you, it is helpful to understand the law or principle of Karma. In the West we view Karma as a type of cause and effect that carries over from lifetime to lifetime. If you do something bad in this life, you will have to atone for it in the next. It is an eye-for-an-eye type of understanding. In Eastern philosophies Karma is viewed differently. They see it as a cause that moves you toward an effect. They believe you must balance off your debt in order to move toward union with God.

When you are not incarnated on the planet, you have a soul life. When you are embodied as a human being, only a small percentage of your soul comes with you into your physical body. Most of your soul stays in Spirit Land and has a whole life there (but not in a physical body) — it has a purpose there. While you are a human, you remember very little of Who You Are, but your soul in Spirit Land is very awake to the whole of Who You Are. At some point in your journey of incarnations, when your physical body passes from one of your lives you will make amends out of benevolence and love for another who you have wronged or who you have caused to feel pain. You will do so because you choose to, not because you have to.

Through the eyes of spirit, Karma is a balancing of energies, not a punishment system. It serves to balance through action. When you return to Spirit Land after your physical death, you review every nuance of this lifetime and decide (because free will also reigns in Spirit Land) to make correct anything you think has been left unbalanced. For example, if you caused another person to feel belittled by your thoughts, words or actions, then at some point in a future lifetime you may choose to experience what it feels like to be belittled.

"Karma is the dynamic force that keeps the Universe in motion."

Karma implies that *every* thought, word and action you take will affect *all* life on the planet (and beyond). Like the stone tossed into a pond (mentioned at the beginning of this chapter), your thoughts, words and actions have a far-reaching energetic effect in the Universe. Karma is the dynamic force that keeps the Universe in motion. It is the sacred rhythm of all life, by which you move the energy of God.

You cannot escape the law of Karma: it is the law of energy and the way it behaves. Although the concepts of space and time do not exist in Spirit Land, it can still take the soul (that has not fully integrated) some time to choose to make amends. Just as it may take you some time to make amends for your past actions in this lifetime, the newly arrived in Spirit Land needs a chance to digest past errors.

To help you understand Karma further and see how it can be revealed in your dream time, it is helpful to broaden your belief systems further to include past lives. Karma works not only in balancing actions you have taken in this life, but in other incarnations as well. The very term "past lives" evokes disbelief in many North Americans because it has not been taught as a truth. But many modern religions teach the exact opposite of this: life continues in a wheel of cosmic Karma or reincarnation. Whether you believe in this concept or not, various aspects of self that have lived before can and will be revealed in your nightly dreams.

In the eyes of Spirit there are no past lives either, but rather a series of concurrent or ongoing lives or energetic experiences (see Figure 6). Time as we experience it here on Earth is vastly different than what Spirit experiences. Time, for the spirit, is not linear with a past, present and future but can be thought of as everything happening at once — a circular type of occurrence. This means that those other incarnations you may refer to as past lives are actually happening right now, at the same time that you are experiencing this life. This may seem confusing to the rational mind because your intellect tends to think in the all or nothing world of extremes or opposites (as discussed in Chapter 8) and in a straight line of past, present and future.

All lives, whether past, present or future, occur and vibrate in the infinite *now*. This is why your dreams can reveal information about your past lives just as they reveal many different marbles of your self. Think of your soul as a large soap bubble filled with smaller soap bubbles. Each one of the smaller bubbles can be said to be a life or past life occurring within the same large bubble.

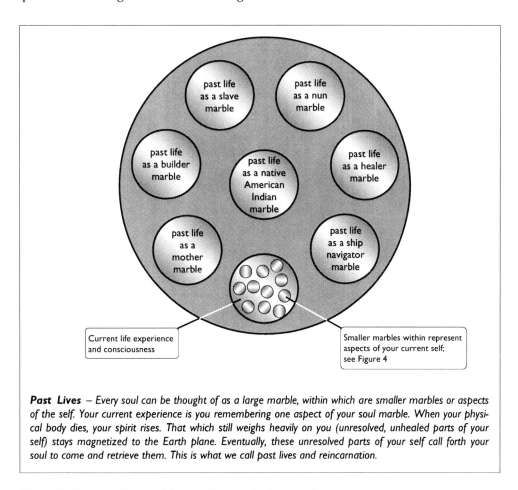

Past Lives – *Every soul can be thought of as a large marble, within which are smaller marbles or aspects of the self. Your current experience is you remembering one aspect of your soul marble. When your physical body dies, your spirit rises. That which still weighs heavily on you (unresolved, unhealed parts of your self) stays magnetized to the Earth plane. Eventually, these unresolved parts of your self call forth your soul to come and retrieve them. This is what we call past lives and reincarnation.*

Figure 6. How marbles explain past lives and reincarnation

❀

Creator or Soul Marbles

Just as each individual is composed of many aspects or marbles (see Chapter 7), so too is your soul self full of different aspects or past-lives marbles (like the bubbles within a larger bubble). Just as all your personal inner marbles are happening all at once, so too are all your Creator or soul marbles happening simultaneously. And just as your dreams point out different inner marbles, the Creator perspective allows you to view one particular soul marble in each dream.

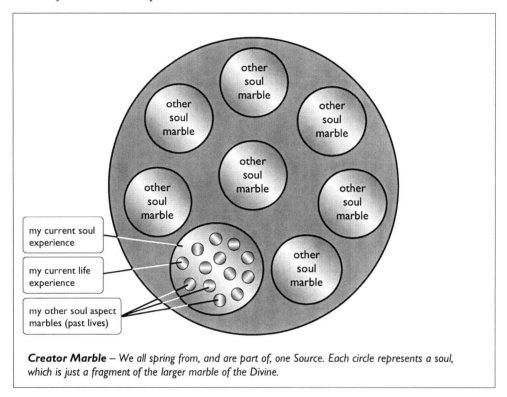

Creator Marble – We all spring from, and are part of, one Source. Each circle represents a soul, which is just a fragment of the larger marble of the Divine.

Figure 7. We are all part of the one Source, the Creator marble

As you progress through your dream work and begin to Know Who You Are (literal level) and Know Who You Are Not (irrational level), you will begin to be shown your Creator self or Creator marbles more clearly. Learning to recognize these parts of yourself can take some study and time, but be assured that this broader perspective of self is offered in every dream.

You may have heard esoteric teachings that report that you are just a spark of the Divine or a splinter of God. This is true, and as you work to Know Your Creator Self, you will begin to see that you are indeed just a spark of the Divine's will here on Earth. This perspective truly gives your current life more meaning and more purpose. In fact, it is here in the Creator perspective that your current life's purpose can be revealed to you. This is a dream request often asked (regarding your life's purpose) and the answers are always revealed, but often in a step-by-step process that guides you toward it.

Traits and Qualities

The following words emphasize some of the qualities and attributes inherent in the Creator perspective. You will likely be able to see your dream trying to encourage you to adopt one or several of these traits as a message from your Creator. When interpreting a dream, use this list to help identify clues about the meaning of your Creator's viewpoint. You can think of these as some of the soul marbles inherent in every human.

abundance	faith	joy	purity
acceptance	forgiveness	liberty	purpose
adoration	freedom	love	rapture
balance	generosity	mastery	responsibility
beauty	grace	mercy	simplicity
benevolence	gratitude	miracles	strength
blessings	harmony	patience	surrender
clarity	honesty	peace	trust
communication	hope	perseverance	truth
compassion	humility	power	vision
courage	humour	prayer	willingness
creativity	integrity	prosperity	wisdom

✿

Universal Laws or Principles

Because the literal perspective deals with our actual experience here on Earth, it would be helpful for dream students to familiarize themselves with some of the basic principles of natural, or universal, laws. These laws have been established by God, the Divine, Great Spirit, Source or whatever you choose to call the Creator. They make it possible for you to have and create exactly what you choose. These laws cannot be violated, nor can they be ignored. You cannot *not* follow these laws, for they work energetically, just as the laws of physics do — and, as you know, you cannot ignore the law of gravity. You cannot step aside from these principles; you cannot operate outside of them. These laws are a fundamental part of everyday life and of the Creator perspective of dreams.

"To be unaware of the laws of the Universe will render you powerless in your life"

If you can understand, trust, and accept that the laws of physics have been scientifically proven, then you can learn to trust and accept that the laws of the Universe are also real and operate in a similar way. To be unaware of the laws of the Universe will render you powerless in your life and subject you to an inordinate amount of pain. So it is a good idea to acquaint yourself with the dynamics of these principles. Once you have leaned how to operate within these laws, your life will begin to unfold more smoothly and you will be able to consciously co-create your reality. You will be able to manifest your goals and desires here on Earth.

Here is a list of some of the universal principles. There are many, many more principles that can be revealed in the dream time; this is an incomplete list drawn from several sources. (If you would like to learn more about these principles, see the bibliography for a list of sources.) These principles can serve as a foundation to understanding the Creator perspective. By having a better understanding of the interconnected nature of all things, you can become more aware of your divine nature. Watch and see how these principles are revealed in your dream time (and your waking time too).

116

1) *Like attracts like.* You will attract like-energy people into your waking hours, and the characters in your dreams will also have similar energy to that of your conscious waking persona. You will also attract what you fear and what you fear draws near. You are like a radio station that constantly emits signals into the Universe. If you are sending mixed signals (like most people are) you will get back mixed information (which leads to confusion instead of clarity). Remember that every person drawn into your life is reflecting/mirroring some part of you.

2) *As above, so below.* This is the microcosm being revealed in the macrocosm and vice versa. It is why the principle of Know Yourself and You Will Know the Universe functions. All that takes place at a microcosmic or quantum level is also taking place in the movement of the planets and stars. Whatever action you take here on Earth affects the tiniest particles and the largest planets. All that is revealed in the spin and function of a single atom is a mirror of the spin of the galaxy. Your dreams work in a similar fashion, revealing marbles that reflect the whole.

3) *For every action there is an equal and opposite reaction.* This is an organized way of understanding Karma. Although Karma is complex, it can be revealed in this principle, which is also a simple principle of physics. Watch your dreams to find out how the consequences of your thoughts, words and actions are being played out.

4) *There is no coincidence, and nothing happens by accident.* This is truly a challenging concept to grasp when faced with a difficult or tragic event. However, your dreams can reveal the deeper meaning behind most occurrences in your life, including illnesses, "accidents" and disasters. Ask questions of your dreams (see Chapter 2) and be assured that the answer is *always* provided. Remember, your answers can come in a dream or while you are awake — through another person, television, a song, or an animal encounter. Be aware and keep your eyes open and you *will* get your answers.

5) *You can be, do and have whatever you can imagine.* Use your dreams to help fulfill any goal or desire. Set your intent and surrender the steps to your God. There is a fine line between what is real and what is imagined. In fact, you are making your whole life up anyway. Trust the power of your higher self to bring you the information you need for your journey so you can begin the co-creation process and manifest your desires here on Earth.

6) *Emotion is energy in motion. When you move energy, you create effect. If you move enough energy you create matter.* This principle speaks of the ability to create through feeling. Remember, your emotions are powerful tools that guide you in your everyday life. Pay attention to your dream feelings, because they speak the truth of your heart. Connecting your energy/emotions with your intent gives you a powerful tool for creation in the physical.

7) *Thought is pure energy. Thought is creative.* The power of the intellect and human mind is tremendous. Sitting in meditation and being aware of your thoughts is one of the most powerful tools you can use to help you understand what you are manifesting in your everyday life. Your thoughts are also revealed in every dream. Pay attention and learn how to direct your own creative power.

8) *Love is all there is.* This principle reveals we all stem from one Source. This is the foundation of the Creator perspective. We used to live in a paradigm of everyone for themselves but this saying is beginning to lose its validity as we awaken to the newer concept that We Are All One. Every person on the planet is like a shard of glass from a large broken mirror. The mirror, if intact, would represent God. You are just a fragment of the whole and the whole vibrates nothing but love. You and every person around you vibrate love within them. Can you see it, sense it, hear it or just conceive that it may be possible?

9) *You are in partnership with your God.* This principle speaks of the co-creative nature of our reality. Use your dreams to help reveal God's design for your life and work in cooperation with this Divine plan. Your life can be much less chaotic and confusing when you realize there are benevolent forces at work in your life. Your dreams can help you recognize that you are never alone and that communication from your God (in the guise of symbolism) is ever present.

10) *You will always be given what you ask for.* "Be careful what you ask for" is a well-known phrase. As soon as you ask for something, the energy of it is communicated to the Universe. The answers may come in a guise you were not expecting. For example, you may ask your God to help you kick your coffee/caffeine habit. After several days of success you may decide to cheat and buy just one cup of java. Then to your dismay, and hopefully your funny bone too, you spill the coffee. You could be upset or see it as an act of a benevolent God who is just giving you what you asked for (in this case, quitting coffee/caffeine). These types of incidents are more frequent than you may realize. Get to know what you are "putting out there." Be aware of seemingly opposite answers coming back your way. Remember that in order to create wholeness, you must first become familiar with the contrary side of your request (that is, you cannot know hot until you experience cold). Most people operate unconsciously, and therefore they are only aware on an unconscious level of what they are asking for. Let your dreams help you to see what you are truly asking for.

11) *Humans are three-fold beings consisting of a body, mind and spirit (trinity).* You cannot escape this principle and you can begin to observe the trinity within yourself, as well as the trinities that exist around our world (such as id, ego and superego; Father, Son and Holy Ghost; past, present and future; unconscious, sub-conscious and superconscious; up, down and centre; and so on). Every dream reveals and reflects this principle.

12) *Your life proceeds out of your intentions for it.* Just as you can set your intent to remember your dreams (a powerful tool discussed in Chapter 2), so too can you set your intent to achieve any endeavour in life. Become aware of what signals you are sending with your thoughts, words and action. Get to know what your intent is for your life by writing down some of your desires. Be clear on what you intend to bring into your life. Watch your dreams for signs of the true reality you are creating with your intent.

13) *Consequences are an element of the Earth plane (relativity) and do not exist in the realm of Spirit (the absolute).* Here on Earth we cannot experience Who We Are until we experience Who We Are Not. This is part of what the Earth plane experi-ence is for — it helps us to see and experience the consequences of our actions. It allows us to have desires and then use the universal laws and principles to try to manifest them in the physical reality. This dynamic does not exist in the world of Spirit — it exists only here on Earth. It can be seen at work through the four per-spectives and is best understood through the irrational perspective. One way to relate to this is by considering what you desire for your life. Perhaps those desires have not actualized in your life. What is wrong? Nothing. The benevolent Universe realizes you have dreams and desires and gives you the playground of the Earth plane to make manifest your desires. Part of your Earth walk is learning how to take those desires, work with the universal principles and literally pull those desires into the physical reality and make them evident.

14) *Truth and God are found in the same place: in the silence.* This principle reflects the deep need for a daily meditation practice. All of your answers can be found within, if you would just take the time to sit quietly and listen to your inner voices. Your wisdom will speak through the chatter — it's just a matter of sitting in silence long enough to hear it. An important scientific study revealed that human brains have more than 10 trillion synapses in the nervous system, whereas there are only 100 million sensory receptors within the body. This means the mind is 100,000 times more sensitive to its internal environment than to its external. It is truly from a place within that you receive and assimilate most of your knowledge. You will hear and see your inner wisdom reflected in the dream time as well.

15) *You have free choice about everything.* Earth is a planet of free will. Nothing you do, say, think or feel is by force. You have choice about everything. Watch your dreams as they show you this principle at work in your everyday life. Accepting the huge responsibility revealed in this principle can be a bitter pill to swallow, but this principle can and will bring you the ultimate gift of freedom.

16) *The Creator does not judge. Only humans judge.* This can be a challenging principle to grasp if you have been raised in a religion that sees God as man-like in nature. Nothing could be further from the truth. God is revealed in your dreams as a sacred witness to your life that gives you ultimate freedom by allowing you choice. Then why would He choose to judge your choices if He has given you this gift? Find your sacred witness's voice in every dream — it is there waiting for you to find it.

17) *You are co-creator with the Divine in your own life. You create your future with your thoughts, words and actions.* This principle is discussed and revealed throughout this book. Allow yourself to co-create. Use your dreams to co-create. Be aware of what you are creating with your thoughts, words and actions.

18) *We are one. We are one large energetic whole, not separate beings as we appear to be.* We are all fragments of God. Earth may look like one solid planet from outer space, but in reality it is composed of billions of people, plants, animals and elements. From a distance we look whole or as one; up close we see the individuals that comprise our planet. This is similar to the marbles that comprise your dream-time self. We can break the self down into smaller pieces or parts for closer examination. But in reality, We Are One.

19) *The law of Dharma reveals that you are on the Earth plane for a purpose.* Dharma means your purpose here on the planet. Dreams are an excellent tool for helping you discern your life's purpose. Use a dream request to get you started walking the path toward your destiny. Understanding and using the four Ancient Egyptian Mystery School perspectives is also a superb way to tap into your Dharma.

20) *Energy can never be created or destroyed. Death is not an end but a beginning.* This principle is discussed at length earlier in this chapter. When viewing the meaning behind death in your dreams, you will realize it is symbolic of a transformation occurring somewhere in your life. Death and rebirth are a part of life — you cannot separate yourself from this principle. If the notion of death as a beginning is new to you, pay attention to the deaths occurring in your dreams. They can help reveal the truth of this rebirth concept and help you to integrate it into your belief system.

Remember that every thought you have, every word you speak and every action you take is helping to create your reality. Waking up to the four levels of the Ancient Mystery School is your key to enlightenment and the road map of how to manifest your desires on Earth. Let these tools guide you so you can learn to take your dreams and desires and manifest them here on Earth. Our planet can truly be a Garden of Eden when you learn how to see from the four perspectives and how to use the universal laws and principles in your everyday life.

Chapter 10

Dream Interpretation: The Mystery School Methods

The Mystic Path Method

This dream interpretation method is offered to those ardent students who would like to understand even greater depths of self. The Seer's Path Method explained in Chapter 4 is used, but in this variation the analysis continues with an in-depth look at the information revealed according to the four perspectives (literal, symbolic, irrational and Creator) detailed in Chapters 6 through 9. This method helps you to further familiarize yourself with the perspectives while you practise the Seer's Path Method. It may be challenging to find information from each perspective to begin with, and it is not essential to fill in every category. Repeated practice will deepen your ability to spot information in every perspective. Use this variation method only if you are a passionate dream analyzer; it can be overwhelming to the beginner.

Overview of Steps

The Seer's Path Method	The Mystery School Perspectives
1 – Feelings	1 – Literal Perspective
2 – Background or Setting	Physical
3 – Most Significant Symbol	Emotional
4 – Theme	Mental
5 – Symbols' Meaning	Spiritual
6 – Dream's Meaning	2 – Symbolic Perspective
7 – Title and Summary	3 – Irrational Perspective
8 – Decision and Application	4 – Creator Perspective

Mystic Path Method Example 1: The Big Scary Monster

This dream was submitted by a 31-year-old woman.

"I am being chased by a monster and I can't get away from it. I am terrified and running away as fast as I can."

First, we use the Seer's Path Method explained in Chapter 4.

Feelings Terror	Background or Setting Darkness only	Theme ▸ Something (monster) is chasing me. ▸ I am running away from something (monster).
Most Significant Symbol Monster	Meaning of Symbols A monster is something bigger than me or will overwhelm me if confronted. The monster will hurt, kill, or just scare me if I face it.	Dream's Meaning ▸ In the last day or two I felt terrified. ▸ A waking-hour event, situation or relationship that I think is "bigger than me" or is too overwhelming to confront is chasing or pursuing me.

Title: The Light Bulb Goes On
Summary: I realize I have to deal with my problems at work before they consume me.

Decision and Application
I will confront my problem.
1) I will rehearse and write out what I'd like to say to my boss.
2) I will think of the worst-case scenario and prepare for it.
3) Then I will think of the most positive outcome and practise visualizing this outcome.
4) Then I will speak with my boss.

Dreamer's Comments on Meaning

The dreamer realized that she had been *running away from* a problem at work. She said the monster is her boss. She has authority issues with him and she has been too *terrified* to confront him. She didn't realize it was plaguing her so badly until the dream content was revealed. Now she understands the urgent need to confront this situation and stand up for herself.

Now, to further analyze the dream's meaning, we also use the Mystery School perspectives.

The Literal Perspective	**The Symbolic Perspective**
Physical – My heart was pounding, I was sweating, I awoke and needed to put the light on.	The symbol "monster" is revealed to represent my boss at work. This is a waking-time representation. At a deeper level it reveals a marble or characteristic of myself. It reveals my inner authority marble and how it interacts or relates to the whole of my self.
Emotional – Fear, terror	
Mental – Core beliefs revealed:	Searching more deeply (i.e., realizing, recognizing and owning that this is a marble of her self) is entirely up to the dreamer. The information must resonate or ring a bell with the individual or it is not appropriate to their path *at this time*. Many people are not able to see the deeper levels of themselves when they begin analyzing their dreams unless they have been on their journey of self-study for some time. But interpreting the symbols in your dreams is like reading an in-depth book – you get more out of it when you go back to read it a second or third time. As you gather information about your self through dream work you will begin to see deeper levels of your self revealed in every dream. Searching more deeply means looking more closely to discern who you are (and who you are not). So there is value in keeping the notes you make of your dreams and reviewing them again in the future; you may see more depth in them next year than you do now.
1) I don't *think* I can get away from "it" (some waking-hour situation or part of self).	
2. I *think* I will be killed if I stop running or confront "it."	
3. I *think* I am helpless.	
4. I have no idea how to deal with this situation other than running away.	
Spiritual – Even though I am not aware of feeling afraid of something in my waking hours, I understand and *trust* that something in my life must be frightening to me. I can also see the dream is trying to tell me that I want to get away from some situation, even though I had no idea at the time what that was.	
The Irrational Perspective	**The Creator Perspective**
Information at this level reveals that I am currently using an old belief system in waking time (see beliefs listed in the section above on Literal Perspective – Mental). The dream reveals how irrational or unreasonable these beliefs (thinking	This dream reveals that I am always in choice about my thoughts, words and actions, and how I react to my feelings. In this case, the dreamer realized she was at choice about dealing face-to-face with

Cont'd on page 126

Cont'd from page 125

The Irrational Perspective
that I'm helpless and not knowing how to deal with scary things) are for me now.

The fact that the dreamer remembers the dream is an indication that the information revealed is something she is ready to deal with in her waking hours. With this in mind, the dreamer announces that the old beliefs no longer serve her well and that she is ready to take the next step (facing her monster/boss) and take a stand for herself.

The Creator Perspective
her boss and dealing with her reaction to him as an authority figure – or not. She realized that she had allowed her feelings to "own her" instead of owning them. That is, she realized she was letting her fear control her behaviours and actions. *Choosing* to own her feelings gave her a sense of empowerment and strength that she was not aware she possessed.

How to Compile the Information
from the
Four Mystery School Perspectives

Step 1: The Literal Perspective

Physical: Identify any body parts that you mentioned in your account of your dream. List any literal sensations that you felt in your body upon waking or that you remember from the dream. An energetic blockage or excess can be revealed when a body part (internal or external) is shown in a dream. This does not mean you will necessarily be aware of it or feel it, but something concerning energy is taking place in this area of your body. This can lead to problems or disease over months or years if an energy imbalance continues without attention or even waking-hour awareness.

Emotional: Identify your dream feelings. Remember these are pointing out the truth of how you were recently feeling in the waking hours. Emotions that go unrecognized are stored within the physical body and can build up over time and cause disease or impairments to health. For example, unexpressed anger, passion or rage (all red-coloured frequencies) can cause hardening of the arteries, arthritis, and heart problems in general.

Mental: Identify dream thoughts, attitudes, beliefs, ideas, perceptions, insights, judgements, opinions, convictions, dogma, rules, stances, demeanour — essentially, the components of your human personality. All these components add up to reveal your mental aspects of self.

It is helpful to locate phrases or expressions that contain such words as *can't, won't, not, never,* and *should*. These are limiting you in some area and are at the basis of some judgement, belief or attitude of yours.

Examples

Phrase in Dream Account	Interpretation
"I *should* be able to do this easily."	▶ demonstrates the dreamer's *judgement* of self
"I *can't* imagine why he did that."	▶ illustrates how the dreamer has an *opinion* about something or someone
"These clothes *never* feel comfortable."	▶ reveals the dreamer's *insight* about something not being comfortable in waking hours

Other strong indicators of beliefs, attitudes and opinions can be found in sentences or expressions that contain the words *realize, know, understand, recognize, can* or *will.* Other helpful words that help you pinpoint mental aspects of self include phrases that begin with "I" or "I am."

Examples:

Phrase in Dream Account	Interpretation
"*I can* drive my car easily." "*I know* how to get home."	▶ both demonstrate a positive *belief* about the dreamer's ability to do something when awake
"*I know* I'll fail again."	▶ shows the dreamer's negative *belief* about some waking-hour situation
"*I am* seeing the situation very clearly."	▶ demonstrates the dreamer's current waking-hour *perception* of a situation

Look for any words that point to a dead-end solution, such as "I feel *stuck* in this situation" or "My car is *blocked* in." Both examples demonstrate your *belief* that you are currently unable to accomplish something in the waking time.

Remember that other people, animals and objects usually represent parts of you, so watch for *he, she, them, they, us,* and *we* as indicators of your own mental parts. The action word (verb) often indicates the mental level as well. Underlining the verbs in a dream account is a handy way to uncover mental beliefs, attitudes and thoughts.

Examples:

Phrase in Dream Account	Interpretation
"*She* is *hiding* behind a wall."	▸ shows the *belief* that the dreamer is hiding or disguising something about herself
"*He's getting* the picture."	▸ indicates the dreamer's *belief* or *perception* about getting or comprehending the truth of a situation
"Lucy is standing with her hands on her hips."	▸ reveals the dreamer's stance or *attitude* of defiance
"The *car* is out of control."	▸ reveals dreamer's *perception* or *insight* that something in his life is out of control
"A *dog attacked* John."	▸ shows how the dreamer *perceives* that some thing or someone is being attacked or criticized in his waking hours

Spiritual: To identify your spiritual aspects of self in a dream, you must first realize what "spiritual" means to you personally. This was outlined in the discussion on the literal perspective (Chapter 6). Take note in the dream if you are demonstrating any of your previously identified spiritual qualities.

For example, if you identify love or compassion as a spiritual trait, are you demonstrating love or compassion for your self or others in the dream? Perhaps you are demonstrating judgement or opinions about your self and others. Often identifying when you are *not* demonstrating what is on your "spiritual list" will help you to recognize when you are.

Remember, spiritual qualities may include trust, faith, hope, humour, willingness, creativity, courage, strength, gentleness, flexibility, peace, passion, clarity, acceptance, openness, joy, unity, consciousness and honesty. Identifying these traits will help you pinpoint when the spiritual level of self has been revealed in a dream.

Trust that the information that is being revealed to you is the truth of Who You Are. That is, the dream feelings are actually your waking-hour feelings too. Also, trust that the beliefs revealed are your true waking-hour beliefs.

Furthermore, you can list what has, so far, been recognized as truth. Accept all feelings in the dream as your own. Whatever beliefs you were able to identify are also your own, and the opportunity to just accept these without judging whether they are good or bad is part of what the spiritual information is offering you.

Your experience in your physical body is your personal spirit quest on Earth, unique and perfect to you as an individual. This level, like all the information, must resonate at a deep level with you. You are on a quest to remember Who You Are, and your higher spiritual cravings and yearnings are revealed in all your dreams. Every time a light bulb goes on or you get an "ah-ha" feeling, you know you have connected with, and remembered, a part of your self. Perceiving self, and making connections, is what the spirit desires. The spirit in you craves and delights in your Knowing Your Self in all its glory. Whether you judge the dream information as good or bad is not what the spirit cares about (it's what the intellect cares about). The spiritual aspect of self sees all awakenings or openings to information as a step toward remembering your spirit/soul self.

Examples:

Phrase in Dream Account	Interpretation
"I see myself as a toddler in the dream. I think I'm really cute and admire my own manners. I want to stick around and help my early self grow."	▸ demonstrates dreamer's *love* and *devotion* to own self and self-growth
"I am hurtling through outer space. Although I am scared, I know I will land in a safe place."	▸ illustrates the dreamer's spiritual self or soul marble has *trust* and *faith* in something larger than herself
"My foot is nailed to the floor and I can't move, yet I find this humorous for some reason."	▸ shows the dreamer's spiritual self *knows* and *trusts* that all of life is a process and she will therefore not be "stuck" in this situation forever

Cont'd on page 130

Cont'd from page 129

Phrase in Dream Account	Interpetation
"A tornado threatens to engulf me, yet I feel no fear."	▸ reveals the dreamer's spiritual self has *faith* in something to save her from a daunting situation

Step 2: The Symbolic Perspective

If you wish to analyze the symbols already revealed in Step 5 of the Seer's Path Method at a greater depth, you can do it here in the symbolic perspective. However, to try to analyze every symbol in a dream is challenging and can often lead to information overload, which beginners especially want to avoid.

Example:

"I see a snake in my dream."

The dreamer fears snakes and so makes the connection that the snake represents something he fears in the waking hours. This is only one level of information revealed to the dreamer. At a deeper level (universally), snakes are symbolic of many other things, including transformation, healing, alchemy, sexuality, initiation, wisdom, resurrection, rebirth, eternity, kundalini, transition and change. It is up to the dreamer to search through his self (all the parts that make up Who He Is) to discover which of these deeper aspects is being reflected at this time (watch for the "ah-ha" moments to help you begin to see these deeper reflections). This type of deeper insight comes with practice and patience. It takes a while to get to know yourself and your symbols. As you progress through dream study and self study, gleaning these deeper meanings will become easier.

Using the Dream Symbol Dictionary (Part 3 of this book) will help familiarize you with universal symbolism and help you discern your own symbolic meanings. When you look up a dream symbol in the dictionary, remember to be aware if the meaning resonates with you, rings a bell, gives you an "ah-ha" moment or otherwise feels right for you. If it doesn't make sense, or you cannot see the relationship between the symbolic representation and your current journey, then the symbol's deeper meaning may not be right for you at this time. In this case, try to delve deeper into what the symbol means for you by reviewing the material on the symbolic perspective in Chapter 7.

Step 3: The Irrational Perspective

To reveal dream information from the irrational perspective, identify aspects of the dream that cannot be reasoned out or rationally explained. Remember that the information you get from this perspective may be irrational and contrary to your intellect.

The information you compile in this section will include identifying imbalances in your belief system and discrepancies between dream feelings and waking-hour feelings. It is irrational to feel one emotion in a dream and not feel it in the waking time. Identify these kinds of irrational aspects of the dream and list them.

Review the information compiled in the Mental section of the literal perspective. List the thoughts, beliefs, or attitudes that were revealed in the dream and compare them with their usefulness in your waking hours.

Example:

This example uses again the first sample dream in this chapter, in which the woman dreamt that a monster is trying to kill her ("I am being chased by a monster that I can't get away from; I am terrified and running away as fast as I can."). She realized the monster symbolically represents her boss at work. The dream clearly points out the perception that she *believes* she will actually die from this encounter (facing her boss). In the waking time she knows this *not* to be true. Herein lies the duality or irrationality of the dreamer's current belief system. She is holding two beliefs, yet she is acting on only one of them. She *believes* she will die if she faces her boss, yet she also *believes* she will *not* die if she faces her boss.

This perspective shows this dreamer, and all of us, that we are being irrational. The irrational level is intended to make you change. In this example, the dreamer's belief that she will die if she encounters her boss face-to-face is outdated and no longer serves her well. Once you are able to spot your own irrational beliefs, you can take steps toward changing them.

Recognizing your irrational aspects of self and beginning to think, speak and act in a manner that moves you toward your intended target (your vision of a whole self) will bring more clarity and balance into your life.

Step 4: The Creator Perspective

This level reveals information about your soul's journey or purpose and offers a glimpse of the Creator's plan for your life. Review and become familiar with the universal laws or principles that govern the Earth plane (see Chapter 9). Once you have accustomed yourself to the existence of some of these standards of reality, then the Creator perspective information will become clearer. This level reveals a higher purpose and meaning to your life and is about detaching from the outcome of events in your life. This is the level where you learn to trust your God's vision for your life. You learn to let go of or surrender your lower will to the Divine's will. Remember, the Creator is always moving you toward a higher purpose and toward your soul's desires. This is done through Karma.

> *"Fear is a gift from the Creator intended to assist you in your spiritual growth by allowing you to have an obstacle to experiencing all of Who You Are.*

All of life is preprogrammed, much like children's video games. All the possible moves have been programmed into the computer prior to anyone playing the game — there is no move or manoeuvre possible that the computer doesn't already know about. You have choice about what moves you make in the game, but none of your moves is truly original — you can only choose from among the options the game presents to you. The Creator has preprogrammed everything, and together with the Creator you co-create what you would like to experience here on the Earth plane.

As discussed in Chapter 9, before you enter your physical body you choose much of what you will experience during your Earth walk, just as you choose what moves to make in a video game. But this does not mean that your life is pre-destined. It means that you may choose to create certain opportunities in your life prior to incarnating in order to experience certain events, feelings, relationships, illnesses or anything that your soul desires. Some of those choices are revealed to you when you examine your dreams from the Creator perspective.

Examine the dream content that has been revealed and identify where you may have an opportunity to change some part of your self. Look for signs of fear in your dream and remember that fear is a gift from the Creator intended to assist you in your spiritual growth by allowing you to have an obstacle to experiencing *all* of Who You Are. The obstacle, the fear, now becomes a tool for your spiritual growth.

Accept that *all* the parts of self revealed (emotional, mental, spiritual and physical) are revealed now for a reason. You may not understand the reason just yet. But accept that the Creator is not judging this revealed information. If there is any judgement about this material, realize it is coming from you. The Creator's intent in revealing information about your life's journey is to help and guide you to a greater understanding and experience of yourself. All information revealed is a gift, despite your rational mind's tendency to refuse to accept seemingly negative aspects of self; remember that all is happening for a far-reaching reason (your soul's remembrance and growth). Many people believe that you are here in this life to learn something — in fact, you are here to remember your Whole Self or Soul Self, and this level of the dream work will begin to reveal those forgotten parts.

Realize that all feelings and beliefs (even if outmoded) serve a purpose and are therefore perfect for your experience at this time. You will only move on and grow when you remember how to accept and love your current self (no matter how imperfect *you* may think you are, in the eyes of Spirit you are always perfect).

Example:

Suppose you had the following dream: *"I am swept up by a tornado and I can't stop myself from being sucked into its powerful funnel."*

To see the Creator perspective in this dream, you must remember that although this is a planet of free will, you are never in control — but you are always at choice. In this dream, it appears that you have no control about being sucked into the tornado. But you still have a choice — you can fight the flow or go with it.

Tornados often represent huge emotional upset or being swept away by strong emotions in your life. The Creator perspective suggests it is perfectly all right to be swept away by your strong emotions. If fact, allowing this to happen (by trusting the divine action in your life and letting yourself get sucked in without resistance) would shift the flow of energy and you would be spit out by the funnel. In other words, allowing the strong emotion to flow through you is the action that will most benefit you. If you choose to fight the flow of this tornado of emotion in your life, you will be trying to fight the Creator's plan for you. Being drawn into emotional turmoil may not be pleasant, but it serves a great purpose and will teach you and guide you if you allow it to. In this case, the dream is suggesting that you surrender or let go of control because the force of the emotion is too strong to fight — what you resist persists, and resisting takes more energy than letting go. Trusting the Creator's vision for what is in your best and highest good is challenging initially, but with practice it can help to bring more peace and balance into your life.

Example:

This dream was recounted by a 46-year-old woman.

"I am holding my cat in my arms as though she were a baby, and she is talking to me (pleading with me to let her go outside)! The situation seems surreal and the images are very vivid. I feel love and tenderness for my cat. I also feel guilty about not letting her outside, but I want to keep her safe."

The dream reveals the dreamer's need to see this beloved animal as an aspect of her self and the need to hold herself like a baby. It also indicates that there is a strong need to open the doors of communication between her self and her inner baby self. In fact, the cat-baby communicates that she needs to be free of constraint or perhaps inner rules, and shouldn't be so afraid of being hurt.

Detaching from outcome is part of what the Creator perspective tries to teach you. In this case, the dreamer is attached to the outcome of her cat being hurt before she even lets her outside. One of the universal laws states that like attracts like. Since the dreamer is sending out the vibration of fear (that her cat will be hurt) and non-trust into the world before she even opens the door, this is attracting the same vibration back. This is an example of "what you fear draws near." In this case, this could mean that the fear the dreamer is sending out is actually attracting unhealthy and non-beneficial vibrations. Realizing what signals (fears) you are putting out is the first step toward changing these signals. You must be aware of your fears before you can change them.

This same principle applies to trusting your God. Practising trust and sending it out will bring more opportunities to trust into your life. In this dream, the dreamer would do well to understand that even though she may not have received the love she needed as a baby, there was a larger plan at work here. Her soul may well have chosen this path (of not being held lovingly as a baby) in order to fulfil a Karmic debt (remember that we freely choose to come back and balance things — nothing is ever forced upon us). She may have chosen to experience this "lack of needs being met as a baby" to strengthen her self as an adult — to show her how to love herself and overcome hurdles that would otherwise have prevented her from achieving self-mastery.

Of course, we may not see the outcome of the choices we make in this lifetime until some time has elapsed. But trusting that your God knows what is in your best and highest good and learning to go with the flow and not resist your feelings or the circumstances that arise in your life will help to make your journey smoother.

Mystic Path Method Example 2: Making a Dream Request
Where Do I Fit In?

Recorded by a 38-year-old woman who had asked a question prior to sleep. She asked, "What is my life's purpose?"

"I am standing in an unfamiliar room looking at a huge map of the world that is made entirely of puzzle pieces. I hold in my hand a piece of the puzzle but I can't figure out where my piece fits. I feel overwhelmed by the sheer size of the puzzle."

Feelings	Background or Setting	Theme
Baffled, overwhelmed	Unfamiliar room	▸ I am somewhere (room). ▸ I am looking at something (puzzle). ▸ I hold something (piece of puzzle). ▸ I can't figure something out (where piece fits).
Most Significant Symbol Puzzle	**Meaning of Symbols** Room – represents an unfamiliar area/aspect/part of self Puzzle – represents something about me that is in pieces, but whole when completed Puzzle piece – a single part or ingredient to help make the puzzle (me) whole or complete	**Dream's Meaning** Dream Request question: "What is my life's purpose?" ▸ In the last day or two prior to the dream, I was feeling baffled and overwhelmed by my life events, issues and relationships. ▸ I am experiencing an unfamiliar part of my self. ▸ I am able to see the whole situation. ▸ I hold the part or missing ingredient. ▸ I can't figure out how to make myself whole or complete.

Title: Life's Purpose
Summary: My life's purpose is to become whole. I realize I am on the right track to becoming whole. I acknowledge how overwhelming and confusing this is for me, and that it is okay to feel this way.

Cont'd on page 136

Cont'd from page 135

Decision and Application

Continue with goals of becoming whole. Three things I can do to actualize my goals:

1) Continue with dream work and therefore self-discovery.
2) Acknowledge emotions and allow them to be/exist without judgement.
3) Become aware of outdated beliefs and choose new ones that will benefit me in reaching my goals. Practise new beliefs by using the affirmation, "I am on my path to wholeness and reach it effortlessly and with confidence."

Dreamer's Comments on Meaning

The dreamer was trying to find out where she "fit in" in the world and has been on her spiritual quest for many years. She has been feeling confused and overwhelmed lately and that is why she asked, "What is my life's purpose?" The dream confirmed what she already was reaching for, namely wholeness. Her life's purpose is to become whole and she realizes that although she is able to see (envision) the puzzle of who she is, the puzzle has not yet been completed.

The Mystery School Perspectives

The Literal Perspective	The Symbolic Perspective
Physical – Hand is mentioned in the dream. In this dream it represents the ability of the dreamer to hold or grasp something (puzzle piece). The key to becoming whole is within her *grasp*. How she chooses to *handle* the situation is up to her.	Many symbols appear here (room, puzzle, hand and puzzle piece), all of which represent aspects of her self.
If she chooses *not* to handle or deal with the situation presented, she could, in the long run, manifest problems with her hands.	
Emotional – Revealed in this dream are the dreamer's feelings of being baffled and overwhelmed.	

Mental – A mental block on the dreamer's part is revealed when she believes she can't do something (a very limiting belief). She believes she can't figure out where she fits into the larger picture of things (represented by world puzzle). On a personal level she desires wholeness, but believes she *can't* figure out how to complete her own image of self.

Spiritual – Dreamer demonstrates her faith in her spiritual endeavours by *trusting* her higher self to guide her (asking questions of her dreams and accepting the answers revealed). She *trusts* that she has a life purpose (demonstrated by making the dream request) and aspires to understand and manifest her goals in this lifetime.

The Irrational Perspective
Beliefs revealed in the Mental section above are irrational or incongruous to her waking-hour goals. Neither of her beliefs serves her well at this time, and she will have to review and change them in order to remedy the situation.

The Creator Perspective
This level reveals there is a higher reason (as yet unknown) for why she does not know how she fits into the greater picture of life or how she will reach a state of wholeness. There could be many reasons why her soul and her (concept of) God do not wish her to have this information at this time in her spiritual development. Her dream reveals that she has the potential to reach wholeness in this life. Patience and perseverance are the sinews of this Creator level of teaching.

❁

The Enlightened Path Method

Now we'll look at how to add the Mystery School Perspectives to the Magical Path Method that was explained in Chapter 4.

Overview of Steps

The Magical Path Method 1 – Feelings 2 – Most Significant Symbol and its Meaning 3 – Waking-Hour Connection	*The Mystery School Perspectives* 1 – Literal Perspective Physical Emotional Mental Spiritual 2 – Symbolic Perspective 3 – Irrational Perspective 4 – Creator Perspective

Enlightened Path Method Example 1: Tidal Waves and Tornadoes

Submitted by 44-year-old man.

"I am in a building with many windows. Outside I see a tidal wave coming. I go to a small room for protection, but I see a tornado through this window. I am afraid and anxious."

Most Significant Feeling Fear	**Most Significant Symbols** Tidal wave and tornado
Meaning of Symbols Tornadoes and tidal waves both represent extreme emotional upset.	**Waking-Hour Connection** The day the man had this dream was also the day of a family get-together. Although these family gatherings were only twice a year, the man made the connection that they inevitably caused him great emotional upset. He was pleased at this insight, which would give him a better perspective

	on the evening's events and the effect on his emotional state. This dream was portending what was to come (the tidal wave of emotion was coming but had not yet hit).
The Literal Perspective *Physical* – Felt fear in gut area. (This is the seat of the emotions. If these emotions are not recognized or validated, over a prolonged period they can cause health problems in the gut/intestinal area.) *Emotional* – True emotion being experienced by the dreamer is fear. *Mental* – The belief revealed is that some situation is overwhelming and there is need for protection. *Spiritual* – Showing an interest in his dream's meaning demonstrates a *willingness* to grow and a *faith* in his higher self and his (concept of) God.	**The Symbolic Perspective** Tornadoes and tidal waves – represent his extreme emotional state (fear).
The Irrational Perspective The dreamer was unaware of apprehensive feelings in his waking hours, which is in contradiction to the truth of his real feelings (fear). Once the dream's meaning was understood by this man, he began to realize how irrational his *belief* was that his visit to his family would be overwhelming (perhaps even fatal) and that he needed protection. He knows this is an old belief system from childhood, when he did feel overwhelmed and in need of protection. However, he now realizes that this old belief no longer serves him well and he can work toward changing it.	**The Creator Perspective** At a deeper level, his soul required growth in this area and therefore the situation was perfect for his spiritual requirements at this time. His feelings (fear) were "perfect" as well, because they led him to be exactly where he needed to be in order to grow, release the past and create a new belief. The Creator gave him this dream at this time so he would realize that his fears about his family are no longer valid. The old patterns of behaviour that once kept him safe are no longer working — it is time for him to review and update them. His dream feelings of fear (**F**alse **E**vidence **A**ppearing **R**eal) were what guided him to this realization.

This wraps up the Mystery School interpretation methods presented in this book. Although these methods are in-depth and can seem overwhelming to the novice, I encourage you to continue using them and integrate them into your dream interpretation practice. It can take years to master these approaches, but reviewing your dreams from these perspectives will provide you with some information no matter how much skill or practice you have.

The Mystery School perspectives are tools to help you remember more of Who You Are. You are not expected to master them in one sitting or one attempt. They are meant to be a process — as is your self-discovery journey. Try to approach these more challenging studies and interpretation tools with an open and gentle heart for yourself and the insights you uncover.

Final Thoughts

The Egyptian Mystery School teachings are not something you learn over a weekend or even several months. Absorbing these teachings is a life-long learning process that takes years of practice to accomplish. But even novices can use these perspectives to learn important things about themselves.

Now that you are familiar with the Egyptian Mystery School teachings and the four levels or perspectives, I would like to anchor within your mind and cells that this material can be used (and was designed to be used) during your waking hours as well as to analyze your dreams. You do not need to have a dream in order to use these perspectives. Absolutely every event, relationship and situation that happens to you during the day can be a tool for your self-growth, insight, inspiration and healing. These tools or levels were designed with living your everyday life in mind. I began by applying these teachings to the dream time because it was easier for my rational mind to learn symbolism through the dreams — my mind had already accepted that I dream in symbols. Applying symbolism to my everyday life and situations was harder for me to get comfortable with and digest.

But I now know that symbolism is abundant in the waking time and its principles operate whether we are aware of them or not. Let's look at a couple of examples.

Example 1: The Nightly News

You are watching the television news and find yourself fearful of the constant negative influence that doing so has on you. Now that you have some familiarity with the four perspectives of the Ancient Mystery School, you can start practising applying this knowledge to just about anything, including how to digest the nightly news in a new way. Here are just a few new ways to view the news from the four perspectives.

Literal Perspective

You can buy into the fear of whatever they are "selling" on the news that particular night. You can allow this fear to become your literal reality.

Symbolic Perspective

Realize there is deeper meaning for you at a personal level. For example, what type of relationship do you have with your own fear? Do you realize it is a tool for your self-growth? Although your fears may feel like an obstacle in your life, they are designed to expand you and make you grow. Notice your reactions when you feel fear. Does your mind make judgemental comments about this feeling? What is your self-talk (what you say to yourself in your head) like? By listening to your own reaction to fear, you will begin to discern what type of relationship you have with this feeling. Many people don't like their fear and literally turn away from it, deny it or try to get rid of it. It would be helpful to see your fear as a small child who needs some comfort and support in fearful times. Do you say comforting words to yourself when you are afraid? Get to know how you treat yourself when you have certain feelings and remember that even though your fear is being triggered by the nightly news, the fear provides you with an opportunity to learn a lot about yourself. Every situation offers you a chance to know yourself better, including the nightly news.

Irrational Perspective

Does your mind go all black and white while watching the news? Do you go to extremes while taking in the material? Can you see the good in the news story or only the bad? Can you hold two opposing views? Remember that every thought you have affects the planet. How will you choose to respond to the fear you feel and think about?

Creator Perspective

Can you trust that whatever is happening on the planet is for the best and highest good, even if you can't see how the outcome will be of benefit? Can you let go or surrender to the outcome and lovingly detach? Remember that what you fear draws near, and what you put out you get back.

If you view the nightly news from a higher perspective it will become easier to digest. You do not have to take everything literally and allow fear to run your life. Be one step ahead and be aware of how these external events are mirroring and affecting your inner life.

Example 2: The World Trade Centre Event

Here are some different (and perhaps controversial) ways in which we can view the events that occurred on September 11th, 2001.

Literal Perspective

There was an attack on the United States; a personal attack of one country, regime, or religion upon another.

Symbolic Perspective

Deeper meaning: This event actually gave people (especially men) the permission to feel and express their emotions openly and with acceptance (a rare occurrence, especially en masse). Realize that this opportunity was beneficial for many and allowed much to be purged (when this type of energy/feeling is released, as it was on September 11th, it allows for great healing on the planet). Realize the date of 9/11 is not random or by chance. 911 is the emergency number used in North America. It was symbolic of a wake-up call and represented the emergency situation (crisis and chaos) that has been building on the planet for many years.

Irrational Perspective

If you spend a moment using the irrational perspective, your mind may ask, "How can this event be helpful?" Notice that, in general, the mind likes to ask a lot of questions and has a hard time accepting responsibility at this deeper level. In this case, your mind may have difficulty acknowledging that we are all responsible for the condition of the planet at this time. We all contributed to this disaster because every thought and feeling of every person on Earth contributes to the greater whole and to the greater consciousness of the planet. It is an awesome responsibility for each of us to realize that we are at choice about larger events such as what happened on 9/11. But choices begin with the self and with awareness of the self. You can consciously begin to make a difference on Earth by exploring your inner reality, because everything that happens in your inner reality — how you treat yourself — will be reflected in your external/everyday reality.

Creator Perspective

From this perspective we realize that old paradigms must crumble before the new can arise (like the phoenix that rises from the ashes). This event shook up the old structures and old ways of being to allow room for the new. Also consider for a moment that, at a soul level, every person who died that day may have chosen to do so to help with the healing of the whole planet. How would that change your perspective on this event?

Waking up to daytime symbolism is one of the greatest joys and gifts I have encountered in my life. It changed my life dramatically and it brought great comfort to know that some Creator or Source was with me all day and all night, and speaking to me in a language I had simply forgotten. The remembering has been sweet and inspiring. I hope you can open your mind to waking-hour symbolism and use this book as a tool for living a good life — a meaningful, full and abundant life.

Part 3
Dream Symbol Dictionary

The purpose of this dream symbol dictionary is to familiarize you with universal symbolism and to get you thinking about your personal symbolism. As you read these entries, observe your own reactions to see if the meaning given here makes some sense to you or resonates with you. If you get an "ah-ha" moment, feel shivers, or just get a sense or a knowing that this is right, then you are using the dictionary correctly. Observe your thoughts too — if you say, this doesn't make sense to me or it's not clicking, then you will have to sort through your personal experiences of the symbol in order to find the correct meaning for you.

I have developed this dictionary after fifteen years of daily personal dream work. I have gathered knowledge and understanding of symbolism through meditation and by observing the universal symbolism inherent in all things living and inanimate. I have also learned a great deal from working with the dreams of others and through my practice of hands-on healing, since layer upon layer of symbolic messages are stored at a cellular level and within the energy fields of clients. In addition, I have gleaned much from continual intuitive insights while observing nature, animals and other people in my community. The information that I present about universal symbolism has been compiled from several different sources, including other dream dictionaries.

Because you are on the Earth to grow and learn about yourself, it is rare for your dream symbols to give you literal information about another person, an object, or a place. Symbols can and do represent other people sometimes, but be aware that re-ceiving this information is an opportunity for your own awaking and self-growth. Symbols are always telling you something about yourself — they reflect something that is within you at a deep level. This is called mirroring. Bear this in mind with every dream element that stands out in some way or catches your attention. See the discussion on marbles and mirroring in Chapter 7 for more information.

All dream symbols mirror you in two different ways or at two different levels. First, they always represent something within you and your inner reality. Your inner reality is what you alone experience; it is comprised of your thoughts, feelings, ideas, beliefs, insights, intuition, desires, emotions, opinions, and your mental chatter. You may or may not share this inner reality with another person. Even if you do try to share this inner world with an intimate friend, you are still alone inside. You alone are responsible for how you treat yourself inside, and it would behoove you greatly to get to know your inner world. Your dreams are an excellent avenue by which to explore your inner reality and the relationship that you have with your inner self. Secondly, symbols can also represent things that are going on outside of you and your private inner world. For example, the symbol of an aggressive bear may represent your boss at work (if you feel that he/she is being overbearing or overly aggressive with you).

Thus, dream characters, objects, and situations are simultaneously a tool for self-examination and a symbolic representation of how things in your waking-life environment affect you emotionally and mentally. It is for you to identify the symbols that appear in your dreams and what information they are conveying to you. In most dreams, each symbol represents something going on in your internal world *and* something about your external world. But keep in mind that it is normal for beginning dream interpreters to see or understand only one level of mirroring. With practice, you will begin to notice both levels.

Let's look at a few examples to show how different kinds of dream symbols can be interpreted on these two levels.

Example 1: A dream about a person

Suppose you dream about a police officer. You may realize that this symbolizes someone in your waking life who you see as an authority figure or as someone who imposes rules on you. This could be the tax man, your father, your boss, a doctor, or a teacher. To identify exactly who is being symbolized at this level, review the past twenty-four hours of your waking life and decide who most likely fits this role during that period. At the same time, you may recognize this to be your inner rule maker marble or your inner voice of authority marble. Both interpretations are correct because both the inner and outer worlds exist and operate in your life. Both levels of symbolism are being presented to you as tools for your self-growth; the external symbolism is *not* a tool to change others or to gather information about them. Of course, your ability to recognize and interpret how the police officer mirrors something in your inner world will depend on how well you know yourself and whether you can "own" this marble as one of your own parts.

For another example involving a person in your dream, suppose you dream of a monster that threatens you. You realize that the monster symbolizes someone in your waking-time reality who is currently intimidating you. But also realize that this may be your inner demon marble, or any part of you that you consider to be a monster, unbearable or threatening. Once again, both levels of interpretation are right.

Example 2: A dream about an object

Suppose you dream about a doormat. At one level you realize that this represents your best friend — you have been worried about her recently because she is acting like a doormat in a relationship. You feel she is being used and that she should speak up for herself. At a deeper level, you realize this dream is trying to get you to connect the dots about how this situation makes you feel. You may also recognize that you would speak up if you felt like a doormat and that you are not willing to be disempowered by another. These are useful insights about yourself, but they won't be helpful in making your friend change. These insights about your inner world are tools for your self-reflection — they teach you about what roles you are willing to play or be involved in.

Example 3: A dream about a place or setting

Suppose your dream takes place in a bar where there is bickering among the patrons and drunken behaviour that frightens you. At one level you realize that this scene represents your perspective on family gatherings — fighting, squabbling and perhaps power struggles. At a deeper level, you may realize that you have internalized your family behaviour patterns and that you currently are experiencing inner struggles and conflict. Perhaps your recent mental chatter has been argumentative, and you have been internally belittling yourself or not being supportive of yourself. Both levels of interpretation are delivering useful information to you, so you can begin to understand how your family gatherings affect you (not how you can change them) and how the partners in your "inner marriage" — your masculine and feminine natures — are communicating with each other.

Dream Symbol	External Interpretation	Internal Interpretation
police officer	someone who you see as an authority figure	your inner rule maker or voice of authority marble
threatening monster	someone who is intimidating you in your waking life	your inner demon marble, or a part of you that you think is a monster
doormat	your friend who isn't standing up for herself in a relationship	recognizing how you would speak up for yourself if you felt like a doormat
rowdy bar	how you feel about family gatherings	you've been arguing with yourself inside, or your inner chatter has been threatening or non-supportive

Keep these examples in mind when looking at the people, objects, and places in your dreams. Try to identify what they mean on both levels. But don't worry if you don't see both levels right away — the more you get to know your own marbles, the easier it will be to identify them in your dreams.

It would be very helpful to start your own dream dictionary so that you can become familiar with your own dream characters and symbols. Appendix A is provided to get you started.

Remember that this dictionary can be used for your waking-time symbols as well. This is an important thing to consider if something during the day catches your attention. If you spot a deer while enjoying a walk one day, you could use the dictionary to help you understand the deeper meaning of this encounter. If you have car problems you can read up on what aspect of self is being mirrored by that car part. On and on you can use this dictionary for insight, inspiration and healing. Make the connections between what is happening to you during the day (external events and situations) to what is happening in your inner reality. Let all of life mirror you and use this dictionary to Know Yourself, to Know Your Symbols, to Know Who You Are Not and to Know Your Creator.

Actions

Remember: These symbolic meanings are just suggestions. If these suggested meanings do not resonate with you, ring a bell, give you an "ah-ha" moment or otherwise feel right, search through your own experience or beliefs about the symbol to find what makes sense for you.

Acting

Reflects how you are acting in your current lifestyle or how you need to act in order to be more in line with your heart and soul. How have you been acting or behaving lately? Do you need to act on a thought, idea or belief? Do you need to put something into action? Are you acting your age or acting out? Are you being a drama queen or acting without thinking? Is your dream acting on a stage and/or do you feel as though you are on centre stage? Are you actively participating in the dream, or are you part of the audience, and feel as if you are not participating in your own life? Perhaps you feel as if you are watching your life pass you by. See Actor in the *People* section and Theatre in the *Buildings and Rooms* section for more information.

Bathing

Suggests that you are cleansing, clearing away the old or letting go — usually at the emotional level if water is involved, but could also suggest cleaning up your act or modifying your behaviours. Could also suggest the need for internal cleansing such as releasing pent-up or held-in emotions. Denotes need to let go of inner frustrations, tension, fears or any emotions that are being held in. May need to forgive, surrender or give up something. Could say you feel clean and freed from recent burdens. Look to feelings to understand if this is a positive release or a need to absolve.

Bending

Suggests flexibility, going with the flow or preservation. Are you bending over backwards and overburdening yourself with responsibilities? Or are you bending to someone else's ways and needs? Note the dream feelings to fully understand if your bending is a healthy reflection of your agility or a negative statement about your ability to boundary yourself. Note whether you are stooping or lowering yourself in some way in your life.

Boiling

May represent a boiling temper such as anger or rage, or a situation that is boiling over in your life. Often it is water that is boiling, which represents emotions. What situation has you boiling mad or reaching your boiling point? If the dream action is "boiling over," search your current situations, events and feelings to pinpoint what area of your life feels like it is out of control or like you may be losing a grip on.

Bouncing

Represents a jolting experience or that you are being shook up. Is there an idea you are trying to bounce off of someone? Do you feel as though you are being bounced around? Look at what is being bounced in the dream and how you feel about it for further understanding.

Bowing

Represents reverence for self or another. May say you need to take a bow or recognize some recent accomplishment. Could also imply respect, honour and humility. May have religious connotation, such as prayer or devotion. May say your pride needs to bend a little or that you feel your will is being bent. Are you being obsequious and weak willed? Or are you unwilling to submit and bend?

Breaking

Have you broken off something lately? Could it be a broken tie (relationship of some sort) or a broken promise? Do you feel as though you are breaking up (inside), or are you breaking up with someone? Is your heart breaking or do you feel broken down? Perhaps you perceive you are having a breakdown (which can also be viewed as a sort of breakthrough, because the new cannot be created until the old structures and systems are broken down). Note what is breaking in the dream and what the feelings are to help you understand if this is a helpful and positive break or a negative experience.

Breaking the Law

Suggests that you feel guilty about some recent thought or behaviour — you knew right from wrong but proceeded anyway. The source of your guilt may be that you broke one of society's rules, or one of your inner rules.

Burning

May represent that your emotions are consuming you and speak of the need to express or release pent-up feelings. Are you burning up or burning mad about someone or something? Do you feel as though you've been burned or ripped off in some way? Burning can also represent purification and transformation. See Fire in the *Miscellaneous* section of this dictionary for further insight.

Buying

Implies that you may have "bought" or accepted something or someone else's opinions or ideas. Are you buying into something? Do you feel you have paid a price or that you are now paying the price? Note the dream feelings for further clarification. Could indicate your sense of "purchasing power" or how much control you feel you have with respect to bringing something into your life. May point to a need you are trying to fulfill or "purchase" through the exchange of money (which represents energy).

Chanting

Chanting is considered a spiritual practice, so it denotes your need to become more open to spiritual matters. Conversely, it could suggest that you are in harmony with your spirit self. Perhaps you need to actually do some chanting and toning to realign your energies. Do you feel in synch with your higher self or your God?

Chasing

Represents that you feel something or someone is after you — perhaps something you cannot face and that you fear. Often experienced in a nightmare, chasing dreams can be very upsetting and you need to shed some light on the situation in order to clear this away. May denote that you feel powerless or helpless. May be pun on "your past catching up with you." Conversely it may have a positive meaning suggesting you are pursuing or chasing a goal or dream. Note dream feelings for greater understanding and see the section on *Nightmares* in Chapter 3.

Climbing

If the climb is tough, it may suggest there is currently a challenge in your life that you find difficult. If the climb is effortless, it may say you are scaling something with ease. May represent achieving your goals or your ambition to achieve them. Do you feel as if you are climbing a mountain or burdened with an impossible task? Could this be a pun on climbing a social ladder or social climbing? Are you trying to climb the ladder of success or do you need to get a higher perspective on something? If you are climbing steps, perhaps you need to take it one step at a time or it may indicate how you are stepping up in life. Note dream feelings for greater understanding.

Closing

This is symbolic of some part of you closing down or being shut down. Perhaps it is a temporary and much needed closing or rest period. If a door is being closed, it means you have missed an opportunity or are about to, or that you may have to close one door before another one opens. It could be that you feel cut off or shut out of a situation or relationship. Ask yourself what you are shutting off or out of your life. A door can be a positive sign if you are ending a chapter in your life or set-

ting strong, healthy boundaries. If a window is being closed, this often represents being closed off from insight, vision or clear seeing. If you are doing the closing of anything, be warned it is suggesting you take responsibility for your own actions and their consequences. Note the dream feelings for greater understanding of whether this is a positive or negative closing situation.

Cooking

Suggests you are cooking up a new idea or creating something in your life. Cooking is about inventiveness and originality, and food often represents the mind, thinking, thoughts, beliefs and opinions. Try to relate this dream to some recent creative mental process in your waking life. Have you been cooking up a storm? Have you been feeling "cooked" (burned out)? For greater insight, note what you are making and how it feels to be in this creative process.

Crawling

Represents a slow movement forward, often arduous. May say you currently feel challenged by something or find it tough going. Has something or someone slowed you to a crawl? Do you find it hard to stand up for yourself or some values? Are you down on your knees, humbling yourself or feeling demeaned?

Crossing

Represents moving from one area of consciousness (awareness) to another. Crossing railroad tracks indicates a switch in your attitudes or thinking. Crossing water can indicate a change in emotional behaviour. Crossing a road suggests you are trying out new ways of being on your journey. Are you at a crossroads? Or do you have a cross to bear? Crossing anything may signal a need to take a different viewpoint or warn that you are going against the flow. Perhaps you are "crossing the line" — often a crossing of some internal rule that you have created or a crossing of behaviour codes or values that society has deemed correct. If the feelings are positive, then it suggests a favourable crossing or journey is underway.

Crying

Denotes that you feel sad, hurt or wounded about something, depending on the depth of the dream feelings. Could be tears of joy or happiness if the dream feelings are positive. May suggest the need to release pent-up feelings through crying (tears are one of the greatest avenues for release, and crying allows energies to flow again).

Dream feelings should help point out what is creating the sad feelings. Try to relate the crying to your current day-time feelings to see if you can connect with the part of you that is seeking expression through tears.

Dancing

Usually a healthy expression of joy, creativity and feelings in general. May say you are in harmony or in synch with yourself or another. Could suggest you need to dance or frolic a little more in your life. May suggest gratitude. Note how you feel while dancing and what type of dancing you are participating in for greater understanding. For example, if you are square dancing and this is unfamiliar to you, it suggests you are moving in new and unfamiliar ways in your life. Note whether you are dancing by yourself, with a partner or in a group. This will help you understand if your expression is happening (or needs to happen) within your self, within a partnership or within a community.

Dating

Suggests you are trying something new or different in your life. Perhaps you are testing the waters of a new emotion or are ready to try your hand at something new. Perhaps you are

153

pursuing a new thought or belief. May be a temporary state of mind or feeling. Could say you are merging with an aspect of your self within inner reality.

Digging

Suggests you are looking for something that has been buried. Maybe you are digging up the past or looking for a lost part of self. Digging usually requires effort, so it suggests you are working hard at some task. Perhaps you need to dig deep or look elsewhere for solutions to current problems.

Diving

Since one usually dives into water, this suggests you are diving into your emotions/feelings. Perhaps you need to take a plunge or a leap of faith. Maybe you need to dive in and do something quickly. Or are you getting in over your head? Could say you are immersed in some feeling — note how you feel in the dream for greater understanding. Could say you are diving into the heart of a matter or may represent a crash dive or overwhelming situation.

Dropping

Represents the need to let go, let things drop or end. Could also feel as if you've let something drop or slip by you. May say you feel as if you have dropped the ball or let someone (including yourself) down. Have you been careless or inefficient? Have you omitted or discarded something? Note dream feelings for greater understanding. If it is a positive feeling, then it could be a useful dropping or ending.

Drowning

Since drowning usually happens in water, it may represent drowning in your emotions. Often associated with overwhelming and disconcerting feelings — usually the feelings that you consider "bad," wrong or not allowed. Perhaps you feel in over your head or in too deep. Note the dream feelings and the clarity and consistency of water for greater understanding. See also the *Water* section of this dictionary.

Exercising

May represent a daunting, hard experience or a joyful and expressive situation, depending on how you feel about exercising. May suggest the need for more physical exercise in your life, or maybe you need to exercise a belief, a right, a value or more control. What do you feel you need to apply, exert or otherwise express at this time?

Falling

Often denotes loss of something. If the feelings are unpleasant or negative, then the dream reflects that you are experiencing, or are in danger of experiencing, loss, defeat or failure of some kind in your waking time. This could be loss of control, loss of emotional stability, loss of respect or loss of status. Perhaps you feel as though you have fallen off the ladder of success, failed to land on your feet, lost your balance in a situation, or don't have your feet on the ground. If the feelings are positive, it could mean you are falling in love. But falling dreams are often fearful and thus denote negative feelings and situation. Perhaps you feel you have fallen from grace, are falling short of a goal or about to take a fall.

You may sometimes have a falling sensation when you "re-enter" your body after a dream. Our consciousness literally leaves, or rather expands, into the space of our whole being; when it (our consciousness) returns to the physical body it can produce a sense of falling. It is a common experience and is normal.

Feeding

Denotes need for physical, emotional, intellectual or spiritual nourishment.

Do you need to care for yourself more? Do you feel empty on some level? Do you crave fulfillment? Note who is doing the feeding and who is being fed. If a baby is being fed, it suggests that you need to nurture yourself as you would a baby or that you are caring for yourself well. Note the dream feelings to understand if this is a need or an indication that you are already "feeding" yourself. In general, any type of feeding represents or requests support and comfort.

Flowing

If water is flowing, it denotes the flow of emotions. If air is flowing, it denotes the flow of the mind or thoughts. Are things flowing smoothly in your life? Are you in the flow and able to manoeuvre well through your everyday life? Note how you feel in the dream. Does the flow feel natural and positive, suggesting you are in choice and control? Or is it a difficult passage, suggesting that you are out of control or adrift?

Flying

Often associated with positive feelings such as exhilaration, flying dreams often denote feeling in control, "the sky is the limit" or seeing things from a higher perspective. There are no current road blocks and you feel free and unlimited. Search your daily life for recent times when you have felt these emotions to help pinpoint what the dream's message is. Perhaps you have just climbed the ladder to success or completed a project. Or maybe you have risen above a situation or you need to rise above something. A negative flying experience may symbolize your literal fear of flying or a fear of taking control of a current situation. Is there something you'd rather not deal with that involves taking control, taking charge or even taking a different viewpoint? You will have to decide the meaning and message based on your current personal experiences and the emotions in the dream.

Forgetting

Denotes unawareness, absentmindedness and distraction. Have you been indifferent, lax or negligent about something? Note what you are forgetting in the dream and how it feels for greater understanding, because these are important clues about what triggered this dream.

Grasping

Represents ability to comprehend, understand or appreciate something. May be a pun on grasping at straws. Do you need to get a grasp or are you already holding on or clinging too tightly?

Hearing

Hearing can be an act of receptivity or active listening. Are you hearing what you need to? Have you lost your hearing and don't wish to take something in? See Ear in the *Body* section for greater understanding.

Hiding

Implies you do not want to be seen, heard or "found." What or whom are you hiding from? Is it your fears, your feelings or some negative thoughts? Are you hiding the truth or dodging important issues? Are you covering something up or blocking something out? Do you feel the need to conceal, bury or disguise the truth? Perhaps you are hiding for protection and safety.

Holding

Suggests clutching, grasping or gripping something. Perhaps you are holding on too tightly to something and need to let it go. Are you holding something lovingly or are you afraid to let go of something? Note what you are holding in the dream, why you are holding it, and your feelings. Perhaps you are grasping at straws or hanging onto something — it may be time to let go.

156

Hopping

Represents ability to move from one place to another quickly or in leaps and bounds. May say you are jumping the gun or moving forward too quickly on something. Hopping suggests you are not staying in one place for very long — perhaps you are moving too quickly to finish or accomplish things. May be a pun on "hopping mad" or "hop to it." Note dream feelings to understand if your leaps are healthy or an avoidance behaviour.

Hugging

Suggests you are in need of, or are providing, some nurturing, holding or embracing. May say you are holding on too tightly or clinging, depending on dream feelings. Perhaps you are openly showing your affections or holding something close to your heart.

Hurrying

Suggests you are moving too quickly and perhaps without enough preparation or thought. Represents a need to slow down and take note of what is going on around you. Why are you in a hurry in the dream and how does that relate to your waking-time activities?

Jaywalking

May suggest you are crossing a line or doing something that you know is illegal. The laws you are breaking may be your internal rules, standards, morals or values.

Jumping

May represent a jump for joy or jumping ship (abandoning yourself, a project, or another person), depending on feelings associated with the dream. Jumping in general suggests moving, so note whether this is a leap forward or just hopping in one place (not moving forward). Jumping may be a symbol of joy, excitement or play, depending on how the jumper feels in the dream. See Hopping for further insight.

Kidnapping

Suggests feelings of powerlessness, helplessness and not being in control. Do you feel like a victim? Perhaps you feel that you need to be rescued. Or do you feel captivated by something, carried away or imprisoned? Do you feel as though you have no choice in some current situation or relationship, or that someone has taken something from you?

Kissing

May indicate desire to be kissed or loved, or need for self-love or self-tenderness. May be seeking security or union with self or another. Kissing is an expression of affection and may suggest you need to express your affections more openly. But "kiss off" is an expression of anger, so note the dream feelings to help you understand what your dream kiss means.

Knocking

May represent opportunity knocking or that you feel knocked about. Could suggest you "don't knock" something or that you are knocking yourself out over something.

Laughing

Suggests you find something humorous at some level of your being. May suggest the need to lighten up or the need to laugh at yourself. Laughter, like tears, is a great release mechanism and may suggest that you need to let go, surrender or vent something. Often our souls find humour in things that our human personalities do not. See if you can make the connection of humour at a deeper level of your being. Note dream feelings to see if this laughing is related to feelings of belittlement or of being laughed at (which can be a painful experience for some).

Lifting

Are you lifting a heavy load or burden, suggesting that you are overwhelmed and overburdened by something that weighs heavily on you? Do you need a lift, a boost or feel the need to be elevated? Do you need to raise your sights or lift your spirits? Do you need to be uplifted and inspired? Perhaps you need more support? Note what are you lifting in the dream to help you understand if this is a positive lift or a heavy burden you are carrying.

Locking

May suggest you feel locked out or locked in. Do you feel like a prisoner? Do you want more freedom? May suggest you are looking to feel safe, secure or protected. Note what you are locking and why. If you are locking a door or window, perhaps you are shutting someone or something out of your life as a protective measure. Do you feel insecure, or feel the need for more safety and security in your life? Are you locking or closing the door on an opportunity? Could say you are locking horns with someone or not seeing their point of view.

Marching

If this is a military march it suggests ridged, controlled and analytical ways of being and acting. Or it could be a merry march of celebration, depending on dream content and feelings. Marching implies movement forward, perhaps going along with the crowd or group thinking. May say you march to a different drummer or that you follow your own beat (or need too). Have you hit your stride and are marching along at a positive pace?

Missing

Depending on what is missing, could say you yearn for, crave or desire something that is out of reach. Ask yourself what is missing in your life. Did you miss the mark, miss an opportunity or miss the point? Note what is missing in the dream and how you feel about it for greater understanding. Know that this could be a positive quality that is currently missing in your own make-up and character, so look to what is missing in the dream to help you determine what trait you may need to develop to become whole.

Mixing

Represents ability to mix, blend, merge or combine something. May suggest you need to blend in or involve yourself more. Could be about your socializing or who you are associating with. Otherwise, could suggest you don't mix well with another or with some new notion or idea. May say you feel you are in mixed company, or that you feel mixed up or confused.

Moving

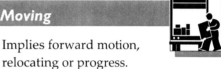

Implies forward motion, relocating or progress. Could also be a moving experience and suggest sentimental emotions. May say you need to move on, move up or move over. Could say you have made a change in your thinking, feelings or attitudes. Moving forward in the dream is a positive step in the right direction that says you are "advancing," not receding. Perhaps you are taking the necessary steps toward your goals and endeavours. If you are moving backward this would indicate that you are backing out of something, back tracking or going back over some situation. Usually negative in its connection, backing up is often about avoiding issues, people or situations. What situations do you not want to face? Do you have a fear of moving forward? If you are moving sideways, it may refer to a lateral move you are taking or suggest you are taking a neutral stance in some regard. Sideways could also suggest not facing something head on or sidestepping an issue. Perhaps you are not being "up-front" or are skirting an issue.

Packing

May suggest your desire to move on, move up or move out of a situation. You may be finishing off a project or a relationship, or you may be experiencing an ending of any type. May say you have gotten it all together in one package. May be pun on "pack it in" or "packing a punch."

Parking

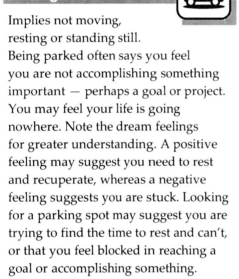

Implies not moving, resting or standing still. Being parked often says you feel you are not accomplishing something important — perhaps a goal or project. You may feel your life is going nowhere. Note the dream feelings for greater understanding. A positive feeling may suggest you need to rest and recuperate, whereas a negative feeling suggests you are stuck. Looking for a parking spot may suggest you are trying to find the time to rest and can't, or that you feel blocked in reaching a goal or accomplishing something.

Paying

The act of giving, settling or expending. What feelings accompany the act? Positive feelings imply you may be settling a score or debt; a negative feeling suggests loss. Perhaps you feel you are paying through the nose, need to pay a debt, or feel that you are paying the

price for something. Is this the price you have to pay or the consequence of some recent actions?

Playing

Playing like a child suggests fun, frolicking, freedom from worry and feeling carefree. Activating the child within is often a healthy representation — note dream feelings for greater clarity. This could say that you need to play more or that you are all work and no play. It could also be about the parts we play or act out in our life. Have you been overly dramatic, performing or acting in an uncharacteristic way?

Plotting

Implies you are planning, preparing or arranging for something. Look to the dream feelings to see if it is a conniving, scheming or manipulating type of plotting, or a healthier calculated design. Are you plotting something or is someone plotting against you? Perhaps you need to plan something, such as goals, intent or aspirations.

Plunging

May suggest you are taking a plunge or a leap of faith. Implies moving forward or driving yourself in a certain direction. Plunging suggests quick movements, perhaps in too much of a rush, which may be positive or negative depending on the dream feelings. You may need to slow down or plunge ahead. If you are plunging a toilet, it suggests there is a back-up of pent-up emotions blocking the flow of your feelings. There is an obvious need to recognize the blocked feelings and allow them expression in order to unclog your system.

Praying

All thoughts (conscious and unconscious) are a type of prayer and heard by your guides and angels. Prayer represents conscious communication with your higher self and your God. Seeing someone praying in a dream may suggest that you are seeking, requesting or begging for something in your everyday life. Could suggest you need to pray more or that prayer will help you in some unseen ways. Could suggest your prayers are being heard.

Pulling

Implies detaching, removing or withdrawing. Is the pulling in the dream a struggle or done with ease? The feelings should help make this clear. Could it be that something or someone is pulling at you or pulling at your heart strings? May suggest you feel that you are pulling your share or that you need to pull harder. Are you pulling a heavy load or are you stretched to the limit?

Do you feel pulled in two directions or pulled apart about something?

Punishing

Suggests that you feel you are being punished for some act, word or thought you had. Do you feel guilty or are you punishing yourself with negative self-talk? Berating the self is almost considered normal in North American culture. It is time to stop punishing yourself and see what healthy boundaries and disciplines the dream may be suggesting. For example, if you recognize that you have been harsh with yourself, realize that you have choices in how you treat yourself inside. You were probably taught these behaviour patterns as a child and it is now up to you to learn new behaviours and new ways of treating yourself. Note who is being punished and realize that their traits are mirrors of some aspect or part of yourself.

Pushing

Implies having to plough ahead against some force or struggle. Whether the pushing in the dream is easy or difficult will help you understand if you are pushing your luck or just shifting space. Perhaps you are pushing the limit or being pushed around or against your will. Maybe you need to push the envelope or feel you are caught in a push/pull situation.

Perhaps you are pushing too hard to achieve an outcome; your dream may be suggesting that you let go of trying to control the situation.

Racing

Implies that you are in a hurry and rushing around. Look to the feelings in the dream to help you understand if this is beneficial for you or a warning to slow down. Do you feel the need to win the race or feel caught up in the rat race? Are you currently involved in a contest, battle or competitive encounter? Are you racing against time? Alternatively, this symbol could be about race consciousness, which includes such things as stereotypes, prejudice, ignorance of "the other," and racial or cultural intolerance. Have any of these been playing a role in your waking life recently?

Raping

A dream about a rape symbolizes that you feel deeply violated, defiled or abused. May represent having something forced on you or done to you against your will. Perhaps someone has taken advantage of you or assaulted you in some way. Do you feel vulnerable, weak or like a victim? Rape represents a deep wound that needs to be addressed.

Reaching

Suggests you have achieved, attained or accomplished something. May also say you have gained, realized or completed something. Have you achieved a goal or received what you needed? Reaching allows you to communicate with, get in touch with, and reach out to others. Could also imply you are reaching out for help, support or nurturing.

Reading

Ability to comprehend, decipher and perceive. May also represent studying or understanding. Implies a search for more knowledge or information, or a desire to learn. Reading is a type of communication or message to the self. Take note of any written words remembered from the dream. Could be a pun on your ability to read someone's mind, suggesting intuitive forces at play. May suggest you need to relax, put your feet up and read for pleasure.

Rejecting

Represents feeling disowned, disclaimed or rebuffed about something. You may be rejecting yourself or feel that others are rejecting you. Note the dream feelings, which are usually unpleasant, for greater understanding. Note if you can connect with anything you have been refusing to accept, be it positive or negative information, a feeling, or an opportunity. Note whether you have rejected someone's advice or discarded a new idea or belief.

Riding

Riding a horse may represent your personal power, freedom and sense of being in control. Riding a merry-go-round suggests you are going around in circles. You may be riding out a storm or going along for the ride. Perhaps you feel that you've been taken for a ride and are not in control. For greater understanding, note what you are riding and how it feels.

Rowing

The act of rowing may represent a current challenge you are facing or how you are steering through the waters of your life — perhaps with a lot of effort and exertion. May be a pun on having a row or quarrel. Are you fighting with something or someone? Rowing can also be a peaceful and relaxing event for some, depending on your personal viewpoint.

Running

May suggest you are in a hurry or going too fast. Are you involved in a race in your dream, which suggests

competition, or are you running for cover? You could be running away from something or running into something. Do you need more exercise or do you need to realize you can't run from this? May say your fears are building or you feel out of control. Some people run for the joy of it, while others find it arduous. Note the dream feelings for greater understanding.

Sailing

Denotes the way you are moving through life, your drive, motivation and spiritual passage. May imply smooth sailing if the dream sailing is a joyous experience. If a negative feeling is associated with the sailing, it may be that someone or something has let the wind out of your sails. It could say you are in the flow or that things are flowing well. May be a pun on the word "sale" denoting a bargain or trading opportunity.

Screaming

A very loud expression denoting great pain, anger or the need for help. Note who is screaming in the dream and why. Is it out of fear, joy, distress or grief? If there is no sound but screaming gesture, it would imply the need to express some disturbing emotions. May suggest you are unable to give voice to your feelings or fears.

Seeing

Denotes your perception, viewpoint or understanding of something. What have you been observing, noticing, regarding or envisioning? Can you see clearly or are you wearing rose-coloured glasses? Is your vision clouded or are you seeing double? To see clearly in a dream means you have clear understanding, insight and thinking about the subject matter. If vision is cloudy, it implies your thoughts are scattered, confused or disorganized, or that you have a poor understanding. May be a pun on the word "sea" and suggesting you are out to sea or not in safe waters.

Seeking

Suggests you are searching for or looking for something in your life. Are you pursuing, questing or aspiring to something? Are you striving, endeavouring or attempting something new? May be a pun on "seek and you shall find." Note the dream feelings to understand if you are in need of something (lack or loss feelings) or positively looking in new directions.

Sewing

Implies expressing your creativity by putting things together. You may be mending, patching, or repairing some-

thing in your life. It may say you are sowing new seeds or creating something. You may be constructing a new self-image or revamping a point of view. Note the dream feelings to understand if it is a positive, healthy creation or an uncomfortable development.

Sex

May represent a union, marriage or a coming together of two things in your life. This could be a new partnership in any endeavour, two ideas or concepts merging, or even the coming together of opposites. Sex in its expression is a creative act and thus could reflect some creative action on your part or the need for some creative action. Sex is also about striving for wholeness and may symbolize your need to balance your masculine and feminine sides, or say that you have achieved a balanced state, depending on the feelings in the dream (frustration or peace). Sex is also about intimacy and knowing another on a personal level. Note if this factors into your life lately or if you have recently made a new intimate friend.

Of course, dreams of having sex may be taken more literally — they may point out your true desires and true feelings of arousal. Some may feel inhibited by their own sexual feelings and these types of dreams will hopefully point out your underlying beliefs about expression of your sexuality and help you understand if you are suppressing your sexual feelings. Many sex dreams are simply an expression of your hopes, desires and wishes, or your frustrations and fears. Note how familiar you are with your sexual self and whether you can "own" the feelings portrayed in your sex dream.

To dream you are having sex can mean a number of things, depending on your personal views about sexual intercourse and the feelings felt and expressed in the dream. It could mirror your desire and/or need for sexual relations, or it may denote the need for love, depending on how you view and feel about the action in the dream. If sex is a positive or uplifting occurrence for you, then it could reflect a positive and fulfilling situation in your life. If sex is a negative experience for you, then dreaming about having sex reflects a negative situation in your life. Because sexuality is a function of the first and second chakras, these dreams also reflect the health and function of these two chakras. Sexuality is your expression of Divinity in the physical and is a powerful component of who you are. The need for and desire for sexual expression is often symbolized by the act of sexual intercourse in the dream time. Consider whether your passion for life or enthusiasm is currently find-

ing any expression in your everyday life or whether it is being suppressed. Perhaps this part of you is craving a way to express itself and is finding fulfillment in the dream time only. Read more about the functions of the first and second chakras in the *Chakras* section of this dictionary.

Shaking

Represents agitation, distress or a jarring experience. Are you shaking in fear, love or apprehension? Are you shaken up over a recent event or do you feel all shook up? Perhaps you need a shake or wake-up call? Is your foundation on shaky ground or do old habits need to be given a jostle? Look to the dream feelings to understand fully what your shaking represents.

Shooting

Shooting a gun off may suggest deadly intent on your part, or the part of another. Are you trying to kill something or someone in the dream, denoting that you are trying to kill off an aspect of self? This may be a pun on shooting your mouth off or expressing yourself in an explosive way. It could also be shooting ahead in a positive way or shooting blanks. Note what is being shot and the feelings connected to it for greatest understanding.

Shopping

Represents buying power, spending power, purchasing power and choice. Could say you are trading, selling or looking for new ideas. Note whether the shopping is a pleasant or unpleasant experience for greater clarity. Could suggest you are shopping around for new understanding or opinions.

Singing

Represents expression, creativity, joy, music and harmony. Allows for expression of truth and alignment with higher self. Are you singing the blues or is the singing bringing you joy? Note dream feelings for greater understanding. If you remember the words to the song, they may be considered strong guidance. Singing also represents that your throat chakra is open and communication is happening. See also Fifth (throat) Chakra in the *Chakras* section.

Sinking

Usually associated with water, this suggests you may be overwhelmed with current emotions and feelings. Do you feel as though something is declining or deteriorating, or that a situation is worsening? Perhaps you feel immersed, in over your head or swamped by something. Do you

have a sinking feeling or do you feel you are sunk? Suggests you require help and emotional expression to raise yourself up again. If the feelings are positive, it could denote that you are letting go or surrendering and that this is the correct thing to be doing.

Sitting

The act of doing nothing, sitting still, not moving forward or being lazy. May also suggest you need to sit and rest or that you are not active enough, depending on dream content and feelings. Note why you are sitting to help you understand if this is a positive or negative position for you to be taking.

Sleeping

May say you are not fully aware of something going on in your life or within your inner reality. Perhaps you are not paying attention or are "dead to the world." Some part of you is cut off from reality and dozing. May say you need more rest or to go within and hibernate.

Smoking

If you are a non-smoker this may represent doing something that's out of character or bad for you. If you are a smoker it may suggest you are repeating patterns of negative thinking or behaviour. You may be setting up a smoke screen or trying to hide behind something. Could suggest you are fuming mad, smouldering or on fire about something.

Spilling

Symbolizes an overflow — perhaps an abundance of feelings or emotion. Maybe your cup runneth over with positive sensations. Have you spilled your guts and spoken without thinking or spilled the beans? Note what is being spilled and the dream feelings for greater understanding.

Spying

Are you the observer or being observed in the dream? Do you feel as though someone is snooping, eavesdropping or otherwise invading your privacy? Or are you watching, exploring or considering something or someone? Recognizing whether the act of spying is comfortable or uncomfortable will help you to understand if it is a healthy exploration or a deceitful intrusion.

Staggering

Suggests feeling overburdened by the weight of something. Ask yourself what weighs heavily on you. Could say you are reeling from something, feel shocked or astonished. Staggering could mean that you are on shaky

ground, or that your current choices are putting you on a collision course or leading you to a fall.

Standing

Implies you can carry your own weight and stand on your own two feet, and indicates that you are "holding up well." Denotes your position, stance, resistance and ability to withstand something. Symbolic of what you stand for, advocate, endorse or support. May be pun on how much you can stand, stomach or otherwise tolerate. May represent your "understanding" or your standing (status or class). Perhaps you need to take a stand, stand up for your rights, stand firm or stand tall.

Swearing

May be an expression of anger, upset or distress. Could also be a pledge, promise or vow. Do you see swearing as a blasphemy, profanity or obscenity? Have you sworn an oath, sworn to God or sworn allegiance? You may have sworn to do something and not kept your promise. Look to dream feelings to help you understand the meaning more fully.

Swinging

May denote that you are going back and forth over something. Note the feelings to understand if this is a positive manoeuvre or not in your best interest. Have you changed your mind about something or been vacillating? Do you need to make up your mind about something? Or perhaps you are going to extremes in your thinking. May also say you are flourishing or having a swinging good time. Could be a pun on "swing music" such as Dixieland, jazz or jive, and therefore be about harmony and self-expression. Are you taking a swing at something or trying something new?

Teaching

Represents ability to educate, enlightenment and impart knowledge. Teachers instruct, prepare, illustrate, demonstrate, explain and describe. Have you been doing any of these things lately? Note who in the dream requires the teaching, or who is doing the teaching. How do they feel about this? Often we teach what we need to learn. If the teacher is someone you know or have known, she/he may represent your own traits (i.e., may mirror your characteristics).

Touching

The act of feeling, handling, contacting or showing affection. The dream feelings will help you understand if the touching is a caress of love or a strike of anger. May suggest you need more touch in your life — more love, affection or tenderness. May say you need to get in touch with deeper levels of self or that you are out of touch. This could also indicate that you've been too touchy about a situation.

Unfolding

Suggests something is emerging, developing, appearing, evolving or maturing in your life. What is unfolding within your self or in your life? Could suggest the need to open, expose or expand something. May say watch for an opportunity to unfold.

Urinating

Represents the ability or need to let go of, or release, something in your life. Often this will be emotional in nature. Note whether this is a pleasant experience or not. Can you find a place to release and relieve yourself or is it not private enough? Do you feel the need to detach from a certain tension-filled situation in life? Does the urine flow freely or is there a blockage or obstruction?

Vomiting

Usually indicates something you can't stomach or something you refuse to take in. Could say you completely reject something, whether it be an idea of another or a belief of your own. Often our desires don't line up with what is actually happening in our lives, which can be overwhelming to even think about (we often express this as "reality sets in"). A dream in which vomiting is portrayed shows you completely refusing this reality. Could even symbolize rejecting another person at any level, or something about yourself that you find completely un-ownable.

Voting

Casting your opinion, beliefs or attitudes for others to see. May indicate making a selection, choosing one thing over another or making yourself heard. Voting could also be an expression of your truth, disclosing or confessing something personal. May say you need to cast your vote and let your thoughts be known.

Wandering

Suggests you may have wandered off course or away from your goals. Have you digressed, departed from or deviated from your regular routines or projects? Do you feel as though you are wandering aimlessly and without direction?

Watching

May suggest you are not taking part in your own life and affairs, or you could be making a positive observation. Look to dream feelings to help you understand if your watching is healthy or not. Perhaps you feel you are watching your life pass you by or that you need to watch something more closely and take the witness role. Note what you are watching and the feelings it arouses for further understanding.

Weeping

Weeping is often associated with the expression of sadness, grief or any painful emotion. However, you can also weep out of happiness and joy, so note the dream feelings for greater understanding. Dream may suggest you need a good cry to release pent-up feelings, or it may say you have cried long enough over something.

Weighing

Suggests you are considering two points of view or decisions at this time. Likely you need balance or are seeking balance through the weighing. Do you need to take stock of a situation or is something weighing heavily on you? Note what you are weighing and the feelings associated with it for greater understanding.

Wishing

Represents what you long for, hope for, yearn for, pray for or desire. May be wishful thinking and imply you don't really think you'll attain something.

Working

Represents what you labour for and strive for, and your driving force. Is the work in the dream arduous or pleasant? Does it represent your struggles and hard work or a positive cultivation of your skills? Perhaps you need to work something out or get the job done. Do you need to find work or employment?

Writing

Represents communication, putting your thoughts together and expression of self. Putting your thoughts on paper or into a computer allows you to see clearly what you are thinking about and creating in your life. Writing by hand connects you with and expresses the subconscious and unconscious parts of self. May suggest you need to do more writing or journal work. May be a pun on righting a wrong or doing the right thing. Note what is written in the dream, who is doing the writing, and the feelings associated with it for greater understanding.

Yawning

A symbol of fatigue or boredom, or may denote routine. Have you been feeling unenthusiastic with life lately? Perhaps you feel listless. Have things been monotonous or tedious?

Animals

Animals bring you significant information about your instinctual side and your basic or primal nature. Animals may also reflect your senses and how you are using them or not using them. Animals (whether in a dream or in the waking time) are couriers of knowledge and often represent your feminine side's intuition. Each animal has its own personality or characteristics that are unique to its species, and these traits reflect something about your self. To determine exactly what is being mirrored about yourself in the animal, simply list or name three characteristics or behaviours you associate with that animal. For example, if your dream animal was a cougar and you listed the traits as courageous, sleek and agile, then this reflects your courage, sleekness and agility. Check in with yourself and see what qualities or characteristics you would personally assign the dream animal.

Note if the animal in the dream is acting on its instinct or not. Instincts are doing what comes naturally — are you doing what is natural for you in your current life? Have you recently been displaying animalistic behaviour such as being sly as a fox or like a snake in the grass? Perhaps you need to roar like a lion or beat your chest like a gorilla. There are many such analogies for animals. Is there one for your dream animal? Do you know someone who's been acting like an animal? For greater insight, ask yourself how you are reacting to the animal in your dream. Are you afraid of the animal and thus some characteristic of yourself being portrayed by the animal? Are you joyfully engaged with the animal? How you feel about the animal will help you determine what aspect of your life, your self or another is being represented.

Wild animals may show you the need to express your uninhibited side, or perhaps you have been too wild and irresponsible. Wild animals often live in groups and may represent group behaviour, group action and cooperation. Have you recently been associated with a group of people? Check in with the feelings to discover whether you are comfortable with the group activity or behaviour.

Domesticated animals and pets often represent our partly trained aspects of self. If the animal belongs to someone else in the dream, it may mean that the person has that animal's traits. Pets in the dream may be showing you your pet peeves or an undisciplined aspect of self, depending on how trained your pet is. If the pet in the dream is your actual pet, ask yourself what qualities or characteristics attract or repel you about your pet. This often points to your own qualities and your acceptance or judgement of them.

In general, animals represent your instincts — your basic or primal nature — or may refer to your senses. Animals, whether in a dream or in the waking time, are couriers of knowledge.

This is a list of some of the animals that seem to come up often in dreams. The brief explanation that accompanies each should give you a starting point for figuring out what the animal means to you.

Remember: *These symbolic meanings are just suggestions. If these suggested meanings do not resonate with you, ring a bell, give you an "ah-ha" moment or otherwise feel right, search through your own experience or beliefs about the symbol to find what makes sense for you.*

Alligator

Denotes ferocity, tough exterior and initiation. Have you recently been uncivilized, aggressive or angry about something? Is there an especially tough issue you are wrestling with, or have you been displaying thick-skinned attitudes and beliefs toward others?

Ant

Ants bring messages about patience and discipline. Because they are highly industrious builders, they may reflect a need to build something in your life at this time. Are you the architect of your own life? Examine your own industriousness and discipline. Have you been patient or do your need to be patient about some aspect of your life? Perhaps

you have recently lost your patience. Ants are small and get squashed easily — does this mirror your feelings of smallness or repression? Perhaps you feel like you'd like to squash a situation, a rumour or another person. May be a pun on aunt, anti (against something) or ante (pay up). See Aunt in the *People* section of this dictionary.

Armadillo

Because of its armoured covering, denotes boundaries, personal protection, discrimination and empathy. Are you able to protect yourself from the judgements and words of others? Is it safe to let your defences down? Or are you overly defensive in regards to a certain subject or situation?

Ass – See Donkey

Badger

Sign of assertiveness, bold self-expression and reliance. Badgers are very aggressive, so they may be telling you about your own aggression or lack of it. This powerful animal lives underground and thus can represent the ability to see below the surface of all things and people. It is an unsociable animal and may indicate that you are currently not relating well with others. Perhaps you are badgering yourself or someone else, or you are being overly persistent. Badgers will fight to the death, so note if you are willing to die for a cause, opinion, belief or anything. They are also fearless and may represent your fearless attitude or stance.

Bat

Represents initiation, transition, rebirth or martyrdom. They also indicate that it is time to face your fears and let go or surrender that which no longer serves you well or suits you. Bats hold the promise of rebirth and coming out of the darkness. A bat symbolizes of facing your fears, often through hardship, but it also holds the promise of empowerment. May also be a pun on going to bat, feeling batty, baseball bats, and something within striking distance. Bats fly on sonar or instinct,

which would indicate the need to go by your intuition, instincts or senses. May also say that you need to have your sonar activated (i.e., to be on alert or on the defensive about something).

Bear

Represents hibernation, self-reflection, introspection and going within to awaken the power of the unconscious. Bears often reflect a need for you to go deep within yourself to find your own answers and/or to give birth to a new idea or project. Bears have lunar ties and therefore often reflect the feminine aspect of self. May be a pun on the bare facts or bearing arms. Have you felt exposed or is there something you have to endure presently? What do you need to reflect on or pay attention to? Is there something you need to bear in mind or reveal? Perhaps there is a situation, relationship, feeling or aspect of self that you cannot bare?

Beaver

Associated with building, construction and teeth. Do you need to build something or in the process of building something in your life? Perhaps you have been neglecting your most basic dreams (life goals and yearnings). Do you need to pay more attention to the words you speak? Beaver's message may be that it is time for action, for building/creating something. Beavers are also associated with building dams and barriers. Does this reflect your own behaviour? Have you been building walls in your own life? Perhaps you are busy as a beaver? The beaver is known for its large, strong teeth; it may be helpful to read about Teeth in the *Body* section for more insight.

Bee

There are lots of possible puns in the word "be." May suggest that you be aware of something. Note where the bee lands and realize that this may be what your attention needs to "be on." Could represent an annoyance in your life — is something bugging you? In metaphysical circles this could denote just let it be or just "be" (be yourself). Bees extract the sweetness out of life — are you taking in the sweetness in your life? Do you hear yourself saying be quiet, be this or be that, or simply demanding a lot of yourself or others? Is something a-buzz in your life or are you feeling stung? May remind you to extract the honey of life while you can and pursue your dreams. Be aware of how you use the word "be" in your own vocabulary — this will likely highlight the meaning of your dream bee. For example, you may say "be happy" or "be quiet" a lot in your head or out loud, and this will

help you discern the meaning more clearly.

Beetle

Beetles denote metamorphosis (change) and resurrection. Are you in the process of some transformation, project or cycle? If so, what stage are you at? Perhaps you need to make a change or resurrect some aspect of your self or your life. Beetles may represent bugs to some people and thus denote that something is bugging you.

Buffalo

Associated with abundance and prayer, the buffalo was a sacred animal to the Native American Indians. The buffalo may be a sign that your prayers have been heard or that you are already abundant. Because buffalo was a major source of sustenance at one time, it may represent gratitude and praise for what has been received. It may signify a time to start praying or to be humble enough to ask for assistance at this time. Buffalos are big, strong animals, so they may represent your strength, physicality and connection to the physical (including the ability to manifest your desires). Buffalos once roamed freely, so they may be associated with your current need to roam free and follow your own senses. Because they have humps, you may wish to read the Camel entry for what humps represent.

Bug

What's annoying or bugging you at present? Bugs of various types often represent small annoyances in your life. Look at your current life to see what you find irritating, frustrating or distracting to help you understand what your dream bug is symbolizing. Sometimes your bug represents another person or a situation that is bugging you. Pay attention to the background of the dream — it can point to where the annoyance is. For example, if the background is your office, you can tell your problem is likely stemming from some minor office irritant. Because bugs are small, this usually indicates that the problem is small — don't blow it out of proportion! For example, a bug on your head can represent a mental aggravation or an irritating or repetitive thought.

Bull

Associated with anger, aggressiveness, inflammation, fertility and the astrological sign Taurus. It may be telling you about a person you know who is a Taurus — which is often a sign of stubbornness (yours or theirs). May be a pun on "bull," as in baloney or nonsense. Have you recently been enraged or provoked? Are you being "bull headed" or full of bullshit? See Taurus in the *Astrology, Planets and the Cosmos* section for greater insight.

Butterfly

Represents metamorphosis (change) and transformation. They are also symbols of beauty, joy, flight and freedom. Because butterflies go through stages of development, ask yourself if you are confronting any issues at the moment — if so, what stage are you at? Do you feel the need to take flight or be free? Are you experiencing joy or needing to change some aspect of yourself, or your life, in order to gather more joy? Butterflies may indicate a need to dance or get up and move and bring some sweetness into your life. Because butterflies are in the air, it may speak of the mind or mental realm. Perhaps you need some clarity to your mental process or are ready for transformation. If the butterfly is not in flight, you need to recognize or absorb some beauty in your life (within yourself), or you may need to rest and take notice of beauty.

Camel

Because of their humps, camels are often symbolic of storage or reservoirs. These are caches of stored forces that can be tapped into and used for your benefit. Often seen on camels and buffalos, the humps indicate that abundance is available to you now and can be tapped into. Camels are also known for their ability to go great distances and for their stamina. Ask yourself if you need to go the distance on something, and know that you likely have the stamina to do it. How the camel feels in the dream — whether its task seems daunting or easy — will help you understand your own viewpoint on the matter at hand. Camels are also known for not needing as much water for travel as other animals do. This may indicate your own thirst or show a lack of emotional response.

Cat

Often represents your connection to the spiritual or intuitive self. Write out three characteristics about your dream cat or cats in general — these characteristics symbolize something in your current life. Cats are also representative of sleekness, slyness, and individuality and expression of it. Mystery, magic and independence are also often characteristics of cat and may be indicating that magic and mystery are about to, or need to, come alive in your life. Cats are also associated with nine lives, unpredictability and healing. Do any of these words ring true for you at this time? If the cat is a pet, note what personality traits you associate with it and realize it is mirroring your own traits, or even your pet peeves.

Chicken

Associated with fertility, sacrifice and a pun on being afraid or foul. Have you been accused of being cowardly? Or has a situation run afoul? Is there foul play happening or does something smell foul? Are you feeling afraid of facing a situation or do you lack the courage to face something (chicken shit)? Do you feel hen-pecked or picked on? What other associations do you make for chicken? Perhaps your diet is lacking in protein and this is a suggestion to eat chicken.

Cougar

Associated with a time of coming into your own power, leadership and feminine energies. Cougar may be telling you it is time to act on your power or with authority. Cougars are known for their sleekness, agility and courage. Could suggest its time to growl your truth or act with ferocity in regard to some issue. Cougars leap, which may suggest you need to leap at an opportunity or move forward at this time. May be a sign that you need to defend or protect yourself or those you love in some way (either through gentleness or forcefully). Big cats are amplified domesticated cat energy, so also see Cat for more information. See also Feminine in the *People* section of this dictionary.

Cow

Associated with being passive, gentle, obedient to authority and going along with the crowd. Have you been overly passive about something or not assertive enough? Do you tend to be submissive to authority figures, or are you going along with the crowd? May be associated with stupidity or with being overweight, depending on your personal views.

Coyote

Associated with both wisdom and folly depending on what is being represented in your present circumstances. Are you fooling yourself or are you being too serious? Are you making things more complicated than they need to be? Also known as the great trickster, coyotes are both the creator and the jokester, but sometimes the magic does not work. Have your actions be wise or foolish lately? Coyotes are also associated with howling, and this may suggest a need to howl or vocalize something. Remember to factor your personal associations for coyotes into your understanding of what coyote is trying to represent to you in this dream.

Crab

Associated with perseverance, possessiveness and the astrological sign of Cancer. Also has the tendency to hold on to things with its pincers. Have you been holding on to something or need to let go of something? Have you been crabby or irritable? Crabs also scuttle and scurry quickly — have you been emulating, or do you need to emulate, this behaviour? May represent someone you know who has the astrological sign of Cancer or be a pun on cancer (something that eats away at you). See Cancer in the *Astrology, Planets and the Cosmos* section for greater insight.

Deer

Deer are a sign of gentleness and innocence. Have you been too hard on yourself or others lately? Are you trying to force things? Deer tells you it is time to be gentle with yourself and those around you. It indicates a time to return to your childlike innocence — perhaps you have gotten too far away from the role that would be most beneficial to you at this time. Deer trails are known to twist through the forest and are a sign that you are being lured into new adventures, so be on the lookout for anything new coming into your life. Deer are also known for freezing when caught in the headlights of an approaching car. Ask yourself if you have been stuck or frozen in fear in the days prior to receiving this dream symbol. Also note the behaviour of the deer in your dream.

Dog

Dogs bring you messages about loyalty, companionship, faithfulness, protectiveness, unconditional love, playfulness and joy. Note your personal associations about dog. If you have been bitten or scared by a dog, then it may represent fear or dislike of something in your life. Are you in need of or lacking companionship at this time? Have you been less than loyal to yourself or another? Do you need to be more protective about something? Perhaps it is time to add a bit of play in your life or time to examine your own territory. Dogs often tell you something about yourself. To help determine which aspect of self is being reflected, describe the dog's characteristics and/ or behaviour with three words. For example, if you choose aggressive, defensive and sly, then this would be mirroring or reflecting your own aggressiveness, defensiveness and slyness. If the dream dog is your pet dog, it may represent your pet peeves, pet projects or your beloved. May represent someone born in the year of the dog (according to Chinese astrology).

Dolphin

Brings you messages about playfulness, the energy of water, the power of your breath/breathing and sound. Perhaps it is time to breathe new life into a relationship, project or idea. Perhaps you need to be more playful or enter into the more watery aspects of life (creation, passion, sexuality). Because dolphins live in water and water is symbolic of emotions, be sure to relate your dolphin dream to your feelings by taking note of the quality of water in the dream. See the *Water* section for greater clarity.

Donkey

The donkey symbolizes stubbornness, patience, humility and wisdom. Are you being stubborn and refusing to move with the flow? May be a pun on ass or buttocks. See Buttock in the *Body* section of this dictionary.

Dragon

Represents mystery, imagination and intuition. May also speak of your own power or resistance at this time. Perhaps you feel the need to slay or terminate some aspect of self or something in your life at this time. May be a pun on draggin' or drag. Have you been dragging your feet or do you feel something or someone is a drag? Dragons also breathe fire — they may suggest that you are full of hot air or that you need to express some pent-up feelings. May represent someone born in the year of the dragon (according to Chinese astrology).

Dragonfly

Dragonfly denotes illusion and light. May be telling you things are not as they seem or may be reflecting your true colours. Dragonfly can be the bearer of messages to gain a new perspective or make a change. May tell you to see through your illusions and let your own light shine forth.

Elephant

Symbol of ancient power, royalty and strength. Also may be making a reference to the trunk or nose, which is about your senses or ability to sense. Because of their size and weight, elephants may suggest a heavy load or burden you are carrying. Elephants are very family oriented and are run by a matriarchy in the wild. How does this association reveal itself in your every-day family life and the role you play? See Nose in the *Body* section of this dictionary.

Elk

Related to the deer family, the elk is known for its incredible stamina and ability to go the distance. How have your energy levels been? Are you burning yourself out? How do you plan to finish or arrive at your goal without burning out? Do you need to go the distance with respect to some endeavour? Elks are also strong and noble, so they may reflect these characteristics within you. Do you need more strength and endurance or are you at the peak of such? Have you hit your stride or do you have to learn to pace yourself? Elk are also about partnerships of all kinds, so be aware of what partnerships are being highlighted in your own life and how they are working for you.

Fish

Because fish live in the water, they often represent the unconscious or emotions. They are also a symbol of Christianity. Fish is the universal symbol of the life-giving, or life-preserving, power of water. May indicate Christ consciousness or your ability to go with the flow and surrender to the currents of life. May be a pun on feeling like a fish out of water, if you have felt out of your element or league recently. Is your dream fish flowing smoothly or fighting the current? This reflects your ability to flow with, or fight, whatever situations you currently find yourself in. Fish represent the astrological sign of Pisces, which rule the feet and your ability to understand. Fish can also be about martyrdom and self-sacrifice. May be a pun on something smelling fishy. Could even imply you need to add or eliminate fish from your diet. See specific fish or list three of your dream fish's characteristics to help determine what personal traits the fish is reflecting about you. See Pisces in the *Astrology, Planets and the Cosmos* section for greater insight.

Fox

Fox brings you messages about slyness, cleverness, camouflage, invisibility and shape shifting. Have you felt out-foxed recently or been described as sly as a fox ? Perhaps it refers to a foxy lady or the dance the fox trot? Have you been blending in, or have you felt invisible? Perhaps it is time to blend in or act invisible. Fox speaks of a sly type of power and ingenious manoeuvres. Being crafty, cunning, wily, and having a deceptive nature are also associated with fox.

Frog

Represents your ability to make leaps, and is associated with fairy tales about transformation. Do you need to make some changes in your life or hop toward a new endeavour? Perhaps you've had a frog in your throat about some issue or relationship and feel the need to express yourself about it.

Giraffe

Symbol of farsightedness or the ability to foresee events. Associated with the neck and therefore with communication and expression. Also denotes

balance and represents an ability to progress. Perhaps you wish you were taller in order to see something more clearly or from a different perspective. See Neck in the *Body* section of this dictionary for further insight.

Goat

Goats address your surefootedness and new heights to be reached. Are you moving into a new area in your life and are you getting support in regard to this? Are you feeling on shaky ground about something and require some support? Are you being flexible about exploring new avenues in your life recently? Perhaps someone is getting your goat or you feel like a scapegoat. Goat is also the sign of Capricorn and may reflect a Capricorn person in your life. See Capricorn in the *Astrology, Planets and the Cosmos* section for greater insight.

Goose

Associated with fairy tales and childhood dreams. May be a pun on "silly goose" or indicate you are being foolish about something. Are childhood dreams beckoning you, or have you been day dreaming about something? May suggest your goose is cooked or something has failed. See the section on *Birds* in this dictionary for greater understanding.

Grasshopper

Reflects good luck, abundance and your ability to leap. Have you been afraid to make a leap? Or have you been making great leaps in your life? May be telling you it is time to make a leap of faith about an idea, project or relationship.

Groundhog/Gopher

Because they live underground, gophers are associated with the ability to go within and tap into your inner wisdom. Like bears, they hibernate and suggest you have the ability to go deep within an area of interest. Groundhogs may appear when a new area of study is to open up. Hibernation also reflects death without dying and therefore represents that you may be undergoing some sort of initiation at this time. May suggest you are just coming up from a long period of inactivity or that some light has finally been shed on something.

Horse

Horses are bearers of messages about freedom, power, energy currents and travel. Horses show you what physical forces are at work in your life and, because they are animals, they can also reflect instinctual or intuitive power. Horses can reflect violent or powerful emotions that you feel, or that are going unnoticed. Note the dream feelings, the colour of your dream horse and its actions. Are you riding the horse or is it out of control? What behaviours is the horse displaying? The horse's actions and the amount of mastery you show over it will help you determine what part of your self is being reflected and to what degree you have control over your own power, energy or emotions. If your dream horse is running free, this may indicate your desire to be free and "in your power" or it could represent a loss of control, depending on the feelings associated with the dream. Dreaming of stallions may represent your sexual energy or desire. Perhaps this reflects your need for horsing around, horse play or horse sense. Training a horse may reflect your active discipline over some event in your life. Have you or someone else been on your high horse (arrogant, pompous or egotistical)? Do you have the ability to move forward at a steady pace? Are you feeling too constricted and need more freedom? Is the horse galloping, indicating moving under full steam (your own power) or being led by someone (indicating you may be being led around or led astray or not taking the lead)?

Insect – *See Bug*

Jellyfish

Jellyfish are the only creatures dependent on movement for their sustenance, and yet they have virtually no ability to move on their own. Therefore they represent your acceptance of the flow of life, or that you are floating aimlessly. A jellyfish may also say you feel spineless or without courage. If you associate a stinging ability with the jellyfish, realize this may be a sign that you feel stung by someone's thoughts, words or actions.

Kangaroo

Known for their great jumping ability, kangaroos may symbolize your efforts to make great leaps and bounds in your life. Because they have a pouch, they may point to your need to contain something or hold something close to you (or even keep a secret). Kangaroos' teeth grow continuously and they are well known for their constant need to gnaw. Has anything been gnawing at you or do you need to speak your truth about something? Because they are associated with Australia, your dream kangaroo may symbolize an Australian you know.

Ladybug

In general, bugs may indicate a small annoyance in your life. But ladybugs are not always viewed as pests and are even considered beneficial by some people. Be aware of what personal associations you have with ladybugs to help you understand what it is representing for you. Because ladybugs are red, they may be trying to get your attention about this colour and its associations — such as first chakra issues or feelings of anger or passion. See the *Chakras* and *Colours* sections for more information.

Leopard

Leopards bring messages about ferocity, valour, feminine energies and the possible need to reclaim your power. Would it help if you were more ferocious about something in your life, or do you need more courage? Have you felt powerless over a situation and perhaps need to assert yourself? Is your leopard spotted and would this indicate your truthfulness or slyness in recent situations? For further clarification, see also Feminine in the *People* section and Cat in this section of this dictionary.

Lion

Relates to the words you speak, assertion, feminine energies and power. Do you need to speak out your truth on a matter? Are you in need of being a little wild and having some fun? Could be a pun on "lying" — either lying around lazily or lying about the truth. Is it a male or female lion you encounter? A male lion could speak of a time to roar like a lion or to be more protective about something. Perhaps you have been feeling threatened or intruded by someone or something and need to assert yourself. Also associated with the astrological sign Leo and may be trying to get your attention about a Leo person in your life. See also Feminine in the *People* section and Leo in the *Astrology, Planets and the Cosmos* section.

Lynx

Brings you messages about feminine energies, secrets and things unseen. Have you been taken into confidence lately and are you keeping the secret well? Perhaps you have let a secret slip or have accidentally learned a secret. Have you shared a secret inappropriately? May be informing you to connect to lost treasures within your self or connect with something forgotten. See also Feminine in the *People* section of this dictionary.

Monkey

May represent high levels of energy and activity or playful energy, depending on how your dream monkey is portrayed. Perhaps you feel like monkey in the middle or that someone is monkeying around with you. Monkey

can also be a type of experiment — to fiddle with something or to tamper with. May suggest you have "monkey mind" or an abundance of foolish thinking. Monkeys can have outlandish, bizarre and curious behaviour — does this represent your own recent behaviour?

Moose

Moose brings messages about your self-esteem, sacred energies (feminine) and the magic of life and death. Do you feel good about some recent accomplishment or do you have a new sense of self? Perhaps you have broken a habit or completed something and have reason to be proud of yourself. Moose may be an invitation to explore your feminine energies. Moose are large animals, so they may represent something that you feel is too big to handle or overwhelming. See Feminine (in the *People* section) to reveal what energies are being offered.

Mountain Lion – *See Cougar*

Mouse

Mouse bears the message of scrutiny and of paying attention to detail. Look at yourself and others closely to see if something is right before your eyes. Perhaps you are not seeing the forest for the trees or getting lost in big dreams and neglecting other aspects of your life. Are you becoming too focussed on one or two activities and not seeing other opportunities? Are you missing something obvious that is right in front of you? Perhaps you are scattering your energies and trying to do too many things. It is time to focus your attention and pay attention to details. Since mice are small, they may represent "small" things, beliefs, attitudes or something seemingly insignificant. For some, mice may represent fear or irrational fright.

Opossum

Since opossums play dead as a diversionary tactic, they are often bearers of messages about diversion and the use of appearances. Expect the unexpected and be clever in achieving your victories. Perhaps you need to play dead or behave in a strategic manner. Do you need to appear fearless or fearful despite how you truly feel? Opossum says it's time to pretend and use your acting skills. Opossums are also survivors (they have been on the Earth since dinosaur days) and may represent your own survival issues or needs.

Otter

Brings messages about playfulness, feminine energies, joy and sharing. Otter may be telling you to play like

a child again and to allow things to unfold in your life. Perhaps you are being too playful and not focussed? Are you getting too serious or worrying too much? Otter points to the need to be in the flow of life and to allow the wonderment of life to enfold you.

Panther – See Leopard

Pig

Pigs are often considered dirty animals and may be a reference to your actual living conditions (living like a pig, in a pigsty or pigpen, or a pun on "you dirty pig"). In fact pigs are quite orderly and clean creatures, and the virtues you associate with a pig will affect the meaning of this symbol for you. Pigs are also known to eat slop or anything put before them and this may be a pun on you pigging out (overeating) or behaving like a pig (slob). Could be you are being a bore (boar) or acting like a swine or lout. Pigs' snouts are strong enough to break up cement and this could indicate either a strong sense (if the nose/snout is emphasized in the dream) or denote your own strength in some area. Some movies (such as *Babe* and *Charlotte's Web*) portray pigs as caring and considerate, so be aware of your own feelings toward pigs and how the dream feelings may or may not line up with the attributes of your dream pig. Pigs are also associated with plumpness or being fat and may indicate your feelings about your own weight (or things that weigh heavily on you). Also consider your personal associations with the well-known Miss Piggy character.

Porcupine

Reminds us about our innocence, good-naturedness, curiosity and sense of wonder. Have you been caught in the chaos of adult life? Porcupine is a gentle reminder to open your heart to those things that gave you joy as a child. It may be time to honour your playfulness and sense of wonder. Because porcupines have quills, they may be telling you about your recent knack for "sticking it" to others, perhaps too sharply and intensely. Are you overly sensitive to the barbs of others, or are old insults and pains still bothering you?

Rabbit

Rabbit may be bringing you messages about fear, fertility or new life. Are you currently afraid of something and worrying overly? Perhaps it is time to face a fear or be more productive. Is there something new that you'd like to begin? Rabbit gives you a sign that it is time to start new endeavours and let go of fears associated with them. Could also be a pun on "hare," "heir" or "hair." See Hair in the *Body* section of this dictionary for more information.

Raccoon

Raccoons wear a mask and often tell of your ability to disguise, conceal or cover up something. Are you hiding behind a mask or misrepresenting yourself? Perhaps wearing a mask will be beneficial to you at this time. Do you need to present a different f ace or are you hiding your true self? Raccoons also speak of your dexterity, proficiency and courage. City dwellers may find them to be annoying pests and scavengers. Have you been searching for something of late or is something irritating or annoying you?

Ram

Represents force, power, seeking out new beginnings and the astrological sign Aries. Rams speak of your boldness and strength and how well you are, or are not, using it. Because of their large horns, they may be presenting you with information about mental activity. New beginnings and the ability to land on your feet are also what ram teaches you. Is it time to begin something new, rather than just think about it? Are you taking advantage of new opportunities and staying balanced? Ram can also mean drive, force, thrust, smash or slam. See Aries in the *Astrology, Planets and the Cosmos* section of this dictionary for more clues.

Rat

For city dwellers, rats may appear as only pesky, invasive vermin, but rats also speak of success and shrewdness because they have managed to thrive among humans. Are you pursuing your goals and perhaps need to be more aggressive? Could be a pun on the common turn of phrase "oh, rats." Perhaps you feel you have missed an opportunity or something is annoying you? Has anyone ratted on you lately or have you ratted about another? May represent someone born in the year of the Rat (according to Chinese astrology).

Scorpion

Often denotes a painful sting from self or another. Perhaps sharp words have been spoken or you have felt stung by another's words or actions. Could represent a Scorpio (astrological sign) you know or that you feel burned about something or someone. Perhaps a smart remark has left its mark on you or you are irritated about something in general. See Scorpio in the *Astrology, Planets and the Cosmos* section for more information.

Seal

Brings messages about feminine energies, lucid dreaming, imagination and creativity. Are you in need of using your creativity or your imagination? May be a pun on the verb to "seal" or close up and lock something away. Do you need to applaud your own efforts or do you need a seal of approval? Perhaps you have sealed your fate or felt closed in. Seals can also be seen as playful mimics and may speak of your need to play more. Associated with water and therefore with the emotions and feminine energies.

Skunk

Because they are known for their spray and smell, skunks often bring messages about reputation, respect and self-esteem. Skunks can either attract or repel, and they often tell you what you are attracting or repelling in your life. How well are you respected lately, whether in the community, by your family, or with yourself? Do you demand respect or are you in need of some respect in regards to some current situation? Perhaps someone has been irritating you or you are irritating others. Examine your self-image for clues as what skunk's personal message is to you. Has your sense of something been offended lately? See also Nose in the *Body* section of this dictionary for more on senses.

Snake

Snakes are ancient symbols of healing, initiation, resurrection, rebirth and transmutation (change). They are associated with wisdom, sexual energy and creative life. Perhaps it is time to change something about your self or your life. Do you need to heal some part of your self, a relationship or an issue? Does something need to die in order for something new to be born? Have you been, or do you need to be, creative? Some may see snakes as fearful, slimy and sneaky. Has someone been a snake in the grass or has someone pulled a fast one on you? May represent someone born in the year of the snake (according to Chinese astrology). Also represents the Kundalini energy associated with the first chakra and the flow of the energy systems of the body. Read the discussion on the First Chakra in the *Chakras* section of this dictionary for further clarity, as this representation is often associated with the functioning of this important energy centre.

Spider

Spiders are ancient symbols of creativity and weaving and represent what you are currently formulating or producing in your life. Spider may bring the message that it's time to create or move toward a goal. Have you been focussed or are you scattered and going in multiple directions? May be a pun on the tangled webs you weave or someone near you is weaving. May also represent something that gives you the creeps or makes you squeamish. For some, spider may denote fear and the desire to squash some aspect of your life. Is there some aspect of your life you'd rather not see, or feel the need to obliterate?

Squirrel

Brings you information about gathering, activity and preparedness. Because squirrels are often quite sociable, they may speak of a need to be more sociable or more active. Are you too active or not active enough right now? Are you planning for your future and gathering the tools that will be necessary? Action is often required when squirrel shows up; sometimes you are collecting too much. Be prepared for anything and gather what is necessary for your current life endeavours. Have you felt harried or caught up in the hustle-bustle of life? Squirrel may also represent a squirrelly or overactive mind.

Tiger

Represents feminine energies, ferocity, power, passion and devotion. Do you need more passion in life or are you expressing your passions appropriately? Have your energy levels been down? Is it time to start a new adventure? Have you been devoted to your goals, self or other relationships? Do you need to be more assertive or ferocious about a recent situation? Could denote the need to roar (voice your opinions or feelings) or protect yourself in some way. May represent someone born in the year of the tiger (according to Chinese astrology). See Feminine in the *People* section of this dictionary.

Turtle

May represent tough exterior, longevity, and Mother Earth. May denote you are moving at a slow pace or that you are hiding in your shell. Perhaps you need to slow down, or to realize that your progress is slow but steady. May indicate a time to connect with Mother Earth and get grounded. Tortoises are known for their longevity and may be a sign that something has either grown old or perhaps outlived its usefulness in your mind. Or they could denote wisdom that comes with age.

Unicorn

This mythical animal can represent mysticism, magic and a creative imagination. Because the horn is in the location of third eye, a unicorn may represent your intuition, vision and insight. Like a horse, it can also denote your

power, sense of power, or powerlessness. Are you in control or riding this magical beast? Are you able to fly on this animal, implying a sense of freedom, choice and a higher perspective on something? Note the dream feelings for greater insight.

Whale

Whales are historically the record keepers of the Earth and bring messages about feminine energies and balance. Whale may also bring you information about your own creativity, voice and inner depths. Because of the sound whales make, it may indicate a time to sing your own song or your unique call. Perhaps it is time to use the voice for creativity and to release tensions. Are you using your creativity appropriately or not at all? Perhaps you need to have a whale of a time, or it could be a pun on "wailing." Have you been lamenting too long about a situation and now it's time to be more imaginative? See Feminine in the *People* section for further clarification.

Wolf

Wolf denotes teachings, loyalty and the wild or free-spirited aspect of self. Wolf teaches you to look within to find your inner teacher. Because they howl at the moon, wolves are linked to feminine energies and may be telling you it is time to howl or communicate in new and powerful ways. Have you been listening to your inner thoughts and words? Do you feel the need to howl or be free? Perhaps you need to connect with your intuition? When you dream of wolf it is time to look for teachings no matter where you are. Some people associate wolves with traits that are sneaky, crafty or untrustworthy — do you? Because wolves run in packs they may be representing your family life and your role in the family or community. See also Feminine in the *People* section and Moon in the *Astrology, Planets and the Cosmos* section for more information.

Zebra

May represent black-and-white thinking or an all-or-nothing attitude. May suggest your ability to blend in with the crowd, or that you are following along with group thinking or behaviour. Similar to Horse in meaning; see Horse in this section of the dictionary.

Astrology, Planets and the Cosmos

Remember: These symbolic meanings are just suggestions. If these suggested meanings do not resonate with you, ring a bell, give you an "ah-ha" moment or otherwise feel right, search through your own experience or beliefs about the symbol to find what makes sense for you.

Astrological Signs

The Zodiac is made up of twelve sun signs. Your date of birth determines which one you are. The information complied here is incomplete but offers a glimpse into your nature and the nature of others who fall under a certain sign. If you know someone's sun sign, your mind may conjure up these symbols as a way to relate to certain character traits they may have. Here are the dates to which each of the astrological signs applies.

Aries	March 21 – April 20	**Libra**	September 24 – October 23
Taurus	April 21 – May 21	**Scorpio**	October 24 – November 22
Gemini	May 22 – June 21	**Sagittarius**	November 23 – December 22
Cancer	June 22 – July 22	**Capricorn**	December 23 – January 20
Leo	July 23 – August 21	**Aquarius**	January 21 – February 19
Virgo	August 22 – September 23	**Pisces**	February 20 – March 20

Aquarius

Astrological sign of the water bearer and therefore is linked to emotions. Could be trying to get your attention about an Aquarius person who figures in your life at this time. Aquarian attributes include being responsible, scrupulous, conventional and practical. They can also be serious and hard-working. Also known to be unforgiving, egotistical and brooding.

Aries

Astrological sign of the ram. May be pun on being "rambunctious" or stubborn. Could be about an Aries person who figures in your life. This is a fire sign and may suggest fiery thinking, behaviour or actions. Aries attributes include being pioneering, competitive, courageous and dynamic. Aries traits also include being domineering, hasty, arrogant and quick-tempered.

Cancer

Astrological sign of the crab. Have you or someone you know been crabby, grumpy, or expressing complaints a lot lately? May be a pun on the disease cancer. Has anything been eating away at you lately? Cancer as a disease often brings on feelings of impending death (symbolic or literal), so ask yourself if you feel as though some part of you is dying or can't go on. Astrologically, Cancerians are sensitive and like a secure home life. Can you relate to these aspects within yourself, or do they represent a Cancerian you know? Cancer traits can also include being tenacious, emotional and materialistic. Other qualities include being too cautious, lazy and selfish.

Capricorn

Astrological sign represented by a goat and often associated with workaholic behaviour or the ability to begin something new.

Or do you know a Capricorn who figures prominently in your life lately? Has anything gotten your goat or your attention recently? Capricorn traits including being practical, prudent, ambitious and disciplined. They tend to be patient, careful, humorous and reserved. On the dark side, they can be pessimistic, fatalistic, miserly and can hold a grudge.

Gemini

Astrological sign of the twins and may represent a Gemini you know or be pointing to the traits Geminis possess. These include their ability to be adaptable, expressive, quick-witted and clever. Also known to be restless, ungrateful, lacking in ability to follow through and scatter-brained. See also Twins in the *People* section of this dictionary.

Leo

Zodiacal sign representing the lion and therefore may represent issues of courage. May represent a Leo you know or attributes of a Leo. Leo traits include being ideal-istic, ambitious, generous, optimistic and dignified. Also known to be vain, boastful, pretentious and overbearing. May be a pun on the need to roar or be lion-hearted.

Libra

Astrological sign of balance and the scales. Are you out of balance? This symbol could also reflect a Libra you know. Libra traits include being cooperative, peace-loving, artistic and diplomatic. They can also be fickle, indecisive and easily deterred. May be a pun on the scales of justice. May indicate the need for more balance in your life and current undertakings.

Pisces

This zodiacal sign of the fish represents the unconscious realms and it rules the feet (your understanding). Also about self-sacrifice and martyrdom, Pisces people are said to be compassionate, selfless, intuitive and sympathetic. Because Pisces is a water sign, it is therefore associated with emotions and feelings. Pisceans are also considered to be secretive, vague, idealistic and sometimes weak-willed.

Sagittarius

Astrological sign of the archer and may represent a Sagittarius person in your life or indicate you are displaying Sagittarian qualities. Has someone been shooting arrows (negative thoughts, words or actions) at you? Positive characteristics of Sagittarians are that they are straightforward, freedom-loving,

broad-minded, generous and enthusiastic. Negative traits are that they can be argumentative, pushy, procrastinating, blunt and impatient.

Scorpio

Astrological sign of the scorpion and may indicate that someone has stung you or that you are stinging yourself. May be representing a Scorpio person you know or indicate that you are displaying traits of a Scorpio. Positive characteristics include being resourceful, passionate, motivated, determined and probing. Negative traits include being vengeful, temperamental, secretive, sarcastic and jealous.

Taurus

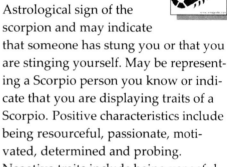

Astrological sign of the bull and could indicate stubbornness or be associated with a Taurus person in your life. Taurus positive characteristics include being patient, thorough, stable, dependable, practical and loyal. Their negative traits include being stubborn, argumentative, short-tempered and materialistic.

Virgo

Astrological sign of the virgin and may indicate a Virgo you know or that you feel virginal in some current undertaking, relationship or endeavour. Virgo attributes include being studious, methodical, exacting and humane, as well as being a perfectionist. Virgos can also be critical, petty and picky.

Planets and the Cosmos

Planets are an important part of our everyday make-up, and astrologers use them to understand the part their collective energies play in our everyday lives. These energies affect us every day, and we all have information about the planets stored in our DNA (similar to how archetypal and universal symbolism is "known" to us at a deep level). So the planets provide important clues about the hidden behaviours and actions that may be driving you without your conscious (deliberate) awareness.

Earth

In general, Earth is about structure and form, and about being grounded (being fully present in your body and in your own life — in the now). It may symbolize something about the material world and/or practical matters. Seeing Earth from a distant view in the dream could suggest that you are ungrounded or that you feel adrift, detached or disconnected from something presently happening in your life. Notice the dream feelings to help you understand if this is a healthy perspective from which you are viewing your life or a negative situation from which you are detaching yourself.

Jupiter

Represents expansion, abundance and tolerance. Notice how these themes may fit into your life at the current time. Do you require some expansion or more tolerance? Is abundance flowing but you are not recognizing it? Some of this planet's keywords include morality, gratitude, hope, honour, and the law. Jupiter is a planet of broader purpose, reach, and possibility. How do these keywords feature in your current undertakings? Jupiter has generally been associated with good luck and bounty. It also denotes optimism and growth (including mental and spiritual growth), and will therefore reflect these areas in your life. Note the dream feelings and understand that the more negative reflections of Jupiter include blind optimism, excess, and overindulgence.

Mars

Often called the Red Planet, Mars may represent your red energies — these are often associated with feelings of anger, aggression and assertiveness, but they are also about your fire or passion for life. See how these feelings currently factor in your life. Mars is also associated with Martians or extraterrestrials and could suggest that something feels foreign or alien to you at this time. Mars is the planet of energy, action and desire, so it may symbolize these in your current life. Mars energy is the push that gets us out of bed in the morning, our drive and desire, and our active energy. Do you need a push or to be more action-oriented? Note how you feel in the dream to help you understand further what this planet may be symbolizing.

Mercury

The planet of day-to-day expression and communication. How well have you been communicating lately? Mercury may symbolize that you have just been curious about some things of late. Mercury may also reflect the need for analysis, sorting or just trying to makes sense of things. How well do you express and convey your thoughts? How do you approach others and information in order to learn and exchange ideas? Note the dream feelings and realize that on the negative side Mercury may represent that you are being high-strung, nervous, nit-picky, indecisive, or overly technical. Mercury in a dream will help show you your individual style of communication.

Moon

Represents the imagination, fantasy and intuition. Also reflects your sensitivity, emotions and your feminine energies (see Feminine in the People section of this dictionary). The moon is associated with the mother archetype and may represent your own mother or feminine energy in general. The moon is both your inner child and your inner mother. It is about your responsiveness, receptiveness, spontaneity and instinctual reactions. The moon is about how you react to certain situation, events and people. How do you instinctively react or respond to problems? The moon represents your deepest personal needs, your basic habits and reactions, and your unconscious. The moon shows how you protect yourself, as well as how you make yourself feel secure, comfortable and safe. Because the moon's cycle affects us so greatly, keeping track of the phases of the moon during your waking life will help you to stay grounded (i.e., stay fully present in the moment and in your body) and can be a helpful guide for when to act or when to be still. The new moon represents a time of fertilization, beginnings and the planting of the seeds. The waxing moon is a time for nurturing and watering what you have planted. The full moon is the coming to fulfillment; it symbolizes fullness, culmination, consummation or fruition.

195

The waning moon is a time for finishing projects, completion and letting go.

Neptune

Represents your inspiration, dreams and psychic (intuitive) receptivity. It may also symbolize your illusions and confusion. If the dream feelings are positive, then Neptune reflects your mercy and compassion; negative aspects associated with Neptune include deception, trickery, deceit, guilt, and addiction.

Outer Space

Represents big thinking and grand ideas, hopes, wishes and goals. May be something that is unreachable or wishful thinking. Could be something you feel a great distance from or alien to. Could represent the great Void or connection to the cosmos and God. May represent freedom to do, be and express as you desire. Could imply big opportunities for co-creation. Conversely, it may suggest that you are "way out there" with your thinking, a space cadet or just plain spacey and ungrounded.

Pluto

Pluto is about transformation and represents subconscious forces — it rules all that is below the surface. On the up side, Pluto is associated with renewal — it represents endings, new beginnings, spiritual growth and rebirth. Conversely, it also symbolizes obsessive desire for power and control, and destructiveness in general. Pluto may signify a time of change, an upheaval, power struggles, and issues of control. It may also denote the need to find deeper meanings, and a willingness to explore and examine your self and the world around you.

Saturn

Associated with restriction and limitation, but it also brings structure and meaning to our world. Saturn may represent something that you find limiting or restrictive in your current life. Could also denote rigid structure or a tough time in general. Saturn may be reminding you of your boundaries, your responsibilities, and your commitments. It may suggest the need for self-control, boundaries and limits. Saturn is often associated with fathers, father figures and other authority figures. The discipline, rules, and regulations imposed on you by authority figures (parents, teachers, religion) when you were a child may not always have been pleasant, but they did help you to understand the world around you. Similarly, Saturn's lessons actually help us to grow.

Sky

Associated with the mental plane and thoughts. A clear blue sky may suggest that your mind and thinking are clear, rational or free from worry. A cloudy sky could suggest a clouded mind, clouded vision, impaired judgement, or worrisome thoughts. May also represent heaven or heavenly thinking, the cosmos, the universe or your connection to the Divine. May be a pun on "the sky's the limit" and denote freedom, choice and unlimited potential.

Star

Symbolizes your celestial body (sixth chakra) and therefore may be your connection to your intuitive, wise self, or your divine/ higher self. May denote celebrity status, the hero (or heroine) within or your sense of stardom/popularity. It could also represent your guiding star or a bright light in the darkness. A star in your dream could symbolize your high hopes or ideals. Perhaps you are reaching for a star or wish to be in the spotlight. A shooting star may symbolize your deepest desires, hopes and dreams (wishes).

Sun

Represents vitality, life force, warmth, energy, heat and Source. The Sun is the giver of life.

May represent light, illumination or insight. May be something you feel is a great distance from you or out of reach. May suggest you need more sunlight or sunshine in your life. May imply you need a little "light" on a situation or more insight. The Sun represents your conscious mind, your will to live, your creative life force, and your life's purpose. It symbolizes your basic identity, and represents self-realization. It is about reason as opposed to instinct and reflects the here and now (whereas the moon may reflect the past).

Uranus

This planet is about being forward-looking, and it may suggest that you balk at tradition and celebrate originality and individuality. Uranus is associated with technology, innovation, discovery, and all that is progressive, so note how these concepts are currently fitting into your life. Uranus may also reflect your sense of enlightenment, progressiveness, objectivity, novelty, and ingenuity. Uranus could also speak of a current rebelliousness or without a cause type of irresponsibility. It may symbolize your reactivity if untamed, or an intuitive sense that can be quite inventive. This may be the spark that furthers your studies or investigations of any kind. Uranus may suggest it is time to stir things up, put a new spin on situations, and go against established thought or order.

Venus

Represents love, feminine energies and beauty. Venus is also related to fertility and partnerships. This planet reflects your grace, charm, beauty, and what you value. Surprisingly, it also symbolizes money, how you spend it and what you spend it on. Venus can also reflect your tastes, artistic inclinations, and what makes you happy. Venus shows how you approach relationships of the heart, as well as what gives you pleasure.

Backgrounds and Settings

The backgrounds in your dreams can offer you clues as to where your concerns are, or where a problem lies. For example, if the background of your dream is in a kitchen or dining area, this could be telling you there is a problem with your thinking (food for thought), digestion, or even a conflict about food ingestion itself.

Like the backdrop in a movie, the dream background sets the tone and mood of your current life situations. The background can help you understand the purpose of the dream. For example, dreams that take place indoors are pointing to particular inner states of consciousness, whereas outdoor dreams may indicate that everything is out in the open or represent external situations.

Use the background of your dream to help orient yourself to which level of your self is being addressed. An ancient setting, for example, may be trying to get your attention about an old or outdated problem or belief. If the background is a battle-field, you can bet the dream denotes some area of conflict in your life.

Remember: These symbolic meanings are just suggestions. If these suggested meanings do not resonate with you, ring a bell, give you an "ah-ha" moment or otherwise feel right, search through your own experience or beliefs about the symbol to find what makes sense for you.

Daylight vs. Darkness

Think of yourself as an iceberg. Only a small part of a massive iceberg is exposed above the surface of the water. The visible tip of the iceberg only portrays a thin slice of its true nature. You are like the iceberg. You are a multi-faceted, multi-dimensional being, but in your waking reality you are usually only aware of or familiar with your tip — the part of you that you are consciously aware of. The majority of who you are is below the surface, hidden from view. But although this large part of you is hidden from your waking-time awareness, it is reflected in your dreams — your dreams are a window into this hidden part of yourself.

Dreams that take place in the daylight or in a brightly lit area reflect the tip of the iceberg — they represent what is "visible" to you in your waking hours (that is, the

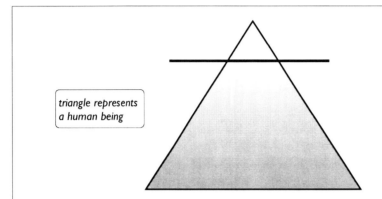

triangle represents
a human being

Dreams that take place in daylight occur in the area above the line, which represents the issues, events, and the conscious parts of your self. These dreams reveal to you something about your deliberate, conscious actions, and choices.

Dreams that take place in darkness occur in the area below the line, which represents the parts of your self that are unknown to you – the subconscious or unconscious parts of your self. These dreams reveal the actions you take and choices you make automatically or without conscious thought.

Figure 8. What daylight and darkness represent in dreams

part of you that is conscious and deliberate). Dreams that take place in the dark or poorly lit areas represent what is below the surface of your waking-time awareness (the part of you that is unconscious and automatic). When attempting to interpret your (or someone else's) dreams, this simple observation about the amount of light present is a quick way to determine how much waking-time awareness you already have of the dream's meaning and therefore how easy it will be to interpret. Dreams that take place in the light are generally easier to interpret than those that take place in the dark, simply because we have some conscious awareness of the light dream's meaning. When starting your dream interpretation journey, it is therefore often easier to start by analyzing the dreams that take place in the light. You may require help with uncovering the meaning of your dark dreams at first, but with practice you will begin to "shed some light" on these hidden aspects of your self.

Nightmares almost always take place in the dark, signifying that in your waking hours you don't have an awareness of or an understanding of the deeper meaning of the dream's content. See Chapter 3 for further discussion of nightmares.

See also the section on *Buildings and Rooms* for further understanding of background meanings.

Airport

Represents a place of hustle and bustle, busyness, crowds and "high ideals." It is a place where you can take off, land or get grounded. May be a pun on a place to connect to higher planes or dimensions. May say you are reaching out toward your goals or feel a new venture is about to "take off." May be a pun on "flying high" or "flighty thinking." May suggest you either need to get moving on something or get your feet on the ground, depending on dream content and feeling. Note what your destination is, or if you have one, for greater understanding.

Alley

Usually alleys are narrow passages with high walls (barriers) on either side. This could represent barriers to thoughts or new ideas. Alleys force you to go in one direction with no choice except to go forward or back where you just came from. Are you feeling confronted with such a choice in your current life? Does your alley lead to a dead end, or where you need to go? Note if it's dark or light in your alley and refer to the discussion on daylight vs. darkness at the beginning of this section.

Bank

May indicate your current financial situation or any money issues you currently face. May be a place of order, business or formality, depending on how you view a bank's atmosphere. Perhaps it is suggesting there is a lot of hustle and bustle in your life, or that you feel overwhelmed by financial responsibility. Any area related to financial matters is likely being highlighted. May be a pun on "you can bank on it" or "it's in the vault." Note the dream feelings to help you understand the positive or negative undertones of this dream symbol.

Battlefield

Represents your inner battlefield, turmoil or conflicts. This may be a familiar battlefield, or an old issue coming to the surface. Either way this speaks of a battle of some sort, either with yourself or with another. This struggle may be triggered by a recent disagreement or confrontation with another or reflect a state of inner turmoil. If the feelings are positive, it may suggest you are conquering new situations or overcoming problems.

Beach

Is your dream beach a comforting and relaxing place? If so, this may indicate your current relaxed state of mind or

201

prosperity. If it is a peaceful beach it may be denoting a spiritual dream, whereas a sandy beach can denote poor footing, poor support or poor understanding. Also note what the water is like and how this reflects your current state of feelings. See the *Water* section of this dictionary for greater understanding.

Bridge

If your background location is a bridge, it suggests you may be bridging or crossing into some new area or situation. May indicate a connection or link between two things, or the act of accessing or joining two things. May suggest moving from one state of awareness or consciousness to another. May say you are bridging the distance or bridging the gap. Could imply change or leaving the old behind as you cross over to something new. Note any new bonds or ties you may have made and see if you can relate them to your dream bridge.

Bull Ring

Implies area of conflict, battle, competition or even a game, depending on dream content and your view of bullfighting. May represent a part of you that is stubborn or looking for a fight.

Campus

Associated with schools or current situations in which you are learning or remembering something. If you are currently on campus, the activity portrayed in the dream likely reflects your current state of mind (for example, is there a hurried pace or relaxed atmosphere?). Campuses denote any type of learning or growing mentally. See *School* in this section for greater insight and understanding.

Cemetery

Cemetery or graveyard may indicate that something has been laid to rest, such as an outdated model of self or an old belief. May represent loss of something or mourning. May also refer to the recent death of part of your self, or warn of an impending death of a part of your self. Dreams of death are about transition in your life (not usually a literal death). If cemeteries scare you, then this may represent your fear about something. Note the dream feelings for greater understanding. See the section on *Death, Dying and Killing*.

City

Cities are often places of much activity and hustle and bustle. This may reflect your inner activity or state of mind. Do cities overwhelm you? If so, this dream

202

may denote a feeling of being over-powered or enveloped by some current project, thinking or situation. Because many cultures, beliefs and customs can come together in a city, this may reflect your inner belief systems and any current clashes among them. A city may represent your whole state of consciousness. Or perhaps you are "out of town" in the dream, which reflects that you are presently in unfamiliar territory. Note how comfortable or uncomfortable you are in the dream city for greater clarity.

Cliff

A dream of standing on the edge of a cliff may represent how you feel in some current situation. That is, you may feel dizzied by some height or overwhelmed by present circum-stances. Do you feel on edge or like you are clinging to the edge? Do you feel you may go over the edge, go crazy or fall apart? Do you have a fear of falling (loss and failure)? If the feel-ings in the dream are unpleasant, you can be sure this reflects an uncomfort-able emotion or stance you are cur-rently experiencing. If the feelings are pleasant and you are enjoying the view, if may denote that you are comfortable with yourself and with your perspec-tives. This dream may also say that you are daring to be so close to the edge. Could say something in your life is a

real cliff hanger. If in the dream you are viewing something from the top of a cliff, it may suggest you have a higher or new perspective on some-thing. If you are faced with climbing the dream cliff, it may symbolize a challenge that faces you in your waking life. Again, your feelings will help with understanding the meaning of your dream symbol. See also Mountain if applicable.

Club – See the entry in the Miscellaneous section

Dark

Denotes inability to see clearly or see what is right before you. May represent your fears or dark emotions. Often dark dreams imply you have *not* got the "light on" or insight about something. Suggests you don't know all the facts or are dim about something. There is a real need to shed some light on this matter. See the discussion on daylight vs. darkness at the beginning of this section.

Dead End

Usually denotes a feeling of being boxed in or having no way out. This may indicate the need to turn around in your thinking or doing. Are you in a dead-end job, relationship or project?

Do you feel trapped? Is your current thinking hitting a dead end?

Desert

Usually a place of dryness — are you parched on your spiritual journey? Are you feeling empty or barren? Depending on how you view deserts (do you like or dislike them?), this reflects what is going on inside of you. Do you need refreshment on any level? Are you feeling alone, abandoned or left high and dry? Perhaps deserts are oases of peace and fulfillment for you. How does your dream desert reflect your inner reality?

Fall (Autumn) – *See Seasons.*

Farm

Often considered a place of hard work — where are you working hard in your life? Or do you see farms as places of rest and relaxation in the country? If so, then this may reflect your need for rest or that you feel relaxed in a current project, endeavour or relationship. Are seeds just being planted? Perhaps you are cultivating something new in your life. Note what is taking place on your dream farm and relate this activity to your current life.

Field

Is your dream field barren, fallow or in full growth? This reflects your current state of growth, emptiness or dormancy. Perhaps the field is denoting that you feel wide open to some endeavour or relationship. Do you need to reap some benefit or sow new ideas? Does an open space gives you a sense of peace and prosperity? Note what is growing in the field to help further determine what it reflects in your waking time.

Foreign Place

A foreign country denotes the feeling or sense that you are experiencing something new or unfamiliar in your current life. This could be an unknown feeling or new relationship, or even a new and uncharacteristic place within yourself. Have you felt alienated from a recent experience or feeling? Are circumstances unfamiliar and strange to you? Foreigners or strangers in your dream may represent new and unaccustomed parts of self that you are meeting and/ or integrating into your reality. Do your life circumstances seem alien or foreign to you?

Forest

Represents growth and fecundity. If your forest is thick with life, then it represents your own fullness and prosperity. If the season is autumn or winter, ask yourself if it is time for a rest or renewal. Perhaps you need to hibernate if the forest is a wintry scene. Are you being productive and fruitful in your everyday life or do you need to be more focussed on your growth? Forests are usually full of life and abundance — is your life? Perhaps you need to get back to nature. Or, a dream forest could be saying you can't see the forest for the trees.

Garden

Deciphering what your garden denotes depends on what is growing, or not growing, and the condition of the soil and plants. Is the garden dormant or fallow? This could indicate your unproductive state of being, or a state of feeling useless and worthless. A garden abundant with life and growth reflects your rich inner world and inner growth. It may be depicting prosperity, harmony, peace and beauty. Are there weeds in your garden? If so, you may need to do some inner weeding (keeping out unwanted thoughts or "bad" seed ideas). If the garden has been neglected, it implies you are neglecting your own needs and you

need to start tending to yourself now. Note what is growing in your garden and how this reflects your current life situations.

Graveyard – See Cemetery

Heaven

May suggest you feel heavenly or that you wish to go home. May say you desire communion with God or the angels. May represent your higher self, your god-self, or a high state of consciousness or awareness. May symbolize that you are longing for comfort, support and love. Note your own associations with heaven for greatest understanding.

Hell

Dreaming of hell usually reflects some sort of torment, agony or misery going on in your life. Depending on your views on what hell means, this may suggest you are in an extremely uncomfortable or unbearable situation or relationship. This could also be a pun on such sayings as, "to hell with it," "go to hell" or "burn in hell." Try to connect your recent words or thoughts about hell to the dream images for greatest understanding.

Indoors

Dreams that take place inside a house or building are reflecting different areas of awareness inside the self (in your inner world or inner reality). Indoors denotes certain mental states of consciousness, such as ideas, opinions, thoughts and attitudes. Be aware of what type of room you are in — is it a familiar place? If not, it may be telling you about an aspect of self you are *not* familiar with. What state or condition is the room in? This will help pinpoint your mental state. For example, if the room is dishevelled, it may be pointing to your scattered state of mind. Note colours and textures in the room, as this adds further clues as to which aspect of self is being revealed (see the *Colours* and *Chakras* sections for further clarification). Be aware of how you feel in this dream room and if you are comfortable or not. See also the *Buildings and Rooms* section of this dictionary.

Island

May suggest being surrounded or inundated by your feelings (which are symbolized by the water). Calm waters denote peaceful and calm feelings, whereas rough waters denote uncomfortable or stirred-up feelings. Do you feel as though you are an island unto yourself and all alone? Island may suggest you require some rest, relaxation or some down time. Could say you feel isolated and apart from the mainstream.

Jungle

Represents a place of fecundity, productivity and wild growth. May be a place of the unknown or untamed aspect of self. May imply feeling caught in a jungle, or in a place of too much activity, restlessness or inner conflict. May be pun on the saying, "it's a jungle out there."

Junk Yard

Implies an area that feels cluttered, old or outmoded, or one that has outlived its usefulness. May be aspects of self you have discarded, thrown out or otherwise rejected. May be parts of self you describe as garbage, trash or stuff. May suggest unwanted things, situations or relationships. The representation all depends on what you consider to be junk in your life.

Lake

Most water dreams are associated with your current emotional state of being. Note the condition of your lake water and if it's wavy or calm, clear or murky to help you understand your current feelings. Waves indicate upheaval and how upsetting the situation is; calm waters often indicate a sense of inner peace or fulfillment. Note the dream feelings and how it feels to be by the lake. If you are familiar with this lake it may denote familiar emotional states, whereas unknown waters may reflect an unfamiliar place (emotion) within your inner reality. See the *Water* section of this dictionary for more insight.

Lawn

Represents the earth upon which you stand, and may also symbolize your materialism. Do you feel the need to keep up appearances by presenting a perfect image to your neighbours? Your lawn is an outward expression of your self and the seed thoughts you have planted. Note how well the dream lawn is cared for, or if it is full of weeds. May represent your connection to Mother Earth and solid ground. If the colour is vibrant green, it suggests health, healing and growth.

Light

Dreams that take place in the light suggest you have some knowledge or insight, or that you can see the situation clearly. May say you feel enlightened or intuitive, or that you are aware of a particular situation. Suggests you have the clarity you need to move forward in your life. May say you are in the Light of God or on your spiritual path to

enlightenment. See the discussion on daylight vs. darkness at the beginning of this section.

Marsh

Suggests you are not on solid ground, or that you feel bogged down or swamped with overwhelming feelings or emotions. Since marshes are watery, this is especially likely to represent your current emotional state of being. Marshes can also be about the unknown or your feelings of being mired. If you think of marshes as a healthy part of the ecosystem and where growth happens, then this reflects your inner state of health/ growth and fecundity.

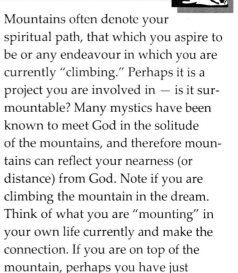

Mountain

Mountains often denote your spiritual path, that which you aspire to be or any endeavour in which you are currently "climbing." Perhaps it is a project you are involved in — is it surmountable? Many mystics have been known to meet God in the solitude of the mountains, and therefore mountains can reflect your nearness (or distance) from God. Note if you are climbing the mountain in the dream. Think of what you are "mounting" in your own life currently and make the connection. If you are on top of the mountain, perhaps you have just attained some high ideal, a higher state of consciousness or reached a goal. How far can you see from your dream mountain? Could suggest a challenging or arduous situation if the mountain climbing is tough. May represent peace, nature or relaxation, depending on the dream feelings.

Neighbourhood

If this is a familiar neighbourhood it may be pointing out a part of your self that you are already familiar with, or a part of self that you live in frequently. (We all have chosen mental states (marbles) that we occupy more frequently than others. For example, you may be driven by your ambition, whereas someone else may be driven by their procrastination marble more often). If the neighbourhood is one from your past, it may denote a past belief, attitude or state of mind that you are still frequenting, clinging to or using. Note if you are comfortable in this neighbourhood. Perhaps it is pointing to a situation or issue that is right beside you (neighbour).

Outdoors

Often outdoor dreams that take place in nature denote a spiritual connection or sense of freedom. If the background setting is one of peace and quiet, it may reflect an inner state of peace and quiet. Scenes from nature often reflect your nearness to your God or spiritual activity (such as climbing a mountain). Note the characteristics of the background — does your dream take place in a darkened alley where you are frightened? This type of background likely indicates a hidden fear or a situation in which you feel trapped. Outdoors can also signify external situations rather than internal ones (inner reality), and knowing yourself well will help you determine whether your outdoor dream symbolizes an internal or an external aspect of your current life. Use the outdoor background clues to help pinpoint which area of your life is being reflected.

Park

Often parks are peaceful places that reflect your inner state of peace. May represent a spiritual dream or relaxed state of mind. Could suggest playfulness or the need to rest or play. May be a pun on the need to park your butt or slow down. Note what feelings you experience in the park to help you pinpoint what part of your life it is trying to represent.

Parking Lot

Being parked in a lot denotes that you are not moving in your life or that you are parked at a standstill. Perhaps there are certain issues on which you feel parked. Could suggest you are at an impasse, stalemate or standoff. Perhaps this represents the need to take a rest from some activity or even from old patterns of behaviour. If your dream feelings are negative or of frustration, this indicates that you feel stuck; if they are positive, this suggests a well-earned pause.

Plateau

Usually represents that you have reached a plateau in some endeavour, relationship, issue or project. Can you move forward at this time? Perhaps you need to rest or "level out" something currently happening in your life. Or you may be reaching a higher state of consciousness. How far can you see from your plateau? This may help you see how far along you are in a current waking-hour situation.

Quicksand

Represents feeling sucked in or sucked under without control or choice. Definitely not feeling like you are on solid ground or that you have a good footing. Suggests you may be bogged down or feeling swamped and overwhelmed. Implies you have no support, no place to make a stand and/or nothing to hold you up.

Railway Tracks

Usually associated with "tracks of our mind" or "train of thought." Can be one-track thinking, getting sidetracked, being on the right track or on the wrong track. This suggests your mind may be set, rigid, unmoving or on a prescribed course. Are you unwavering? Is your thinking limited, boxed in or unoriginal? May also indicate that it is hard for you not to think in a particular way or pattern. Means you are on a thought path of least resistance — the path that comes easily to you (be it positive or negative). One-way thinking or black and white thinking are also denoted here. May imply harsh inner rules that you think by — a prescribed way of thinking that is not necessarily original. Train tracks may also symbolize old patterns, behaviours and beliefs you are still "riding."

Rainbow

Often denotes a spiritual dream or connection to God. May indicate God has heard your prayers or a promise of a new beginning. May reflect that something you found hard has come to an end. May symbolize blessings or a sign of better times to come. If rainbows have a special meaning to you, that's what the dream rainbow reflects. Because rainbows contain all the colours of the chakras, a rainbow may symbolize your chakra system.

River – See Water section of this dictionary

Seasons

Each season reflects a different phase or need in your life. Spring brings a freshness to current projects and issues. It's time to water the seeds that have been planted in your mind; time to cultivate, develop and enhance some project, relationship or endeavour. Summer denotes a fullness of life, fecundity, growth and productivity. Are you in full blossom with some project, relationship or endeavour? Do you need to bring something to ripeness? Fall/autumn is a time of fruition, harvest and culmination. Is your fall scene a pun on the word "fall"? Do you feel in decline or diminished in some respect? A wintry background may reflect a need to hibernate, rest or relax. Inner work can be dealt with in the wintry months, so this may reflect the need to go within and be silent (meditation).

Skating Rink

Because ice is frozen water, it often denotes frozen emotional states you are currently experiencing. This can be any emotion you deem bad, wrong or useless.

Often ice is associated with fears or worries, but skating can be a freeing and exhilarating experience. So look to the feelings in the dream to help you understand if you are running on fear or experiencing something liberating in your life. Could be a pun on "skating on thin ice" or feeling that you are not on solid ground (because you can fall easily on ice).

Sky

Associated with the mental plane and thoughts. A clear blue sky may suggest that your mind and thinking are clear, rational or free from worry. A cloudy sky could suggest a clouded mind, clouded vision, impaired judgement, or worrisome thoughts. May also represent heaven or heavenly thinking, the cosmos, the universe or your connection to the Divine. May be a pun on "the sky's the limit" and denote freedom, choice and unlimited potential.

Snow

Snow is comprised of frozen water, and therefore it reflects your emotional state. Frozen emotions are usually ones of fear, anxiety, dread, or any other emotion that you dislike or judge as being bad or wrong. Snow can also be fun and playful, so note your dream feelings to help you understand if this dream is trying to address an emotion or suggesting you are relaxed and at play in some current situation.

Spring – *See Seasons*

Summer – *See Seasons*

Sunny Day

Suggests you have insight and the ability to see a situation with clarity. May represent sunny feelings, hope or lightheartedness. May imply carefree attitudes, playfulness or optimistic outlook. May reflect that you feel free from burdens, and full of choice and/or control.

Swamp

Do you feel swamped or overloaded by some situation, workload or emotion? This symbol suggests an overwhelm, crisis or impending deluge of feelings. Perhaps you are in an emotional bog or feel bogged down. Are you in over your head, up-ended or consumed?

Swimming Pool

Because water is a refection of emotions, so too will the swimming pool reflect your emotional state. Since swimming pools are usually calm and clear, this reflects peaceful and/or tranquil emotional states. Pools further reflect your spiritual life or con-

nection to your God. Are you sinking or swimming in your dream pool? Are things (emotions, relationships, situations, business deals, issues) murky or clear to you presently? The extent to which you are immersed in the water represents how involved you are in your own spiritual life. Pay attention also to whether the feelings you have in the dream are positive or negative. For example, cheerful or optimistic feelings suggest that you feel certain about or have clarity about the way you are moving through life right now. Negative feelings suggest you are unclear about or feel insecure about what you are currently undertaking. See the *Water* section of this dictionary for greater clarity.

Valley

A wide open valley may indicate your sense of being out in the open. (Is this a positive or negative feeling for you?) Valleys connect you to nature and God, and thus reflect your spiritual pathways. Is your dream valley vast (representing vast ideas) or a low spot (representing lower ideals or low thinking)? Do you feel enriched or diminished in your valley? This reflects how you feel in your waking hours. Is your dream valley full of fecundity and growth or barren and uncultivated? Once again, this reflects your inner state of mind or being.

Water – *See Water section of this dictionary*

Winter – *See Seasons*

Woods – *See Forest*

Zoo

Represents your internalized animal nature or instincts. May symbolize a kind of prison, confinement or caged feelings. For greater insight, note what animals are in the zoo and see the *Animals* section of this dictionary.

Birds

In general, birds represent flying and freedom. Because they soar close to the heavens, they also denote spiritual forces and your ability to go with the flow and/or to surrender. Look at the events and feelings in your current life to see if you are soaring, taking flight, or expressing yourself in a joyful way. Because birds sing, note the ways in which you have been using your voice — have you been singing songs of praise or sorrow, talking your truth or barely chirping? Perhaps you need to sing your own song or drum out a new beat (like a woodpecker). Birds may also represent harmony, flexibility and light-heartedness. Because birds are in the air, they may symbolize the flow of the mind, your thought processes and thinking.

It is important to note whether your dream bird is caged or flying free. Caged birds can represent your lack of feeling free or your feelings of restriction. Do you feel caged, imprisoned or otherwise limited, controlled or confined? Birds that are in flight or soaring high may indicate you have gained a higher, better or new perspective on something going on in your life. Could suggest you are soaring toward or have achieved some goal or dream. Note the feelings associated with the flight to see if this is a positive insight or a negative viewpoint you are taking.

Because birds come in many sizes, shapes and varieties, note what your thoughts are about the specific type of bird and then try to relate it to yourself. List three characteristics about your specific dream bird to help you understand what parts of yourself are being mirrored. For example, if you dream of an eagle and your three descriptive words about eagle traits are powerful, dynamic and wild, your dream mirrors your power and dynamism (possibly untamed).

See the specific bird type for further information.

Remember: These symbolic meanings are just suggestions. If these suggested meanings do not resonate with you, ring a bell, give you an "ah-ha" moment or otherwise feel right, search through your own experience or beliefs about the symbol to find what makes sense for you.

Blackbird

Red-winged blackbirds represent new surprises and a new understanding of the forces of nature. Since blackbirds like to nest near water, there is likely a strong emotional component connected to this symbol. See Black and Red in the *Colours* section of this dictionary for further clarification.

Blue Jay

Because jays are associated with being bold, noisy, assertive and powerful, they may mirror these traits within you or be a sign that you need to be more assertive or bold in some endeavour. They are also related to discipline, responsibility, dedication and resourcefulness and may indicate the need to use your power wisely or not allow others to dominate you. Have you been acting boldly or assertively? Do you require more discipline or resourcefulness? May also represent the colour blue. See Blue in the *Colours* section.

Budgie

Most often associated with a caged bird or pet, the budgie may represent that you feel caged, unable to express yourself, or lacking freedom in some other way. Do you feel restricted or limited in any way at present? Could be a pet peeve or pet project if the dream bird is an actual pet. Could represent trained or disciplined aspects of self. May represent something you cherish, adore or nurture, depending on feelings about the dream budgie.

Canary

Most noted for their singing voices, a dream canary may imply the need to express yourself more vocally or that you are squawking too much. Often these birds are caged, so ask yourself if you feel confined, limited or restricted in any way. Canary often indicates a need to sing your song or praises in some way. Canaries are so sensitive that they used to be used in coal mines to detect gases. Canary may be telling you about your own sensitivities and how they may be heightened at this time. Because they are most often associated with the colour yellow, you may wish to read about this in the *Colours* section of the dictionary for further insight.

Cardinal

Associated with the colour red and therefore with vitality, passion or even anger. Often indicates a time of renewed life, endurance or stamina, and an opportunity to recognize your self-importance. Female cardinals may reflect a need to assert your feminine qualities. May be a pun on religious cardinals or men of authority and power. Note your own thoughts and beliefs regarding cardinals of a religious nature. See also Feminine in the *People* section and Red in the *Colours* section for further clarification.

Chicken

A domesticated bird, the chicken often represents fertility, "egg laying" or hatching new ideas. This flightless bird may mirror your challenges at taking off, or represent how you feel limited or restricted in some way. Chickens may be considered pets by some and therefore may represent your pet peeves or pet projects. Chickens are also a source of food and nutrition and therefore may be an indication from your body to eat more of this. May be a pun on something being foul in your life or that you feel you have fouled up in some way.

Crow

Associated with magic, mystery and intelligence. Crows are the sentinels or watchdogs of the forest. Do you feel there is some situation you need to safeguard? May be a reminder to watch for the mystery and magic in everyday life. May represent something that is annoying or disturbing to some. Note if you are "cawing" in an appropriate manner — if you aren't, a crow may suggest the need to use your voice (and assertiveness) in new and bolder ways. See also Black in the *Colours* section for further clarification.

Dove

Associated with peace, maternity and harmony. May also indicate lovebirds or an intimate relationship. Note if you require more peace in your inner or outer world, or if you have just experienced some calm composure. See also Feminine in the *People* section.

Duck

Associated with water and therefore emotions or spiritual life. Often a pun on sitting duck or ducking an issue. Do you feel as though you are in a vulnerable position? Or are you avoiding something? May indicate a need to pay attention to your emotions or to learn how to move through the waters in your life.

Eagle

Represents the ability to soar high and your sense of freedom (or not feeling free). Because of the great height at which they fly, eagles are often considered a sign of spirituality or closeness to God. But may also denote superiority, loftiness or supremacy. Eagles may also represent illumination of spirit, healing, creation and inspiration. Symbol for the United States of America. Eagles teach about balancing your high ideals with your earthly reality. Bald eagles represent feminine energies and golden eagles represent masculine energies. Have you got your head in the clouds or do you need a greater perspective on a situation? Have you been feeling dominated by or superior to others? Perhaps you desire freedom from a situation or need to soar above something. The height of a soaring bird is a sign that you may have gained a new, higher or better perspective on something.

Goose

Often associated with fairy tales, a goose may be calling you to play, imagine or prepare for new adventures. May also stir up childhood memories and can reflect the quest you have been on since childhood. Since geese mate for life, it may reflect your belief in having one special life partner. Because geese fly in formation and encourage the whole group's movement with their honking, this bird may be mirroring your need to "honk" within a group setting (speak your truth) or to keep with group behaviour and/or guidelines. May also be a pun on "your goose is cooked" or suggest you are waiting for the goose to lay a golden egg.

Hawk

Often seen as messengers, bearers of great vision and power. These raptors may be a sign of an answer to a prayer or be reflecting your inner powers. They have keen eyesight and may mirror your clear seeing of a situation or your lucidity. Because hawks are often harassed and attacked by smaller birds, this may imply you have felt attacked by others or have been the target of harassment. May represent your ability to soar to new heights, achieve your goals or see from a new perspective. Hawks can awaken your vision and inspire you to follow your life's purpose. May be a pun on "to hawk your wares," dispense or sell something.

Hummingbird

Represents joy and the nectar of life. These tiny birds can fly in any direction (including backwards) and hover. This suggests great manoeuvrability on your part and flexibility in the directions you choose. In fact, they cannot walk, which may reflect your need to either keep moving or that you have been keeping too fast a pace. May suggest you need more joy and sweetness in your life, or that you are full of joy at the moment. Are you getting enough sweetness, joy, rewards or fulfillment in your life?

Ostrich

Well known for burying their heads in the sand, these large birds may be implying just that. Have you been trying to hide from a situation, issue or relationship? Do you wish something would just go away so you wouldn't have to deal with it? Ostriches can run fast, are aggressive and live in hot, dry regions. They cannot fly, which may imply you feel imprisoned, confined or restricted in some way. May suggest you don't feel free or don't have the ability to "take flight." Conversely, because they are flightless, ostriches are associated with being grounded or fully present.

Owl

Known for its silent wisdom, vision of the night and magic, this bird reflects your inner wise knowing, the feminine, the moon and the night. It is the bird of magic, prophecy and darkness. "Owl medicine" is associated with clairvoyance and astral projection. May represent new vision coming to you and the awakening of your sixth sense. Because they regurgitate, it may imply that you need to eliminate or let go of something. Perhaps you already have and it indicates success. Owls may also represent your courage, playfulness or fearlessness.

Parrot

Known for their ability to mimic, this may reflect your copycat behaviour or imply that you have been imitating something. You may have been repeating what you've heard, or parrot may suggest unoriginal thinking or acting. Parrots are also known for their colourful feathers and may imply that you are displaying colourful emotions or behaviour.

Peacock

Because of its showy, colourful feathers, peacocks are most often associated with vanity and pride. Have you been showing off, bragging or strutting your stuff lately? Peacocks are protective and powerful birds, so they may represent your wise vision or watchfulness. They can be a reminder to laugh at life and they are also an ancient symbol of death and resurrection.

Pelican

Associated with the water and therefore the feminine, the unconscious and your emotional life. Although pelicans' pouches are used for scooping fish (not storing them), it may reflect a need within you to store or horde something. Pelicans are well known for their unselfishness and may be mirroring this trait in you. They are a symbol of renewed buoyancy and suggest you have the ability to stay afloat despite heavy burdens. Pelican can teach you how to rise above life's troubles. See also

Feminine in the *People* section of this dictionary.

Penguin

Because of its colour, this bird may suggest your thinking has been all black or all white, or that you currently think in an all or nothing perspective. Its unique waddling pace may suggest you are either plodding along or moving at your own pace. Because they do not fly, it may suggest you feel limited or restricted in some ways. Their home is in the water, so they may speak of your emotions, feelings and spiritual life. At a deeper level, penguins are reflective of lucid dreaming and astral projection (out of body experiences). May say that you are going to be doing more dreaming, especially lucid dreaming.

Phoenix

Mythic bird known for its ability to resurrect out of the ashes of the old. Has something recently crumbled in your life? If so, the phoenix may be a sign that something new will now be gained or created. Perhaps some old patterns of belief, habits or relationships are ready to die so that something new can take their place. If this is the case, surrender and let phoenix bring the hope of a new tomorrow and new beginnings.

Pigeon

Known as city-dwelling birds, this may reflect your ability to cope, blend in or adapt to challenging situations. Pigeons have historically been used for their homing sense and thus reflect your own need for home, security and settling down. May reflect your ability to find your way home when feeling lost and remind you of the importance of family. Realize that if you find pigeons to be annoying, this may be a sign that there is some small annoyance presently in your life.

Raven

Similar to crows, ravens represent magic, shapeshifting and the act of creation. There is a lot of mysticism associated with this bird and this may be considered the messenger of Great Spirit. Raven can help motivate you toward action, shapeshift, and/or disguise or camouflage yourself in different ways. Have you been "cawing" out your truth, or do you need to speak in a more assertive or bold way? Expect magic to occur when raven appears. See also Crow in this section.

Robin

Known as the first sign of spring, robins can reflect new growth within yourself or around you. Expect new growth to occur and be aware of new territories opening up when robin shows up in your dreams. Their singing voice may imply the need for improved communication or suggest you need to be more vocal or sing your own praises. The red breast may be significant, therefore read more about Red in the *Colours* section of this dictionary.

Rooster

May be telling you it's the start of a brand new day with its crowing. Roosters are associated with sexuality, watchfulness and resurrection. They may imply the need for more vigilance in your life or suggest you have been overly cautious or watchful. May reflect a need for you to be more direct, eccentric or colourful. It is a sign of enthusiasm and humour in the Chinese astrological calendar, and may represent someone born in the year of the rooster.

Seagull

Associated with water, and thus reflects your emotional life, the feminine and the unconscious realms of creation. Often seen as nuisances or annoyances, these birds have learned to thrive among people and may mirror your instinctual traits of survival and ability to adapt. They are well known for their raucous voices and may suggest the need for improved communication

skills or mirror your great ability to give voice to your feelings and thoughts. Seagulls reflect the need for more responsible behaviour on your part or your need for lessons in more proper behaviour.

Swan

Known for its grace, beauty and power, this bird may reflect these qualities in you. Because they are also known for turning from the ugly duckling into creatures of great beauty, this may reflect your powerful ability to transform some aspect or part of your self. Its long neck places emphasis on the throat chakra and communication. Perhaps you need to speak your truth or awaken to your own inner beauty. Swan teaches you how, and brings the energy of grace and blessings into your life. See Fifth Chakra in the *Chakras* section of dictionary.

Turkey

Known in North America as food to eat during family gatherings and cultural events, turkey may represent a group meeting or group consciousness. Do you partake in eating turkey during holiday celebrations? If so note if there is something you are celebrating at present; the turkey represents the rewards of this situation. Turkeys are also about shared blessings and harvest, and are a symbol of all the blessings the Earth contains. Do you recognize the blessings in your life? How well are you currently using them?

Turkey Vulture

Ancient symbol for death, rebirth and new vision. Although homely in appearance, this raptor has the ability to soar high and implies that you may be flying to new heights in some endeavour, or in the achievement of a goal. Vultures can soar with little effort, which implies you may not have to expend much energy to achieve your goals at this time. These birds keep the environment in balance and may speak of your need for balance or suggest you

are making strides in your ability to be balanced. Turkey vultures display confidence, dignity and patience.

Vulture – *See Turkey Vulture*

Woodpecker

Associated with rhythm and discrimination, this bird may be suggesting you should try to find your own rhythm or that you have already found it, depending on dream feelings and content. It may stimulate new rhythms coming into your life and suggest that you learn to discriminate more closely. It indicates that it is now safe to follow your own rhythm or patterns and to march to the beat of your own drummer.

Body

All diseases, illnesses, injuries and anything else pertaining to the physical body and its condition can be seen as a disturbance or disruption of energy at a deeper level of your being. Before anything can manifest in your physical body, it is first energetically weakened in your subtle bodies. Disease starts in the spiritual body — the energy field surrounding your body — and makes its way down to the physical level. Disease does not start in the physical body.

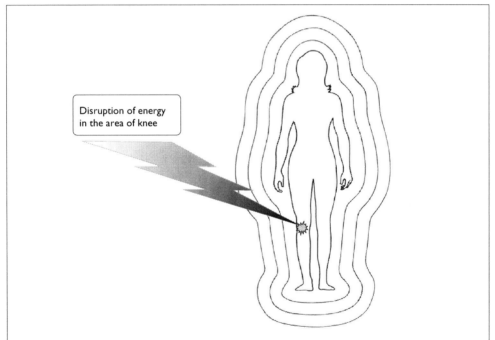

Each layer of the human energy (auric) field contains symbolic information and meaning. When a disruption of the field takes place and causes illness or injury (in this example, to the knee), you must address each layer of information in your auric field before complete healing can take place in your physical body.

If the injury is to your knee, the symbolic issues to be addressed may be related to pride, your ability to bend and be flexible (physically, mentally and emotionally), how well you are standing on your own two feet, and/or whether you are moving forward in your life.

Figure 9. The symbolism of a knee injury (in a dream or in your waking life)

221

There is much to learn about your physical body in the dream time, and if you wish to improve your physical condition or health, it is imperative that you understand that what is affecting your physical body has already affected your other bodies (that is, your auric field). Before any disease or malady becomes manifest in the physical body, it alters the vibration of the emotional, mental and spiritual bodies. Therefore, in order to heal the physical body you must take into account the other levels of your being and heal them as well. All this information, about each level and its health, is reflected in every dream.

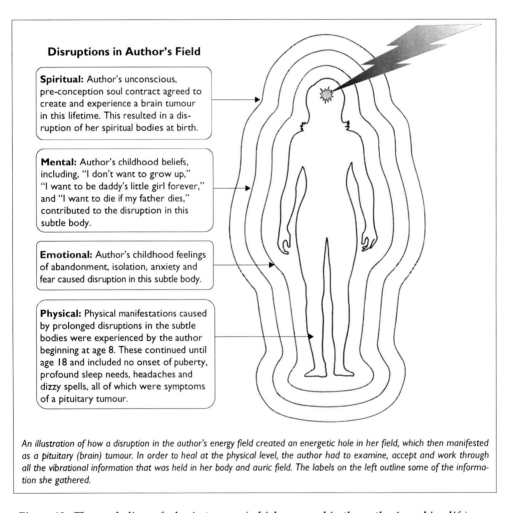

Disruptions in Author's Field

Spiritual: Author's unconscious, pre-conception soul contract agreed to create and experience a brain tumour in this lifetime. This resulted in a disruption of her spiritual bodies at birth.

Mental: Author's childhood beliefs, including, "I don't want to grow up," "I want to be daddy's little girl forever," and "I want to die if my father dies," contributed to the disruption in this subtle body.

Emotional: Author's childhood feelings of abandonment, isolation, anxiety and fear caused disruption in this subtle body.

Physical: Physical manifestations caused by prolonged disruptions in the subtle bodies were experienced by the author beginning at age 8. These continued until age 18 and included no onset of puberty, profound sleep needs, headaches and dizzy spells, all of which were symptoms of a pituitary tumour.

An illustration of how a disruption in the author's energy field created an energetic hole in her field, which then manifested as a pituitary (brain) tumour. In order to heal at the physical level, the author had to examine, accept and work through all the vibrational information that was held in her body and auric field. The labels on the left outline some of the information she gathered.

Figure 10. The symbolism of a brain tumour (which occurred in the author's waking life)

Getting to know your own symbolism is a great way to get to know your physical body and attend to its needs. The physical body and its parts have symbolic meaning, and it's especially helpful to understand the symbolism if you have an illness or problem. Using symbolism, you can uncover a deeper layer of meaning behind the illness or problem and help that area to heal more quickly. Insight and awareness into an illness/issue always begins the path to healing.

Illness begins when the energy field is depleted in a particular area. It affects the spiritual level of your self first, followed by the mental energy field surrounding your body, and then your emotional energy field. Finally, you will feel the effects of this energy depletion in the physical body. In order to heal the physical body completely, you must also heal the other levels/layers of self — the emotional, mental and spiritual parts of self. Healing these parts gets the energy flowing back to the physical body in a healthy way.

If you are asking a question of your dreams about your body, be aware that your answer will come symbolically through imagery in the dream. Homes and cars are common examples of images that may contain your body symbolism. However, any symbol can represent a body part or aspect of the body's functioning. For example, the womb can be symbolized by a garage or any container or receptacle, including a bag, basket or bin.

Other body symbolism may be found in colours in your dreams. They may indicate the need to eat food in that colour group, such as dreams containing the colour green or persons named Mr. or Mrs. Green. Balloons can be about the lungs and electricity about your nervous system. Often car parts represent body parts and as such point out where problems are occurring. Plumbing may refer to your own digestive processes, whereas running out of gas in your car could indicate a lack of energy or fuel in your body. Perhaps you will dream of drain cleaner, which indicates a need to cleanse your own pipe system (bowels).

If you ask a question about your physical body, be aware of such things as liquids representing bodily fluids like urine, blood, or even saliva. If you ask about your muscles, this may be represented by meat (most North American meat product is animal muscle). Your spine may be represented by something like a cane, stick or even a serpent and feature curvatures or disk problems. Watch for puns on words like a disk in your back being represented by a compact disk or floppy disk. Your bones may come up as dog bones or a pun on a name, like *Star Trek*'s character Bones (the doctor's nickname). Other puns may be showing you things that need to be cleansed by portraying dishwashers, washing machines, showers and bathtubs.

This will all be revealed depending on your dream question.

A pun on your physical joints may be represented by dream items such as marijuana or pot, or anything that attaches and pivots like a ratchet tool. Your heart could be represented by anything that pumps or needs to be pumped, such as pumping up a ball or tire, and even pump-up shoes. Feet could be represented on a ruler or in "de-feat."

Remember: *These symbolic meanings are just suggestions. If these suggested meanings do not resonate with you, ring a bell, give you an "ah-ha" moment or otherwise feel right, search through your own experience or beliefs about the symbol to find what makes sense for you.*

Adrenal Gland

Represents your total belief about your support systems (adrenal glands support your body's whole system by producing adrenaline). These glands represent your enthusiasm and energy, or lack of it. They are connected to the energy of the third chakra and therefore to your intellect and lower will power (the will power of your ego or personality as opposed to your higher will power, which comes from your higher self or spirit self). Having the ability to "fight or take flight" is part of adrenal glands' message.

Ankle

Represents agility and flexibility in your ability to stand for something. Also reflects support you received or now receive from your parents (right side indicates father and left mother). Are you supported by your feminine or masculine energies, or is there a lack of support in this area? A weak and/or broken ankle indicates a possible disconnection in the area of support.

Anus

Can represent that you are anal retentive or rigid and fixed in your thinking and actions. May also represent great humour in this puckered and pinched part of self. Have you been rigid in your thinking, judgements or opinions? Have you been defensive or close-minded?

Arm

Represents the ability to hold something, nurture, reach out, create, carry and, in general, the ability to do or take action. What is the condition, position or health of the arms revealing to you? Arms crossed at the chest may indicate you are taking a stance about

224

something or refusing to let in new ideas. Perhaps your arms are raised in celebration, excitement or victory. Are you armed with new ideas or thoughts? Are you bearing arms in your life or bearing gifts? Are you opening your arms to something, or are you closed and defensive (crossed arms)? Your left arm may represent your ability to reach out as a woman and the right arm represents how you reach out as a man.

Back

Represents support, alignments, kundalini flow, responsibility, dependability and strength. Backs are about support, so ask yourself if you are supporting yourself in a healthy manner or supporting too much weight (responsibility)? Have you got your back up about something? Are you going backwards? Have you felt stabbed in the back (betrayed)? Are you backing out a situation? Perhaps you are turning your back on something, lacking backbone (courage) or are bent out of shape. How does the back in your dream appear to you? This reflects something in your current life in regards to the above.

Birthmark

In general, birthmarks can be seen as a past-life carry-over indicating an old wound, mark or brand. This may be where you had an injury in a past life. Birthmarks are soul marks that draw attention (wanted or unwanted) to whatever body part the birthmark is on. Birthmarks also reflect something unique about you and to you. See the applicable entry in this section of the dictionary for further information.

Bladder

Related to feelings and being "pissed off" or irritated with someone or something. Are you able to express your emotions easily or are they being held in? Note comfort of bladder in dream for further clues as to what feeling are trying to be represented.

Blood

Signifies your vital life force, energy and the colour red. Because blood flows, this could indicate whether you are in the flow or not. Are you feeling vital and alive, or are you bleeding and losing your vitality? Sometimes bleeding indicates you are "pouring out" too much of yourself into a project, attitude, relationship or situation. Perhaps you are donating blood and giving away your vitality. If you are bleeding or losing blood, note what part of the body the blood loss is from for greater clarity. Blood loss of any kind is a warning that you are losing energy and vitality at some level. See also Red in the *Colours* section of the dictionary.

Bone

Bones represent your framework, structure and support. Bones are also about strength, endurance and toughness. Perhaps you have a bone to pick with someone or with your self? How well are you "holding up" with something, or do you feel as though you are falling apart? Noting which part of the body the bone is in will help you determine a more in-depth meaning. For example, a backbone may be about support and how much weight you are carrying. Or perhaps you lack support within the community, your family or peers in regards to some endeavour of yours. Backbones in dreams may be bringing you a message of courage or the need for courage in regards to some area of your life. A leg bone could also be about support, but it represents your ability to support yourself and your own weight. Leg bones could also be about the ability to move forward or stand on your own two feet. Chest bones and ribs often relate to emotional support and issues of freedom. For further understanding, see also the dictionary entry for the specific area of the body.

Bowel Movement

Represents the need, or ability, to let go and release old habits, thoughts, beliefs or attitudes that no longer serve you well. Are you straining to let go of something or is there something preventing you from releasing? May say you have just relieved yourself of a heavy burden, absolved yourself of something or discarded an outgrown way of being. A large bowel movement can say you have a lot to unload or get rid of. Note what slang words you use for your bowel movements and see how they factors in. See also Excrement, Constipation and Diarrhea in this section.

Brain

Represents your thoughts, thinking, mentality or cognition. Can also represent your wit, intelligence and your understanding. Left-brain and right-brain thinking refer to masculine and feminine energies (or intellectual vs. intuitive functions, respectively). May be a pun on "it's a no-brainer" or referring to someone as brainy. Perhaps you need to think about something or use your brain.

Breast

Represents the feminine aspects of self, such as the ability to nurture, comfort, give or sustain. May also be a sexual symbol depending on what aspect you view it as in the dream. Are the breasts bare? What is it you have to "bear" in your life at this time? Breasts are also associated with the chest or area of feelings. How well do you nurture yourself? Perhaps you need to care more for yourself.

Buttock

Represents the "rear view" or perhaps the end of something. Perhaps you are feeling like the butt of a joke. Also could be getting to the bottom of things. Or, are you "behind" in some endeavour? Is your butt bare and exposed and all can see your most private issues or feelings? Could be a pun on the word "but," meaning "however" or "except." Notice if you say or think the word "but" frequently.

Constipation

Represents holding on to old material, ideas, thoughts or beliefs that are no longer needed. Often related to feelings, emotions, and not wanting to deal with indigestible experiences. Over-thinking on a subject can also lead to constipation (linked to the second and third chakras). Do you find something to be a "waste" of time in your life? See also Bowel Movement and Excrement in this section.

Diarrhea

Represents letting go of something too quickly without processing it, or that whatever is occurring is indigestible

to you — perhaps something unpleasant that you would prefer not to experience or deal with. Often connected to emotions (second chakra) issues. Are you feeling overwhelmed by emotions and feelings? This often results in loose bowel movements and feelings of loss of control over emotions. See also Bowel Movement and Excrement in this section.

Ear

Ears represent what you are hearing or not hearing in your life. What is the condition of the ears in the dream and how does it feel? If they are plugged there is an inability to hear or listen to someone else's point of view or to hear your own inner voice/wisdom. Ears are about receptivity and your ability to take in. Are you turning a deaf ear on a situation? Perhaps it is indicating an actual ear problem on the physical level. Irritated ears are also about poor hearing or an unwillingness to listen, heed or obey what you hear. Have you been receiving an earful lately?

Excrement

Often represents whatever you consider to be the crap or shit in your life. This may be any endeavour that you find you don't want to deal with. Often associated with anger and first chakra issues. Excrement often represents old ideas, habits, beliefs, thoughts or situa-

227

tions in your life. In some cultures, seeing excrement means that money will be coming into your life. Excrement in a dream may be what you refer to as your stuff, your shit or your crap. May be a pun on "that's a load of crap" or saying you won't take any more crap. Could be a pun on not giving a shit, that's a load of shit or any other colourful phrase you may use in the realm of your thinking and expressions. See also Bowel Movement, Constipation and Diarrhea in this section.

Eye

Eyes are full of puns on the word "I" (ego, self) and things to do with seeing. How are the eyes functioning in the dream? Are you or someone else blind, cross-eyed or wearing glasses? These are indicators of how well or not well you are seeing or perceiving things, situations or other people in your life. Perhaps it is another person's point of view that you can't see. Have you a blind spot and are not seeing a situation clearly? Eyes are often considered the windows of the soul and imply insight, perception and understanding. Perhaps there is something you do not wish to see, or maybe you are wearing rose-coloured glasses. Nearsightedness reflects the willingness to see yourself but not the big picture. Farsightedness reflects that

you don't want to see yourself but that you will at, or from, a distance. Astigmatism denotes that you want to see things your own way. If your eyes are strained, perhaps you are straining to see something ahead of you or in your future. Eyes are what you can and cannot see spiritually, emotionally, literally or symbolically. Note if your thinking or speaking includes a lot of "I" phrases to help you make the connection between your dream eyes and your self.

Face

Your face is often your identity. What do you currently identify with? This may be your senses, self-esteem, appearance or self-recognition. What do you need to face in your life? Who or what can you face or not face? What challenges are before you, and are you willing to face them? Could be a face-off of sorts or facing facts. Is someone or some issue in your face? Perhaps there is the factor of losing face or the need for courage to face the facts. Perhaps you need to face your fears. Whatever your face is emphasizing may help you zero in on what the dream is trying to inform you of.

Feces – See Excrement

Fibroid

Fibroids are associated with the uterus (womb) and therefore reflect your creativity and issues of feminine orientation or how you view and use your feminine energy. Fibroids build walls between your heart (your truth) and your self. They reflect the sense that you don't feel safe and that your creativity is blocked. If you suffer from fibroids, it is often representative of an issue with your male partner, your own masculine energy or any dead-end situation/issue in your life. If it is a dead-end relationship, it is as if your womb is saying, "You can have your way with me, but you are not getting to the truth or centre of me." This is often a sign of sexual unhappiness and could be a sign that your inner self is rejecting the masculine identification in your life. See also Womb for greater insight.

Finger

Extension of your creativity and may have to do with the work you do or create. Fingers often show you how you are creatively expressing yourself, or not.

▸ *Forefinger:* Is often an accusatory or authoritative stand you or someone takes. Has someone you know recently shaken their finger in your face? This is often an unwelcome gesture and can heighten your defences. Forefingers can also point you in the right direction or be pointing something out. Note to whom, what or where your dream finger is pointing for greater understanding of dream's message.

▸ *Little finger:* May be seen as a sign of snobbery or vulnerability.

▸ *Middle finger:* Usually used as an insulting signal or used when angered and/or annoyed by another. Can often indicate your stubbornness or opinionatedness.

▸ *Ring finger:* May indicate a heart or soul connection (like a wedding ring), or may be telling you of a latent talent that has gone unnoticed until now.

▸ *Thumb*: Could be about an approving (thumbs up) or disapproving (thumbs down) type of attitude. Are you implying an all thumbs type of situation? Or are you thumbing your nose at others? Thumbing a ride like a hitchhiker could imply you are riding on someone else's coattails.

Foot

Because feet are the part of the body upon which we stand, they represent your foundation, your understanding and the beliefs upon which you stand. What do you stand for? Do you need to take a stand? What principles, values and morals do you stand upon? Do you currently have cold feet about something going on in your life? Are your feet bare or covered in the dream — are you covering up your beliefs or exposing them? Feet can represent your grandparents or parents and issues concerning support from these people or lack of it. Left foot is typically symbolic of your mother or your own feminine support systems, and the right representative of the father and masculine support issues. Feet are often about gratitude and the ability to say to yourself "now I heal." Perhaps you feel like a heel or a fool. Could be a pun on the word "soul" and your spiritual essence. Arch of the foot represents support or lack of it. Are the arches fallen or high? Could be indicating fallen belief systems or lack of support of belief systems. Are you able to support your own weight (responsibilities)? See also Heel, if applicable.

Gallbladder

Represents your ability to digest or process something going on in your life. What is galling you or irritating and annoying you? Have you recently heard yourself say that you need to cut through the fat, cut to the chase or get to the point about something? What issues may need to be clarified or cleared up? Could it be your perception about the gall of someone (the nerve of him)?

Hair

If the hair is on the head, it represents your thoughts. More specifically, it represents the outward manifestation of your thinking — that which you show to others. The colour, length and style tells you more about your thinking. For example, red hair may be telling you about recent angry thinking or thoughts of passion. See different colours in the *Colours* section of this dictionary for further clarification. Curly hair may show that your ideas have not yet been straightened out, that there are kinks in your plans or that your thinking is twisted. Long hair may show you are over-analyzing or are "long on your thoughts" about something. A hair cut may indicate the need to cut short your thoughts on a subject, or that you have nicely trimmed up your excessive thinking on something. What is your opinion on the hairstyle being shown? Is it a hairstyle from a particular era, or an old style you once wore? These are all clues to help you pinpoint what area of thought you are exhibiting or revealing at this time. May be a pun on "heir" or "hare."

Hand

Hands are about creativity and how you "handle" things. Are you being creative in your life or do you need to create more? What is at hand? Are you handling things lovingly, demandingly or roughly? Have you a grasp (handle) on things or are they out of your grasp or out of reach? Do you avoid hand outs or hand-me-downs? Do you feel you are handling things well in your current life? Could you use a hand out or helping hand and perhaps are not accepting it? Check in with the feelings to help further clarify how the hands are reflecting your current situation. Note how you used your hand in the dream and if a particular finger was emphasized. This could indicate the strength or weakness or your current creation or endeavour. Other things to look for with respect to hands include

▸ *Open hands:* a gesture of acquiescence or surrender

▸ *Closed hand or fist:* May indicate fight, aggressiveness or willpower

▸ *Left hand:* Representative of your receptivity, openness and what you need to create

▸ *Right hand:* Symbolizes what you need to do (what action you need to take), or it could be about high-handedness or about being right. See also Finger, if applicable.

Head

Symbolizes the mind, intellect, thinking, thoughts, ideas and logic. If you bump your head or get a concussion, ask yourself if you are "getting ahead" of yourself in some area. Or, do you need to knock some sense into yourself? A bowed head can be a sign of humbleness, acknowledgement or gratitude. The top of the head may indicate the crown chakra or spiritual connection and higher thinking. Are you currently heading up something or do you need to head something off at the pass or before it begins? Are you using your head, creating headaches for someone or being big headed? If the head is enlarged, it could say you are thinking big or that your ego is over-inflated. If the head is very small, it suggests small thinking, or that you lack self-confidence or self-esteem.

Heart

Represents feelings and the ability to feel for others. Also symbolic of love, compassion, passion and change. The heart is the bridge between the masculine energies (in the lower chakras) and the feminine energies (in the upper chakras). It is also the place of judgement and can reflect a judgemental attitude, depending on dream feelings. Has your heart been open to others or closed? Heart problems are often a sign of a closed heart, the inability to feel your feelings or the inability to change. What is at the heart of the matter for you? Are you experiencing a broken heart? May also be about your hopes, desires and concerns. Does your heart ache for something or someone? In both waking life and in dreams, heart problems such as arteriolosclerosis and high blood pressure often indicate a limited, restricted or rigid personality — especially regarding thinking, judgements, attitudes, opinions and beliefs. Dreaming of heart problems could also be a literal warning about your heart function, so take appropriate steps to investigate this possibility.

Heel

May represent your ability to heal (get well) or heel (as in asking a dog to heel or stay). Heel may be your vulnerable point (Achilles heel) or weak spot. Do you feel as though you currently have a weak spot that others are seeing in you? Or, are you in need of a little healing (rest and recuperation)? Perhaps you feel like a heel (idiot or fool) in something your recently did. See Foot for greater understanding.

Hip

Represents your ability to be mobile, flexible and free. Right hip often represents how you relate to men and as a man, or could represent your male partner. Left hip often represents how you relate to women and as a woman, or could represent your female partner.

Hips are also symbolic of your ability to learn to be flexible within a partnership. Are you shooting from the hip with your partner (talking straight or truthfully) or just winging it? May be a pun on being hip or in the groove of things.

Immune System

Symbolic of your ability to be or feel secure. Also represents your ability to recognize when you are being violated, threatened, attacked, used, abused or inhibited by either yourself or another. This could be about an attitude or relationship that dishonours your true self or the truth of your heart. Are you able to neutralize and/or eliminate what threatens your truth or your sense of what is right for you?

Infection

Symbolic of issues that need to be looked at in your life and what you need to fight. What or who is invading your space, or who is attacking you? This is likely an issue of boundaries. What do you invite into your space? Are your attitudes, thoughts and beliefs poisoning you? Could indicate a time for forgiveness of self or others, and definitely indicates it is time to do something about the problem.

Intestine

Represents your ability to absorb or take in something in your life. Are you digesting a new concept, idea or recent experience? Would it behoove you to take some time to digest what is currently going on in your life? Your emotional chakra sits right over the intestines, making them the focus of disease and discomfort when your emotions are overwhelming or when you are numb to your feelings. See also Bowel Movement, Constipation and Diarrhea.

Kidney

Represents your ability to discern and discriminate. Also your wisdom, judgement and wit. Also about the filtering of your ideas, thoughts and emotions. Seat of childhood emotions and feelings. Can you listen to your heart and discern/filter the truth? Lots of puns on "kid" apply to the kidney, such as "who are you kidding" or "you must be kidding." Relates to childhood perceptions or attitudes. Kidneys may represent your ability or inability to process something, and are often associated with childhood (kid) attitudes.

Knee

Symbolic of your flexibility — the way in which you move or carry yourself in life. Do you bend easily, or are you too prideful to bow to another? Also about your siblings and peers (right knee is symbolic of your brothers and male friends; left knee represents sisters and female friends). Can also be about competition and applying what you know to be true. May be a pun on "nee" (born or maiden name). Your knee may also denote betrayal of self or others. Knee problems may indicate that you are no longer able to compete, and therefore a sense of humility is associated with the knees. Arrogance and the ability to kneel or prostrate yourself is also associated with the knee. Have you been eating humble pie lately, or has your pride been broken or bruised?

Leg

Represents your ability to stand, walk and support yourself. Are you walking forward or standing still in the dream (and therefore in your current life)? Do you feel as though you have a leg to stand on? Are your dream legs strong and supportive or weak and unsupportive? Perhaps you need a leg-up or help from an outside source. Your legs represent your strength, power and brawn. See also Ankle, Knee and Thigh for further consideration.

Lip

Relates to the words you speak. Are you paying lip service or being lippy? Perhaps you are holding a stiff upper lip. Note if the dream lips are pouting, frowning or smiling for further understanding of the feelings related to the lip posture.

Liver

Liver represents your ability to digest your environment, your life and negativity. Liver is often a pun on how alive you experience yourself as. Much digestion of thought processes is indicated, as well as your ability or lack of ability to take in and process your thoughts, attitudes and beliefs. How much negativity are you exposed to, and how well do you deal with it? This is an indicator of your liver's overall function. The liver is considered the seat of anger in Chinese and Eastern medicine. Therefore your dream liver may be telling you about how much anger you have stored within you, and may speak of the need to release pent-up feelings.

Lung

Lungs are symbolic of your ability to expand, to feel restriction and to feel freedom. Because the lungs are in your chest, they can also be about emotions of the heart or feelings. How are your lungs shown in the dream or what is the waking-time condition of the lungs in question? How freely the lungs are able to function will help indicate

whether the waking-time issue is about restriction or freedom. For example, suffering from asthma or experiencing a restricted ability to breathe in your waking-time or in your dream reflects feelings of not being able to express something in a way that is true to your heart — part of your being feels, and is being, repressed.

Are you seeking more freedom, autonomy or liberation about something in your everyday life? Do you need to expand your horizons or develop your emotional expression?

Lungs could also represent an over-inflated view of self, depending on how the lungs are portrayed in the dream.

Lymphatic System – *See Spleen*

Mouth

Associated with the words you speak, your expression and eating. Your mouth represents what you will and will not say and indicates whether you need to build up the courage to say something. Are you speaking out, taking in food for thought or being closed mouthed about something? Have you been swallowing your words, swallowing your pride or giving voice to an opinion? How do your words affect you and those around you? Are you using cutting words or nurturing and sustaining words? Have you been mouthing off or been a mouth piece? Perhaps you've been just plain mouthy, cheeky and loud. The feelings in the dream will help indicate if your words have been carefully chosen and healthy, or poorly chosen and not serving you well. See also Teeth and Lip.

Muscle

Muscles are an indication of strength — strength of will, ego, and strength of the mind or lack of it. Wasted muscles indicate a waste of energy going into the mind and not to the spirit. Pumped up or muscle bound may represent an overinflated ego, depending on feelings. They may represent healthy pride if you have recently felt strong in accomplishing a task. Note which body part is highlighted with muscles for further indication of area of strength. For example, arm muscles denote the ability to do and/or act and may indicate a recent follow-through on an idea or thought. In contrast, a leg muscle attests to your ability to stand up for yourself or stand on your own two feet. Could be a pun on muscling someone or forcing them to do it your way.

Neck

Represents issues of will and the expression of your will. Also symbolic of pride and whether you will swallow your pride or other people's ideas. Your neck is home to your voice box and therefore it is about voicing your opinions, singing, laughing, talking or not speaking up for yourself. It could also imply misuse of your words or speech. A stiff neck may be telling you that you are inflexible about a certain subject or issue, which will hinder your perceptions a great deal. Are you sticking your neck out or is something in your life a pain in the neck? Your neck is also the home of your thyroid gland, which is about regulation or control issues. Is anything choking you up or making you gag? Communication, healthy or not, is being highlighted when you dream of your neck.

Nerve

Represents your paths of communication or how you talk to yourself. We all carry on an inner dialogue with ourselves. How aware are you of yours? How effectively do you communicate with yourself? Do you have constant internal struggles, or do you feel at peace with yourself? Nerves are often portrayed as a home's inner wiring or electrical system. Any problems with the nervous system indicate a problem with how you are communicating within yourself. This could be with the giving or receiving of messages inside your self. A breakdown of the nervous system (a nervous breakdown) will immobilize you and limit your ability to cope with everyday situations. How well is your wiring or electrical circuitry functioning? Do you have nerves of steel? Are you nervous or tentative about something currently going on in your life? Perhaps you need more nerve, backbone or courage. Could be a pun on "you've got a nerve."

Nose

Brings you messages about your "sense," intuition and instincts, because your nose links directly to your third eye (the sixth chakra). Your nose is an organ of discernment and therefore represents your perception, realization, understanding, wisdom and consciousness ("your nose knows"). Could be you are nosy and inquisitive or a pun on "no" or "no-no." Are you sticking your nose where it doesn't belong or not using your common sense? Perhaps your nose is out of joint (taking someone the wrong way or seeing things differently than someone else). Since you smell with your nose, it may be telling you something about smells. Have you recently exclaimed, "it stinks" or "something smells rotten" or "it's a smelly (offensive) situation"? Examine what these bad smells mean in your life. Perhaps something smells funny or doesn't smell right? Perhaps you are

not able to make "sense" of something, or you feel some current situation or relationship is nonsense. Are you not discriminating as you should or not recognizing something?

Ovaries

Symbolic of your ability to "release" new ideas, thoughts or projects into tangible creative manifestation. Creativity, fertility and femininity are all aspects of the ovaries. What do you want to give life to or beget at this time? The act of creation or the need to create something in your life is linked to ovary symbolism.

Overweight/Obese

May imply a burden or something that weights heavily on you. Could be the heaviness of your thoughts or emotions. Have you been under a lot of stress, strain or pressure lately? Being overweight in a dream implies that you have over-done something. Could be a pun on "wait" or the need to be patient or to delay something. Could be about the weight of a situation — its enormity or gravity.

Pancreas

Represents your ability to take in the sweetness of life and process it. What are you processing or trying to purify in your life? How do you perceive the sweetness in your life? Is there any sweetness in your life? Diabetes and other pancreatic disorders can develop in your waking life when you perceive there is no more sweetness or worthwhile meaning left in life. The pancreas is also related to digestion and may say you need to digest, comprehend or realize something, usually in a new way.

Penis

Represents masculine sexuality or drive. May indicate your sex drive or your ability to stand erect and express your creativity. Is the penis fully functioning or is there an impairment? Are you currently able to express all your creative ideas and plant new seeds in your life? May suggest your hormones are raging or that you are horny. May imply the need for action-oriented behaviour or suggest that you are all fired up about something or someone. If the penis is fully functioning, it implies you are ready for action.

Pituitary Gland

Represents control or mastery. Also symbolizes peace and your sense of things. Are you experiencing peace of mind? Since the pituitary links to the third eye (sixth chakra) and also the pineal gland (which links to the crown

chakra), this is also about intuition, "vision" and spiritual connection.

Rectum

Represents things that you store or hold onto. Are you holding onto beliefs, thoughts or ideas that no longer serve you? Are you storing them in an unhealthy way? Could be a pun on you acting like an ass or someone you know is being an ass. May also imply someone is being anal retentive or rigid in their thinking, behaviour or actions. See also Anus and Buttock.

Scar

Symbolizes a wound that has healed or is healing. Old scars represent old wounds, whereas fresh scars denote a more recent pain, hurt or injury. A dream scar may indicate that you have not let go of old wounds or that you have not forgiven yourself or another. You may feel you are stained, marked or defiled in some way. Note what part of the body the scar is over and read the applicable entry in this section for greater understanding.

Skin

Your skin is the protective outer layer of your body and therefore represents your ability to protect yourself. Skin is also about sensitivity, touch, feelings and vulnerability. How does the skin appear in the dream? Is it wrinkled or damaged in any way? Wrinkles can be a sign of wisdom or fear of old age. Damaged skin can indicate an inability to protect yourself from another person's words or actions. Are you thin skinned or thick skinned? Do you take in what other people say, or do their words bounce off you? Skin diseases are a reflection of a deeper issue that is showing itself on the surface to get your attention. Your skin is also an organ of elimination and may indicate how well you are letting things go or releasing that which no longer serves you well. This dream symbol may be about the "bare facts" or an underlying or hidden issue.

Sore Throat

A sore throat may be informing you that you have things you'd rather not say and/or speak up about, or perhaps you are swallowing your pride, ideas or feelings.

Spleen

Represents filtering. The spleen is a lymphatic tissue and filters blood, so it represents your ability to process your current life's challenges, issues, and any "life" situation. It refers to your ability to take something in, digest it and make use of it — or cause disease with it. "It" can be anything from another person, a relationship, an idea or any part of

yourself you may or may not be accepting well. What are you currently processing or not processing in your everyday life?

Stomach

Represents your ability to stomach something or take it in and digest a situation. Usually represents the area of thought (food for thought), including ideas, attitudes and beliefs. Have you recently said to yourself, "I can't stomach this"? Do you hunger for something or has something whet your appetite? Perhaps you are currently enduring a situation you'd rather not have to. Your stomach is in your third chakra area and issues to do with this chakra often present with stomach problems. See Third Chakra in *Chakras* section of the dictionary for greater understanding.

Teeth

Represent the words you speak and how they affect you and those around you. What is the health of your dream teeth? Teeth falling out may be telling you that you have lost control over your words and/or are speaking without thinking. Words are powerful tools of creation and can cause harm or healing, depending on how you choose to use them. If you are not choosing your words carefully then you may have loose teeth, false teeth, crooked teeth or rotting teeth. Are you speaking your truth or are you being critical of others? A tooth being pulled out indicates a need to eliminate certain words or speaking habits. Do you constantly open your mouth and speak without thinking of the consequences? Have you been baring your teeth or expressing angry words? May be a pun on the expression, "it's like pulling teeth," which indicates that information is being forced out of someone, or even that you are forcing information out of your self.

Thigh

Represents your strength, power of moving forward (or backward) and the power to do or stand for something. Also represents goals and expectations (often expectations of self). Thicker thighs may represent heavy expectations put upon your self. See Leg for greater understanding.

Throat – See Neck

Thyroid

Organ responsible for body metabolism or the ability to process at all levels of your being. Underactive thyroid or sluggish thyroid is the inability to process some aspect of your life. This could be the inability to assimilate anything in life from a relationship to an attitude or a belief about yourself. Overactive

thyroids also indicate the inability to process something in your life, but in this case it is because the situation may be over-analyzed or simply too overwhelming to take in and try to assimilate. See also Neck.

Toe

Represents your balancing ability and the power to support yourself. Can also symbolize grandparents (who may represent your own wisdom) and support or lack of it. Is your wise self strengthening you? Do you need to toe the line in regards to an issue? Perhaps you need to keep on your toes. May be a pun on "tow," as in towing a car or being pulled in a certain direction. Toes point us in the direction we are headed. How are your toes in the dream — what direction are they pointing you in?

Tongue

Sticking out your tongue implies you may be rejecting someone's (or your own) words, behaviour or actions. Also suggests you may be challenging the status quo or being resistant, defiant or rebellious See also Mouth.

Underweight

May symbolize that you think "too little" of yourself or that some part of you feels undernourished or even unsupported. May suggest you feel starved for affection or praise from self. Feeling drawn, wasted or haggard could also be represented by a dream of being underweight.

Urine

Represents release or letting go. Because urine is liquid, it usually represents an emotional release. Note whether it is a pleasant sensation to urinate, indicating whether or not you are pleased by the surrender. Urine is our emotions in a fluid state and often we desire to let go but can't find a suitable setting within ourselves to "let it go." This may be portrayed in a dream by not being able to find a place to urinate. See Urinating in the *Actions* section.

Vagina

May represent a private part of self — a part only known by yourself — or may denote some part of your self that you wish to keep private. If exposed, you may feel uncovered or bare in a current issue or situation. Also reflects the feminine, the sacred and the mysterious parts of self. Also represents feminine sexuality. How do you personally feel about this body part?

The dream feelings will help pinpoint what your dream vagina means.

Womb

Represents your creativity, your ability to create, and your ability to give birth. Also symbolic of your feminine energy centre, which is sometimes called the hara, one-point, second chakra or Dante en. The womb is an area of great power and receptivity. Are you open and receptive to new ideas, opinions, beliefs or relationships at this time? This is the place where seed ideas are born and created. It also represents fertility and your ability to create something new in your life. Could literally mean you are pregnant, depending on feelings, but often means you have a new idea, thought or project you'd like to create and give.

Wrist

Represents your ability to be flexible. Since it is part of the arm, this may have to do with flexibility when doing something or when you are taking action. Are you being flexible in your current endeavours in life? Note whether it is your right wrist (denoting masculine energies) or the left (denoting feminine energies).

Buildings and Rooms

Buildings can represent the various states of your consciousness or awareness (i.e., private, social, decaying or under construction/repair). Each type of building represents a different state of consciousness. Buildings also reflect your general belief system and the associations you make. Buildings, especially houses or homes, often symbolize the whole of your being — all four levels of your self (mental, physical, emotional and spiritual). Individual rooms then speak of a particular area of awareness. For example, the kitchen is often associated with the mental level because that is where we prepare, take in and digest our food for thought. Being inside a building symbolizes that you are currently in that particular state of consciousness. For example, dreaming of being in a hurried business setting may denote your current state of hurriedness. Consider what your own associations are to this type of building, and if it is a place in which you work or are employed. A dream building may be a pun on the need to build something in your life, whether it is a relationship, a new belief about something, or a new attitude.

Try to use your dream house as a tool for gaining greater insight into your self. Note which rooms you encounter most frequently in your dreams and which rooms you rarely or never find yourself in. For example, perhaps you always find yourself in a cluttered or windowless room. Try to observe patterns in your "selected" dream rooms and homes, which will help you to recognize patterns of behaviour within yourself. Your dream images of settings, buildings and rooms are mirrors of your inner reality, which is, in turn, mirrored in your external (everyday) world.

This section of the dictionary is divided into the following subsections:

- ▸ types of buildings
- ▸ parts of buildings
- ▸ rooms
- ▸ condition of the building

Remember: These symbolic meanings are just suggestions. If these suggested meanings do not resonate with you, ring a bell, give you an "ah-ha" moment or otherwise feel right, search through your own experience or beliefs about the symbol to find what makes sense for you.

Types of Buildings

Airport

Airports are usually busy areas with lots of hustle and bustle, so they may reflect a part of you that feels harried, hurried or generally busy. Perhaps your space is feeling crowded or your mind is cluttered with thoughts. Airports may indicate that a new idea or venture is about to take off or has taken off. Have you departed from your norm lately? Are you about to depart or embark on something new? Has something new arrived or is something impending? Perhaps you have high ideals or lofty thinking. What plane of consciousness are you experiencing? Are you having flights of fancy? Or do airports remind you of your fear of flying? See Airplane in the *Vehicles, Their Parts and Actions* section.

Apartment

Apartments are often temporary living spaces and can therefore symbolize a temporary state of mind or thinking. Have you recently taken a new stance or are you trying out a new perception? There are often a lot of comings and goings in apartment buildings — could this represent a lot of ideas or thinking lately? If the apartment in your dream is where you actually live, it represents your current way of thinking or state of awareness.

Arena

Often associated with group behaviour or situations, this type of building may represent your going along with the crowd or group consciousness. If a sport is being played, note whether you are participating (playing an active role in a group) or sitting on the sidelines (being a spectator of your own life). Note dream feelings and whether you feel buoyed by this place or diminished by the group thinking.

Art Gallery – See Museum

Asylum – See Mental Institution

Bank

Indicates your "financial" state of being. Money represents your current energy levels and therefore the bank reflects your energetic currency. What are your current resources? Perhaps your bank is a reflection of financial worries or burdens you currently carry. It may represent your wealth on any level of your being (mental, physical, emotional or spiritual). Banks symbolize financial or material things, savings, and the investment of time and money.

242

Are you feeling prosperous or do you feel as though you need to rob a bank? May be a pun on "you can bank on it" or rely on it. May reflect your self-worth (or lack of it) or may say you feel bankrupt on some level, depending on the dream content and feelings. See Money in the *Miscellaneous* section of this dictionary for greater detail.

Bar

What do you associate with bars? Is a bar a meeting place where good times are experienced or a place to drown your sorrows? Is it a place of clarity or addiction? How have your moods been lately? Could the bar represent an escape from your reality or a happy place to let loose and express yourself? Note the dream feelings to help you understand whether this is a healthy, positive place to be or an indication that a negative situation is brewing.

Barn

Often houses animals and may represent your animal instincts or desires. Perhaps you grew up on a farm and associate barns with part of your past or a part of your state of awareness. Barns can be vast spaces of your consciousness and indicate a need for relaxation or a greater need for expanded thinking. What are your personal experiences of barns and how

did it feel to be in one or see one in your dream? If you are an urbanite, it may suggest this is a foreign or unfamiliar aspect of your self.

Bookstore

Often indicates a state of mind having to do with the intellect or gathering of knowledge. Have you been "in your head" a lot lately or thinking a great deal? This is a place of information gathering and may be associated with bookish thinking. What do you associate with books? See Library for greater understanding.

Castle

Seen as fortresses and may represent a rigid or confined way of thinking. Perhaps you see it as a place of safety or security, depending on how you feel about the castle. What century is associated with this castle and does this offer a clue about how up to date your thinking is? Perhaps you see castles as denoting wealth, prosperity and abundance in your life. It may represent your hopes and dreams or that you are building castles in the sky. Because castles are usually large, it could be about thinking big or symbolize that you have many parts of self to explore and grow into. Could your castle represent a magical place within your self, a dungeon or a mansion?

243

Church

What are your personal associations with the church in your dream? Are churches a place of worship and connection with your God, or are they places of constriction and rigidity? A church in your dream could represent the sum total of your spiritual beliefs or morals. Is this a comfortable state of mind or symbolic of dogma or out-dated thinking? Do you find comfort and solace in a church or does it represent disturbing past associations? Consider how you feel in the dream church; this will help you understand how the church reflects your current life.

Courthouse

Courthouses are where judgements are made and sentences passed. Are you feeling judged in your life currently or have you been judging others? Are there legal matters on your plate or are you reaping what you have sown? Do you feel that some situation is "justified" or that an injustice has occurred? Do you feel pressured to conform to some sort of law or dogma? Is there something or someone you are "courting," romancing or pursuing? Are you courting disaster? Do you feel the scales of justice are working in your favour ? Note how you feel in the court setting to help you

understand what the courthouse currently represents to you.

Dentist's Office

Often seen as a place of discomfort and pain, to dream of being in a dentist's office may indicate that you are in a place of discomfort within some current situation, relationship or place within your self. Do you literally need any dental work? Otherwise, ask yourself what feelings are conjured up for you in the dream dental office and see if you can relate them to any emotions you are feeling in your everyday waking hours. Because dentists work on your teeth and mouth, they represent the words you have been speaking. Ask yourself if you have recently been running off at the mouth, gossiping or otherwise being careless with the words you have been speaking . Perhaps you need to pay more attention to what you say. See Teeth in the *Body* section of this dictionary for greater understanding.

Doctor's Office

Usually associated with the health of the physical, emotional, mental or spiritual body. Do you feel that you need some attention, nurturing or guidance on any level of your being? Ask yourself how you feel when you are in a doctor's office to help you understand if this denotes a stressful or helpful environment. If the doctor's office in your dream reminds you of a stressful place, note what may be currently stressful in your life. If the dream office feels supportive and helpful, look to see if there is currently any need of this in your life. If a doctor's office reminds you of authority figures, ask yourself what current situations, events or relationships you can relate to conditions of control, dominance or authority. However a visit to the doctor's office makes you feel will likely point out the current feelings you are having about some area of your life. May imply that you feel as though you are waiting for something or that you have to wait something out. Could imply you need to repair, restore or heal something. May be a pun on "I'm sick and tired," "I'm sick to death" or "I'm sick of hearing that." Remember to ask yourself if you are literally in need of a doctor's advice or other professional advice in some area of your life.

Factory

Often denotes repetitive work or labour. This may symbolize repetitive thinking and doing in your everyday life, perhaps the same old thing or run-of-the-mill ideas. Symbolic of predictable or unchanging patterns, beliefs and thoughts.

Garage

If your dream garage is attached to a house, it can be an extension of your awareness, consciousness or beliefs. This can be a place where storage happens and may indicate some stored-up or pent-up emotions or frustrations. A garage is a car's resting place and may suggest you need a rest. A cluttered garage may be trying to tell you to unclutter your life. Could represent a body part that is a container, such as the stomach or womb.

Gas Station

A place to refuel your car and therefore represents the need to refuel yourself. Do you need to tank up or increase your energy levels? Have you been feeling run down? At gas stations you also get repairs done and check under the hood. Do you need some maintenance, help or support on some level? If this has a service station aspect to it, it may be indicating that it's time for a physical check-up. What repairs are necessary in your life at this time?

Gym

Often denotes a place of activity and exercise. Do you feel like you've been on a treadmill or is your life rushing by at a hurried pace? Do you need to get in shape or work out some glitches in your life? What type of activity is happening in your dream gym? Perhaps you need more physical exercise or need to exercise some discipline or control in other areas of your life. May be a pun on a person named Jim who you know or are acquainted with.

Home

Usually implies the whole of you or represents you on all levels of your being (mind, body, emotions and spirit). If the home in your dream is where you currently live, it represents a current viewpoint or perspective you are taking on some matter. If it is a home you once lived in, it denotes the state of awareness or consciousness you held at that time in your life. For example, if you dream of your childhood home, it may represent childhood feelings or beliefs that you held at that time. This often tries to tell you that you are still using beliefs or feelings formed in childhood in your current life. These old patterns of thinking and expression are usually *not* serving you well anymore and need to be reconsidered. If it is a home you are not familiar with, it may imply a part of your self or level of your being that you are not familiar with, not comfortable with or just have been unaware of to this point. Unfamiliar homes are trying to tell you about some

aspect of your self that you have not paid any attention to. Therefore, take note of the condition of the home and how you feel about it for greater insight. The individual rooms of the house express which particular level of awareness is being represented. See the discussion on Rooms further on in this section for greater understanding.

Hospital

A place to heal, refresh, get better, restore, mend or recuperate. Perhaps you need to recover from a recent stressful event, situation or overwhelm of some kind. May represent current healing needs are being met or that you need to address a health issue. May suggest that a part of you feels sick, ill or unattended to. Note what is happening in your dream hospital and whether you are the patient or the doctor. Do doctors or nurses represent authoritarian figures to you? If so, how does this type of dominating personality factor in your current life? Perhaps you require more "patience" in a current situation or relationship. A hospital may be telling you that you require rest or restoration on some level. Does some part of you feel like it's dying or needs to die off (be let go of) in your life? Do you feel a sickness or illness on any level of your being? This dream may be a warning to seek professional advice. Hospitals can create fear in some and therefore be symbolic of some current fears you are holding.

Hotel

Because one usually uses hotels for short temporary periods, this represents a temporary state of mind, feeling or phase you are going through. If the hotel is bustling with activity, this may reflect your constantly active mind and the comings and goings of ideas. If you actually live in a hotel, it symbolizes your current state of mind, viewpoint or perspectives. You may associate hotels with work, leisure or vacation time. See also Motel.

Jail – See Prison

Library

Holds vast amounts of knowledge, information and ideas, and therefore is associated with the mind, intellect, and analytical thinking or thoughts. May depict a time in your life when you were full of knowledge, or may symbolize that you are full of knowledge at this time in your life. Conversely, dreaming of a library may symbolize that you require more insight and knowledge in a particular area of your life. If you may find libraries to be a type of sanctuary, a dream library

may reflect the need for some peace of mind, inner reflection or quiet time. Have you recently acquired new knowledge about something or need to investigate something more deeply?

Mall

May represent a busy or active time in your life — a hurried or harried pace — or the consciousness of the masses. Malls are where things are purchased and a lot of money (which represents energy) is exchanged. How are you "spending" your time and energy lately? Is there too much hustle and bustle or not enough? Malls are about materialistic things and may reflect your materialistic or greedy nature, the need for security or your physical being in some way.

Mental Institution

Symbolizes a psychological state of being or the mental realm in general. May represent a frayed mind or delicate mental state. Is your life feeling a little crazy or have you been saying, "I am going crazy"? Perhaps you need some support on the mental level or require the services of a counsellor or therapist. May be symbolic of "I'm losing my marbles" or "I'm going crazy." Asylums may feel similar to a jail or rigid institution and can therefore represent fixed thinking, limited thinking or feeling like you are a prisoner of your own mind/thoughts. See Prison in this section for further insight. See also Padded Wall, if applicable.

Mosque – *See Church*

Motel

Represents a temporary state of mind, feeling or phase you are going through. Note if the motel is seedy or run down. This will help you understand if a part of you feels run down or neglected in some way. May represent rest, vacation or travel to some people. See also Hotel.

Museum

May depict old feelings or ancient issues in your life, or a time when many thoughts and ideas are coming to the surface. What is "on display" in your life currently? Are old memories creeping to the surface for review? Museums are usually large places and may represent thinking big or the need to explore the vastness of your self. What part of the museum do you see in your dream and how does this fit into your current life?

Office

May be symbolic of a hurried pace, rigid rules, great satisfaction or a job well done. Is there something in your life that needs to be accomplished or addressed? What type of office is depicted and how does this factor into your current life? If it is your actual place of employment, how do the environment and the politics of this place affect you? Do you feel it is a place of joy or a prison? Often offices are where we plan, create or research, and where we are held accountable. May imply analytical thinking, logical thinking or the mental realm in general. What is happening in your dream office and how does that apply in your everyday life?

Prison

May denote that you are feeling trapped or imprisoned in a relationship, situation or within your own mind and/or feelings. Do you feel caged or ensnared in a particularly tough issue or belief? Is anything restricting or limiting your movement, thoughts or desires? Do you require or long for freedom? Do you feel boxed in or feel the need to break out of a situation? Prisons or jails impose tough rules and may denote your rigid beliefs, attitudes or ideas, or your limited ways of thinking. Have you been overly harsh on yourself, berating or beating on yourself — are you a prisoner of your own ways of relating to yourself?

Restaurant

Usually associated with food and therefore with the mind or food for thought. What have you been taking in mentally and digesting lately? Implies a place of new ideas or perhaps something that is indigestible or unpalatable to you. Restaurants represent a reprieve or social event to some and therefore a place of fulfillment and enjoyment. They can also be busy, noisy and harried atmospheres. Take note of the mood, surroundings and ambience of your dream restaurant to help you understand if it symbolizes a hurried part of your self or a contented one. A buffet may represent many ideas or opinions to choose from. Fast food may suggest you are not taking time to take in and digest something. What type of food is being served and is it appealing to you? Your dream may be suggesting you either avoid or include certain foods in your diet. Look to dream feelings to help you decide. Perhaps you crave some mental stimulation or need a new attitude. The type of restaurant and what is going on there will serve as clues about the meaning behind this symbol.

School

Usually denotes a place of learning or "life's schooling." Do schools represent a repressive, rigid place of rules to you, or a soothing and nurturing environment? The type of school in your dream will give a clue as to the meaning. A kindergarten setting indicates you are just learning something new, or have reverted to childlike thinking. A university speaks of higher education and therefore higher levels of thinking and thoughts. Have you been thinking big or dreaming big? What is your current level of learning or need for learning? Is growth or awareness required in a certain part of your life? Do you require more knowledge at this time to deal with some aspect of your life? What lessons do you need to learn? Or do you require more discipline in some area of your life?

Store

A place of transaction, sales and supplies. Are you lacking in something on any level (physical, emotional, mental or spiritual)? May suggest you are storing up or accumulating something. Perhaps you need to stock up, take stock or stockpile something. What kind of store is revealed in your dream? A clothing store may reflect the need to "dress up" a situation or be more aware of what actions or attitudes you put on, wear or show to the world. Trying on new clothes in the store may indicate that you are currently trying on new attitudes, beliefs or behaviours in your life. Perhaps you find yourself in a grocery store and in need of nourishment on some level of your being? The type of store will help pinpoint the area of consciousness being revealed.

Synagogue – *See Church*

Theatre

A place where action and drama occur. Note if you are being dramatic in the dream and perhaps overly dramatic in your own life? Or are you part of the audience and not participating in your own life? Have you been acting out or acting up? Perhaps you need more action in your life. Do you feel on stage, upstaged, or in need of expressing something? Note what performances are happening in your dream theatre (if any) and how it feels to be onstage, participating or acting. See Acting in *Action* section of this dictionary.

Parts of Buildings

Ceiling

Represents your mind or intellect. A dream ceiling indicates the health or functioning of your thoughts, thinking, beliefs, ideas and attitudes. Have you reached your limit, maximum or ceiling? Is your thinking leaking or intact these days? Are you having trouble moving beyond the limits you have set for yourself? Perhaps some creative thinking would benefit you. If the ceiling is leaking water, it suggests an overwhelm of mind and emotions.

Closet

Represents a part of your self that has been in storage, or a place within yourself where you store, reserve, accumulate or hide something. Have you recently felt the need to conceal some part of yourself or hide away from your reality? Perhaps you have put something into deep storage — an old memory, feeling or issue. Do you feel closed off or separated from anything in your life or from a part of your self?

Door

Can act as a barrier or open you up to new places, spaces, people and aspects of self. How is the dream door revealed — is it closed or open? Do you feel closed or open in your everyday life? The material the door is made of may offer clues as well. Is it made of solid gold and representing a golden opportunity? Or is it heavily armoured and representing a heavily protected part of your self? There is a well-known phrase that says, "when one door closes, another door opens." Does this expression fit your current life? Keep in mind that if the dream door is closed, it may be a beneficial closure; if the dream door is open, then new possibilities and opportunities may be around the corner. How does your dream door represent some part of your life, relationships or inner world? Does your door represent that you have an open mind or a closed mind? Does your door allow freedom or represent a no exit or no escape situation in your life? Is the door a front door denoting accessibility, or a back door denoting private or hidden parts? Perhaps there are many doors (many choices) in the dream or no doors (no chance, no opportunity, no way out). A revolving door could point to a situation in which you feel you are going in circles, or it could be a pun on an evolving situation. Storm doors denote the need for extra protection; a screen door may be telling you to be cautious or to defend yourself more.

Drawbridge

Castles and fortresses often have draw-bridges, which are used to keep people out. This symbolizes a need to be secluded or safe, or a need for protection. Could say you are being overly defensive or protective of something. Who or what do you feel you need to be distanced from? See also Bridge in the *Streets, Roads and Paths* section of this dictionary.

Fireplace

Since the fireplace is often the heart or centre of a room or home, a dream fireplace represents the heart or centre of your self — your inner reality or your relationship with God. If there is a fire burning, it may symbolize warmth, coziness, and a sense of belonging. If it is cold and barren, it may represent your feelings of loneliness or separation. Do you feel barren and empty, or without passion or fire? Has something or someone sparked your interest of late? Or do you have a burning desire to do something? See also Fire in the *Miscellaneous* section of this dictionary.

Floor

Often denotes the beliefs upon which you stand or your foundation. What type of floor is in your dream? Is it a solid foundation or shifting, broken boards? This will help you determine what type of support (stable or not) you are currently experiencing in your life. Floors can represent a stand you are making or the principles upon which you stand. A dream floor that is new could represent new beliefs or principles, whereas an old floor symbolizes old standards. A rotting or uneven floor represents a poor foundation or poor understanding of a situation. Wet floors imply an emotional component or overwhelm of feelings.

Foundation

Represents support, groundwork and basis. Is the foundation crumbling, suggesting your support systems are not working? Or is the foundation sturdy, suggesting you are holding up well? A cracked foundation may symbolize that you are in need of some repair. Do you receive adequate support from yourself and others? Or do you need better support structures in your life?

Hall

Halls and hallways often represent times of transition. They are the in-between or transitory stages in life. It may be a pun on a long haul or something that feels drawn out. Halls are about change and going from one state of being to another. May be a pun on "overhaul," or symbolize many changes or stages. Halls are connecting links and imply transition from one state of thinking or feeling to another.

Padded Wall

Suggestive of mental asylum rooms used for the protection and preservation of one's body and mind. Do you feel as though you are going crazy? Do you feel you need some safe place in which to unload the chaos of your mind? Perhaps you just need to soften the blows and protect yourself from real harm. Note the dream feelings and connect these feelings to your everyday waking hours for greater understanding.

Roof

Often denotes the mind or mental states. Note what type of roof and the condition it is in. Roofs offer protection and therefore represent your sense of protection, or lack of it, within your mind and consciousness. The condition of the roof depicts your mental state. A leaking roof may be telling you that your thoughts, attitudes and beliefs are out of alignment with your truth. Water on the roof indicates emotional overwhelm. Roofs in need of repair speak of the need to address stressful states of mind or states of overwhelm, and the need to resolve and solve conflict. In contrast, a new roof indicates the integration of a new belief, attitude or thought.

Wall

Can be either a sense of protection or a barrier. How does this dream wall feel? Does it provide a sense of safety or is it stopping you from achieving some goal? Are you currently experiencing any obstacles in your life or do you need to learn to boundary (i.e., set or create healthy limits around) something or someone? Walls can represent your limits or old, limited thinking patterns. Do you need to break down some old patterns or walls? Sometimes walls are needed to protect us from overwhelming fears and situations. Is it time to take down this wall and see

what is on the other side? Does your wall serve you well? Or is it an old, outgrown behaviour pattern trying to get your attention? See also Padded Wall, if applicable.

Window

Often symbolizes the "window of the soul" or your unique perception of the world. How do you currently view recent events in your life? Is the dream window clean and clear or is it dirty? This will help determine whether you are seeing the situation clearly or whether your viewpoint is clouded and unclear. Windows are also about insight, clarity and your outlook on life. Looking out a window may represent your approach, attitude and opinion on something. Can also indicate that you are needing a new outlook on life. Looking in a window indicates a need to look within or do some soul searching.

Rooms

In general, rooms symbolize states of consciousness, awareness or a particular level of your being (mental, physical, emotional or spiritual). Note the type of room and its condition. Are there windows or doors (indicating an accessible part of your self), or is the room closed off? Is the room comfortable or uncomfortable (symbolizing an acceptable or unacceptable part of your self)? Familiar or unfamiliar (a well-known or foreign aspect of self)? Note the colour and content to help discern what part of yourself is being represented by the room. See the individual entries for rooms for more clarity.

Attic

May symbolize lofty or elevated states of consciousness, or could indicate a "crowded mind." If the attic is used for storage, it could denote a place within your self that is hidden or secret. Because attics are high up within the house, they often represent higher levels of thinking or the mind (that is, thoughts that are conceived from the higher mind rather than from the intellect).

Basement

Symbolizes unconscious or subconscious states of mind (those parts of self that are below your everyday awareness). "All that is not realized" in the waking hours can be said to be unconscious. You still create your everyday reality with the unconscious parts of self, so be aware of what is going on in this dream basement to help you understand what you are manifesting in your everyday life. The lower levels of thinking and the mind are represented by basements. Lower levels of thinking are often generated by the intellect or ego parts of self, whereas higher thought is gathered from Source or the Universal Consciousness.

Bathroom

Represents a need to cleanse or release at some level of your being. May be an emotional release that is needed or the need to let go of old limiting beliefs, attitudes or other weighty concerns. Often an old pattern, behaviour or habit needs to be liberated in the bathroom setting. If you can't find a place to "go" in your dream, that may be telling you that you don't feel there is any acceptable way to release pent up feelings or old patterns. There may be an urgency to the need, which indicates the urgency of your present need to let go or cleanse a certain part of your self — which could be at the physical, emotional, mental or spiritual level. A blocked-up toilet indicates an emotional or mental blockage in your life; you have a great need to express yourself but are unable to do so at this time. Urine in a dream represents emotions and feelings, while feces represent old ideas, habits, beliefs, attitudes and patterns that need to be liberated. Bathrooms are also cleansing places — are you cleaning yourself in the dream? Do you feel the need to do a physical cleanse, or do you need to cleanse emotionally? Is the tub or shower draining well? This could indicate how well you are letting go or surrendering in your life.

Bedroom

Denotes an area of privacy or an issue that is private or that only you are aware of. Depending on whom you share the bedroom with, may indicate who else is privy to the private part of your self being revealed in the dream. Bedrooms can also represent your intimate parts of self or sexual parts of self. How is the bedroom being used in the dream? Are you making the bed and need to connect with the well-known phrase, "you make your own bed and therefore have to sleep in it" (i.e., you are responsible for the consequences of your actions)? Discerning what you use your bedroom for in your waking time the most will add helpful clues in understanding the symbolic meaning of the bedroom in your dream. Do you equate your bedroom with rest, relaxation and sleep, or with quarrelling with your mate? Do you need more rest, relaxation or sleep, or do you need to address a recent conflict with your mate? If your bedroom is a safe haven from the outside world, ask yourself whether you are afraid of having your space invaded or feel in need of some security.

Change Room

Denotes that you feel you are changing in some area of your life. Note the dream feelings and whether this is a comfortable and easy change or a difficult, uncomfortable situation. A change room in which you are trying on new clothing indicates you may be trying out a new way of being in the world, new feelings, a new belief or new attitudes. A change room related to sports may indicate your readiness to participate in some group endeavour or situation.

Classroom

Often related to places of learning, education or testing. Note the dream feelings and whether this setting is comfortable or stressful for you. Are you on a learning curve and enjoying the process, or do you feel you are being tested or under scrutiny (examination)? Perhaps this is a pleasant educative experience in your life or a burdensome one (depending on dream feelings). Do you feel there is something you need to learn or that life is like a school and you are here for lessons?

Dining Room

How the dream dining room is being used will help you understand its symbolic meaning. Most often the dining room represents a place of gathering to eat meals. So this may represent a place where you take in and digest something (mentally). Have you been pondering any new ideas or issues that need to be "digested"? Dining rooms can also represent social gatherings and sharing. Do you need group support or need to take in a group idea? Dining rooms are often places of discussion, sharing and evaluating ideas. Have a look at how your dream dining room is being used to help you discern what it is reflecting in your current life.

Kitchen

Because the kitchen deals with food, it is often equated with the mental realm or place of food for thought. This is where you prepare, take in and digest things mentally. Have you been "cooking up a storm" in the new ideas department? Are you formulating, analyzing or designing new beliefs or patterns of thinking? Are you mentally digesting, thinking over or absorbing something new? Could also represent disposal or letting go of old patterns of thinking or behaviour. Do you associate kitchens with being the heart of the home or centre of activity? This will help you understand if the dream is about your levels of mental activity or about whether you've taken something "to heart." Note what actions are being performed in your dream kitchen and the feelings associated with them for greater understanding.

Laundry Room

Associated with cleaning, cleansing or the need to let go. Are you in need of a physical cleanse or emotional clearing? Do you feel dirty, unclean or soiled? Perhaps you feel corrupt, defiled or tainted in some way. Maybe you need to clean up your act or wash away some problems. Indicates a time to get straightened up or organized, or to tidy yourself in some way.

Library

Represents a part of your self that is knowledgeable, in the act of learning or studying. May suggest you have great resources at hand or unlimited information available at this time. Can denote great potential, intellect and mental activity in general. May suggest you need to "brush up" on something or use your resources more wisely.

Living Room

May symbolize a busy central point of your home (self) or it may be a place you seldom frequent (an unknown part of self). Could be a place just for show and represent a false front. If your living room is used every day, a dream living room indicates a part of your self that you inhabit every day or are very familiar with. It could represent a familiar belief system or mental outlook that you occupy every day. For example, if you are perpetually conservative in your approach, this attitude could be the aspect of self you "live in" or dwell in on a daily basis.

Nursery

Inhabited by infants, this may represent infantile behaviours, attitude or feelings. Could represent a place of new ideas or growth, depending on the activity in the nursery and your feelings associated with it. May imply the need for nurturing, tender loving care or a safe place in which to grow and feed your self.

Operating Room

Since this is where surgery or repair is carried out, it suggests you are in need of some major attention or healing in some area of your life. Are you in crisis or in great need? Do you require support or health care? Are your basic needs being met or are you in need of

emotional life support? An operating room may also imply a process or a place where you implement action. How does this correspond with any actions you are currently undertaking? Could also be a pun on a part of you that is a "smooth operator."

Rest Room – *See Bathroom*

Storage Room – *See Closet*

Waiting Room

May imply the need to wait, rest or pause on your journey. Note the dream feelings to understand if this is a positive need to slow down or a negative implication that you are being impatient. Could also represent an expectation or anticipation. Have you been aspiring or envisioning something new and just waiting for it to expand and come to fruition? Are you in a hurry and need to relax your pace a bit? Could be a pun on "weight" and imply you are over-burdened by some weighty concern.

Condition of the Building

Decaying

A building in a state of deterioration or in need of repair indicates a need to tend to something in your own life quickly. It implies that something is

crumbling or falling apart in your life. Can you relate to this? Do you feel as though you are breaking down, run down or near collapse? Do you feel fragile and as if you could easily crumble? Are you in need of some fixing, mending or restoring? The amount of decay or disrepair of the building directly mirrors your inner state of need. Pay attention and get the overhaul or service your body, emotions, mind or spirit may need.

Demolishing

Represents that something is being destroyed, crushed or wrecked in your life. Not all destruction is negative. In order to make room for the new to come into your life, the old must first die or crumble. Is anything tumbling down or tearing apart in your life? Note how this feels to get a sense of whether this is a positive crumbling or a more serious collapse or decline. Perhaps you are obliterating old belief patterns or systems. Or it may be a pun on the "break up" of a relationship or tearing down of old walls. Note the type of building for greater understanding of which part of your self is being "torn down."

Large

May indicate an expanded state of consciousness or that your awareness is big enough to hold many ideas or concepts. Could say you are being broad minded, or expansive in your thinking, or have unlimited potential for growth.

New

Suggests that something new is starting to grow within you or around you. Perhaps it is a new idea, thought, belief, opinion or state of awareness. Perhaps you are building a new relationship or partnership, or allowing for the growth of a new mental or emotional state. Perhaps you have just started a new project, had an innovative idea or launched a new business.

Old

Could represent an old or possibly outdated way of being, thinking or doing. What shape is the building in and how do you feel about it? Perhaps old concepts, beliefs or ideas on the verge of collapse are being indicated. Are you repeating old habits or patterns of thinking, or using outmoded behaviours? Have you gone back to former ways of expressing your self or are you using early emotional models (i.e., using emotional patterns or expressions that you learned in childhood, probably from a parental role model)?

Small

A small house may indicate that you feel diminished in some way or that your role is minor in some situation. Could suggest a limited scope of a situation or narrow-mindedness. Perhaps your thinking has been small or you feel "less than" in some way. Note how you feel about the small building or house to help you understand if it represents an emotional "smallness" you feel or a need to step back and reassess your position or feelings on something. Sometimes "playing small" can serve you well temporarily or in certain situations. A miniature house or doll house may indicate an even more limited view of your self or of others and the roles they play in your life. A doll house may suggest you feel something is child's play or insignificant.

Under Construction or Renovation

May indicate you are in the process of building or manifesting something new in your life. Are you currently laying a new foundation in a relationship, career or other area of your life? Perhaps you need to update, remodel or reconstruct some aspect of your life. Is a new belief being assimilated or taking shape? What inner work have you been focussing on? Or have you accomplished something new? Have you made any improvements to yourself, been working on your self-development or remodelling?

Ceremonies, Events and Situations

Remember: *These symbolic meanings are just suggestions. If these suggested meanings do not resonate with you, ring a bell, give you an "ah-ha" moment or otherwise feel right, search through your own experience or beliefs about the symbol to find what makes sense for you.*

Anniversary

May reflect any event, situation or circumstance that happens annually or seasonally. The dream may be trying to symbolize a ritual, habit or recurring event in your life. Are the dream feelings pleasant or unpleasant? This will help you pinpoint if the dream anniversary reflects a pleasant or unpleasant situation currently happening in your life. Or is this a reminder of something from the past, either coming back to haunt you or as a celebration? An anniversary may reflect your relationship with a significant other or any person with whom you are intimate (personal). May reflect celebratory feelings or feelings of love, affection or union in general. Note the type of anniversary in the dream for greater insight. For example, a wedding anniversary could symbolize something you feel committed to or have loving feelings for, whereas the anniversary of a death represents a "death" (change or transformation) within or around you.

Announcement

Represents that you have recently declared, proclaimed or disclosed something. The feelings in the dream will help you understand if this has been a positive or negative event in your life. When you announce, you make something clear to everyone around you. What have you recently revealed, made public or released?

Ballet

May suggest you require more balance or need to be on your toes. Could say you have been moving with grace, poise, agility and harmony. May suggest you need to dance, prance or do something light and airy. Note the dream feelings and your personal associations with ballet for greater insight.

Baptism

Symbolizes an initiation, a new beginning or the launching of something new. What new endeavours, relationships or ideas have you recently initiated? Perhaps you feel reborn in some way, or that you have been given a second chance. Have you debuted something or been inducted recently? Do you associate this with your religion or belief systems? If so, a dream baptism may be tied to your religious beliefs or spirituality. May represent something sacred or holy in your life. Note your personal associations about baptisms and the dream feelings for greater insight.

Bar Mitzvah

Refers to the coming to age of something and may represent a rite of passage. Could suggest you feel you have accomplished something or are prepared to enter the next level of something. If tied to your religious beliefs, this symbolizes your religion, your spirituality, or something sacred and holy in your life. Linked to the age thirteen, this is a time when children are obligated to observe the ten commandments. What have you had to observe lately? Or does the dream bar mitzvah reflect your inner rules, morals and codes?

Bazaar

Represents a place (often within yourself) of bargaining, haggling and/or congestion. Have you been haggling with yourself or another? Do you find yourself bargaining with God? Is your inner reality congested with uncomfortable thoughts or feelings? May be a pun on how things feel "bizarre" or odd at this time. May say you are currently confronted with a lot of choices.

Birthday

Represents a celebration, ritual or observance of some kind. Note your personal feeling about birthdays and whether being a year older is difficult for you or triggers you in some way. May represent a birth of any kind — a new beginning, a pioneering project or the start of something new.

Bullfight

Suggests an inner conflict or external struggle of some kind. Could represent a game, depending on how you feel about bullfights. May say you are talking a lot of bull or nonsense. Could suggest you are a "raging bull" and symbolize the need to get your emotions under control or express them in a healthy way. May say you should not take any more bull from someone or with respect to a recent situation.

Carnival

Represents amusement, entertainment and frivolity. Could say you are in a festive mood, feeling light and balanced. On the other hand, it may denote foolishness or falsity, depending on how you feel about carnivals. Do you feel as though you've been taken for a ride or that everything is all fun and games? Are you partaking in foolish games or going in circles on the rides?

Christmas

Depending on your personal view, Christmas may represent Christian values and morals. It could also symbolize a time of celebration, family gatherings or being spoiled. May suggest that you have been overly materialistic, or may represent the Christ in you. May speak of your spiritual gifts or your own Christ-like qualities.

Church Service

Depending on your personal views and the dream feelings, this may denote a special, holy or sacred time or event in your life. If you are against religious services or feel disdain, this could represent those beliefs and feelings. Perhaps you feel the need to be "of service" in your community, or maybe you are already being of service and

this needs to be recognized. Again, the dream feelings will be most helpful in understanding how this church reflects your current endeavours, viewpoints or actions.

Circus

Symbolizes fun, frivolity, acting and putting on a show. May suggest a temporary situation or a lot of pomp and ceremony. Does your life feel like a three-ring circus? Or are you walking a tightrope or doing a balancing act? Perhaps you have been clowning around, or you need to lighten up and enjoy your life. See also Carnival.

Concert

A musical performance, a concert may suggest you are freely expressing yourself and/or are in harmony or balance. Conversely, could say you are acting out in an unruly manner. You may require more expression or music in your life. May suggest you are "in the groove," in the flow of things or otherwise in synch (often within a group situation). Note the type of music being played and how you feel about it.

Eclipse

Creates clear and distinct moments of endings and beginnings. Often symbolizes the death of one thing in your life and the awakening of something new.

Emergency

Any emergency situation in a dream reflects your inner cry for help. Something is building to the point of a crisis, overwhelm and chaos. Can you pinpoint where the warning is coming from? Are unexpressed emotions building inside of you, or are negative thoughts consuming you? Either way, an urgent situation is trying to get your attention. May be a pun on something trying to "emerge" from you.

Examination

Symbolizes feelings of being analyzed, reviewed, or scrutinized. Do you feel pressured or prepared in the dream? Do you feel as though someone is observing or probing you in an uncomfortable way? Do you fear failure or that you are being tested? Exams and tests are often a reflection of your self-esteem and confidence. Are you ready and willing to take the test or are you afraid to face it? Note the feelings in the dream for greater understanding.

Fireworks

Represent a celebration, an observation or merriment. May say you feel explosive (have pent-up feelings) or repre-

sent cheerful expression. May denote your fire, passion and enthusiasm. May represent a recent lavish display, showing off or ego aggrandizement. Perhaps you are seeing fireworks because you are in love or having feelings of love.

Funeral – See the Death, Dying and Killing section of this dictionary.

Graduation

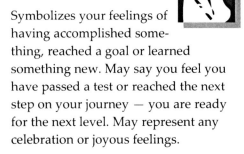

Symbolizes your feelings of having accomplished something, reached a goal or learned something new. May say you feel you have passed a test or reached the next step on your journey — you are ready for the next level. May represent any celebration or joyous feelings.

Parade

Suggests a festival, celebration or any expression that needs to be displayed openly. Note the dream feelings to determine whether you have felt scrutinized and "on parade." Or have you been boasting, strutting or exaggerating lately? Could say you need to get out in public and express yourself more. May imply that you are side-tracked from your regular routine or goals by some spectacle or eye-catching situation.

Picnic

Symbolizes rest, relaxation and possibly feasting on a variety of food for thought. May represent family ideals, your roots and your tribal values. May say you feel life is a picnic (or perhaps no picnic) these days, or may suggest the need for more leisure activity — especially with loved ones. May also denote that you have been feeling relaxed and at peace about something or a relationship.

Rehearsal

Represents exercise, practice or preparation for something. May say you have been rehearsing or going over something, or may symbolize the need for more discipline.

Seminar

Represents being in class, studying, learning and gathering knowledge. Could say you are gaining wisdom, insight or expansion of the intellect. Some learning is at hand.

Test – See Examination

Vacation

May suggest a need for rest and relaxation. Vacations are usually taken to break up routine, so you may need to get away from current troubles or distant yourself from anything that weighs heavily on you. Perhaps you need a change of pace, to explore new places or just do something different. Do you need a vacation from your own thinking or emotions? You may need to recharge your batteries or vacate the premises. Conversely, dreaming about a vacation may symbolize that you are feeling rested, relaxed or refreshed about something.

Valentine's Day

Represents the heart, loving feelings or the need for love, depending on feelings in the dream. Could say you need affection, romance or nurturing. Could also symbolize that you are bursting with love and that positive feelings are overflowing from you.

War

Suggests an internal or external struggle, turmoil and conflict. Have you been berating yourself? Do you feel as though something is killing you? May also represent a recent battle or conflict you have had with another person or with a group. Do you feel as though you are battling or at war with group consciousness? See the section on *Death, Dying and Killing* in this dictionary for greater insight.

Wedding/Marriage

This is the universal symbol of the union, dedication and commitment of two persons or two things. Any two things that have come together recently in your life can be symbolized by marriage. Could be two ideas, businesses or partnerships of any kind. Also symbolic of cooperation, love, togetherness and co-creation. May symbolize that the male and female energies within your self have been "married" or merged in a healthy, harmonious way. Perhaps you are experiencing oneness or union with your higher self. Note the dream feelings for greater insight. For example, if the feelings are negative or intolerable, it may suggest that "this marriage" is something you have to live with or tolerate. Positive feelings suggest you are pleased at whatever union has taken place or commitment has been made.

Chakras

Just as a prism refracts light into the seven colours of the rainbow, your Soul Light refracts into the seven colours of your chakra system when you take physical form (a physical body). Your chakras contain the blueprint material that is collectively called your soul or Soul Light.

The chakras are spinning vortexes of energy that look like mini tornadoes. Similar to a compact disk, the chakras store information about you — your soul records. Your chakra system is a metaphor for your life.

Each chakra vibrates at a different frequency and wave length, so each is associated with a different colour.

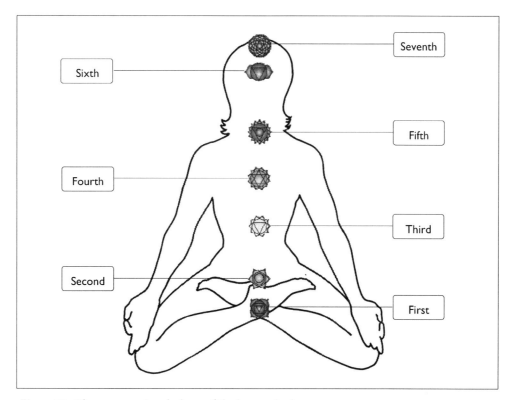

Figure 11. The seven major chakras of the human body

Chakras and the Auric Field

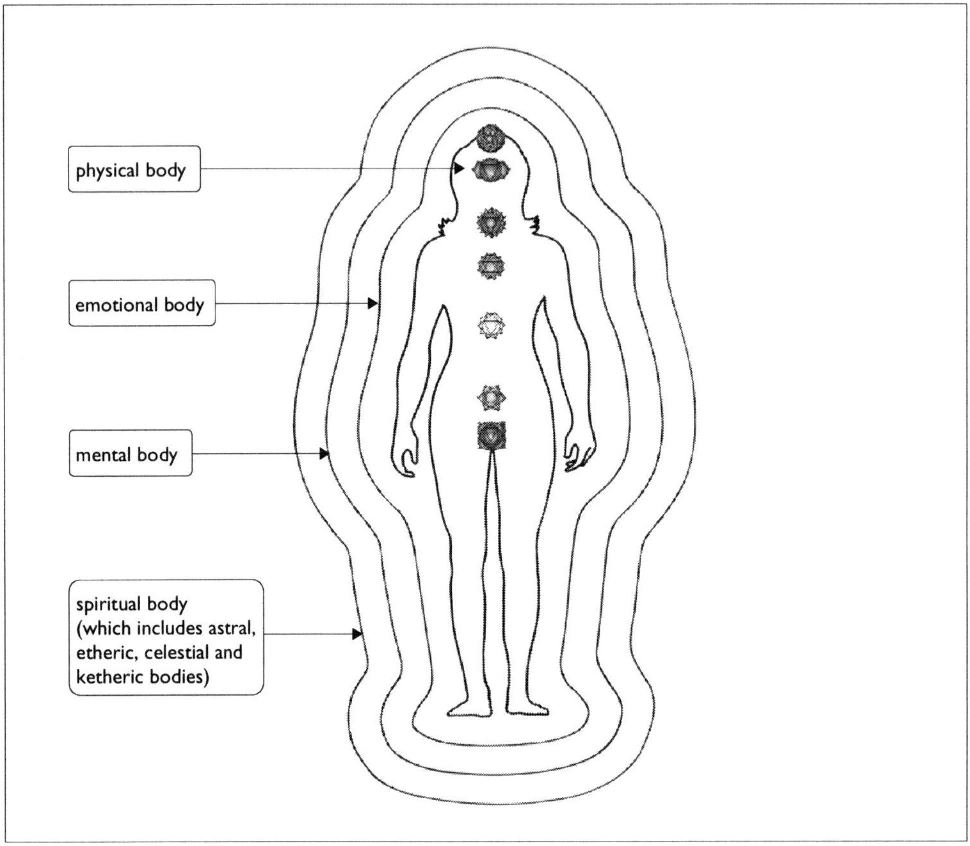

Figure 12. Chakras and the auric field

Your energy field or auric field is made up of layers that are created by the spinning of your chakras. Each of these layers, which are also called subtle bodies, vibrates at a certain frequency and is associated with a colour — the same colour as the chakra that creates that subtle body.

The physical body can be considered a very dense and slow-moving vibration (when you consider all the vibration that exists in the Universe). Each layer of the auric field vibrates a bit faster than the one before it and the particles are spinning so fast that the human eye cannot detect it. However, the auric field can be photographed and measured by modern scientific instruments. People who are clairvoyant are able to detect these spinning molecules in the auric field and are therefore able to see the different coloured layers of the field.

Within your aura is imprinted all the information that you need for this life, including

- ▸ your genetic and ancestral lineage
- ▸ a record of your past lives, karmic contracts, and the lessons that you intend to resolve in this lifetime
- ▸ all the information that has been "programmed" into you since your birth in this lifetime

The energy patterns within the layers of your aura are like compact disks full of vibrating information; these are the chakras. You may understand and recognize this material to be your emotions, thoughts, beliefs, viewpoints, intuition, insight, higher self, and much more — all the parts and information that make you who you are today are quite literally stored in a vibrational code within your chakras and energy field. And these patterns of information affect every nuance of your life. As you become aware of these energy patterns, you will understand how they can influence you and how they are reflected in your dream time. Learning to recognize these energy patterns will help you to expand your understanding of yourself and those around you; enhance your clarity and perspective; and increase your intuitive/psychic awareness.

The aura is a bridge to the unseen or greater mystery in life. Through it you are able to attune to subtler dimensions of Spirit and gain greater understanding of what has contributed to making you who you are today. The stronger your aura, the easier it is to receive helpful messages from your higher self, spirits, guides, and angels, and in your waking and sleeping dream times. The weaker your aura, the more likely you'll draw negative energies and illnesses into your life.

The fourth layer of the auric field (associated with the heart chakra) is called the astral body and it is here, in the astral plane (dimension) that dreaming takes place. If you have had an out of body experience (OOBE) you will recognize this level of dreaming (similar to a lucid dream experience).

Chakras and your auric field are the very matrix of who you are. I suggest that you read further on this subject to help you understand how significant a role chakras play in the dreamtime information.

Chakras in Your Dreams

Your dreams constantly reflect the chakras and your energy field by using metaphors and the colours of the rainbow. For example, if you dream about a door on the second floor of a building, this may be a metaphor for your second chakra. Noticing whether the door is open or closed is important, since an open chakra is considered healthier and better able to function than a closed one. Anything that opens or closes, such as a window or a drawbridge, can symbolize a chakra in the dream time.

The colours in your dreams reflect the chakra that corresponds to that colour. For example, if the colour red figures prominently in your dream, this could symbolize the feeling or the chakra associated with the colour red. Anger and passion are the feelings associated with red, as is the first chakra and the information (compiled about you) that is stored within this spinning disk.

Chakras can sometimes be represented by vortexes, tornados, whirlwinds or anything that spins in your dream time — even a child's spinning top. Note the colour of the object to discern which chakra it symbolizes.

Other Symbolic Links with Chakras

In addition to the above, there are animals and elements associated with each of the chakras. These animals and elements in your dreams may symbolize your chakras. Table 1 shows the animals and elements associated with what are traditionally viewed as being the seven main chakras of the physical body.

When you dream of an animal, use the table shown here to check which chakra it is associated with. Note the animal's behaviour and actions to help you understand how it is reflecting the health of your chakra. For example, a dream about a sleeping snake may be telling you that your first chakra is dormant or inactive, whereas a hissing or moving snake may denote an active and awakened first chakra.

Use the Element column of Table 1 in the same way to help you understand the symbols in your dreams. A dream about great gusts of wind, for example, may be telling you about your third chakra (and the state of your mind and thoughts) or about your fourth chakra (and the state of your heart and feelings).

Table 2 lists some simplified traits associated with the seven chakras. Use these traits and characteristics to help you discern what (within yourself) is being mirrored or represented by your chakra dream symbol. Note that each chakra is also associated with a body part or parts, so they can help reveal the health of that part of your body. For example, a dream in which you try to talk or scream but can make no sound may indicate a dysfunction in your fifth chakra, which in turn symbolizes your ability (or inability) to express yourself. The age of your dream characters can correspond to a chakra and will reflect its health and needs. For example, a crying infant may reflect the needs (possible neglect or love) of your first chakra.

Table I

Chakra	Animal	Element	Ages (approx.)
First	snakes	fire or earth	0 to 4
Second	aquatic animals	water	age 7
Third	birds	air or fire	age 12
Fourth	four-legged mammals	earth or air	age 18
Fifth	humans and the Archetype of the Hierophant (spirit teacher)	ether and sound	age 25
Sixth	Archetypes*	light	age 45
Seventh	Kachina (supernatural beings)		ageless

* **Archetypes** are universal symbols based on patterns derived from historical roles in life, such as the Mother, the Child, and the Servant, and universal events, including Initiation, Birth, Death, and Rebirth. The collective unconscious (and information about the archetypes) is inherited (genetically encoded) rather than developed. See also the *Numbers* section of this dictionary and associated tarot card archetypes referred to under each number from one to twenty-one).

Note that the key words in the Related Issues column can be dream symbols. For example, dreaming of a family situation or about the roots of a tree may represent your first chakra. Dreaming about money or your sexual feelings may represent your second chakra and its functioning.

Remember: These symbolic meanings are just suggestions. If these suggested meanings do not resonate with you, ring a bell, give you an "ah-ha" moment or otherwise feel right, search through your own experience or beliefs about the symbol to find what makes sense for you.

Table 2

Chakra	Colour	Location	Related Issues	Related Body Parts
First	red	tail bone	*security, trust, roots and family, "what grew you"* This is your connection to the Earth, your body, your family, your culture and your community.	ovaries, testes, legs, feet, pelvic area
Second	orange	between belly button and pubic bone	*money, sexuality, creativity, emotions* Also about relating to and relationships with others.	uterus, intestines, bladder, lower back area
Third	yellow	solar plexus	*self-confidence, the mind, ego/personality, intellect, beliefs* Seat of personal power, issues of authority and issues of control. Reflects your "lower" will power.	mid-abdominal area, including adrenals, pancreas, stomach, gallbladder, spleen, liver, kidneys
Fourth	green	heart	*love of others, humanity, compassion, patience, higher emotions, and the ability to take others in* The heart is the centre of the energy systems and is about balance and your sacred "inner marriage" (relationship with self).	chest and mid-back area, including heart and lungs, shoulders

Chakra	Colour	Location	Related Issues	Related Body Parts
Fifth	blue	throat	*self-expression, "higher" will power, voice, speaking the truth, speaking up, speaking out, commitment and perfect timing* Connects to etheric blueprint or energy pattern of higher self. Also associated with clairaudience ("clear hearing").	throat, neck, ears
Sixth	purple or indigo	brow area, between the eyes (also called the third eye)	*insight, intuition, and clairvoyance (clear seeing)* Often called the third eye, it relates to "predicting" the future based on past patterning.	eyes, nose, mid-head area
Seventh	white or purple	top of head or crown	*spirituality and connection to higher-self Spirit, soul self and God* Depicted as a halo in works of art, it represents union with the Divine.	top of head, cranium

Clothing

Clothes indicate what you "put on" or wear for the world (and yourself) to see. Clothes can be symbolic of your mood or state of mind and may represent your idea of how you look or present yourself to others. These are the attitudes you put on to show to the world. They also imply your sense of style, fashion or overall self-esteem (or lack of it). What do you associate with the type of clothing seen in the dream? For example, wearing a dress may indicate your femininity whereas pants may indicate your masculinity. Are you wearing a specific colour? This would indicate a certain mood, emotion or chakra (see the Colours and Chakras sections for further insight). What is highlighted about the clothes? See that specific item of clothing. Whatever the item, you can be sure it is trying to tell you something about your "posture," attitude, stance, mood, and the way you portray yourself in your waking time.

Remember: These symbolic meanings are just suggestions. If these suggested meanings do not resonate with you, ring a bell, give you an "ah-ha" moment or otherwise feel right, search through your own experience or beliefs about the symbol to find what makes sense for you.

Apron

May represent work in the kitchen and therefore work in the mind or mental aspect of self. How do you feel wearing an apron? Is it women's work or is it a time for creative play? Do you feel a slave to your lifestyle, or old and matronly in the apron? An apron is a type of protection, so it could speak of your need for more security, safety or control.

Armour

Symbolic of feeling in need of emotional, mental or physical protection. Do you feel safe in the armour or ready for war? What issues have been surfacing for review or expression lately? Do you feel you need protection from certain feelings? May indicate that you have been acting defensively or that you are resisting some change. Perhaps you feel "hardened" about a subject or relationship, or that you are being rigid and inflexible about something.

Bath Robe *– See Housecoat*

Bathing Suit

Depending on how you feel in your dream bathing suit, it may symbolize how you have felt comfortable or uncomfortable in a recent event or experience. Perhaps a bathing suit represents that you have felt overly exposed in a recent relationship or encounter with another. Do you feel sexy and playful in your dream bathing suit? Could suggest you are ready to "get wet" or get involved with looking at your feelings. May be associated with feelings of relaxation if you are on a beach.

Beautiful Clothing

Depicts recent acts or behaviours that you deem beautiful or attractive. This could be a recent incident where you felt gracious, generous or benevolent toward yourself or others. Clothes in which you feel beautiful, attractive or elegant may represent any act of kindness. Usually suggests a positive attitude and feelings of security and self-confidence.

Belt

Because belts are used to hold something up, it may symbolize that you feel something is slipping away or that you need to be held up and supported in some way. Perhaps you need to belt something out or express yourself in a big way. Maybe you have felt "belted" or berated by yourself or another recently. May indicate your need to tighten your belt or be more thrifty and frugal.

Bikini *– See Bathing Suit*

Blouse

Represents how you express your feminine nature. Are you comfortable in the dream blouse? Are you comfortable in expressing your feelings and the truth of your heart? See also Shirt.

Boots *– See Shoes*

Borrowed Clothing

May indicate that you have recently taken on someone else's point of view, opinions or ideas. Have you borrowed attitudes or beliefs of others recently? Are you freeloading or sponging off others? Note how you feel wearing the borrowed clothes for greater understanding.

Bra

Symbolic of how you support your feminine self or how well you align with your feelings. Is the dream bra comfortable or uncomfortable (denotes whether you are comfortable with your feelings)? Is the bra new or old (denotes new feelings or old ones)? Is it supportive or unsupportive (denotes how supported you are, or feel you are, by your self or others)? How you feel in the bra will help determine its meaning more clearly. Perhaps you are not wearing a bra in your dream, which may indicate that you need support for recent feelings or issues of the heart.

Button

Because buttons hold two things together, they symbolize the need to hold something together. They could also represent that it is time to let go of something that is holding you in a fixed position.

Children's Clothing

If you are an adult looking at or wearing children's clothing, it may indicate that your recent behaviours or thinking have been childish. Look to recent events in which you may have acted in a childlike way. Could also suggest you need to play more or be more free in your expression.

Coat

Symbolic of how you may cover up or hide what you don't want others to see.

Perhaps you hide certain behaviours or attitudes behind a cloak or cape. A coat could also be a protection of your attitudes, beliefs or opinions, depending on how you feel wearing the dream coat. A raincoat could indicate that you are covering up emotions and feelings, or that you feel you need protection from your own emotions or those of others. An overcoat could denote that you feel the need to cover some aspect of your self and not show it to others. A winter coat may indicate the need for comfort or that you are feeling cold or abandoned. Note if the coat is new or used and how you feel wearing it. May be a pun on riding on someone's coat tails.

Costume

May indicate the need to present yourself in a different way, or symbolize that you are presenting yourself in a false way. Do you feel the need to disguise your thoughts or feelings? The type of costume and how you feel wearing it will indicate why you feel the need to put on an act or hide under false colours. Perhaps it represents a playfulness that needs to be expressed.

Diaper

If you are an adult wearing diapers in the dream, it may indicate that you have been acting in a babyish way or that your attitudes have been babyish. On the other hand, perhaps you are in great need of treating yourself with extreme gentleness and nurturing — the way you would treat a baby. How you feel about yourself in diapers will be a big clue about the meaning of this symbol. Changing diapers in a dream indicates the need to change some babyish aspect of yourself or change an old, outgrown attitude or belief. A messy or dirty diaper may have a similar symbolic meaning — the need to clean up your act or recent actions.

Dirty Clothing

May indicate a need to clean up your act or that you feel you have been acting "dirty." May imply that you have had unclean or lewd thoughts recently. Have you been acting in a disgraceful, improper, or shameful way? Perhaps a recent event has left you feeling polluted, corrupt or tainted. Has a messy situation or encounter with another left you feeling violated or unclean? Do you consider yourself to have a dirty mind and therefore in need of some cleansing? May imply you are not caring for yourself well and need some attention.

Dress

Represents how you feel about being a woman (or about the feminine aspect of your self) or how you relate to women.

How does it feel to be wearing this dream dress? Do you feel confident, comfortable and strong? Or do you feel uncomfortable, demeaned or small in any way because of the dress? The feelings will help you understand how you feel in your feminine nature. A dress may also represent how receptive and nurturing you have been to yourself and others lately.

Favourite Clothing

Often represents attitudes, postures or ways of being that are comfortable and familiar to you. These are behaviours and habits that are known, acceptable and even cozy to you. Represents states of mind or perspectives you experience daily.

Formal

Depending on how you feel about formal attire, this symbol may indicate rigid, conventional or stuffy ways of thinking and being in the world. Or it could represent elegance, graciousness and refined states of being. May express a particular attitude of grandeur or recent prideful state. Do you feel luxurious in formal attire, or feel as though you "have it all" in the dream? Look to recent events in your life to hone in on the precise meaning of your formal stance.

Glove

Brings messages about covering up how you are "handling" things. May indicate whether you have a grip on a situation or not. Are you handling a current life challenge with kid gloves or with a rough hand? Are the dream gloves a type of work glove and therefore referring to how you are handling things at work? Or are they evening gloves and more suited for elegance? See also Hand in the *Body* section.

Hat

May represent the many hats you wear in your day-to-day life and encounters, the many jobs or talents you have. A hat could also represent your thinking, or those thoughts that you try to cover up. Either way, your dream hat is about your mental state of being and may protect or reveal your state of mind. Note what type of hat you are wearing and whether it is specific to a particular job or talent. This will help you understand what your attitude is toward that job or talent. Trying on a hat in a dream represents that you are trying on new (or used) attitudes, beliefs or opinions. You may also be trying on a new stance or behaviour. Many hats may denote that you have many talents, abilities or expertise in a particular field. Perhaps you can change hats easily and switch from one mental state to another with

ease. A helmet or hardhat may indicate hard or limited thinking. Or perhaps you feel in need of protection and don't want to take in another's point of view or beliefs. The type of hat will be a great clue about the meaning of your recent type of thinking or thoughts.

Housecoat

Often represents a comfortable attitude or belief that you are currently "wearing" or displaying. Or it may denote a more private and personal aspect of self, not often seen by others. How do you feel wearing the housecoat? This will reveal what the dream housecoat symbolizes for you.

Jeans

May indicate how comfortable you have been in recent situations or events. Do you wear jeans often, or is this an uncommon piece of clothing for you? Do you consider them work-type clothing or a statement of free thinking? If old and faded, they may represent your old attitudes that are still being shown to the world.

Mending Clothing

May indicate that you are mending, repairing or updating healing attitudes, beliefs or ideas that no longer serve you well. Perhaps you are making amends for a recent thought, word or action that did not align with your beliefs or attitudes.

Negligee

May denote feelings of sensuality or sexiness. Who is wearing the negligee and how do they feel? May say you feel exposed or that someone has "seen through" you. May represent shame or embarrassment, depending on how you feel about wearing negligees.

New Clothing

May symbolize new ideas, thoughts and beliefs. Perhaps you are testing out a new attitude or way of being in the world. Have you had any new perceptions or insights lately that are represented by the dream clothing? How do you feel wearing the new clothes? Do they represent a change in your understanding, self-esteem or self-confidence?

Old Clothing

May indicate old attitudes, beliefs or behaviour patterns. May symbolize that your thinking or "posture" is out-dated or in need of replacement. Are these clothes suitable in your current life? Are you comfortable in your old habits and behaviours? Are you clinging to the past and old ways? If the clothing

is old-fashioned or from another era, it may be telling you that this is a past-life dream.

Pajamas

Reflect attitudes of comfort and reassurance. Depending on how you feel about wearing pajamas in your waking time, could also represent personal issues or indicate that you are feeling exposed in some way. May indicate the need for more rest, sleep or down time.

Panties

May symbolize a feeling of exposure if you are caught in your panties in the dream. Or may reflect personal issues and feelings. Panties reflect the feminine or female point of view, so the Feminine entry in the *People* section of this dictionary may be useful to you. What feelings are elicited by wearing panties in the dream?

Pants

May reflect masculine point of view or attitudes, depending on what type of pants are worn in dream. May be a pun on "who wears the pants" or issues of control. See Masculine in the *People* section for more in-depth understanding of male attributes. Feminine pants would reflect feminine attitudes and tendencies.

Purse

Symbolizes issues of identification, value, worth and money. What do you keep in your purse and how much value do you place on it? Understanding this will help you decipher the meaning of your dream purse.

Shirt

Since shirts cover the heart area, they often denote feelings and expressions of the heart. How do you feel in your dream shirt? Are you comfortable? Is it, or does it feel like, a familiar shirt? A shirt that is new or uncomfortable in some way indicates new feelings that you are trying on to see how they suit your lifestyle and image. See also Blouse.

Shoes

Denote the beliefs and foundations upon which you stand. Shoes are the "basis" of your understanding and represent everything you stand for. The type of shoes worn (or not worn) in the dream will help you pinpoint the type of support you are or aren't receiving. If the shoes are stiff, uncomfortable or inflexible, it may denote a barrier to your understanding, poor support of your self or poor support from another. Comfortable and flexible footwear may indicate that you are comfortable in a certain stance you have taken recently and that you are flexible in your understanding and thinking. Note how you feel in your dream shoes. Are they too tight, indicating a less than flexible or desirable foundation? Or are they just perfect like Cinderella's glass slipper? Are you barefoot and comfortable in your chosen beliefs and support systems? Or does going barefoot represent poverty and the inability to move freely for you? Perhaps your dream shoes are boots, which may represent your need to protect your beliefs or defend your understandings. Boots could also be a tough exterior which you show to the world, or symbolize your need for security. Are your dream shoes old or new? Old shoes represent old beliefs and understandings; new shoes mean that you have taken on or adopted new beliefs. How well do the shoes support you? What kind of foundation are you standing on? Safe and secure, or flimsy and unsupportive?

Skates

Represent your ability to glide through life or through a current challenge. May suggest you have good balance presently, or indicate that you need more balance in your life. If you have never skated, they may suggest you are trying something new or that a challenge is before you that will require patience and practice to perfect. See also Skating in the *Sports and Games* section.

Skirt

Symbolizes the feminine and issues of how you feel as a woman (or about the feminine side of your self) and how you relate to women. Feminine qualities may include tenderness, receptivity, openness, creativity and nurturing. May be a pun on skirting an issue or hiding behind a skirt.

Socks

A reflection of the beliefs and foundations upon which you stand. Are the socks comfortable or well worn? This will help you understand if they symbolize comfortable beliefs that you endorse or old, worn-out beliefs. See also Shoes.

Soiled Clothing – See Dirty Clothing

Sweater

Often associated with the chest and heart area, a sweater may reflect your feelings and the truth of your heart. In your waking life, do you consider sweaters to be casual wear or for more dressy occasions? This will reflect

whether you feel comfortable in your thoughts and feelings.

Tie

Usually worn by men, a tie reflects masculine points of view and attitudes, including attitudes about aggression, protection, dominance, action and authority figures. May be a pun on the ties that bind us or any type of physical, emotional, mental, or spiritual tie that you have. Could also represent karmic ties, financial ties or religious ties. May be about bonds, such as love bonds, marital bonds or bonds of malice. Perhaps you feel tied to a situation or relationship, or all tied up in knots emotionally or mentally.

Torn Clothing

Are you feeling divided or torn about something? Do you feel as though your recent thoughts are flawed or in need of some repair? Or do you feel shabby in some way about the way you have recently presented yourself in some situation or relationship?

Trying on Clothes

Often denotes that you have recently "tried on" a new attitude, belief or stance to see if it fits your lifestyle.

Note how you feel in the clothing you are trying on — does it feel comfortable or awkward? Your feelings are further clues about the meaning behind your trying on something different or new.

Underwear

May reflect a sense of exposure, depending on how you feel in the dream. May indicate personal issues or those parts of you that others don't see. Could relate to feelings of comfort or constriction, depending on how you feel about wearing the underwear in the dream. See also Panties.

Uniform

Depending on the type of uniform, this could point to issues of control, dominance or feelings of obsequious- ness (subservience). Also reflects work- related or group issues, depending on the type of uniform being worn. Army uniforms may relate to issues of disci- pline, assertiveness and orderliness. Police uniforms symbolize issues of law, authority, judgement, or what is considered right and wrong. Nursing uniforms may reflect issues of health, nurturing and compassion.

Used Clothing

May symbolize that you have adopted another person's point of view or atti-

tudes. Did a recent event in your life make you feel "used" or manipulated? Have you been making decisions based on others' beliefs or opinions? Look to how you feel in the dream's used cloth- ing for further clues about the symbolic meaning.

Veil

Denotes something that is partially or completely hidden from you. What do you currently experience as not being fully in focus for you or that you have a blind spot for? Veils often relate to issues of mystery and hidden or secret knowledge. May imply feelings of modesty, sexiness or insecurity. May denote flirtation or temptation. Who is wearing the dream veil and how do they feel wearing it? Are they hiding behind it or using it as a deliberate tool, such as for deception?

Vest

Often related to issues of the chest and heart. May reflect how you currently feel about some issue or relationship, or reflect the truth of your heart.

Washing Clothing

May indicate you feel in the need to cleanse or clean up your act or your actions. Perhaps you need to forgive yourself or another or release some emotions. Note whose clothes you are washing, since this is an important clue about whose attitudes or beliefs need to be cleansed or changed.

Wedding Dress

Symbolizes issues surrounding marriage, purity and innocence. May also be about two things or ideas coming together. May denote issues of love and devotion, depending on how you feel about the wedding dress. Could also reflect issues of commitment and service. Feminine in nature, it may also indicate your femininity and relationships to men.

Colours

Colours in your dreams reflect your emotional states, moods, attitudes and thoughts. They also correspond to the seven major charkas in the body (see the Chakras section of this dictionary for more information). Note how bright or dull colours are and what your personal opinions are of that colour. It is more common to dream in colour than not.

Dreaming in black and white is most often associated with an "all black or all white" type of perception, that is, an unbalanced perception of a situation. This type of all or nothing attitude or belief is most likely not serving you well. Black and white is often our judgement in the extreme. Something is either all good or all bad, all right or all wrong or even all good and or all evil.

Black and white dreams may also symbolize being cut off from your feelings, or that you are totally numb to your emotions or those of others. Is there any colour or brightness in your life or are there only shades of grey? What feelings are associated with your black and white dream? These will often indicate the area of imbalance. Cheery black and white dreams may represent that you are comfortable with your way of seeing the world. If your dream feelings are negative, this tells you that the imbalance in your perceptions needs to be corrected in order for your sense of harmony and peace to be restored.

Remember: *These symbolic meanings are just suggestions. If these suggested meanings do not resonate with you, ring a bell, give you an "ah-ha" moment or otherwise feel right, search through your own experience or beliefs about the symbol to find what makes sense for you. Always note what your personal links are with each colour.*

Black

Represents a deep spiritual connection with the Void, the unknown, mystery and darkness. Are you in a black mood? Is this an all black or all white situation? May indicate hatred, malice, spite or death, depending on how you feel about black. If there are positive feelings in the dream, black can represent spiritual gifts and talents that have been judged or gone unrecognized.

Blue

The colour of the fifth chakra, blue symbolizes the higher will power and your connection to the will of your higher self as opposed to the will of your personality or ego. It is also about your voice, expression or the ability to express. Blue is about communicating, and can also denote truth, wisdom, spirituality and "true blue." Are you expressing your self or is there a blue feeling overriding your ability to communicate? Is the blue clear, which indicates clear communication? Are you speaking your truth? Are you feeling blue or out of synch with your true self? Have you or someone else been talking a blue streak? Blue is the colour of your etheric blueprint and the first level of the higher self. See Fifth Chakra in the *Chakras* section of this dictionary.

Brown

Indicates earthy or grounded feelings. May represent filth or muddied, dull or drab feelings. Also represents practicality, orderliness, being materialistic or being physically oriented. May indicate depression, lack of ambition or negative attitude.

Gold

Often symbolizes striking it rich or feeling great about something in your life.
May represent spiritual rewards or the attainment of some goal, desire or approval you've been seeking. Is gold within your reach (say, in the twenty-four to forty-eight hours prior to your dream) or do you already have it? Anything that is dear to or prized by you, or that you consider valuable, could be represented by gold in a dream. For example, gold could represent a wealth of information or wealth of knowledge.

Green

Represents envy, healing, nourishment, compassion and love. Also denotes growth, hope, balance and fruitfulness or productivity. Are things growing in your life? Are you green with envy? Are you balanced in your emotions toward others? Green is the colour of the fourth (heart) chakra and our ability to feel for others; it indicates a higher feeling (the feelings that you have for others, such as compassion, love, judgement) rather than the second or orange chakra (your own feelings, such as anger, sadness, joy). Green reflects your ability to take something in and nurture it in a loving, balanced and compassionate way. It is the colour of loving receptivity. See Fourth Chakra in the *Chakras* section of this dictionary.

Grey

Often indicates a grey or sullen mood

or way of thinking. It often denotes fright, depression, a grey area of thinking, or an undefined or unclear situation. However, because we often think in an all black or all white manner, grey could be a positive symbol representing a middle ground or balanced way of thinking.

Orange

Symbolizes your creativity, sexuality and feelings (such as anger, sadness, joy) as opposed to feelings you may have for others (such as compassion, love, judgement). Orange is often about your emotions and how comfortable or uncomfortable you are about your own feelings. Whether the colour appeals to you or not is a good indicator of how at ease you are with emotions in general. Because orange is the colour of creativity, note if there are creative opportunities in your life at this time and whether you are taking advantage of them. Perhaps you need to be more creative about something or need to explore your sexual energy and how it is currently being expressed in your life. Colour of the second chakra (see the *Chakras* section of this dictionary).

Pink

Represents love, divine love, universal love flow, unconditional love or Christ consciousness. Are you feeling tickled

pink about something? Pink often denotes an exciting kind of joy and happiness in your life and a sense of fulfillment. Since some people associate pink with feminine qualities, note what your personal links are with this colour.

Purple

Represents royalty, intuition, insight and the ability to feel on a higher level of compassion (feeling for the world or all of humanity). Purple is the colour of the sixth chakra (the third eye) and signifies clairvoyance. Purple (insight) denotes the ability to see how your past actions have created your current experiences. Do you wish to continue creating the same things in your life? The vibration of the colour purple offers you a chance to predict your future based on past behaviour patterns. Purple is also the colour needed for visualization — for imagination and creation at a pretend level. Do you need to play more with your ability to picture (create) your future? Purple has been worn by royalty in many cultures for hundreds of years. This reflects the better insight and perception associated with purple, and therefore symbolizes that the wearer is a superior leader. Are you in the proper position to take on a leadership role in some endeavour? Do you need to step up and take charge? See the *Chakras* section of this dictionary for greater insight.

Red

Symbolizes anger, passion and your basic energy drive. Red is raw energy, vigour and aggressiveness, as well as action or the power to love and hate. May be related to your sexuality or your driving desires. What are you passionate about? Although our current culture often judges anger negatively and frowns upon expressing it, red in a dream can really help move you forward — it is, in fact, a positive energy to have. It means you have built up enough energy to move forward or move in new directions. How you choose to express (or repress) this energy is up to you. Even when you are "seeing red," this is still a positive energy that you can use for benefit. Note the variations possible with the colour red and whether it is mixed with another colour (more orange-red or blue-red), and refer to that colour as well. Colour of root chakra; see First Chakra in the *Chakras* section of the dictionary.

Silver

May represent intuition, God's grace (blessings) or energy. May denote quicksilver or money, especially coins (since loose change is often referred to as silver). Note whether you are wearing or in possession of the silver-coloured symbol in the dream; this will help you understand whether you are accepting the blessings in your life currently. For example, if silver bracelets were on your wrist in the dream, this represents that you accept the blessings in your life; if the bracelets are on someone else's wrist, it could represent that you have not owned or recognized your wealth or blessings.

White

Represents purity, wisdom and perfection or holiness. May also represent black and white thinking, depending on whether black is also manifested in your dream. White is the colour of the seventh chakra, and it often relates to your spiritual connection. It may also symbolize an aspect of your higher self. See the *Chakras* section.

Yellow

Represents your intellect, mind, thinking, reasoning and the will power of your ego (as opposed to the will power of your higher self). Yellow is also the colour of the sun and great energy and vitality. May represent a sunny outlook or positive thinking. Is anything glaring you in the face? Sometimes associated with cowardice or negative thinking. Colour of the third chakra (see the *Chakras* section of this dictionary).

Death, Dying and Killing

Dreams of dying and death are common. They symbolize letting go, ending, completion or termination of something so that something new can begin. Death represents transformation and is a teacher of wisdom. In reality, it is only a dying of the physical body because the soul lives on in spirit world. Death is similar to falling asleep — your soul leaves your body and your consciousness continues to exist in a different time, space and vibration. Death is actually a joyous occasion for the soul.

Look at what is going on in your life currently to understand the meaning of your "death or dying" dream. Do you actually desire to see someone dead or out of the way? More likely, a dream about death signifies the death of a part of your self. This part could be something that is no longer useful to you, such as an old belief or attitude, or the death of something that you have outgrown, such as a job, project or relationship. Nothing is more alive than death and something new is always born out of what has ceased to be. Can you identify what you need to let go of in your life? Has an idea or feeling died within you? Has anything ended lately or do you have a deeper sense that something new needs to be started? Dreams that symbolize the death of an old habit or negative thoughts can be very positive ones.

To unravel the meaning of your dreams that are about death and dying, you must first consider the feelings in the dream. Was it a positive experience or was it frightening? For example, if in the dream you feel regret or concern over the death, this may symbolize that a positive quality or talent of yours has been allowed to die because of neglect. On the other hand, positive feelings in the dream may alert you to success in overcoming an outmoded image of yourself, or to the letting go of a way of thinking.

On rare occasions, death dreams are about the actual death of someone, but then the feelings of the dream will help you understand if this is an ESP warning or not (see the discussion on ESP dreams in Chapter 3 to help clarify). If the death in the dream feels like an ESP warning about your own impending death, you may wish to explore this dream with your medical doctor to ensure that your health is fine. It is not common to receive such information about your own actual death, but it will help allay any worries or concerns the dream raises for you. Consider the details and the feelings in the dream to help you fully understand the meaning.

Dream about a Dead Loved One

Positive feelings associated with a dream about a dead loved one most likely indicate an actual encounter with that person's spirit or soul energy. Just as your auric field vibrates faster than your physical body and goes mostly undetected by the human eye, the energy of the dead and spirit energy vibrate faster than the human eye can detect. Your ability to communicate with the dead is heightened in the dream time because you are more aware of the whole of your self when in the dream state — you are more alive and sensitive to vibration and can easily detect and discern energies at higher frequency. Actual communication with the dead is very common — it's just not often discussed in Western society for fear of judgement. Sometimes visits from the spirits of dead loved ones in the dream time also bring up old issues that have yet to be forgiven or released. Enjoy your visit and watch for signs that a message is forthcoming about your relationship with that person.

Unpleasant feelings associated with a dream about a dead loved one indicate that the dream is actually about you. The characteristics or personality that you associate with that person in your waking life are being mirrored by the character in the dream. Remember that almost all dream characters — dead or alive — symbolize an aspect of you. If the feelings are negative and/or fearful, the dream probably represents the death of an aspect of your self that no longer serves you well. See the *People* section of this dictionary to help you determine which aspect of your self has died.

The death of a loved one in your dream could also represent an aspect of your self that you feel is dying or in great neglect. Look to the feelings and the dream details for further comprehension, and be mindful of how you treat yourself in your inner world. Do you beat and berate yourself to the point of feeling dead or killed? Have you been thinking or speaking words such as "something is killing me" or "I wish [something] was dead"? This type of thinking creates the very pictures/symbols we dream about, so be aware of your self talk (what you say to yourself in your mind).

On occasion our alive loved ones visit us in the dream time to let us know they are planning to leave the earthly plane. This warning may come up to a year in advance and can be shown to you in numerous ways. For example, you may see your loved one getting on an airplane and waving goodbye. The dream feelings will be most helpful in understanding whether this type of dream is an ESP type or a reflection of yourself.

Dream about Killing

Killing someone in a dream may symbolize that you are beating yourself (or an aspect or quality of your self that you dislike or judge as being bad) to death. The key to identifying which undesirable trait you are destroying often lies in whom you are killing. The characteristics and personality traits you associate with that person reflect or indicate which qualities within yourself you are killing.

For example, say you dream about killing your next door neighbour. Do you currently have any disputes or arguments with this person in your waking life? If not, then the qualities you associate with this person's personality are the aspects of your self that you want to kill. (Note that this principle applies also to dreams about killing an animal or destroying an object.)

Note what your intent is in the dream — do you kill someone deliberately or is it accidental? This will help you understand whether you are consciously choosing to destroy some aspect of your self (likely one you don't like) or totally unaware of your own actions (usually these types of actions are internal, such as thinking and responding to your feelings).

Dream in Which You Witness Someone Being Killed

If the dream symbol is another person being killed, then it is still often just a reflection of your own part that you wish to kill off. To determine which aspects it is reflecting, simply describe the character and personality of the person in the dream. Even if you don't know them personally, you will often get a sense of their demeanor. List three traits and realize that this is a reflection of self. Seldom will dream characters represent another person, and almost always be a reflection of your own character. Note if the killing was accidental or deliberate. This will help you understand if the destruction (death of an aspect of your self) is being done consciously or unconsciously.

Ask yourself the following questions to help uncover which area in your life is being mirrored in this type of dream.

- Have you been angry with yourself lately, or have you said or done something you'd like to retract?
- Have you said that something is "killing me," be it a job, a relationship or attitude? Thoughts such as these may be killing some part of your self, because your subconscious mind takes these thoughts literally and translates them into a picture of death in a dream.

▶ Do you find something in your life is intolerable, unbearable or insupportable? The feelings in the dream reflect the depth of your need to be rid of this part of your self or part of your life. Often, these are parts that you judge as not good enough, bad or simply intolerable. You can't or don't want to face or deal with these parts of your self and therefore try to get them out of your mind and your life. But it is important to understand that this is a part of you, and you can never be rid of it. Learning to accept this part without judgement will always help you to balance the issue in a healthier way. All parts of your self serve a purpose and are useful, even if you don't currently see the beauty behind them.

Remember: These symbolic meanings are just suggestions. If these suggested meanings do not resonate with you, ring a bell, give you an "ah-ha" moment or otherwise feel right, search through your own experience or beliefs about the symbol to find what makes sense for you.

Death of an Animal

Represents the death of some instinctual part of self. What qualities do you associate with this animal? The answer will help you understand what aspect of your self has died in you. See the *Animals* section for further clarification.

Death of a Baby

Often symbolizes that some new project, idea or relationship has ended or been terminated. Have you "dropped the baby" with respect to some responsibility? Has some hope died within you? Are you treating yourself so poorly inside that you need to recognize the baby within (i.e., take care of yourself and nurture yourself as you would a baby)?

Death of a Bird

Birds often represent freedom, so this dream symbol may denote the death of a sense of freedom or autonomy over something. What within you feels lost or has died recently? Have you been soaring high and had high ideals that have ended? What has terminated or been completed recently?

Death of a Stranger

Denotes that some part of your self (that is unknown to you) has symbolically died or left you. Look to the feelings and details of the dream for further comprehension. Is the stranger's face visible? Is there something you don't want to face, or are you dreading some encounter or situation? What is unresolved at this time in your life? To understand what part of your self is represented by the stranger, describe three qualities or characteristics you would attribute to this shadowy figure. Despite the fact that you can't recognize the stranger, you will still have a sense and feeling about him/her. For example, you may only be aware that you don't like him — the next step is to ask why. Is it because he is sneaky or underhanded? Whatever characteristic you believe the stranger has is the very aspect of your self that you are not recognizing and owning. In this case, the dead stranger symbolizes that you completely dismiss (consider dead) this part of your self. It is hard to claim the parts of self that we do not like. Allow this to just be information for you, rather than a judgement about what is good and bad about you.

Destruction on a Large Scale

Could symbolize that you are doing some massive and serious harm to your self, or that there is a major crisis and chaos within you. Are you being self-destructive in a big way? Is a habit destroying you? Are you eating away at yourself with negative self-talk? Alternatively, this could be an ESP warning of a large scale disaster. Look to the dream feelings to help you understand if the devastation is within you or external to you. See the discussion on precognitive dreams in Chapter 3 for further information.

Execution

May represent the death of part of your self or that you are killing yourself in some way in your inner world. This is severe and harsh punishment that is usually rooted in self-loathing, very low self-esteem and self-hatred. Allow this information to help you recognize what parts of your self are so intolerable for you. Realize that this is just information to help you to recognize, accept and heal this incredible hurt inside. We often try to kill off (get rid of) parts of ourselves that we don't like (judge negatively), so this may relate to your dream execution. Note the dream feelings about this, since positive feelings may indicate the need to "execute," accomplish or begin an endeavour. It may also say you feel persecuted, totally denied or ignored by someone in your life. Again, allow the dream feelings to help you understand who or what is creating these feelings.

Funeral

Is the dream funeral a celebration or a mourning? The dream feelings will help you understand whether this funeral represents a useful shedding of some part of your self or something you have outgrown. For example, if the funeral is for a child, describe the attributes of this child and realize that he/she symbolizes the part of you that has died. It may represent some childish behaviour that you now recognize you no longer need. Or, if you describe the child as a brat or brute, the dream may be saying that you recognize these qualities within yourself but are not letting them go. If there is great grief at the funeral, it may represent your sorrow about losing someone or something in your life. Can you recognize what in your current life feels like it has died, been lost, been transformed, or been otherwise changed in a dramatic way? What are you grieving?

Killing

Killing is often our attempt to get rid of or remove parts of ourselves that we judge. For example, you may be aware of your mental chatter always nagging you to do something, or perhaps you have an inner critic that won't shut up. In our minds we often respond to these voices negatively — "Oh, I wish this voice inside would just go away, shut up or die." This sends a direct image to the mind (in symbolic picture format) and we use that symbol (killing) as a way to depict what our actual thoughts have been. Are you angry at yourself lately or have you said or done something you'd like to retract? The feelings in the dream will reflect the depth of the need. These parts are often just parts we judge as not good enough, bad or simply intolerable. We usually

don't want to face or deal with these parts of self and therefore try to get them out of our minds. It is important to understand that this is a part of you and you can never be rid of it. Learning to accept this part without judgement will always help balance the issue in a healthier way for you.

If the dream symbol is another person, remember that it is likely just a reflection of a part of your self that you wish to kill off. To determine which aspect is being symbolized, simply describe the character and personality of the person in the dream. Even if you don't know them personally, you will often get a sense of their demeanour. List three traits that apply to that person and realize that this is a reflection of your self.

Be aware of the words you have been saying lately, since the dream killing may be reflecting these words. For example, if you catch yourself saying "my job is killing me," your dream killing may be trying to draw your attention to your feelings about your job and how they are affecting you. If you say "my spouse" or a certain situation is "killing" you, realize that these words are also trying to get you to connect your feelings to the person or event and how they are affecting you. See also the dictionary sections on *Tools and Weapons*.

Massacre

Something is being annihilated, obliter-ated or killed off. Is it an aspect of your self that you are butchering with harsh words, actions or judgements? Do you go off on inner tangents, berating and hating your self? This may be what your dream massacre represents.

This could also symbolize that you are following a "mass consciousness" and experiencing an inner death because you aren't following your own truths.

Suicide

Dreams in which you kill yourself are often warnings that you are being overly hard on yourself. Do you beat yourself up inside with your thoughts? If you are not aware of this already, you need to become more attuned to your inner dialogue. On the other hand, killing yourself in the dream may describe the death of an unwanted, old or bad habit. Have you been trying to eliminate some unwanted aspect of your self? Note the dream feelings to discern if this is a helpful transformation or a warning of severe depression or impending inner crisis in your actual life. Suicide dreams may also indicate that you feel as though you have no control or choice about something, or they could symbol-ize that you would like to abandon, bail out or leave an overly demanding or stressful situation or relationship. If accompanied by feelings of hopeless-ness and helplessness, this type of dream may be a warning that you actu-ally feel suicidal — seek appropriate help or share your dream with someone.

Disease, Illness and Medical Treatment

Remember: These symbolic meanings are just suggestions. If these suggested meanings do not resonate with you, ring a bell, give you an "ah-ha" moment or otherwise feel right, search through your own experience or beliefs about the symbol to find what makes sense for you.

Amputation

May suggest you feel "cut off," ignored or uncared for. Note the dream feelings to help you discern whether the dream is depicting a helpful letting go or a painful situation. An amputated leg may denote that you don't feel you have a leg to stand on, or that your not able to take a stand for something. An amputated arm may say you feel you can't grasp a situation or hold on to something. Either way, the dream probably represents a painful, debilitating or otherwise over-whelming situation.

Bandage

May say you feel wounded and in need of some nurturing and tender loving care. May symbolize that you are covering old wounds (or something else) up. Or, could represent that healing is taking place and that you are caring for yourself well.

Blindness

Dreaming that you are blind is a signifi-cant omen suggesting that you cannot see your way clearly in some regard. This could be anything or in any area of your life — a relationship, event, situa-tion, belief, habit or way of thinking. Usually we are blinded by our own emotions, which inhibit us from seeing things clearly or as they really are. Note the dream feelings to help you discern if this blindness is a healthy way of dealing with your current reality or a warning to wake up and see the situa-tion in its truth. The blindness of some-one else in your dream likely mirrors a part of you that cannot perceive its reality clearly, or is dazed or confused.

Blood Transfusion

Indicates that you feel a loss of vitality and vigour and are in dire need of some help, or a boost to your morale. Red may be associated with anger, rage or passion. Notice whether you feel low or cut off from these feelings (in the dream and in your waking life) and how this links to what is currently going on in your life. May suggest you need to express these feelings more. May also imply you are low on energy or vitality and need support or encouragement in some way. Loss is likely at the root of this problem, so try to connect this dream symbol with recent feelings of loss or decreased vitality (exhaustion). Red is the colour associated with the first chakra, so this symbol ties in with the first chakra energy. See the *Chakras* section (first chakra) of this dictionary for help in discerning what your blood transfusion signifies.

Broken Bone

May represent that you feel broken, betrayed or otherwise divided about something. Have you felt separated, invalidated or crushed lately? Perhaps something or someone has shattered you, or you feel in pieces (mentally anguished or distraught). Does something currently cut you to the bone or have you pulled a boner (done something foolish)? Do you feel hurt or wounded in any way? Perhaps you are in need of some deep healing or repair of some kind. Could this represent a broken heart or broken promise? Note the dream feelings for greater insight.

Bruise

Indicates that you have recently been wounded on some level of your being — perhaps your feelings have been hurt, or angry words have been sent your way. All types of insults, belittlements or harsh words bruise or harm us at an energetic level (which eventually manifests as disease or illness, or can make you prone to physical injury). Note the dream feelings and try to connect this to some recent daytime event, situation, issue or relationship.

Burn

May suggest you feel burned or otherwise betrayed by someone or some current situation or event. Does this depict a painful feeling, a useful separation, or even a beneficial purification? Have you recently lost something and feel cheated or deceived? Do you feel wounded or in need of some tender loving care? Perhaps some sort of "surface" (external or seen by others) situation has hurt you to the extreme. Burn can also symbolize your anger, rage or aggressive feelings coming to the surface for you and others to see. What currently burns you up or creates rage within you? Do you feel burnt out or worn out?

Cancer

Known for its ability to destroy things, observe what issues, relationship or situations currently eat away at you. Are you being self-destructive or otherwise self-abusive? Note your personal feelings and associations of this disease to help you understand what it symbolizes for you. For example, if you think cancer denotes certain death, make the connection to what you perceive as currently dying around or within you. Death can also be about transformation and change, so note how things are changing around you and how you feel about that. Also note your current choice of words — have you been expressing such things as "this is killing me"? Or do you feel that you can't go on in a certain way?

If the disease cancer creates fear in you, then realize that cancer in your dream likely represents some big fear that you are currently facing or experiencing. In order to resolve or transmute these powerful circumstances, you need to make the connection to some recent event, feeling or issue. Perhaps you feel helpless or out of control and cancer is the manifestation of these fearful feelings.

The dream symbol may even refer to the astrological sign of Cancer (the crab), so it would be useful to read about this in the *Astrology, Planets and the Cosmos* section of this dictionary. May be a pun on "crab" — have you or someone you know been crabby, grumpy, or doing a lot of complaining lately?

Cast/Sling

Wearing a cast may symbolize that something feels broken or a part of you needs to mend. May be a pun on feeling typecast (stereotyped) or set in a certain role. Could this be a pun on "casting a shadow" or feeling cast aside and uncared for? A sling can be about hurling an insult or feeling that you're in a sling (bind). Could also denote the need for support (either from yourself or from others). See Broken Bone for greater insight.

Cold

A dream about an influenza type of cold represents a generalized state of confusion and the need to rest in order to sort things out. A cold feeling in the body indicates a numbness or disconnection from that particular body part. See the applicable entry in the *Body* section of this dictionary to determine what you may be disconnected from. Puns on "cold" may include cold shoulder, needing a cold shower, or putting something into cold storage.

299

Crutches

Symbolizes something that assists you in walking (moving forward) when you've been wounded. Do you require assistance on your journey at this time? May suggest you need some help or that you have a crutch to bear. May suggest you are leaning or relying on something or someone too much. Crutches can also denote an excuse for not doing something.

Cut

Indicates you feel wounded at some level of your being. Perhaps someone has used cutting (harsh, angry, insulting) words about you (or maybe you have turned these words in on yourself)? A bleeding cut symbolizes that you are losing energy or vitality. Have you recently felt "loss" with respect to some event, situation, issue or relationship? A cut probably indicates the need for "management," help, insight or tenderness. It may be a pun on something cutting deeply or cutting you to the quick. It could also say that something cuts like a knife or that you wish someone would "cut it out" (behave differently). Have you been wanting to cut someone or something out of your life? Do you feel as though you can't cut it?

Deafness

Dreaming that you are deaf indicates that you are not hearing something or someone clearly. You may not be taking yourself or another in, or not hearing the truth of someone's (or your own) words. Whether you are turning a deaf ear on purpose or unconsciously, now it's time to hear the truth. If someone else is deaf in your dream, realize that the attributes or characteristics that you ascribe to that dream character are the parts of you that are unable to "hear" what's being said. It could also suggest you are not hearing the symbolic meaning (as opposed to literal meaning) of someone's words. Learning to listen for the deeper or hidden meaning is an attribute of the fifth chakra and associated with clairsentience (clear hearing). Are you playing deaf in your waking life for a reason? Perhaps it is an act of self-protection or self-preservation — if you don't hear something, then you don't have to acknowledge it or act on it. See the entry on the fifth chakra in the *Chakras* section of this dictionary for greater insight.

Dental Examination

This symbol is associated with the words you speak. May say you have been speaking false words (lies, deceit or gossip) or that you have been speaking out of place. If the check-up is for cleaning, it suggests the need to clean up your words. Getting a clean bill of health may suggest that your recent words have been healthy, well chosen and/or inspiring and truthful. Have you been scrutinizing or analyzing your own words (or those of another) lately? Note the dream feelings to help you discern how you have been using your words. Could suggest you are putting pressure on yourself to speak clearly, correctly or otherwise communicate in a perfect way. If seeing a dentist brings up fear for you, realize that this dream symbol may represent some current fears you are experiencing. See Dentist in the *People* section and Teeth in *Body* section for greater insight.

Fever

May suggest the build-up of feelings or unexpressed emotions. Could symbolize that you are enraged or "hot" about something, or "all burned up." May represent your actual internal temperature is rising to defend you against an invading virus or bacteria.

Flu – See Cold

Headache/Migraine

May suggest there is mental anguish, confusion or a battle of wills taking place in your inner reality. Also implies a blockage of first chakra energy or the build-up of anger or some other heated emotion. If these emotions have no outlet, they build into a dream migraine or a migraine in your waking life. Anything that you hold on to can build up pressure within your thoughts and thinking processes and create pain. This can be old beliefs, habits, attitudes, or any negative thinking. See First Chakra and Seventh Chakra in the *Chakras* section of the dictionary.

Heart Attack

Signifies a closed or hardened heart. It may also be a wake-up call for you to change your habits or current lifestyle. May suggest that you have been overly judgemental about yourself or others, or that your ability to be compassionate is not functioning well. The heart is the place of love, so dreaming of a heart attack may indicate your lack of love, loss of love or great grief. It could also symbolize that you are under attack from yourself or from another. Do you feel pressured by a group or by group consciousness? May suggest you feel under assault, harassed or bothered by something or someone. Understanding the function of the heart chakra would be very beneficial if you are dreaming of heart attacks. Read about the Fourth Chakra in the *Chakras* section of this dictionary.

Illness

May denote feelings of being disabled, frail, weak or impaired at some level or in some area of your life. Any held-in emotion, chronic negative thinking or dissatisfaction with your life can cause disease within the physical body. Have you been saying "I'm sick of" something or that something is "killing" you? The subconscious mind reads your internal dialogue as real, so over time these messages can manifest as illness. Any illness or disease in the dream may denote that you have a literal illness brewing — you should seek medical advice to be sure. Have you been making yourself sick with worry, guilt or other unexpressed feelings? Your dream illness may be trying to get you to pay attention to your thoughts, feelings, words and actions. Could say you are sick and tired about something, or that you are being drained by a relationship, addiction or repetitive negative thoughts or feelings. Have you caught yourself thinking or saying "this makes me sick"? Could be a pun on a sick joke or something you find abhorrent.

Infection

Often symbolizes a sense of being invaded at some level. Perhaps your privacy or space has been invaded. Do you feel contaminated while in a certain person's company? Is your mind being poisoned by your negative thinking or by someone else's negative thinking? Could indicate that you have a literal infection brewing within your body — perhaps you need to get medical advice.

Injury

May denote that you have been harmed, hurt or damaged on some level of your being, either by your own negative thinking and feelings or by someone else's. Note what part of you is injured and if any healing has begun. May point to the need to forgive yourself or another for wrongs inflicted. Wounds can be caused in many different ways and require understanding, compassion and a nonjudgemental approach in order to heal. See the applicable entry in the *Body* section for greater insight.

Intravenous Drip

Indicates a need for more hydration or fluids. Could say you feel all dried up or emotionally spent. May require some self-care — more tenderness, loving and nurturing.

Laryngitis

Losing your voice signifies you feel you have no "voice" or opinion, that your words are not being heard, or your words don't count or matter.

Perhaps you feel insignificant or un-worthy of expression. Are you speak-ing your truth or have you lost energy to false words (lying, gossiping)? There is definitely a problem with communi-cation or self-expression when laryngi-tis is present in the dream (or waking time). Try to discover what significance your voice has in your current under-takings or relationships. Note the dream feelings to understand if this Is a healthy silence you are holding or a loss of energy because of you are unable to express your truth. The func-tioning of the fifth chakra is greatly in-fluenced by any dreams related to the throat, so it would be most helpful to read about this in the *Chakras* section of the dictionary.

Life Support System

If you dream of being on a ventilator (breathing machine), this is a clear warning that you need more support in your life. Are you undermining yourself with negative thinking, self-betrayal or self-hatred? Are you surrounded by judgemental, negative and unsupportive people? You need to "wake up" and re-create new support systems in your life. May symbolize that your energy reserves are so low (exhaustion) that they have reached a critical point. This is a crisis in the happening. It may symbolize your literal health, so seek appropriate medical advice.

Medical Examination

Represents getting checked over by a professional and may suggest an encounter with authority, depend-ing on your viewpoints and associa-tions with medical personnel. Could say you feel scrutinized, analyzed (by yourself or another) or otherwise under pressure to perform or accomplish something. Note the dream feelings to help you understand whether you need some encouragement or more attention on some level. May suggest you feel ill or sick about something (see the entry on Illness for greater insight). Have you felt like a victim or that things are out of control recently? If you have felt dominated by someone else, then this symbol could be about your issues with authority. Perhaps you are seeking advice, support or positive feedback lately. May suggest you actu-ally require medical help, so keep this in mind when discerning the meaning of your dream examination.

Menopause

A time when women learn to hold in their own energy (blood) and therefore become a resource (wisdom) for loved ones and the community. Menopause is a time of great power in a woman's life, and it represents a time of freedom to use your gifts of perception for the greater good of all. Women at this stage of life are often referred to as crones or hags (wise ones). Note your personal associations with menopause and whether you see this as an empowering time or a time of misery. This symbol suggests change or transformation in some area of your life. Issues of self-esteem or self-empowerment are usually denoted here. Can also represent something you feel hot (angry) about or a heated issue, debate or situation. Could say that you feel like you are going to boil over, blow up or blow your top. Note the dream feelings for greater insight. See Hag in the *People* section for more insight.

Menstruation

Menstruation is symbolic of letting go and going within so that the new can come. It is part of a natural cycle that follows the moon cycles. Remember that women bleed but they do not die, so dreaming of menstruation may reflect your victim consciousness or your strengths, depending on how you view menstruation. Menses is a time of power and strengthening of the self. Because it is associated with bleeding and blood, blood loss in the dream may represent loss of power, energy or vitality, depending on the dream feelings. Your own associations about your own menses will be most helpful in discern-

ing what this dream symbol means to you and what it represents in your life.

Miscarriage

Indicates that you have lost something near and dear to you, probably something you have been working on or developing recently. May be a pun on "miscarriage of justice" or, if you are actually pregnant, it may be a warning to seek medical advice. Have you had to let go of anything unwillingly lately, or has something been taken from you without your permission or blessing?

Operation

If you dream of a surgical operation, note what is being done in the procedure. Is something being removed, cut off or taken away? Ask yourself if there is something that you need to cut out of your lifestyle. An operation can also symbolize how you are handling something or a transaction that is currently taking place, such as a business action, venture, project or any current undertaking. Could be pointing to an actual health problem, so take note of what body part is being operated on and seek appropriate medical advice. See also the *Body* section of this dictionary for further insight.

Pain

In general, pain symbolizes that you feel pain or hurt — physical, emotional, or mental (psychological) — at some level of your being. Your dream pain may symbolize anything that currently creates a hurt or suffering for you. The words, actions and opinions of others cost us dearly at an energetic level. What causes you pain in your everyday life? It could be heartache or something that "gives you a headache." Note your choice of words and thoughts to see if you have been saying such things as "it's a pain in the neck" to do something, or "he's a pain in the rear." Your language creates your reality and your dreams use your everyday words to help you see what situation you are creating. Be aware of your language and try to catch what moments in life are painful for you. Your need for some comfort, TLC and self-support are indicated when you are in pain.

Paralysis

Denotes that you are stuck and feel that you can't move on or move forward. You are unable to do things for yourself, feel victimized, or feel crippled by something. Perhaps you feel out of control or without choice. Or, this could represent that you feel deadened, hopeless and helpless. You are obstructed, deadlocked and

incapacitated in some way. Fear often paralyzes us, as do uncertainty and doubt. This is a warning that you are not in a healthy place; keep in mind that it can be tough to remobilize yourself without help. You need to gather energy in order to move on. Seek help from others to help you understand why you feel powerless to move forward.

Parasite

Parasites are invaders, freeloaders and loafers. Are you feeding on others or is someone sucking your energy from you? Is someone overly dependant on you, irritating you or being totally non-productive? You could even be draining yourself with old patterns of thinking, old attitudes, old behaviours and outdated ways of processing your emotions. May say you actually have parasites, so seek appropriate medical advice.

Pills

Symbolize medicine, a remedy or a treatment. May imply you need to care for yourself in a different way or need to digest and take in the need for caring for self. Painkillers imply you are wounded or in pain at some level of your being and therefore this is a call for help and attention. Could be a pun on a bitter pill you have to swallow.

Pregnancy

Dreams of being pregnant and/or giving birth are common and usually denote that you are trying to give birth to something new in your life. Something is developing within you — whether you abort this or give birth to it is up to you. This could be a new idea, attitude or belief, or a new project or relationship. Anything that you can conceive of is possible to create and give birth to. What have you been trying to accomplish lately? Are you brimming with ideas and feeling pregnant with energy and creativity? Whatever you are pregnant with needs to be nurtured or cultivated in order to bring it to fruition. If you are a woman of childbearing age, the dream may portend that you are actually pregnant. If you are already pregnant, the dream may be giving you information on your condition or the baby's condition.

Prescription

Suggests the need for care, therapy, a remedy or treatment. Note the dream feelings to see if this is a positive need, such as a prescription for love, or a negative message suggesting you have prescribed to a fixed notion or to something that is not your truth. Ask yourself what you prescribe to or how you

define yourself. May also suggest you require healing on some level.

Rash

May be a pun that something is "getting under your skin" or that you are being irritated at some level by someone or something. Perhaps you are being hasty, imprudent, reckless or impulsive.

Sickness – See Illness

Tumour

Whether they are benign or malignant, tumours are about abnormal growth. How do you view your emotional, intellectual and spiritual growth? Has anything been eating away at you or bothering you to the extreme? Note how you feel in the dream and your general associations with tumours to help you understand this more clearly. For example, if you believe that a tumour means certain death, then be aware of what may be dying or ending in your life to clarify the representation. If even the word "tumour" arouses fear, then try to associate this feeling with something you find fearful in your current waking life. Note also what part of the body the tumour is growing on and see the applicable entry in the *Body* section for further clarification of the tumour's meaning. For example, a dream about a lump in your breast relates to your ability to be nurturing and tender with yourself, with someone else, or with respect to some event or situation.

Vaccination

Associated with needles and therefore may indicate being stuck with something or feeling stuck. Could say you are stuck up or that you need to "get the point." Also associated with something that may make you sick, or better, depending on your viewpoint. May represent something you are forced to do against your will. Maybe you need to boost your physical immune system or become immune to something emotional or psychological. It may symbolize something you feel you need protection against, or it may represent your resistance to something.

Voice Loss – *See Laryngitis*

Warts

Since warts are generally thought to be ugly and contagious, they may symbolize how you feel about yourself. May represent low self-esteem, low self-worth or poor self-image. Take note of where the wart is and see the applicable entry in the *Body* section of this dictionary for greater understanding.

X-ray Machine

Represents being able to see below the surface of things — to see to the heart of a matter or through someone's defences. Note what is being x-rayed and see the applicable entry in the *Body* section for greater understanding.

Food

Food in general is related to the mental plane of your being. This is the area of thoughts, thinking, beliefs, ideas, attitudes and opinions. Any dream food may indicate that you need that particular food in your diet, or that you should eliminate it from your diet. Note your feelings in the dream and whether you are attracted or repelled by the food. In this way you will discern the truth of what your body desires. Say, for example, that you dislike carrots in your everyday diet but have a dream of eating carrots (with alacrity). The body and the mind have varying opinions on what is the "right" food to take in. In your waking hours, it may be your mind that makes the decisions about what to eat, but through the dream your body is trying to tell you that it desires this food group.

Note also the colour of the food, as this is often a strong indicator of a need for this colour (vibration) in your life (energy field). It may be helpful to read about the chakra associated with the colour as well. That is, red for first chakra, orange for second, yellow for third, green for fourth, blue for fifth, purple for sixth, and white for seventh.

Because we prepare, take in and digest food, it often symbolizes the need to prepare, take in or digest something mentally. For example, you may need to rethink some plans, arrangements or even a conversation you recently had. What thoughts, words and actions do you need to digest? Are you prepared psychologically for some upcoming event? Note whether the dream food seems repulsive or indigestible to you. Or perhaps you gobble it down, reflecting your great desire to take in something.

Remember: These symbolic meanings are just suggestions. If these suggested meanings do not resonate with you, ring a bell, give you an "ah-ha" moment or otherwise feel right, search through your own experience or beliefs about the symbol to find what makes sense for you.

Objects and Actions Related to Food

Back Burner

What have you left on the back burner lately? Is there anything that you are avoiding or putting aside to deal with later? Look to projects, ideas, relationships or other issues that may have to be dealt with now and not put off until tomorrow.

Banquet

Often represents a plethora of new ideas or mental stimulation (perhaps overstimulation) being offered to you. A feast for your mind or food for thought.

Barbecue

Often associated with relaxing times or perhaps a cottage setting, depending on your personal experiences with barbecuing, so this setting may suggest that you are relaxed and at peace mentally. Note the dream feelings to understand if this is something you are taking in well (peaceful feelings in dream) or perhaps not taking in well (frustrations associated with dream). Note what is being barbecued and whether this indicates your need to eat, or to avoid, this type of food.

Buffet

Indicates a choice to be made in your life currently. Perhaps you have many things to choose from or many ideas to choose from. What type of food is being offered at your dream buffet? Is there fresh healthy foods to choose from, has the buffet been picked over, or does it offer foods that you don't enjoy? The type and amount of food will help you understand what is currently being offered in your waking time.

Choking

Indicates there is something unpleasant in your life that you find hard to swallow or impossible to take in. Look to see what has been offered lately that you are reluctant to embrace or accept — this could be a thought, concept, piece of information, idea or relationship.

Hungry or Starving

A common phrase is "I'm starving to death," and this symbol may represent that you are starving or undernourished on one or all levels of your being (physical, emotional, mental and spiritual). Are you currently unsupported in some endeavour? Do you or others support your belief systems? Lack of food can often symbolize a lack of mental stimulation, ideas or choice. No food may indicate that you have no support or nourishment of your emotions, mind or soul; that your mind has nothing to grow on; or that you are neglecting to feed yourself on different levels.

Picnic

Usually associated with relaxation, family and a break from regular routine. May indicate your preparedness to take something in with pleasure or without fuss or worry. Because picnics are usually outdoors, it could suggest you have open-mindedness or fresh ideas about something. It could also speak of an easy-going manner you have recently adopted, or the need to unwind and take a break from your regular routine.

Pot-luck

Usually denotes a coming together of many ideas, or may represent group thinking and behaviour. Are all the dishes presented at pot-luck the same or is there a variety? Do you need to bring some outside ideas into your own opinion pool or vary your thinking? Note the dream feelings to help you understand how open or resistant you may be to others' ideas, thoughts, opinions or beliefs.

Preparing Food

Symbolic of what you are or are not prepared to take in and digest. What are you currently willing to swallow in your life? Is the food being prepared something you like or something that appeals to you? This will indicate how accepting (or not) you are of this idea,

Foods and Fluids

Alcohol

Something you choose to take in and can represent a thought, idea or attitude, depending on your beliefs regarding alcohol. May represent shame, loss of control, addiction, weakness, insecurity, self-judgements, or a way to escape true feelings. What are you swallowing? Do you feel less

inhibited when you drink? In the dream it may represent you letting go or letting loose of something. How and why is alcohol used in your dream?

Apple

May represent the fruit you are currently bearing in your life or that something has come to fruition. Often associated with forbidden fruit, in which case look to something in your life that you feel you are not worthy of receiving at this time.

Banana

May indicate a need for bananas in your diet, but is often a phallic symbol representing repressed urges or desire for love or sexual expression.

Beef

May depict the need to beef it up or that you have a "chief beef" or complaint. Perhaps it indicates an actual need for more meat/protein in your diet. May be a pun on being "full of bull."

Bread

May represent the bread of life or the need for sustenance (strength and support) on one or all levels of your being (mind, body, emotions, spirit). May be a pun representing your pay cheque or wages earned (i.e., money).

Butter

May be a pun on being buttered up or flattered by someone or something. Could be related to "bread and butter" or income earning. Could indicate the

need to be kinder to yourself (butter yourself up).

Cake

May represent your desire for something sweet in your life. Is there a lack of sweetness or pleasing situations in your life currently? May be a pun on sayings such as "piece of cake," "you can have your cake and eat it too," or "let them eat cake."

Candy

Often associated with feeling sweet or something sweet going on in your life. Could be pleasant feelings and a sense of overall happiness about someone or something. May also indicate the need for more sweetness in your life. Note if your feelings in the dream are more of longing, emptiness, fulfillment, or even a sense of reward.

Cheese

May symbolize the need for more dairy/protein in your diet, or may be a pun on something cheesy in your life (cheap or not valuable). May be a pun on the need to "say cheese" or smile for the camera (which may be a reference to a fake smile or put-on smile).

Chicken

May represent a pun on being afraid or foul. Have you been accused of being cowardly? Or has a situation run afoul? Is there foul play happening or does something smell foul? Are you feeling afraid of facing a situation or do you lack the courage to face something (being a chicken shit)? Do you feel hen-pecked or picked on? What other associations do you have for chicken? Perhaps your diet lacks protein and the dream is a suggestion to eat chicken.

Chocolate

May represent indulgence, sweetness in your life (or lack of it), excessiveness or cravings for something. Could say you need to indulge in something or that you are depriving yourself, depending on the dream feelings.

Coffee

Often used as a "wake me up" stimulant or as a source of sharing and friendliness. Do you need a wake-up call in some area of your life, or do you need stimulation about a old pattern or new idea? Do you associate coffee with companionship, gossip or the sharing of yourself? If the coffee is brewing, perhaps you are brewing or seething about something.

Cookie

May represent some long-cherished memory (if you ate cookies as a child) or suggest that you are taking in something you consider to be good (if you are eating cookies in the dream). Do you allow yourself to eat cookies in general, or are they taboo? Could this represent something you are holding back from or not allowing yourself to take in at this time? May symbolize something you perceive as sweet or good but because of your beliefs you aren't moving toward it or embracing it. If you think cookies are just for special occasions, they may represent something special or out of the ordinary for you. It may also be a pun on the computer term cookies, so be aware if this is a known term for you and how it relates to your life.

Corn

Is there a "kernel of truth" in a recent situation? Or perhaps a corny situation has occurred lately. Have you planted something and now watch or wait while it grows to fruition?

Dessert

Are you craving some sweetness in your life or are you waiting for some? Do you need to reward yourself for some current effort, or do you feel you deserve some treats in life? May be a pun on "just dessert" or indicate some indulgence you crave. May also indicate a sugar craving or hypoglycemia, depending on how sugary the dessert is.

Drinking

Consuming or taking in food for thought or perhaps quenching your spiritual thirst. What are you drinking in the dream and how does it feel? Drinking lemonade may suggest the need for aid or help. Are you finding something hard to swallow? Are you thirsting for something more in your life?

Egg

Symbol of creation and the womb. May mean cholesterol problems or the need to hatch something new in your life. Because eggs are food they can often denote food for thought or be a pun on such things as egging someone on or egg all over your face. May also symbolize a seed idea, wholeness or oneness. Eggs are traditional symbols of original state or beginning.

Fast Food

Do you perceive fast food as reward food, nourishing food or junk food? This will help you understand what area of your thoughts, thinking, ideas, beliefs or attitudes are at issue here. Is there lack of preparation for something in your life or are you attempting to undertake an endeavour without much thought or thinking? Perhaps a belief or attitude is not serving you well and is hard to digest.

Fish

Often associated with spiritual food, and may be a pun on sole/soul. Fish is also a symbol for Christ, wisdom and wholeness. May be a pun on something fishy in your life. Since fish swim in water, they may indicate a need to go with the flow or to get in touch with your feminine side or intuition. May indicate that you need fish or fish oils in your diet.

Fruit

Symbolic of the results of the seeds you have planted. What projects have you recently brought to fruition or culmination? Is the fruit in your dreams ripe and healthy-looking or rotten and diseased? This will help you understand how well your project has been supported and cared for to date. Ripe fruit that is ready to pick indicates that whatever idea, relationship, project or endeavour you have been working on is now ready for harvesting.

Grain

Are your dream grains planted or waiting to be planted? Do you have, or are you in need of, some seed ideas (new or inspiring ideas)? Are the grains cooked and ready to be eaten, indicating that you are ready to take in and digest something? Perhaps you are sensitive to grains in your waking life and need to pay attention to what type of grain is being presented in the dream.

Grapes

Associated with fertility and the sweetness of life. May indicate a cluster of ideas or some idea or concept that has come to fruition in your life.

Gum

Is there anything in your life that you need to chew on? Or perhaps a sticky situation that needs to be dealt with? Is anything gumming up your ability to express yourself or are you having trouble expressing yourself?

Hazelnut

Indicates protection and represents the spiritual thread that cannot be destroyed by the powers of ignorance and darkness.

Herbs

The specific herb mentioned or seen in your dream may indicate a need for that herb. Each herb has its own healing properties, which can be found in a herbal dictionary. Herbs in general can "spice up your life," so look to see if you need a little zest in a specific area of your life at this time.

Honey

Symbolic of the sweetness of life. Is there a lack of sweetness or fulfillment in your life currently? May be a pun on a special name you call your sweetheart.

Junk Food

Often associated with thoughts, ideas, beliefs or attitudes that do not serve you well at this time. Is the junk food in the dream appealing? Do you crave it? Do you give yourself permission to eat junk food on occasion or do you exist on a steady diet of it? Noting this will help you understand if this is a usual pattern of behaviour being represented here or an indication that you need some moderation in your actual diet.

Meat

May indicate a need for more protein in your diet, or may be symbolic of your current food for thought or mental processes. Note puns such as "the meat of the matter." If you are a vegetarian, a meat dream may indicate something repellant or distasteful to you. Perhaps you have not taken in a recent thought or way of thinking well, or maybe you don't want to think along these tracks.

Milk

Have you or someone you know been milking a situation or taking more than is necessary? Milk is often seen as nutritious and nurturing (mother's milk). Do you need to feed yourself something nutritious on any level of your being (mental, emotional, physical or spiritual)? Many people are allergic to milk without realizing it. Depending on the feelings in the dream, milk may symbolize either a need to drink more of it or a need to eliminate it from your diet.

Nuts

Has someone or something been driving you nuts? May indicate the need for nuts or protein in your diet. Likely a pun on the word "nut," such as "it's a hard nut to crack" or "in a nutshell." Discover who or what is the nut in your life currently. May also indicate a seed idea or potential for growth.

Onions

Often symbolic of tears because it is hard not to tear-up when cutting an onion. Do you need to express some tears or feelings but are finding it difficult? Is someone or some situation causing you to cry or be sad? Onions also spice up a dish and may indicate the need to add some zest or flavour to a situation or relationship.

Potato

Since potatoes are a staple in some diets, this may represent a necessary element, or your need to include a "must have" in your waking life — a routine, habit, relationship, or just about anything you feel is necessary as a part of your everyday life. Noting whether you like potatoes will help you understand the meaning.

Soup

Because most soups are liquid, this may represent your emotional life or the feelings you are currently having. Are you taking the dream soup in or just observing it? Are you taking in your own feelings or just observing them (perhaps without feeling them)? Soup is often seen as warming, fulfilling and nurturing; it may speak to your need to include these attributes in your life, or suggest that you are feeling filled up in a good way. Note whether the soup is hearty or thin and how you feel about this and the thought of eating it, because some people see soup as not being sustaining or filling.

Tea

May be associated with a ritual or repetitive behaviour on your part, depending on whether you usually have tea in the traditional British way as an afternoon social ritual. Others may associate taking tea with a calming or relaxing experience, so be mindful if tea is a part of your routine or not. If not, it could represent the need for more routine or ritual in your life. Tea also contains caffeine, so it may represent a "pick me up" or a stimulant. Do you associate tea with companionship, gossip or the sharing of your self?

Turkey

Known in North America as food to eat during family gatherings and cultural events, turkey may represent a group meeting or group consciousness. Do you partake in eating turkey during holiday celebrations? If so note if there is something you are celebrating at present; the turkey represents the rewards of this situation. Turkeys are also about shared blessings and harvest, and are a symbol of all the blessings the Earth contains. Do you recognize the blessings in your life? How well are you currently using them? Turkey may also indicate the need for more protein in your diet.

Vegetables

What type of vegetable is shown in your dream? Note the colour, since this may be an important indicator of the meaning behind the veggie. Vegetables can indicate the need for more of this particular type in your diet. Note whether it is a vegetable you like or dislike, as this is a clue about whether you are taking in this particular food for thought.

Furniture and Household Objects

In general, furniture symbolizes your thoughts, thinking, ideas, concepts, beliefs, opinions and attitudes. Everything that takes place in the realm of the mind can take shape and represent the state of your mind at the time of the dream. It therefore is important to note the condition of the furniture in the dream. Furniture that is in disrepair indicates that a belief, attitude or idea that you currently hold is not serving you well and it is important to consider "mending" it. If the furniture is something that appeals to you, the dream may indicate the need to take in or stand firm on a particularly appealing project, idea or belief.

Remember: These symbolic meanings are just suggestions. If these suggested meanings do not resonate with you, ring a bell, give you an "ah-ha" moment or otherwise feel right, search through your own experience or beliefs about the symbol to find what makes sense for you.

Furniture

Antiques

Symbolic of old ways of thinking, doing and behaving. Look to see what you may have recently outgrown in the way of your thoughts, attitudes and beliefs. On the other hand, if you collect antiques and care for them, it may represent thoughts, thinking and principles that have stood the test of time and support you well. Look to see how you feel about the antiques being presented in the dream, since this will help you identify whether the current situation they represent benefits you or not.

Bar

A bar in the home may represent an area of relaxation or indulgence, depending on how your dream bar is viewed. Does having a drink mean a little rest and relaxation to you, or an addiction? Is your dream telling you that you want to indulge? Or that you should drink less? A bar may be a pun on something barring or blocking your way. Perhaps your dream bar is indicative of an impaired perspective or skewed thinking on your part.

Bed

Often seen as a private or safe and secure place. May represent your private thoughts or thinking that you share only with yourself or perhaps a partner. A bed offers support to whomever is lying in it — are you feeling supported in your private place/issues? A bed may also represent your sexuality, depending on what your personal views are about beds and bedrooms. Have you recently "made your own bed" and now you have to sleep in it? In other words, do you have to deal with a situation of your own creation? A bedspread may symbolize that you cover up your private life, or may represent warmth and secure feelings.

- ▸ *Double bed:* May represent your marital state and your relationship with your sleeping partner.
- ▸ *Single bed:* May denote the single life or perhaps feeling alone about something.
- ▸ *Mattress:* May represent the foundation of your relationship (with self or another).
- ▸ *Water bed:* Often represents emotional turmoil within the "bedroom"; that is, either within your relationship or within your private inner world. A water bed may also symbolize play or fun, depending on how your dream water bed is being used and how you view water beds in general.

Cabinet

Place to store or hide parts of yourself — perhaps parts of your personality you don't want others to see because you feel ashamed of or embarrassed by them. What is in your dream cabinet? Is it locked or accessible to all?

Carpet – *See Rug*

Chair

Represents your position or "seat" in life. What kind of chair is it? Is it a throne or a recliner? Is it a plastic chair or a lawn chair? Each type portrays a different symbolic meaning. For example, a plastic chair may represent a false position or viewpoint you are currently taking. A recliner or lazy-boy chair may symbolize that you are in a comfortable position within some current situation, relationship or dealings. Conversely, it may be telling you that you have been lazy or are sitting too much. A throne may represent your dominant thoughts or thinking, or that you are in a position of authority and control. A rocking chair may mean that you are not taking a stance on some matter or are hesitant about a certain situation. Chairs represent your seat, your rights and your stance on matters. What perspective or viewpoint is your dream chair showing you?

Chest

Usually contains something. Note if your dream chest is a treasure chest or a chest of drawers. These could represent you as a container of wealth (treasure chest) or as a container in which you store your thoughts, old ideas or attitudes, perhaps in order to hide them from others. May be a pun on your body part, the chest, and symbolize your lungs or heart. Perhaps you need to get something off your chest or become aware of the feelings associated with your heart. See also Lung and Heart in the *Body* section, and Fourth Chakra in the *Chakras* section for further insight.

China Cabinet

Often used for display, so ask yourself what type of behaviours, attitudes or feelings you have been displaying to others. Note the dream feelings to help you understand whether your pride is a healthy one or whether you are just showing off. May symbolize your finest qualities, or that you feel fragile. Could suggest you feel as though you've been on display, analyzed or judged recently. May say that you are storing away your best qualities — is it time to bring them out and use them?

Couch – See Sofa

Crib

May suggest you need to nurture or baby yourself in some way. Perhaps you have been displaying childish or babyish behaviour. May suggest you feel small, inadequate or even caged (not free) about something. Perhaps you need to cradle yourself or otherwise act gently toward something. Note the dream feelings to help you understand more fully what this symbol represents in your life.

Desk

Used for work or for play, desks are instruments of our will power and intention. Can you relate your recent mental activity, analytical thinking or creativity to your dream desk? Was the desk cluttered or tidy in the dream? This may help you understand whether your thinking or your mind are cluttered or clear and orderly. Perhaps you have some unfinished business at hand or need to work out some problems. What responsibilities, work or tasks do you associate with a desk? Relate this to your current waking-hour events to help you understand the meaning of your dream desk.

Dresser

Similar to a chest of drawers, a dresser contains something. Have you been storing something at a thought level or mental level? Do you need to contain or hide anything? Have you been hiding from something? What thoughts, attitudes and beliefs are you currently storing or "containerizing"? Stored ideas, thoughts or opinions include dreams that you aren't pursuing and ideas that you aren't moving toward manifesting in your waking life.

Filing Cabinet

A place of stored information, a filing cabinet may represent your memories, old ideas or anything that currently feels stored or in need of safekeeping. Perhaps you need to put something in order or get something straight. If the dream cabinet is not accessible, it may symbolize something you don't want revealed or disclosed. If it is open, it may represent something that is "out in the open." What information is filed in the cabinet? How does this relate to your current endeavours or relationships?

Lamp

Ask yourself whether you need a little light in some area of your life. Are you not seeing some situation or relationship clearly, or do you need more clarification on a matter? Is the light on in the dream or are you in the dark?

This will help you discern whether or you have any waking-hour awareness of what the situation is about. Lamps can also be about enlightenment, insights and awareness in general. Could say someone lights up your life or that you need to lighten up (be less serious).

Mirror

Represents reflection and symbolic mirroring; you are seeing a reflection of some part of you. What traits or characteristics are being revealed to you in the dream mirror? Perhaps you need to do some self-reflection with respect to a recent situation or event. Perhaps you need to take a good look at yourself or become more aware of your self-image. What are you reflecting to others at this time? To the world? Is there anything you currently don't want to face? A broken mirror may represent bad luck or a distorted self-image.

New Furniture

Depicts new ideas, concepts or beliefs, or ones that you may be currently forming. May symbolize that you have changed your thinking or thoughts for the better, or that you are feeling refreshed and renewed by your current choices.

Old Furniture

Old ideas, thoughts, concepts or beliefs. May or may not serve you well, depending on the condition. For example, broken-down pieces of furniture are perceptions that are no longer relevant or meaningful in your life; the dream is showing you that you need to revamp or revise them. Could be outdated patterns, habits or behaviours you are still expressing.

Picture

A picture hanging on the wall symbolizes what you are showing or representing to the world. What is the dream picturing portraying? This will help clarify what area of your life is being represented. What impressions does the picture stir up in you? May be a pun on "picture this" — can you picture yourself doing something? Or does a picture paint a thousand words? If the picture is of you, it may represent that you need to take a good look at yourself. Pictures often capture a moment — is there something you want to remember or hold dear to you? If you are taking a photograph, perhaps you need to get a clear picture or get a clear grasp on something. A picture of another person may be symbolic of how you see yourself.

Rug

Because a rug is under your feet, it usually depicts something upon which you stand. Often this has to do with belief systems and things that you take a stance on. A rug may cover a part of your self you don't want to see or have others see — perhaps a belief, thought or opinion. A rug may protect your beliefs or offer you protection. Since rugs also get walked on, ask yourself if you have been walked on recently. Conversely, a rug may represent beauty to you, or something in which you take pride. Note the condition of the rug for greater insight.

Shelf

Represents an area of storage or where you may shelve an idea. Is there some activity, belief or relationship that you have outgrown, or that you need to suspend or delay? Perhaps you have stored or shelved some memories or concepts that now need to be brought back into use. Note what is on the shelves for greater insight.

Sofa

Often a place of relaxation and leisure, so ask yourself if you need some down time or need to put your feet up. Conversely, the dream may be pointing out that you are being too much of a couch potato and need more activity. How is your dream couch being used? This will help you pinpoint where you need more rest or activity in your current life.

Table

Can be used for a variety of activities — how is your dream table being used? Is it for recreation, dining or to work something out? The exact meaning of this symbol depends on how the table is being used.

▸ *Buffet table:* Symbolic of many ideas, thoughts, beliefs and opinions. Denotes much freedom of choice and variety. Implies you may need to help yourself in a current situation, serve yourself, or put yourself first in some area of your life. Perhaps there is something you must do for yourself that no one else can do (serve) for you.

▸ *Conference table:* Usually associated with the workplace. Is there some thing that needs to be worked out? Perhaps you are in confrontation with someone or something? Does something need to be hashed out or communicated in a business-like way? Is there another point of view you could take, or do you need to work out some differences?

▸ *Dining table:* A place to take in and digest food for thought and new ideas. Perhaps seen as a place for sharing thoughts and ideas with family and friends. Also a place to communicate opinions, beliefs and thoughts.

▸ *Kitchen table:* Usually associated with cozy or confidential talk. Is there something you need to express and you need a place to do it or a person in whom to confide? Kitchens in general are related to the mental realm, so ask yourself if you need any food for thought in your life currently. Perhaps your dream kitchen speaks of personal matters or private, confidential situations. If kitchens represent the heart of the home for you, a kitchen table in your dream may symbolize a situation, event or relationship that is a central focus in your life.

Household Appliances and Electronics

Air Conditioner

May suggest you need to cool down, chill out or otherwise stand back and review things. Perhaps you are hot and bothered by something and need a new perspective. May suggest you feel heated about something (anger, rage) and feel the need to thaw out those feelings. Note your own associations to air conditioning to help you understand if this is much needed relief from something or a situation that leaves you cold.

Blender

May represent the need to blend two or more things together — perhaps the blending of ideas, concepts or beliefs. May be a pun on a "blended family" or your need to blend in to a certain situation or environment. Blenders also make a mess of things and stir things up. This could also represent an emotional whirlwind or overwhelming feelings. Because blenders spin, they may represent one of your chakras — see the *Chakras* section of this dictionary for more information.

CD Player

If associated with watching television or movies, may suggest you need some entertainment or are bored with something. Could say you are just watching your life go by or not actively participating, depending on dream feelings. If associated with music playing, may indicate the need for more music (beauty, harmony) in your life, depending on feelings and the type of music being played. See the entry on Tele-vision or the *Music and Musical Instruments* section of this dictionary for more insight. May also be that these

spinning disks represent one of your chakras, so note the colour or feelings and read the section on *Chakras* for greater insight. May be a pun on you or someone being a player, in the sense of being deceptive or manipulative.

Coffee Maker

Is there something brewing in your life? Do you need perking up? Since coffee is often associated with caffeine, it may represent your need for or addiction to caffeine. Do you need to "make" something in your life or prepare for something?

Computer

Symbolic of your thinking, intellect, rational mind, or mental activities. Your core beliefs can be likened to what is stored on your hard drive. What belief systems are driving or motivating you lately? Perhaps it's time to review some old ideas or attitudes that no longer serve you well. Do you use your computer daily? Does it represent your work life, stress or strain in your life? Perhaps it represents something that is invaluable and something you can't live without? What do you need to compute? Or is there a situation that you need to gauge? Computers also symbolize stored information, games played, and access to great knowledge. Computers are links to others, the world and endless information. A "crashing" computer may represent your inner sense of failure. A crashing computer can also symbolize pent-up emotions that need expression, or a build-up of negative thinking that needs venting. Could be a health warning of a coming breakdown, collapse or illness of some kind. A computer that crashes repeatedly may imply you are overloaded, overwhelmed or in need of a rest. May be a pun on "something does not compute" or add up correctly in your mind.

Dishwasher

Represents the need to clean up something in your life. Perhaps you think something is dirty or unclean. May say you have recently cleaned up your act or cleared your plate of something. Perhaps you are putting on a sparkling facade or just feel the need to cleanse yourself of something unwanted. Could be a pun on feeling washed out.

Dryer

May suggest you feel as though you are going around and around about something or tossing around an idea. Perhaps you feel you are tumbling, falling or losing something. Do you feel all dried up, exhausted or spent? Or is there too much heat (pressure) in some area of your life? Perhaps you can't stand the heat. Are you hot and bothered or feeling parched in some way? May be a pun on being sarcastic, having dry humour, or being droll and wry.

DVD Player – *See CD Player*

Freezer

Is there something your need to put on ice, put aside for now or be silent about? Because liquids freeze here, it may represent frozen emotions or fears. Perhaps you are in the midst of a "deep freeze" in some present undertaking, or maybe you need to thaw out some aspect of your life. May also represent ideas, thoughts or opinions that are stored and not currently being used.

Fridge – *See Refrigerator*

Furnace

Since this is a place where things heat up, warm up or generate heat, it may represent your passion or anger, depending on how the furnace is functioning. Are you in need of a little warmth, love or tenderness? Perhaps you have recently had a heated argument, debate or encounter. Is the dream furnace functioning properly and generating warmth? Are you generating enough warmth in your relationships? May also represent your sense or source of power or powerlessness.

Iron

May depict your strength, a rigid way of thinking or that you have a firm handle on things. Could denote your endurance, your willpower, or say that you are being inflexible. If you view ironing as "woman's work," it may symbolize your feelings about your role within the home. Do you need to smooth or iron something out? Are you steamed up or steaming mad?

Kettle

Suggests something or someone is boiling — usually boiling mad. Could be a situation, relationship or any event that has recently reached a boiling point. Could be a pun on "this is a fine kettle of fish" and imply that you feel you have recently made a mess of things or that you are in a predicament. May also symbolize that you feel steamed up about a situation.

Keyboard

Symbolizes getting your thoughts together, communicating your thoughts, and dexterity. See also Computer for greater insight.

Printer

Brings your words to life and makes a "hard copy" (reality) for you. Note what words are being printed and consider them direct communication to yourself. Perhaps you feel you need something in print (require proof) or perhaps you have been making demands on yourself to create and reproduce something (perhaps perfectly).

Radio

This communication device symbolizes your need for communication or that some communication in your current life is one sided. Are you tuned in or receptive at this time in your life? Are you listening to life's little messages? Is your dream radio playing or disconnected (turned off)? Are you really hearing what's being said?

Refrigerator

Have you placed something on hold or are you being cool about a situation, event or relationship? Usually associated with food, a dream fridge may represent your storage of some thoughts, attitudes or beliefs. Is there something you don't want others to see about you? Perhaps you need to cool off about something, or have taken a chilly attitude of late. Are you hungry for new ideas or stimulation of some sort? Do you need to "chew" on something, or do you need a snack or treat for yourself? What food for thought is on your mind? Perhaps you need to thaw out or chill out about something.

Stove

Is there something cooking or brewing in your life? Perhaps you have put something on hold or on the back burner. Do you need to cook up some new ideas or generate some warmth in your life? Are you boiling mad about something or just simmering about it? Perhaps it's a pun on "now you're cooking"! Conversely, a stove may symbolize something that you feel chained to or a slave to. How does a stove and cooking fit into your everyday life?

Tape Recorder

May represent your ability to remember, register or express something. Do you need to account for something, arrange your thinking differently or disclose something? Also related to communication, so it may symbolize your need to express yourself clearly or to be heard clearly. Is there something you need to listen to more attentively? Or perhaps you are running old tapes from your childhood within your mind

without really being conscious of it. We are all programmed by our parents, grandparents, schools, religion, and so on; as adults we often play these old recordings without any conscious thought.

Telephone

May symbolize your need to communicate something or get connected. Perhaps you are out of touch with yourself or someone near to you. Who are you phoning in your dream? Do you dial 9-1-1, representing a need of help or a feeling that you are in a desperate situation? Perhaps you need to connect with the person you are phoning in the dream or with the aspect of your self that is symbolized by that person. Is the telephone plugged in and functioning well? Are you plugged in and ready for communication? Is the line full of static, indicating a bad or poor connection within yourself or with another? Is the telephone ringing and trying to get your attention about something? Ringing can mean that some message is trying to get through.

Television

May represent entertainment, relaxation or a source of information. How do you feel about television? Is it a source of laziness or annoyance? Is it usually just background noise in your life? Do you use it as a babysitter for your children? Are you tuned in or tuned out these days? Perhaps there is something you need to see or view. Are you connected in a deeper way or feeling psychic? Do you need to watch something or take a different approach or perspective? There is much variety and choice today on television — do you need more choice or variety in your current affairs?

Toaster

Represents something that needs to be warmed up, or perhaps something popping into your mind. What has popped into your life recently? Note if your dream toaster is burning the toast, which may represent you feel burnt about something or frazzled over a relatively small issue.

Typewriter – See Keyboard

Vacuum Cleaner

Indicates the need to cleanse, wash, absolve or purge yourself of something. You may need to let go, surrender or release something. Since vacuum cleaners are used for pulling dirt out of carpets, a dream vacuum cleaner may have something to do with the beliefs upon which you stand, your

"understanding" of something, or your core values. Because vacuum cleaners suck, a dream vacuum may be a pun on someone, something, or some situation that is sucking the life or vitality out of you.

VCR

Is your life a drama or have you been acting up or acting out? Since a VCR is used for viewing something, it may symbolize that you need to take a different point of view or consider a new perspective. It is also a recording device, so it may suggest that you need to be more aware, attentive or attuned, or that you should be listening to or watching something more closely. May even suggest you are just an observer in your own life. Note the dream feelings for greater understanding.

Washing Machine

Represents the need to clean something up in your life or clean up your act. May symbolize that you have recently cleaned, cleansed, cleared or otherwise been trying to improve something. May say you have felt dirty about something (words, thoughts or actions). Perhaps you feel unclean or unclear about some recent event, situation, relationship, feelings, thoughts or actions. Maybe you need to clean up old habits, "dirty" thoughts or poor attitudes. Perhaps you need to forgive yourself or feel the need for purification. May be a pun on "squeaky clean." Since washing machines often clean clothes, this symbol may mean that there's

something you have "put on" in public that you feel the need to come clean about. See the section on *Clothing* and note what or whose clothes are being washed for greater insight.

Kitchen Items

Bottle

Bottles often contain fluid, which represents emotions and feelings. Is your dream bottle open or capped? Are you bottling up your emotions or are they able to flow freely? Perhaps something needs to pour out of you emotionally or through an act of compassion or forgiveness.

Bowl

Symbolizes your receptivity and the feminine aspects of self. Perhaps you need to sit quietly and let yourself become a receptive vehicle to "hear" your higher self or spirit. What does your dream bowl contain, if anything? Perhaps it contains food for thought, or new ideas and beliefs being offered to you. In your dream, do you eat from the bowl and take in what is offered? Or are the contents unpleasant and repulsive to you? If you are using it for cooking, it may represent cooking up a new idea. See Cooking in the *Actions* section for more insight.

Broom

Does something need to be swept under the carpet? Is there some area of your life that needs cleaning up or straightening out? Perhaps you need to make a clean sweep or clear your mind of some clutter. How is the broom being used? An idle broom indicates that you need to get a handle on something.

Can

Often a pun on "I can" or "I cannot" do or achieve something. Perhaps you need a kick in the can to get you motivated. Does your dream can contain anything? If so, what is the purpose of the contents? Is it food for thought or an empty container (mind)?

Can Opener

This tool for opening something represents your need to either be more open (minded) or to be open to new ideas, concepts and opinions.

Cooking Utensils

Associated with preparing and taking in food for thought. Perhaps you are cooking up some new ideas or stirring the pot. How is your dream utensil being used?

Cup

Similar to a container or bowl, the cup represents receptivity. Is your cup full, half full or empty? Does your cup runneth over or are you a bottomless cup? Is this your cup of joy or a cup full of new ideas, thoughts and attitudes? Perhaps you need to "pour out" your feelings, or you are overflowing with emotions. In tarot cards, cups represent emotions — is there a connection between your current emotional life and your dream cup? See Glass.

Dishes

Hold our ideas, thoughts and emotions. What are you dishing out or what are you serving up? Dishes have to do with preparation and serving up food for thought. Is your plate empty and you are feeling receptive and open? Or is your plate full and you feel overwhelmed or burdened by thoughts and emotions? Are you washing the dishes and need to clean up your thoughts or words?

Dreaming of your best china represents putting your best foot forward or making a good presentation. Conversely, your everyday dishes denote routine or well-known patterns of thinking and feeling.

Fork

Dream forks symbolize bringing food — thoughts and ideas — to your mind. May also be a pun on "fork it over."

Glass

Since drinking glasses usually contain fluid, they represent your emotions and feelings. Is there fluid in your dream glass? A full or overflowing glass represents overwhelming emotions or an overactive mind; an empty glass represents openness and receptivity. A clear glass may symbolize clear thinking and feelings, and a cloudy glass may represent clouded thinking and feelings. Could be a pun on "drinking it all in." Note the type of fluid in the glass as well — the dream glass may be telling you to drink more or less of that liquid in your waking life. See Cup.

Jug

Represents a container, receptacle or womb. See Container in the *Miscellaneous* section or Womb in the *Body* section of this dictionary.

Knife

When used as an instrument of harm, knives often denote the mind and its ability to be cutting (in thought or in speech). Negative thoughts are as harmful to the target of those thoughts (either yourself or someone else) as speaking the actual words — energetically, they still "cut." Perhaps you want to cut something out of your life or out of yourself, such as a personality trait that you judge as being bad or wrong. Self-judgement is common in North America and our words and thoughts can be sharp and cutting.

Have you been "throwing daggers" or do you need to sharpen your wits? Have you heard yourself saying "cut that out," "I need to cut down on this," or "it cuts like a knife"?

Mop

What needs to be mopped up in your life? What needs to be cleaned up or straightened out? Since mops are usually associated with water and cleaning, it may represent your emotions or feelings in some way. What feelings need to be cleared up or cleared out?

Other Household Items

Blanket

Often seen as a symbol of comfort, warmth and security. Do you need some love, support, comfort or security in some current situation or relationship? Conversely, you may feel the need to cover up some issue, thought or recently spoken words. How is your dream blanket being used? This will help you discern the meaning.

Clock

Your dream clock may be telling you it's time to do something. What is currently plaguing you to get done or pressing in on your time? Do you have a project or endeavour that has a deadline, or is time running out on something? Clocks can also indicate that time is flying by, or time goes on, or time is passing. Could be a pun on "the time of your life" or a message to watch your timing. Is a particular hour associated with the dream clock? What meaning does this time have in your life currently? See the *Numbers* section for more insight.

Coat Hanger

Symbolizes your ability to suspend judgement or the need to get the hang of something. Could say you have a hang up or that you are hung up about something. Do you need to "air" something, or expose or let go of an entangling situation? Are you hanging by a thread or loafing around? Could be a pun on an airport hangar and therefore a place of safety for your thoughts, desires and goals.

Electrical Cord

May denote your inner wiring or nervous system. Have your nerves felt frayed or have you been feeling electric? Do you feel wired or haywire? Since these cords also channel energy, it may symbolize your need to plug into something or become more aware of a situation. How have your energy levels been recently? Are you plugging into the extra energy available for you? Perhaps this speaks of your connection to Source (God), or a higher power. Do you have the ability to regulate the flow of your own power? Do you feel grounded (present) and plugged into your reality?

Ironing Board

Used for smoothing things out or ironing out the details. Could suggest you are steamed up or steaming mad. Represents "flat" emotions or the need to be soothed emotionally. May suggest your thoughts need smoothing out, polishing or refining.

See also Iron in the Appliances section above.

Laundry

Suggests the need to cleanse, release, absolve or purge yourself of something that no longer serves you well. May imply that you need to release emotions through tears. Could suggest you need to clean up your act or wash your worries away.

Light Bulb

Denotes that you've had a "light bulb" of awareness in some area of your life. Have you recently had an "ah-ha" moment or a sudden inspiring thought or occurrence? On the other hand, a burned out dream light bulb may symbolize that you are in the dark about something. Do you need more light on a situation in your waking life, or more awareness?

Linens

Fine napkins, tablecloths, and other expensive linens are usually reserved for fine affairs or guests. This may represent luxury, wealth or the need to refine some of your behaviour. Perhaps you need to set a "fine" example or treat yourself in a more luxurious or gratifying way.

Pillow

Pillows offer support for the neck and head. Do you need support in some area of your life? Or in some mental activity? Perhaps you have been sticking your neck out about something and now need more support from yourself or others. Also, pillows can be about comfort and the need for more comfort in your life.

Pin

A straight pin with a sharp point may symbolize that someone is trying to pin something on you. Do you "get the point" or not of an issue or situation? Are you holding on too tightly to someone or something? Safety pins, on the other hand, fasten or hold things together. Do you feel unsafe? Do you need more protection or security?

Quilt

May indicate comfort, a sense of being at home, relaxation, a reminder of the past, or whatever associations you make to quilts. Note how you feel in the dream for further understanding of the meaning of your dream quilt.

Sink

Usually a place of cleansing or cleaning. Do you need some emotional cleansing or need to "let go" of a sticky situation? How is your dream sink being used? Is it stacked full of dirty dishes or are you scrubbing it clean? Dirty dishes may represent an overload of emotional feelings and the need to scrub yourself clean of some offending feelings, thoughts or beliefs. May also be a pun on the need to "sink or swim." A clogged sink indicates clogged emotions or that you feel blocked in some way.

Suitcase

May symbolize that you are still carrying around some emotional baggage that weighs heavily on you. This may indicate the need to express old emotions or be aware of which attitudes or beliefs you carry that are a burden to you. A heavy suitcase may represent any burden you are currently experiencing. Depending on how you feel in the dream, the suitcase could also represent that you feel you have it "all together." A suitcase could also represent freedom, travel or movement, depending on how it is being used in the dream. Look to recent events, situations and issues to help further clarify the meaning.

Thread

Threads hold things together and allow for creation. May denote the threads you have woven to create your life to date. Are the threads strong or in a tangle? Have you been hanging by a thread or do you feel threadbare?

Toys

May represent your ability to play or the need for more play in your life. Could be "fun and games" or speak of child-like behaviours. Perhaps you have you been dabbling, tinkering or puttering with something? Could say you are toying with an idea or a person, or playing the fool (or any part). It may suggest you need to immerse yourself totally in the act of playing, creating and generally having fun. Look to the dream feelings for greater understanding. Note that this entry applies also to gadgets, knickknacks or any plaything.

Umbrella

Used for wet weather and therefore may be associated with your emotions and feelings. Usually used for protection from your feelings or any outside influence. May speak of your need for security and safety.

Valuables

Often symbolize valuable and worthy traits within yourself. Are the dream valuables being found or lost? This indicates whether you have tapped into something precious within your self or lost a valuable aspect of your self. Can you see the worth and uniqueness of yourself? Perhaps it indicates a new gift or talent that has been hidden until recently, or a new understanding of your self. The loss of valuables in a dream is a fear of some loss in your current life and may indicate loss of self-worth or self-esteem. What do you fear losing?

Vase

Usually a container for flowers and therefore implies a receptacle for growth, abundance and blooming. An empty vase may reflect that you feel empty, vacant or barren. Note what is being held in your dream vase and what the dream feelings are for greater understanding.

Jewellery and Gems

Jewellery tends to emphasize a particular part of the body and represents your gifts and talents. It may denote your values in general or your spiritual gifts that are beginning to unfold. If you are wearing the jewellery, then you have likely "owned" or recognized these abilities/gifts of yours. If someone else is wearing the jewellery, it is likely that you have not owned or recognized this gift or talent. But regardless of who is wearing it, jewellery in your dream represents your talent.

Where the jewellery is worn indicates the area in which the skill lies. For example,

- jewellery on the fingers or hands is related to your creative ability and talents connected with the use of your hands
- jewellery worn on the ears accents your hearing and listening skills (see Hearing in the *Actions* section)
- necklaces accent the throat chakra and therefore represent expression, talking, will power and perhaps indicate a talent for speaking or song
- bracelets are worn on the arm and therefore emphasis your power to do and act.

If gemstones are on the jewellery, note the colour and what your associations are with that particular gem and that particular colour. For example, you may associate a diamond with love, marriage or wealth. Perhaps it is a birthstone that you are familiar with and/or associate with a particular person.

Each stone, crystal, rock or gem carries a unique vibration and therefore a unique effect on the wearer. There are entire books devoted to helping you understand the healing qualities and vibrations available through each individual stone. I suggest that you buy one as a guide to help you identify the stones that appear in your dreams and their symbolic meanings. Often you will dream of a crystal or gem because in your waking life you require the special vibration energy and healing properties it offers.

A few of the more common gems and crystals are listed here to help you understand your dream's meaning, as well as more information about what different types of jewellery may represent.

Remember: *These symbolic meanings are just suggestions. If these suggested meanings do not resonate with you, ring a bell, give you an "ah-ha" moment or otherwise feel right, search through your own experience or beliefs about the symbol to find what makes sense for you.*

Amethyst

Known for its ability to help you remember dreams, amethysts are also strong protectors and healing stones. They are said to enhance your intuitive/psychic abilities and your spiritual awareness. Amethysts can also calm the mind and transmute negative energy. They may also enhance your visualization skills and meditation.

Body Piercing

This is often a form of expression that denotes either a sense of freedom or an act of rebellion — often against the norms of society. Have you felt put off by some recent group consensus or lost in the crowd? It may also indicate a sense of belonging, depending on how you view body piercing. Also note the dream feelings to help you understand if this reflects a stance you are taking or defending, or denotes a recent liberating experience.

Bracelet

An arm bracelet enhances the meaning of "arm" (power to do) and what you are doing with your power (read more about Arm in the *Body* section). Note what type of material the bracelet is made of and what that means to you personally. For example, wearing a charm bracelet may imply that you can "turn on the charm" or be charming.

Brooch

Often worn on the chest, a brooch may symbolize how you feel for others, love, or even a judgement of yourself, depending on whether you like and are attracted to the brooch. If the brooch is old-fashioned, it may represent outdated thinking or feelings on your part. Note how you feel about the brooch to help you understand if it is symbolic of an accepted part of your self or one that you dislike. Also, read about the heart chakra (Fourth Chakra) in the *Chakras* section to help you understand what issues the brooch may be related to.

Costume Jewellery

Depending on how you view costume jewellery, this dream symbol may represent a feeling of cheapness, vanity or unworthiness. It may be telling you that you are putting on a false front or have feelings of low self-esteem. On the other hand, it may symbolize a fun and playful part of self that desires expression for the sheer enjoyment of it.

Crown or Tiara

Accents the crown chakra and head in general. Will therefore emphasize anything to do with the head such as thinking and thoughts. May also depict royalty or feeling like a queen/princess or king. Could represent a sense of mastery over something or someone or domination and control, depending on how you feel in the dream. Perhaps you are feeling like a ruler or have great responsibility. Emphasis on the crown chakra indicates your connection with your God, Creator, or whatever you believe in. It may be telling you that your crown chakra is open. For more information, see Seventh Chakra.

Crystal

Crystals magnetically attract certain energies or repel unwanted ones. Each resonates at a different frequency and has a unique function. They can store, transmit and receive information. Crystals seem to have a magical quality and can represent magic and the unknown in your life (unless you are already familiar with and working with crystals). Crystals can enhance meditation, deepen your connection with self and Spirit, offer protection, and

strengthen positive energies. Note the colour of your dream crystal and look that colour up for deeper meaning. If you know the type of the crystal that appears in your dream, find out more about it in a crystal book or online. Dreaming of a crystal often means that you require whatever qualities it has to offer.

Cufflinks

Since these are usually worn by men, dream cufflinks may represent your male/masculine energy in general, and denote whether you can own your admirable masculine qualities. Note who is wearing the cufflinks and what you associate with that person. Understanding whether you are attracted or repelled by this person will help you understand whether you accept or disown your own male traits. May also represent your "link" or connection to someone — usually a male person. See also Masculine in the *People* section of this dictionary.

Diamond

May represent clarity, wealth, marriage or success, depending on how you view the significance diamonds in your life. They are also April's birthstone and symbolic of Christ consciousness. Diamonds are often associated with marriage and may be telling you about your inner marriage or an external event of two things coming together. Diamonds aid in amplifying energy; wherever they are worn, they magnify the qualities of that area.

Earring

Usually emphasizes the sense of hearing. Perhaps you are picking things up on a different level and the dream is asking you to pay more attention to your inner voice or intuition. May indicate you are becoming clairaudient (able to hear Spirit or your higher self clearly). May also denote that you are hearing or not hearing those around you, or perhaps that you have been turning a deaf ear to someone or something. Are you really listening to your self and others?

Emerald

Often associated with creating harmony in the heart, from which vitality can flow. They enhance joy and the positive qualities of life. Also known for their ability to give equilibrium on physical, emotional and mental planes. Emerald fosters positive qualities and promotes truth and loyalty. Emeralds are the stone of domestic love and can bring domestic bliss. They can also inspire deep inner knowing and aid memory. See also Green in the *Colours* section for further insight.

Jade

Symbol of purity and serenity. Jade increases love and releases negative thoughts, soothing the mind. A protective stone that brings harmony, jade also calms the nervous system and channels positive energy in constructive ways. Note any personal associations you may have with the colour green and/or with the Orient (as jade is often associated with this part of the world).

Gold Jewellery

Gold is considered one of the "wealthiest" of metals and is therefore associated with wealth, power and even control. It has a long history of being associated with royalty or those in command or in power. Do you have the Midas touch or are you in need of some inner wealth and support of self? Perhaps a golden opportunity is presenting itself or you are in need of some type of riches. Wherever worn, gold jewellery emphasizes the body part on which it is worn.

Locket

Usually worn over the heart area, lockets often contain pictures or memories of loved ones. May indicate your need to connect with a loved one or connect with love to your self. May be a pun on the word "lock" and indicate that your heart feels closed or hurt. Note the feelings in the dream to help you understand if this is a positive, loving connection or a negative association.

Necklace

Emphasizes the neck and its functions, as well as the throat chakra and its functions. Jewellery in general often indicates talents (often hidden or not yet "owned"). May indicate your communication or words that have been well spoken or received, or that your strength lies in your ability to speak well. Conversely, a necklace may indicate you have not been using wise words or communicating well, depending on the type of necklace and how it feels wearing it in the dream. For example, a choker may represent your inability to get the words out or that you are all choked up about something. Necklaces emphasize the throat chakra, which is about your higher will power, your creative abilities and the concept of perfect timing. If the necklace hangs down to the heart chakra you may wish to read about the Fourth Chakra. Note the type of necklace, its colour and its features to help further clarify the meaning.

Opal

Known for its ability to induce visions and enhance cosmic consciousness.

Also brings loyalty, faithfulness, spontaneity and enhanced dynamic creativity. Opal is the birthstone for October, and it can strengthen your memory.

Pearl

The traditional symbol of wisdom, pearls are known for their ability to transform from one state to another. Have you been undergoing any transformations lately? Do you require a pearl of wisdom? Pearls are also known as symbols of purity, truth and understanding. When worn around the neck, they may indicate your ability to speak words of wisdom.

Quartz

Well known for its excellent healing abilities and as an energy amplifier. It can double your auric field, storing, releasing and regulating energy on physical and mental planes. Cleans and enhances subtle bodies and enhances intuition and psychic powers. Note colour of quartz and read further on that colour for deeper meaning.

Ring

Emphasizes the hands and fingers and their symbolic function (grasping, holding, doing, creating). Have you yet to recognize a talent you have for using your hands? Have you been grasping things well lately or have you been able to hold a new concept or idea? Have you been creating with your hands? Perhaps a ring points to the need to pay more attention to what you create and how you create it. Rings have personal meaning for every wearer. Was your dream ring one you own, an old one or a new one? Can you own your own talents and creative abilities? Perhaps the ring symbolizes a commitment such as marriage or a strong bond with another.

Ruby

Rubies stimulate the heart chakra and its function (love issues, compassion or judgement). May encourage you to follow your bliss or be true to your heart. Rubies are also known as energizers and balancers. They aid in retaining wealth or passion, but they can also overstimulate and bring up anger or negative energy for transmutation. Rubies can help to open your heart chakra and aid in survival issues. May represent valour and bravery to some. Read more about Red in the *Colours* section for further understanding.

Sapphire

These gems come in a variety of colours, including yellow, blue, green, black and purple. Each colour has certain energetic properties associated with it. Note what colour your dream sapphire is and see sections on *Colours* and *Chakras* for greater insight about that particular gem. The most recognized of sapphires is the blue sapphire; this stone helps align the physical, mental and spiritual planes, restoring balance within the body. It also aids in calming the mind. A dream of a blue sapphire may point to the need to release unwanted thoughts and mental tension.

Turquoise

Often associated with Native Americans, this stone was used for healing and protection. It promotes spiritual attunement and has an elevating effect. Its purifying effects can dispel negative energy, and it can balance masculine and feminine energies. Turquoise helps heal the whole body.

Watch

Emphasizes the wrist area (ability to be flexible, to do and to serve). Also symbolic of time and how you use time. Have you been out of synch lately or running late? Has time passed you by? Are you using your time wisely? Are you living on borrowed time or is time slipping away? If you've lost your watch, perhaps you are losing touch with time or need a time out. May be a pun on "watch out" or be alert.

Music and Musical Instruments

Musical instruments in the dream time are symbolic of your creative talents and expression of your self in the physical. They are about your ability to harmonize with self or with others. Depending on the feelings in the dream, musical instruments may indicate that you are currently in harmony or that you lack harmony in your life in general. Note if you feel in synch with, in rhythm with, or in tune with your life, your relationship, or even with the Universe.

Musical instruments denote that you can "make beautiful music" or that you have the ability to encourage yourself or others. Music is about expression, so it is important to note if you like or dislike the music in the dream and what your feelings are about it. If you are able to play a musical instrument in the dream time but not in your waking hours, this could symbolize that you have overcome or mastered something previously foreign or unknown to you.

Music is often symbolic of your emotions and how they flow (or don't flow). Always note how the music or musical instrument makes you feel to gain greater understanding of the representation. Music is a type of sweetness in most peoples' lives — a pleasure — so be aware of whether you currently have "music" in your life.

The word "instrument" may be a pun on being instrumental (active, involved, helpful) in some endeavour or relationship. It could also say you are an instrument for another person, or an idea or concept, to come through.

Always note your personal viewpoint and understanding of the instrument or music presented in the dream, as your first impressions and feelings of it will likely be the most accurate interpretation for you. For example, if you don't like jazz music in general and it is playing in your dream, you may correlate this with something that is currently happening in your life that you don't like, or something that is not agreeable to you about your own character, traits, habits or thinking.

Remember: These symbolic meanings are just suggestions. If these suggested meanings do not resonate with you, ring a bell, give you an "ah-ha" moment or otherwise feel right, search through your own experience or beliefs about the symbol to find what makes sense for you.

Drum

Implies your rhythm or lack of it. May indicate the need for more rhythm in your life or that you need to beat to your own tune. Perhaps you march to a different drummer or need to follow your own beat. Have you been taking a beating or beating yourself up lately? May symbolize need to actually beat a drum and get some aggression out of your system.

Fiddle

Could imply tampering, tinkering or experimenting. Perhaps you are fiddling with something, either dabbling or playing with it. Similar to Violin.

Flute

Symbolizes the expression of your creative self. Note if the dream flute is in harmony and rhythm or acting as an irritant. Dream feelings will help you understand if there is a need for more harmony and balance or a sense of discordance in your life. Some people consider the flute to be a feminine instrument, so it may reflect your feminine side or the gentle side of your nature.

Guitar

Represents your ability to create, express, harmonize, have rhythm or produce something. Ask yourself if you are "strumming" your truth at the present time. Are you in tune with what is going on around and within you? Do you need to create more sweetness in your life? What type of music is being played (if any)? Is there an absence of music in your life? Could be expressing your emotions, either joyous or sad, through sound. Note the dream feelings for greater insight.

Harp

Often associated with angels, harmony and heaven. May be healing for the soul, spiritual enrichment or enlightenment. May indicate that you need to align with your angels or harmonize your thoughts, words and actions. Could be a pun on harping on yourself or others.

Horn

A loud horn may be trying to get your attention about something that is currently going on in your life. Are you trying to get someone's attention by blowing your own horn? Or do you need to pay more attention to some details? Also denotes the ability to express, create and be harmonious. May be a pun on "horn of plenty" or "locking horns" with another. Could also be an alarm, a signal or a cry for help.

Music

Represents your creative expression and ability to be in harmony. Note what type of music is being played and whether it appeals to you. If it does not, it could suggest you are not "making music" out of your current endeavours or undertakings. Unpleasant music could also suggest that something is grating on you and not harmonious with your beliefs or truth. Beautiful music suggests harmony, grace, peace and fulfillment.

Organ

Often associated with church music and therefore your religious beliefs or spiritual connections. May represent group consciousness or the ability to be in harmony with group thinking. May be a pun on any appendage you call an organ or represent any internal physical organ, depending on your associations with the word. Since organs offer a variety of controls and buttons to produce variations in sound, this may represent a current situation where you feel you have a lot of choice or control. See also Piano.

Piano

Many homes have a piano, so it may represent a family or familiar situation. If you had or have a piano in your home, note who played (plays) it the most and see if this relates to your dream piano in any way. It may also symbolize your ability to "make music" or harmonize. Note if your dream piano is in or out of tune. Take note of who is playing the dream piano and how they feel. Are they playing with enthusiasm or is it something that is being forced upon them? This will help you understand whether this dream indicates a need to get in harmony or in synch with some part of your self or your life, or whether you are already playing a beautiful melody.

Trombone – See Trumpet and Horn

Trumpet

An instrument that can be loud and that makes a definite statement, so dreaming of a trumpet may indicate your need to take a stand for yourself or make yourself heard. Could mean you are blowing your own horn or that you need to. See Horn for further insight.

Tuba – See Trumpet and Horn

Violin

Often associated with romance, relaxation or fine dining. May suggest you need more music or pleasure in your life. Could be very up-tempo music and indicate the need to pick up the pace. Depending on the type of music being played, it could also indicate sad or melancholy feelings. Similar to Fiddle.

Numbers

Numbers are universal symbols whose meanings are held deep in our unconscious memory. So unless the number seen in your dream has some personal meaning to you, this section will help you understand the universal symbolism attached to each number. It is important to know a bit about numerology in order to derive the correct meaning of multidigit numbers.

Numerology is the ancient, sacred study of numbers and their hidden meaning. It dates back to humanity's early beginnings. One technique in numerology is reducing multidigit numbers to a single digit by adding the digits together. The reduction is done in a series of steps until only one digit remains.

> *Example*:
> The number 2,399 would be added as follows: **2 + 3 + 9 + 9 = 23.**
> The number **23** is then reduced to one digit: **2 + 3 = 5.**
> The final one-digit number of **5** is the number to look up and use symbolically, *not* **2,399.**

> *Example*:
> The number 10,081 would be added as follows: **1 + 0 + 0 + 8 + 1 = 10.**
> The number **10** is further broken down: **1 + 0 = 1.**
> The resulting one-digit number of **1** is the number to look up the meaning of.

> *Example*: Phone numbers and numbers with dashes or dividers between them are treated somewhat differently.
> **387-3950** would be added in two parts.
> First add **3 + 8 + 7 = 18; 1 + 8 = 9.**
> Then add the remaining digits: **3 + 9 + 5 + 0 = 17; 1 + 7 = 8.**
> Now take the two single results and add them together for a final single-digit result: **9 + 8 = 17; 1 + 7 = 8.**
> The number you would look up for symbolic meaning is **8.**

Exceptions to these reduction rules apply to master numbers, such as **11, 22** and **33,** which are not often broken down to single digits. Other numbers that have special meaning to you would also not be reduced to a single digit. For example, this includes the number **13** if you believe it holds superstitious powers. Any number can hold special meaning to you, and it is up to you to choose what resonates most in reference to your dream's meaning.

If you are interested in the study of tarot, each of the Major Arcana (numbers zero to twenty-one) are mentioned briefly in the appropriate entries in this section. Tarot is an ancient system of knowledge that has been taught for centuries in Mystery Schools all over the globe. Tarot numbers and their meaning are also part of all humans' unconscious memories. Since only brief mention is made here, refer to a book on tarot for more information if you wish to learn more about this subject.

Remember: These symbolic meanings are just suggestions. If these suggested meanings do not resonate with you, ring a bell, give you an "ah-ha" moment or otherwise feel right, search through your own experience or beliefs about the symbol to find what makes sense for you.

Zero

Represents nothing, nil, void or emptiness. It is infinity, endlessness and the absence of quality. Zeros can also represent inner gifts or potential resources. When seen behind another digit, zeros may increase the strength of that number's meaning. For example, the numbers 30, 300, 3,000, etc. could indicate an emphasized or intense 3. In the tarot, zero is represented by the Fool and refers to individuation.

One

Represents self, the "I," wholeness or unity. It is about impulses, originality, beginnings, and leadership. One also relates to pioneering or things that come first, and may represent a new endeavour of yours. One is a yang or masculine energy and can also represent creativity and confidence. May be a pun on "I'm the one" or "all for one," or may indicate a need to be more self-full or selfish. May be a pun on "won." In the tarot, one is represented by the Magus or Magician and refers to initiation and communication. Refers also to the first chakra, so see also the *Chakras* section of this dictionary.

Two

Represents duality, division and the subconscious mind. It is about receptivity, cooperation and balance. Twos are about the world of opposites, and may also denote twice the strength or twice the weakness of something. In the tarot, two is represented by the Priestess and refers to intuitive knowledge and hidden powers. See also Second Chakra in the *Chakras* section of this dictionary.

Three

Represents expression, sensitivity, great strength, creativity, fate, the merging of opposites into unity, and trinity. Trinities include:
▸ mind, body, spirit
▸ id, ego, superego
▸ father, son, holy ghost
▸ subconscious, conscious, superconscious
▸ physical, non-physical, meta-physical
▸ energy, matter, antimatter
▸ past, present, future

Three can also represent the third chakra, and in the tarot it symbolizes the Empress or femininity. See the *Chakras* section for greater insight.

Four

Can represent earthly reality, basic structure and stability. Four is about process, orientation and the material realm in general. It is about groundedness and doing things in a material or practical way. It can also mean hard work, inflexibility and practicality. Because it can create a square with four sides, it also reflects limits, barriers or obstructions. In the tarot, four is represented by the Emperor and refers to leadership qualities and law. May also

symbolize the function of your fourth (heart) chakra. Refer to *Chakras* section of this dictionary for greater insight.

Five

Fives go beyond the earthly or given reality of the four (see above) and reveal hidden meaning. Four represents structure like a box, a square or a fortress and usually symbolizes the physical/material world. The five takes us one step beyond the ordinary reality and into the unknown, unconscious or hidden world. Seeing a five in your dream usually represents some sort of change in your life or changes that you'd like to make. May imply the five senses, freedom and discipline. In tarot, the five is represented by the Hierophant and refers to the spiritual teacher and religion. See also the *Chakras* section of this dictionary, since five may symbolize information about your fifth (throat) chakra.

Six

Denotes union of opposites and is symbolized by the six-pointed star and by the hexagrams of the *I Ching*. Six can represent perfection, beauty and harmony. It is also about acceptance, vision and strength. It can imply completion of a cycle or the end of something in your life. In the tarot, six is represented by the Lovers and refers to love relationships and the union of opposites through love. See also the *Chakras* section of this dictionary — a six in your dream may represent your sixth (brow) chakra.

Seven

Represents the Divine and earthly harmony. Considered a lucky number by many, it may also refer to the seven chakras or seven planes. Seven also denotes balanced spiritual forces, perfection and victory. It is also about trust, openness and creation. Seven in the tarot is represented by the Chariot and refers to meditation and imminent new beginnings. May also represent your seventh (crown) chakra and its function. See the *Chakras* section of this dictionary for greater insight.

Eight

Represents truth, justice and balance. Also about abundance and the power to do or be. It may refer to material gain, wealth, success and money. In the tarot, eight is represented by the words Adjustment or Strength; it symbolizes the balancing of opposites and being more self-conscious.

Nine

Denotes consecration (dedication), contemplation and endings, Nines are about completion and termination. May

also refer to integrity and wisdom. In tarot, nine is represented by the Hermit and refers to going inward and searching for wisdom.

Ten

Represents perfection or a strengthened one (1 + 0). See One and Zero. In tarot, ten is represented by the Wheel or by the word Fortune and refers to the wheels of life or life in general.

Eleven

Pertains to mastery of something in your life, usually something physical. Also considered to represent enlightenment, intuition, spirituality and achievement. If you have not realized or used your ability to master something in your waking life, then it could represent a two. In tarot, eleven is represented by the words Justice or Lust and refers to truth and great vitality.

Twelve

Represents the boundary of time, divine power and strength of Spirit. Can also be about spiritual perfection and divine order. May work as a three. In tarot it is represented by the Hanged Man and refers to surrender and/or sacrifice.

Thirteen

Often associated with superstition of bad luck. However, it also often denotes endings and beginnings, change and transition. May also signify a four. In tarot it is represented by the word Death and refers to transformation and endings (which then result in new beginnings).

Fourteen

Symbolizes help when needed such as having a prayer answered. May also work as a five. In tarot this is represented by the words Art or Temperance and is about alchemy and integration.

Fifteen

Represents the full moon and therefore ripening or maturation. May also be a four. In tarot it is represented by the word Devil and refers to procreative energy and/or materialism.

Sixteen

Denotes hardening and rigidity. May pertain to sweet sixteen. May also be seen as a seven. In tarot it is represented by the Tower and refers to transformation through the destruction of old patterns.

Seventeen

Relates to new hope. May also be reduced to eight. In tarot it is represented by the Star and refers to self-recognition and connection to universal intelligence.

Eighteen

In the tarot this number is represented by the Moon and refers to illusions, wrong turns and struggle with the subconscious.

Nineteen

In tarot this number is represented by the Sun and refers to highly creative energy, awareness and the source of spiritual energy.

Twenty

In the tarot this number is represented by the words Aeon or Judgement and refers to discernment, self-judgement and regeneration.

Twenty-one

Symbol of wholeness, or may be reduced to a three. In tarot it is represented by the Universe or World and refers to cosmic union, burning off Karma and time.

Twenty-two

Considered a master number. This could represent mastery over any area of your life, especially the mental realm of thought, beliefs and attitudes. If that interpretation doesn't seem to fit, then it may refer to four.

Thirty-three

Considered a master number. This usually represents mastery over the spiritual plane. It may refer to a six if this interpretation doesn't seem to fit for you.

9-1-1

If you see this number in a dream or are telephoning it, it suggests an immediate call for help and attention at your physical, emotional, mental or spiritual level. It is a warning sign that crisis is impending or already happening. Are you reaching out for help or do you feel in crisis? If not, be aware that some part of you is likely quite anxious, concerned or otherwise feeling chaotic when 911 appears in a dream. This number may also represent the September 11th, 2001 attack on the World Trade Center in New York City. Note your personal feelings and viewpoints about this event to help you understand what significance this number has in relation to a current experience, relationship or event in your own life.

People

Ninety-five percent of the people who appear in your dreams, whether they are strangers or someone you know, represent a part of you. So these dream characters are not giving you any literal information about the other person — they are telling you something about you. You are on the Earth to grow and learn about yourself, so it is rare to be given any information about another unless it is in the context of how that person's behaviour, attitudes or actions affect you. Bear this in mind with every character that you dream of, especially if the dream character stands out in some way or catches your attention. See the discussion on marbles and mirroring in Chapter 7 for more clarification.

However, any dream symbol, but especially people characters, mirrors you in two different ways or at two different levels. On the deeper level, the character reflects or mirrors some aspect of yourself. You must know yourself fairly well to recognize this level of symbolism — you must be aware of your inner relationship with yourself or how you treat yourself within your inner world to pick up on how this dream character represents some part of you. On another level, you may recognize that the character represents someone you actually know. For example, a police officer in your dream may represent your boss in your waking life, who is an authority figure to you or someone who imposes rules on you. Or a monster that threatens you in a dream may symbolize someone in your waking-time reality who is currently intimidating you. Both levels of interpretation are right, and both work at all times. So dream characters are simultaneously a tool for self-examination and a symbolic representation of how the people in your waking life affect you emotionally and mentally. Keep this in mind when looking at the people characters in your dreams, and try to identify what they mean on both levels.

Dream characters may represent either beautiful attributes of yourself or unwanted traits. Either way, they are almost always aspects of you that have gone unclaimed or disowned. The way to determine what traits are being shown to you is simple. List three words you would associate with the dream person's characteristics or personality (their traits as seen in the dream and as you know them in everyday life). Even if you don't personally know the character in the dream, you will often get a feel for their character and nature. If the person is someone you know, then simply reference what you immediately think of that person's personality traits and these will be the biggest clue as to what parts of yourself are being depicted.

For example, if your dream depicts a neighbour, then ask yourself what characteristics you associate with that person. If your answer is nosy, gossipy and talkative, then this could be telling you about your own gossipy self. Then ask yourself, "Have I been overly talkative about others and in need of some awareness about this?"

Always take note of the sex of the character, for this will tell you immediately if this is a feminine or masculine aspect of self that you are dealing with. Feminine energies in general are representing your own ability to nurture, be receptive, hold, yield, be soft and intuitive. Male dream characters or masculine energy would indicate your ability to act, do, support, protect and be aggressive. Of course these traits will depend on your own experiences of male and female energies and your personal point of view. For a deeper insight into your own beliefs around masculine and feminine energies, see those entries in the *People* section of this dictionary.

Our systems are constantly striving for balance and equilibrium when it comes to masculine and feminine energies (this is the core energy of the self) and because of this, male and female characters will play a pivotal and constant role in your dreams. See Chapter 8 on the irrational perspective for more information on yin and yang energies (masculine and feminine) and the constant striving need for balance in our lives.

Family members are also common dream characters. Family members who you don't live with in your waking time often represent your own inner family; i.e., your inner marbles and how you view them (see more on marbles in Chapter 7).

Understanding Who's Who in Your Dreams

Because other people who appear in your dreams are almost always representations of some aspect of your self, here is a good method for keeping track of them. Make a list of your dream players, their association to you and three personality traits or characteristics that you ascribe to each one. Before bed, ask that these characters continue to play that part or ask that they only represent yourself — you choose, and stick to the reprogramming of your choice for several nights. Over time as you evolve and grow, you may see the characteristics change with your own perceptions of that person.

The exception to the rule of thumb that ninety-five percent of others represent some part of you is often seen in the people with whom you live. Sometimes spouses or children will play themselves in the dream. Determining who is playing who or which characters are representing you may take a bit of reprogramming. Just as you can ask to remember your dreams, you can ask for clarification on dream players before sleep. Keeping a journal of your dream players is the key to reprogramming your dream symbols.

By keeping this list of who's who you begin to program your mind and your dreams to use the characters as they are described in your list. Yes — you can easily influence your dream character's meaning by writing down what you believe the representation to be.

Using a blank piece of paper or the chart provided in Appendix D, make a three-column chart like the one shown here. As you make your list, tell your subconscious mind that these characters are to have the meaning attributed to them that you have formulated in your list. Be clear that they are either playing themselves or *only* the traits ascribed to them. Now you will have a quick and easy reference chart to refer to for dream interpretation. Remember that characters will change their traits in your dreams, as you change your own behaviours and attitudes.

Example of Identifying/Categorizing Dream Characters

Dream Character	Relationship	Characteristics, Traits or Meaning
Bob	brother	arrogant, conservative, rigid
Doris	wife	plays herself
Willy	friend	outgoing, clown, humorous
Betty	co-worker	creative, intelligent, determined
Brian	father	plays himself

Remember: These symbolic meanings are just suggestions. If these suggested meanings do not resonate with you, ring a bell, give you an "ah-ha" moment or otherwise feel right, search through your own experience or beliefs about the symbol to find what makes sense for you.

355

Aboriginal

May reflect the savage in you or the highly evolved spiritual side of your self, depending on your view of native or Aboriginal Peoples in general. May reflect connections to the Earth and walking through life in a balanced and reverent manner. Could be a pun on "Indian giver." How do you feel about the Aboriginal person in your dreams? Since natives may be seen as being benevolent or wise, your dream Indian may be a spirit guide. Note your personal feelings and attitudes about Aboriginals for further insight into the deeper meaning this symbol has for you.

Actor

If your dream features a famous actor or movie star, then list three characteristic or personality traits you associate with this person. Those traits reflect the part of you that is being revealed. Are you familiar with this part of yourself, or are you putting on an act? If you are the actor, then realize that all of life is an act. Are you comfortable in the action or is this something that needs to be integrated into your life? See Acting in the *Actions* section for more details. See also Movie Star.

Adolescent – See Teenager

Alien

Represents an aspect of your self that is so unfamiliar or alien to you that you cannot recognize or "own" it and its qualities. Does the dream alien conjure up fearful feelings or curiosity? Would meeting this un-owned marble of yours create the same feelings? This unknown, new or untried aspect of self is presenting itself in this form for your examination and inspection.

Angel

Angels in the dream time may represent an angelic act recently performed by you, or they may represent your angelic self or the higher aspect of your self. It could also be a visit from your guardian angel or any one of the countless angels in the hierarchy of angelic beings. An angel may be your conscience getting your attention about a recent act or behaviour of yours, or an answer to your prayers. Angelic encounters are abundant in the dream time.

Athlete

Athletes may be seen as competitors or team members. Have you or someone you know been competitive lately? Note the dream feelings to help you understand if this is healthy competition or if you have an adversary to be wary of. Have you been working out and feeling in shape — perhaps ready for a challenge or confrontation? This may indicate that you feel ready to move forward with some endeavour. May suggest you are feeling healthy and in tip top shape. Note if you are involved with any group activities right now and how the dream athlete relates to this. Are you a team player or participating to the best of your ability? Is the dream athlete a jock and how do you feel about jocks in general?

Audience

May symbolize that you feel as if you are observing your own life and actions rather than being an active participant in your own life drama. Are you taking a back seat or just playing a part in your own life? Could also be feelings of judgement coming from a larger group or society. Check your dream feelings and content to help further clarify.

Aunt

Denotes a female relative or someone close to you. May reflect an aspect of your self that you are close to but not connected with. If the aunt is known, describe her personality and characteristics with three words in your list of dream characters. This will help you understand which aspects of your self the aunt may be representing. May be a pun on the words ant, anti (against

something), or ante (pay up or divvy up). See also Ant in the *Animals* section.

Baby

A new baby in a dream represents a new project, belief, concept or idea you have just given birth to, or a new responsibility, creative endeavour or concern that is your "baby." Search your memory for recent ideas you plan to develop or put into action. Since new babies often need much attention and care, ask yourself what you have been devoting your time to. How well are you caring for your dream baby? Feeding the baby suggests that you are nurturing and taking care of your ideals and goals. Dropping a baby in dream time may suggest that you have dropped or sacrificed hopes, dreams, projects or ideals that were precious to you. Losing a baby in a dream implies you may have lost hope or lost sight of your goals. If the baby dies, it may represent the death of a creative idea, belief or opinion. An infant can also represent an infantile aspect of yourself, so search your recent behaviour for signs of immature or childlike behaviour. May represent first chakra.

Boss

Symbolizes an authoritarian aspect of your self — perhaps a controlling, dominating or ruling aspect of your self. Do you admire or loathe your dream boss? The feelings and dream content will help you understand what the dream boss symbol is reflecting. Could be a pun on being bossed around or being your own boss. Could symbolize loss of freedom or hard work, depending on how you view having a boss. May refer to how you feel about your actual boss or an interaction you have had with an authority figure lately.

Bride

An aspect of your self that is about to make a commitment, take an oath or pledge devotion. Feminine aspect of "union" or the greater whole of self. May represent the spiritual integration of self.

Businessman

Related to the material world, rational thinking and concrete thinking. Also denotes analytical thinking, boxed or limited thinking. May suggest your thoughts are constructive, creative or logical. Note whether the dream businessman is trying to show you that you have had clear and sensible reasoning on your side or whether you need to revamp the way you view things. Are you over-analyzing, judging or scrutinizing anything or anyone (perhaps even yourself)?

Captain

Reflects how you steer or command your way in your life. Are you the captain of your own ship? Do you feel in control and in choice in your life? May reflect an authority figure or inner ruler. How do you feel about the captain in your dreams? Are you admiring or disdainful? This will help you understand what quality within yourself is being reflected.

Cheerleader

May depict your need for support or that you are already supporting yourself well, depending on how you feel about the cheerleader in your dreams. Could be a pun on the need to cheer up or feel uplifted about something. Perhaps you need to support some part of your self more.

Chef – See Cook

Child

Represents innocent, playful aspects of self — perhaps aspects that are not fully grown or mature and are in need of more nurturing and love to support your self to adulthood or maturity. How is the child behaving in the dream? How you judge the behaviour indicates your self-judgements or how much you accept your emerging or growing self. May be undisciplined aspects of self or childish attitudes, beliefs and perceptions. If it is a specific child, list the characteristics or behaviours of that child in order to get an accurate reflection of which part of your self the child is symbolizing. Note the child's age and realize that this may reflect one your chakras, since each chakra is associated with a different age group, as follows:

▸ *First chakra:* womb to age 4

▸ *Second chakra:* age 4 to 7

▸ *Third chakra:* age 7 to 12

▸ *Fourth chakra:* age 12 to 18

See the *Chakras* section of dictionary for greater insight. See also Baby or Teenager.

Clergyman, Cleric – *See Minister*

Clown

Denotes permission to act foolish, to clown around or to act like a sad clown or a happy clown. How is your dream clown acting? Do you need to lighten up a bit in your life? Have you been acting too serious? Perhaps you are not taking life seriously enough, or maybe you need to laugh more.

Comedian

Reflects a humorous or funny aspect of self. Perhaps you need to be less serious or to act out a little. May be pun on the need to ham it up or to laugh more in your life. There may be a need to laugh at yourself or a recent behaviour.

Construction Worker

Usually associated with building, constructing or making something, this reflects your own actions (or inactions) with respect to creating something in your life at this time. You might be building a relationship or a new foundation, or perhaps you are building up the courage to take action. Note what is being built (or not) in the dream to help you understand what this character symbolizes about you. Since construction workers are usually male, the dream construction worker likely represents some masculine attribute of your self, so note how you feel about this character and what you think (perhaps judge) about him. See also Masculine in this section for greater insight.

Cook

Represents your ability to prepare food for thought. Anything to do in the mental realm such as thinking, opinions, thoughts, ideas, judgements, attitudes and beliefs may be symbolized by cooking and cooks in your dreams. May suggest you are cooking up new ideas or in the process of creating on some level. Note the dream feelings and what you are preparing for greater insight.

Cop – See Officer and Police Officer

Crone – See Hag

Dentist

May bring up fear for some people or denote that something is going to be (or has been) painful. If a dentist means "fear" to you, then note if there is something or someone in your life right now that frightens you. Because dentists work in your mouth, they may symbolize the words you speak and whether you have been speaking your truth lately. Could represent something or someone that is to be tolerated because it's the right thing to do. Note what associations you make about dentists to help you understand whether this is a symbol of a helpful aspect of your self or an enemy waiting to hurt you. See Doctor in this section and Teeth in the *Body* section of this dictionary for greater insight.

Detective

Symbolizes an aspect of your self that is inquisitive, determined to find the truth, or curious. May be a part of you that is searching or longing for something. May also represent a very analytical or detailed aspect of your self, or the side of you that strives to know it all. Could also symbolize a puzzling situation or denote something that you haven't yet resolved (or solved). Detectives are often authority figures and associated with rules and codes of behaviour (similar to police officers). See Police Officer for further clues as to meaning.

Devil

The devil often represents fear or evil depending on your upbringing and, especially, your personal views on what a devil is. Because the devil is considered the opposite of an angel, this could denote extremes in thinking or acting on your part or that of another. Note the dream feelings to understand if this is a playful devil that represents devilish, mischievous or impish behaviour, or a nasty devil that represents villainous or beastly behaviour or thinking. Have you or anyone you know been acting like a fiend lately? Do you have an adversary? Did the "devil make you do it"?

Doctor

Represents a healer, helper or authority figure, depending on your view of doctors. May reflect an aspect of self that aspires to help others, or the healer within. Could represent arrogance or over-inflated ego. Do you feel in need of some help on your healing journey?

What does the doctor recommend, if anything, in the dream? May signal the need to actually see a physician in your waking life.

Drunk

Could reflect a dissociated part of your self or a part that is not willing to be fully present. Have you the need or desire to "numb out" or be disconnected from something or someone in your life? Could be telling you that you are drinking too much, depending on how you feel about the drunk and the details of the dream. Could also be "drunk with desire" or drunk in a happy sort of way.

Dwarf – *See Midget*

Family

Your family represents the energy that grew you — the total energy of all parts of your self. At the level of self, family represents your inner family or all the parts that comprise the whole of you (all your marbles and how they function as a whole). Family members in a dream mirror your inner peace and cohesiveness or lack of it. Does your dream family get along or is there mishap and fighting? This symbolizes your sense of inner harmony, happiness and satisfaction. Is the dream family supportive or

indifferent? This may show you where you need to fortify your beliefs about yourself or where you lack self-support. Describe family members' characteristics or personality traits to help pinpoint your own strengths and weaknesses. If the dream depicts your actual waking-time family, remember that these are the people you grew with — how comfortable does the dream portray you to be while you're with the family? Is this behaviour conducive to your life now, or are changes in behaviour needed or shown to you? Your family also symbolizes your first chakra and its overall functioning and health. See the *Chakras* section of this dictionary for more insight.

Father

May represent masculine traits such as provider, do-er or action-oriented part of self. Depending on your personal experiences, this may represent authoritarian, assertive or a dominating figure or part of self. Note how you feel about or view males in general. Look to the qualities you perceive as being inherent in your own father to understand how this dream father may reflect or mirror traits about yourself. Father may also symbolize responsibility or leader, or may be a pun on "man around the house." Could also point to someone in your life who is a father figure or someone you admire.

Feminine

Feminine energies are represented by the female characters in your dream. Any female may be mirroring your own feminine energy, which is always striving for balance and harmony with your masculine energy. By studying your female energies you can see where you are balanced or in need of balance in your current life. As with all symbolism, your sense of your own feminine energy will be the most appropriate interpretation.

There are, however, many universal representations for female energies, including the ability to be nurturing, yielding, soft, receptive, discriminating and intuitive (psychic). Other universal or shared understandings for feminine energies include humanitarian, graceful, merciful, powerful, silent, empty, holding, creative and insightful. Female archetypes include the maiden (or virgin), seductress, mother, warrioress, and crone.

Feminine energies are a characteristic of the upper chakras (fifth, sixth, seventh and higher). List your beliefs about what being female means to you (or about the feminine side of your self). Your list may be very different from the list of universal feminine qualities, depending on your personal experience and impressions of females. If this is the case, you can be sure that you have some imbalance (often represented by struggle or strife) in your dream time, in your actual day-to-day relationships, and in your own inner world. This is something for you to be aware and to use as a tool for your own growth and insight. Allow your own list to help point you in the right direction for you. Refer to the relevant sections in Chapter 8 to help you further identify your feminine energies.

Firefighter

Often seen as helpers in emergency situations, ask yourself if you need any help right now or if you are in a state of crisis (either within yourself or with something happening in your waking life). Because they fight fires, this symbol may represent that you feel burned about something or are on fire (usually denoting anger or rage) about something. Or it could represent the fires of passion, so note the dream feelings to help you understand whether this is some part of your self crying for help or a positive fiery energy that will help move you forward. Firefighters are most often male and therefore likely represent your masculine energy. Note what role he is playing in the dream and what you think about this to understand what part of your self (what role) is being portrayed by this character.

Gardener

May imply that you need to tend to yourself or symbolically pull some weeds and do inner work in some way. Gardeners reflect your ability to care for yourself and to be responsible for your growth and well-being. Your dream gardener may represent what "seeds you are planting" and how well you are treating yourself. Note the dream feelings to help you understand whether you are feeling good about how you treat yourself. For example, a gardener who is annoyed by his garden's growth (perhaps there are too many weeds) may represent your impatience with your own growth (and whatever that implies to you), or that you are feeling overwhelmed by too much work and not enough reward.

Ghost

May reflect something you thought was dead but now appears not to be. Could be that you feel something has come back to haunt you or that you feel invaded on some level. Are you afraid of the dream ghost? If so, what is it that frightens you about it? This will help you understand the meaning of your dream ghost and what part of yourself it symbolizes.

Giant

Symbolizes an enlarged or bigger than life aspect of self. Are you in awe of the dream giant and see it as a representation of your higher self or God-self? Could reflect something that you feel is "bigger than you" or too big to handle." Perhaps you need to think big or bigger about something.

Grandfather

Similar to Masculine, but added wisdom and patience are associated with it. Grandfathers in general are responsible, leaders and action-oriented. Whatever traits you associate with your own grandfather(s) are most valuable in understanding what this symbol reflects for you.

Grandmother

Similar to Feminine, but added wisdom and patience are associated with it. Grandmothers are often referred to as nurturing, giving, receptive female role models. But could be any trait you associate with grandmothers in general, especially your own grandmother(s).

Groom

An aspect of your self that is about to make a commitment, take an oath or pledge devotion. Masculine aspect of "union" or the greater whole of self. May represent the spiritual integration of self.

Guard

Do you feel in need of protection? Guards symbolize protection, guardianship and security in general. They are also usually male and therefore may be associated with issues of authority, control and dominance. Do you feel the need to be on guard about something or someone? Have you been feeling insecure in any area of your life? Perhaps you are defensive about something or feel the need to defend yourself, a belief, or an opinion.

Hag

Represents a woman of wisdom. A hag or crone is someone who has reached menopause and can now hold her own energy (blood) in and therefore can now be a resource for loved ones and the community. Hags bring you messages about the richness of your inner wisdom. Have you been acting wisely or do you need to cultivate your wisdom? See also Feminine.

Indian – *See Aboriginal*

Jester

Similar to a clown, a jester may imply you are being a fool or creating your own folly. Could say you are being funny, comical or "the comedian." May be a pun on "surely you jest" or about a recent gesture or display of yours. Court jesters were a source of entertainment and inspiration, and they were often seen as being magical and/or enlightened. Note the dream feelings and who is "jesting" for greater understanding.

Judge

Represents an aspect of self or another that is usually an analytical thinker and makes decisions. What current situation in your life requires mediation or arbitration? Is there something that needs negotiation? Are you feeling judged? If so, by whom? Does your dream judge symbolize someone else who is judging you? Perhaps you are judging yourself harshly — look to the behaviour of the judge in the dream to determine whether the judgement is beneficial or harsh. What has been your personal experiences of judges?

King

Symbolizes rulership, authority and dominion. May also reflect an over-inflated ego or a controlling aspect of your self. How does the dream king impose his rule? This reflects whether you are ruling yourself with benevolence and kindness or imposing harsh rules on yourself. Are you ruling with an iron hand? Perhaps you are being arrogant about something going on in your life currently — do you think you are mightier than those around you?

Knight

This masculine symbol reflects parts of your self or another that you perceive to be brave, courageous and worthy. May reflect responsibility, the search for truth or high ideals. May be a pun on knight in shining armour or white knight. Could also represent the word "night" and refer to darkness (any emotion or situation that you think of as dark, sad or something to be kept secret) in your life.

Magician

May suggest you have something magical happening in your life or some inner transformation is taking place. Does the magician appeal to you or create a negative feeling? This will help you understand if the magician is a welcome potential within yourself. Can represent an aspect of self that feels it can do anything, re-create or transmute negative into positive. May suggest you need more magic in your life.

Maid

Represents a helpful, dutiful aspect of self or feelings of unworthiness, depending on what you think of maids' work. May be a play on the word "made." Have you felt made to do something or serve someone lately? May represent that you feel unappreciated or grateful, depending on how you feel about maids in general.

Mailman or Mail Carrier

Denotes a message being delivered or an aspect of your self that is trying to communicate a message. May be a pun on a "male" person in your life or your own masculine side. Have you delivered the goods or posted a job? Have you made good on a delivery, delivered a speech or dispensed advice lately?

Man – See Masculine

Manager

May represent an authority figure or controlling aspect of self, depending on how you view managerial positions in general. Could be a need to manage your affairs, your emotions or some situation in your life.

Masculine

Universally, men are symbolic of the action part of self, the do-er, and the physical provider. Masculine energy is also symbolic of the energy of the mind, ego, personality and intellect. It is an "outgoing" energy that can be used for acting, doing and building. It represents the lower three chakras and the lower will power. Masculine archetypes include the boy, warrior, hero, father and warlock. Often represents your sense of support, safety and security. Your beliefs around masculine energy will often be based on your early childhood programming. Males in your dreams, whether strangers or familiar people, are trying to reflect something about your self or a male energy in your life. To help you determine which aspect of your self is being represented, identify three characteristics or personality traits to describe the male character in your dream, and realize these are aspects of your self that are trying to be revealed or brought to your consciousness.

Merlin

Symbolizes a positive, powerful masculine aspect of self. Merlin is able to do anything and has magical powers. Also says you have power to create whatever you want or transform some situation or aspect of self in any way

you want. Your Merlin aspect represents your abundant potential.

Mermaid

Associated with the water and feminine energies (see Feminine). Often represents a warning against vanity, pride and lust.

Midget

May symbolize that you are feeling small about something or that some aspect of your self is underdeveloped in some way. May suggest that you need to think or act in bigger ways. May reflect that you feel diminished, not part of the crowd, or the focus of some unwanted attention.

Minister

May represent an authority figure, friend or wise advisor, depending on your personal association with clerics. How does it feel to be in the presence of the dream character? This will help you understand whether the aspect presented is friend or foe, dominating or flexible. May reflect a spiritual advisor, mentor and kindly support. If you have had a negative experience with the clergy, then it may represent a controlling, powerful negative aspect of your self that is ruling you in a disadvantageous way. Further negative associations may be ego-aggrandizement, self-righteousness, pompousness and a holier-than-thou attitude. May represent your religious or spiritual beliefs.

Monster

Reflects some situation, issue or person whom you find frightening, threatening, intimidating or otherwise unable to face. Could be another person that you fear or an aspect of your self. Often associated with nightmares, monsters could reflect an overwhelming inner controlling part of self or an aspect of your self that you once needed to keep you safe but have since outgrown the need for. These parts of self continue in the same roles until we have a chance to get to know them and give them new tasks to do. Confronting the monster with questions will often illicit a meaningful answer. See the discussion on nightmares in Chapter 3 for more information on how to resolve frightening dreams.

Mother

Consider the traits that you associate with your own mother first when discerning what the mother symbol means to you. Universally, the mother archetype is considered to be nurturing, loving and receptive, but your personal experiences will lead you toward the most appropriate answers here.

Mothers can also reflect the female authority within yourself, or symbolize a teacher and friend.

Movie Star

Often represents aspects of self that desire fame and fortune. What characteristics draw or repel you to the dream movie star? These traits are important clues about which of your traits are being reflected by the dream star. Perhaps this movie star represents your ability to act out or put on an act. Have you been hamming it up or been in a space of make believe? Note what special qualities you associate with the movie star or what behaviour of theirs implies a quality of your own. See also Actor.

Musician

Portrays an aspect of self that has creative abilities and is looking for expression. Is the musician playing an instrument in the dream? If so, what kind? Identify how you feel about the music and how you respond to the instrument. May refer to your ability to uplift or inspire others. Could also be a symbol of inner harmony that you have recently achieved or your need to harmonize. May be a pun on "music to my ears" or the need for more music or inspiration in your life.

Neighbour

Symbolizes something that lives right next to you or beside you. This is likely an aspect of self that you know about but have not fully recognized or integrated within your self. For example, although you recognize a certain quality about yourself, say your controlling self, you do not yet fully understand its role or rulership in your inner reality. May refer to a nosy neighbour or gossip, depending on how you feel about your own neighbours. May represent a situation or issue you cannot get away from or is right next to you.

Nun

A nun in your dream may represent your spiritual or religious beliefs. She may symbolize a friend or wise advisor, depending on your personal associations with nuns. How does it feel to be in the presence of the dream character? Some orders of nuns isolate themselves from the public, so this may denote that you have been isolating yourself from something or from a group endeavour. May be associated with an ascetic lifestyle and therefore represent your frugality or perhaps a severe stance you are currently taking. A nun wearing black and white may symbolize your own black and white nature or thinking (an all-or-nothing point of view). Because nuns tradition-ally wear habits, it could be a pun on something about one of your habits — either a bad one or a good one. May also be a pun on "none" and suggest you are "having none of it."

Officer

Offices often symbolize authority figures, rulers or rule makers. May also represent an analytical, practical or reasoning aspect of self. May suggest you feel in charge or in control of a situation. A military officer may symbolize an aspect of your self that serves, feels devoted to a country or a cause, and/or feels like a warrior, depending on how you view military personnel. Note if your officer is male or female — he or she may represent a masculine or feminine person in your life whose traits include being dominating, controlling, or whatever you associate with officers. Alternatively, your dream officer may symbolize a masculine or feminine aspect of your self. Are you are imposing harsh rules on yourself? Do you live by a code or creed that is useful or harmful, too strict or too disciplinarian? We often have a hard time discerning what rules we hold in our inner reality because we get stuck in patterns of behaviour and patterns of thinking. Symbolic characters such as an Officer are meant to help us see our patterns and behaviours in a new way. Can you own these traits? Note the dream feelings to help you understand this symbol further. Ask yourself what your personal associations are about officers and use this as a guide to understanding this symbol. Also see Police Officer.

Orphan

Represents an aspect of your self that you may have abandoned or that feels abandoned and alone. How does the dream orphan feel? Can you relate to these feelings and see what part of self has these emotions? May reflect feelings of being unloved or unwanted. Orphans are without parents — do you feel you have been without nurturing or guidance lately?

Pastor *– See Minister*

Patient

Symbolizes an aspect of self that feels in need of some care, nurturing or tenderness. Are you feeling wounded or in need of rest? May be a pun on the need for more patience or that you have been displaying lack of patience.

Pilot

May reflect an aspect of self that feels in control of things. Does the pilot know what he/she is doing in the dream, or does the plane seem out of control? Are you flying high or soaring about something going on in your life? Is your dream pilot flying or grounded? Note the dream feelings to help you understand what part of your self the pilot symbolizes. Also note your personal associations with pilots and use them to gain insight.

Pioneer

Reflects an aspect of self that is breaking new ground or at the forefront of something new. May represent your own daring, courage and will power. Perhaps you are finding new and better ways to move through life, or you are inventing something new. Have you been more adventurous or started a new project lately?

Police Officer

Often represents authority figure, rules, rigid behaviour or black and white thinking. Are you imposing stiff and hard rules on yourself or others? Do you feel judged or pressured into doing something? Are you feeling caught in the act or guilty about something? Perhaps police represent a sense of peace, security and protection to you. What do you think and feel about police in your community? Are you punishing yourself for some of your thoughts, words or actions? See Officer for greater insight.

Politician

Symbolizes an aspect of your self that is outspoken, gregarious or an authority figure, depending on your view of politicians. Do you admire or loathe your dream politician? May also represent cunning, public service, leadership skills or diplomacy. May be a pun on the fact that you have been playing politics or that you have been saying a lot and doing little. Have you been speaking your truth or just trying to get votes?

Priest – *See Minister*

Prince, Princess

Represents an aspect of self that feels special, royal, majestic or noble. May also refer to parts of yourself that are learning rulership or learning how to be a controller of affairs. Is there a positive or negative feeling associated with the dream prince or princess? Have you been acting like a princess who is spoiled and gets her way, or is there a need to treat yourself royally? A not fully grown (into its role) aspect of self.

Prostitute

Symbolizes an aspect of your self that feels used, wanton or exploited in some way. Has something made you feel cheapened, degraded or demeaned lately? How does the dream prostitute feel, or how do you feel about her/him? Have you been "prostituting" yourself lately or have you sold out your values and truth? May tell you that you have compromised yourself in some way.

Psychiatrist

Associated with mental health, this character may reflect something about your psychological self and how your mind is functioning in general. Depending on your personal associations with this type of doctor, you may find it reflects a helpful, caring side of self or a harsh, analytical aspect. How do you feel about the dream psychiatrist? Have you been analyzing yourself lately, or do you feel someone else is analyzing you? Do you view psychiatrists as being generally helpful or do they raise fears of having another person see the truth of who you are? Do you feel in need of help, especially at the mental level? Do you feel like you are going crazy? See Doctor for more insight.

Queen

Reflects rulership, authority and dominion, but with a gentler hand than that of a king. May also portray an over-inflated ego or a controlling aspect of self. How does the queen impose her rule? This reflects whether you are ruling yourself with benevolence and kindness or imposing harsh rules on yourself. Are you ruling with an iron hand or are you coming from a place of self-aggrandizement about something going on in your life currently? Do you feel like a queen or do you need to treat yourself like a queen?

Rabbi – *See Minister*

Repairman

Reflects that you need help at some level. The need for mending, restoring or correcting an attitude, belief, thought, idea, opinion, judgement or feeling. Ask yourself what you can do to improve, rectify, remedy, fix or renew some aspect of your self or your life.

Salesperson

May symbolize someone or something that is helpful or annoying, depending on your personal experiences with salespeople. Do you feel you need more attention in some area of your life, or that your needs are not being met? Note the salesperson's demeanor and how that reflects either your current behaviour or that of someone you know. Do you like the "service" you have been getting at home, at work, or elsewhere?

Security Guard – *See Guard*

Servant

An aspect of self that is obsequious, submissive or passive. May reflect feelings of lack of authority or unworthiness. Have you been serving others at the cost of your own energy? Do you need to serve yourself more and others less? Do you feel dominated or out of choice or control? Who or what are you serving in the dream and how do you feel about that? If you are being served in your dream, note how this feels and whether you are in need of some service in your waking life or have been feeling royally treated. Or perhaps you view something as being self-serving at this time in your life.

Shadow

These are usually vague images, which indicates they are parts of self or another that we don't see very clearly or don't know very well. Shadows often have a negative connotation or denotes something bad or wrong. This is not necessarily true — in fact, your shadow parts often reveal great gifts, talents and creative parts of yourself that have just been hidden from your view. Shadow parts are often aspects of self that have been pushed aside or buried due to childhood programming. For example, you may have been told repeatedly that some part of you, such as your anger, was inappro-

priate and should not be displayed.
If this is constantly reinforced, you
suppress your anger and it becomes a
shadow aspect of yourself — hidden,
vague and unfamiliar to you. In fact
anger is a positive and extremely useful
energy if used and expressed in a
healthy way. Shadow parts are often
the ones we treat the hardest, judge the
most harshly, and dislike intensely.

Singer

Denotes expression with song and
therefore the need to use your voice as
expression. Do you need to express
yourself more, express your truth or
speak up in general? Is the singer adept
and capable or out of tune? This will
help you understand whether you are
out of tune with something or someone, or feeling confident about your
abilities to express yourself. Do you
need to sing someone's praises
(perhaps your own) or vocalize an
opinion? Note the dream feelings to
help you understand if this is a joyful
or sorrowful expression. If this is a
famous singer, see Movie Star for
greater insight.

Slave

Suggests that you are feeling held
hostage, prisoner or against your will
in general. Do you feel a slave to your
job, to your children or to other responsibilities? Perhaps you are labouring,

toiling or working hard to achieve your
goals and ideals. Have you made a
commitment that you feel you cannot
break? Are you doing, thinking or
acting in any way against your
free will?

Soldier

Symbolizes an aspect of self
that serves, feels devoted to
country or a cause, and/or that feels
like a warrior, depending on how
you view military personnel. Is this a
fighting aspect of self? Who is he/she
fighting? Are you ready for or spoiling
for a fight? Do you feel the need to be
defensive or on guard? Is there a cause
that you are willing to defend or fight
for? How prepared are you to fight for
something? Do you feel the need to kill,
harm or otherwise do what is needed
to protect or justify your position? Are
you being defensive with a stance,
viewpoint or with your beliefs?

Stranger

Aspect of self that is unknown to
you. These are usually referred to as
shadow parts of self or those aspects
that you have disowned, judged or
otherwise viewed as wrong or bad.
These parts go unrecognized and unac-
cepted, which creates inner conflicts,
worries and struggles. How do you feel
about the stranger in the dream? Look
to the feelings to help you realize what

aspect of your self you are denying. Remember that we often deny positive aspects of self, too. See also Shadow.

Student

Represents learning or being in an environment of group learning. May be an aspect of self that is underdeveloped in some area, depending on the age of the dream student. The grade or level reflects what level of learning you are at. Perhaps the student represents an old pattern of behaviour you've had since grade school, or it could be that this is about an advanced learning environment. Depending on how you view school, it may represent an aspect of self related to boredom, control, opportunities, socializing, group consciousness or restriction.

Teacher

May represent an aspect of self that is trying to convey a message or a teaching. Could represent learning opportunity, support, friend or wise mentor, depending on your personal experience of teachers. Could also represent authority figure, control or strict codes of behaviour. Teachers are sources of knowledge and this could be what your dream teacher is reflecting. Is there something you need to learn at this time in your life? Could be a pun on someone trying to teach you a lesson.

Teenager

Teenagers are usually at that in-between stage between childhood and adulthood. This could suggest your dream teenager is an aspect of your self that is caught in the middle of some situation. Teenagers also represent that period when life can be fraught with frustration, upset and confusion. Search your recent feelings to see if you have been feeling this way. Or perhaps you have been teen-like in feeling insecure, awkward or rebellious.

Thief

Reflects that you feel either threatened by loss or that something has been stolen from you. May symbolize an aspect of self that is shadowy or deceptive. Has someone taken from you emotionally or have you felt manipulated in some way?

Twins

May represent a balanced time in your life or the need for more balance. Could mirror an aspect of self that you can identify with or see clearly. May represent the need to pair up with someone or some project for greater balance. Could be a pun on "double trouble" or duality within self.

Uncle

Symbol of a masculine aspect of self, a dream uncle is best interpreted by referring to the traits of your own uncles. In general, males are action-oriented, providers and supporters. Uncles are often seen as friendly male influences, depending on your personal experiences.

Vampire

Represents a frightening aspect of self, or could indicate that you have been attacking yourself on some level. Have you been bloodthirsty for anything lately? Or have you felt your life force being drained away by another person's words or actions? Either way, you are losing energy to something or someone. Be on the lookout for those around you who suck the vitality out of you. Be mindful of your negative or self-berating thoughts.

Waitress

Represents an aspect of self that feels in service, helpful or unworthy, depending on how you feel about waitresses. Do you feel as though you have been taking orders lately or that you are serving everyone else's needs and not your own? Perhaps you feel over-worked and underpaid, or that others are not grateful for your services.

Witch

May symbolize your strong, wise, powerful and magical feminine aspect. Or could be a negative, nasty aspect of self that is cruel and ugly. How do you feel about witches in general? Do you see them in a positive or negative light? How did you feel about the dream witch? Has someone or something bewitched you lately? Or have you been acting "witchy"?

Woman – *See Feminine*

Sports and Games

Sports and games in the dream time are usually indicative of the games you play (the game of life) or the games people play (group interactions). Of course, your actual experiences and your memories of sports and games you have played are the most important clues about the symbolic meaning of your dreams.

Playing on a team may represent that you are going along with the crowd or group consciousness, which may or may not serve you well. Look to the dream feelings to discern whether you are playing along in a healthy way or need to be more of an individual. How does your participation in the dream tie in to current group endeavours or your participation in a group in your waking life? Are you part of the team (at home, in your community, or at work) at this time in your life? If in the dream you find yourself alone or singled out, it may suggest that you are trying to accomplish something by yourself when it may behoove you to get more input from others.

If your dream is about an individual sport, it may symbolize something you are doing on your own in your waking life. Winning a game in your dream (or just enjoying playing the game) may represent that you are accomplishing things successfully on your own in your waking life.

Sports are also about competition — with yourself or with others. Are you trying your best at some current endeavour or do you need to pick up the pace? Are you winning or losing? Are you currently involved in a rivalry, or struggle with yourself or someone else? Perhaps you are even at war with yourself or someone else. A conflict on a playing field often reflects these types of confrontations.

Any sport may also suggest that you have strength, endurance, agility and a sense of control at this time in your life. Dream feelings will often help pinpoint the personal symbolic meaning for you.

Games of all types are about the tactics and strategies you use in your everyday life. We all have ways in which we manoeuvre through life — whether by manipulating, orchestrating or handling things. The way in which you accomplish goals and get what you want is often symbolized by games dreams. These types of dreams are simply trying to familiarize you with whether your actions are deliberate (conscious) or automatic (without consciousness). Pay attention to the dream feelings to understand if you are playing healthy games or if you are deceiving yourself or others. Playing an unfamiliar game in your dream, or one that you're not skilled at, may represent a challenge you should prepare for, one that you are currently facing, or one that you have met successfully.

Remember: *These symbolic meanings are just suggestions. If these suggested meanings do not resonate with you, ring a bell, give you an "ah-ha" moment or otherwise feel right, search through your own experience or beliefs about the symbol to find what makes sense for you.*

Baseball

Represents that a game is being played on some level. Are you a team player or competitive in the dream game? Are you batting around new ideas, opinions or thoughts? Do you need to strike out on a new adventure, or are you dreaming of striking it rich? Do you feel you've had three strikes at something and now you've struck out? May say you are following group consciousness or that you need to be more group minded in some present undertaking. Getting to bases may be a pun on how far a man can get with a woman sexually (first base, second base, home run). A foul ball in the dream may represent that you think you have fouled up a situation or relationship, or failed at something.

Basketball

May represent ideas, thoughts or opinions being bounced around. A game is being played either in your inner reality or in your waking time. Are you enjoying the game? Is it a competitive experience or a friendly exchange? Are you a sports enthusiast or is this a challenging encounter? Is the fact that it is being played on a court a factor in your current life? Is there something or someone you are courting or pursuing (especially in a competitive way)? Perhaps you are courting disaster. Also represents team playing or group consciousness. Note the dream actions for further clues as to symbolic meaning. For example, if you or someone else is blocking a shot, it may represent that you feel blocked about something in your waking life. Being awarded a free throw indicates you are feeling rewarded or justified by some current situation or development. Dribbling the ball may symbolize that you feel you are in control or choice at this time in your life.

Bicycling

Suggests you are in balance and handling things well, or symbolizes the need for more balance in your life. How well are you riding in the dream, and how does it feel? Is there a sense of being in control, or does it feel shaky and difficult to manoeuvre? Are you labouring or finding it easy to ride the bike? May represent your strength, endurance or stamina. If your bike has training wheels it may suggest you are preparing for something or require a bit of extra support and help in a current undertaking. May say you are playing it safe or symbolize dependence.

Board Games

(such as Monopoly, Scrabble, Clue, Risk, etc.) Board games can represent the games you play or how you manoeuvre in your everyday life. What tactics are you aware that you use? Do you plot or calculate your next move in life or do you prefer to take chances or risks? Are you manipulative or controlling? Do you like to win or dominate? Board games can represent your intellect and how you think (strategize). Note the type of game being played and if it is one you are familiar with or not.

Bowling

Represents a game being played at some level in your life. Are you a team player or following group consciousness? Are you in a league of your own? Perhaps you need a little relaxation or more social interaction. Dreaming about gutter balls may reflect a disheartening experience or that you feel you have fallen into the gutter (lost status). It could also symbolize that you feel like a loser, or that you are not able to accomplish something. Getting a strike may symbolize that you feel rich ("striking it rich"), that you have accomplished something recently, or that you feel elated or like a winner. Getting a spare in your dream may say you are settling for less or that something is the next best thing. The dream feelings will help you pinpoint what is being reflected by this dream game.

Boxing

May represent an internal fight, conflict or confusion (feeling punch drunk). May imply that you are taking a pounding, feel like you are going down for the count, or feel beaten up in some way. May suggest you are dancing around in circles or trying to find your place or footing in the game of life. However, it may also suggest you feel in total control or choice at this time in your life, depending on the dream feelings. Try to relate the feelings to some current situation in your life for greatest insight. May suggest you have great endurance and strength at this time, especially if you are going a lot of rounds. Can also be a pun on "going another round," that someone or something is a knockout, or that you are playing the ropes (pretending to be weak).

Bridge

Usually involves intellect, reason, logic and skill. May symbolize your competitive nature. May be a pun on the "games you play" or the need to accept the hand you've been dealt. May be a pun on a bridge you need to cross or a distance you need to bridge. Note what type of hand you receive and how you play it, and try to relate these to a current situation in your waking life. For example, a grand slam symbolizes your feelings of having a big win or doing something impressive lately. Being the dummy may suggest you feel dumb (stupid, regretful, or inadequate) about some recent thoughts, words or actions, or could suggest you are not actively participating in something (perhaps your own life). Bidding may reflect your secrets or current ways in which you express yourself. See also Card Games.

Card Games

May symbolize your competitive nature, your mental facilities or your luck. Implies the games that you play or the need to accept the hand you've been dealt. May be a pun on you being a card, clown or fool. Note the dream feelings and type of card game being played. If it is a familiar game, then you can bet it represents a well-known "game" or event — a game you have played before.

Chess

Represents a battle of wits, the mind, logic, reason and the intellect. Could be about the mental games you play, or about your competitive nature. May imply current strategies you employ, your approach, tactics and cunning. A checkmate may reflect that you feel like a winner or that you have no choices left. A stalemate may suggest you feel that no one has won or that you have not been able to accomplish something.

Darts

A game of skill to many, this may represent a challenge you are currently undergoing if you are not familiar with the game. May say you feel targeted or that there is a need to get the point. May be a pun on being in a hurry, darting to and fro or rushing.

Exercise

Exercise is about working out and may symbolize how you work out solutions. It may also be about sweating and reflect that you are working hard at something. Does the dream exercise feel rewarding and fulfilling? This will help you understand if you are feeling satisfied with the work you are currently doing. It also lets you know how well you are using your time and energy. Do you find exercising laborious or too much work? Perhaps this symbolizes something you feel you have to do (or are doing) without any heart or commitment. May imply you need some physical exercise in your waking life, or may suggest that you "exercise caution." Perhaps you are exercising control in some area of you life or you need to exercise more patience or control. Note the dream feelings for greater understanding.

Football

Represents that a game is being played at some level. May represent the game of life and how you feel about it currently. Are you having a rough and tumble experience in your waking life? Are you being a good team player? Are you playing aggressively, or do you need to assert yourself in some group endeavour? Could represent a conflict within yourself or within some area of your life. Notice whether you

are playing offence or defence and relate this to current actions or stances you have taken. Do you feel as though you have dropped the ball, or are fumbling your way through something. Do you need to call the play or take a leadership role at this time? Perhaps you are benched and feel penalized or as though you're sitting and watching rather than participating. Have you been caught offside? Or have you been caught in some error or feel that you've made a mistake for all to see?

Gambling

May symbolize that you are currently involved in taking a risk, a gamble or a wager on something. Could say you are speculating on a venture or taking a chance. If you gamble regularly, this may speak of your addiction or craving to gamble. May say "what have you got to lose?" or "what have you got to gain?"

Golf

Represents a game being played at some level in your life. May represent your view of the game of life. Is the dream experience serene, lonely, single-minded or stressful? May suggest you feel alone in the game of life or that now is the time for independent thinking rather than group endeavours. Perhaps you are having a "swinging" time in your life, or maybe you need some rest and relaxation. Golf can be a reflection of the mental realm and your thoughts, thinking and attitudes.

Hockey

Implies team or group consciousness or activity. May be games you play or denote the right to fight. Perhaps you feel you need to toughen up or play harder. Because hockey is played on ice, this may denote frozen or hard feelings. May symbolize walking with your fears or skating on thin ice. Have you been caught offside? Or have you been caught in some error or feel that you've made a mistake for all to see? Scoring goals may reflect your recent accomplishments and how you feel about them. Have you been impressing the crowd or do you deserve some applause? Notice how aggressively you play the dream hockey to help you understand your assertiveness or aggression lately. Stick handling may reflect how well (or not) you are handling something in your waking life. Being in the penalty box may suggest you feel you are being penalized (either justly or unjustly) or as though you're sitting and watching rather than participating. See also Skating in this section and Ice in the *Water* section of this dictionary.

Marathon

May suggest that your lifestyle is hurried, fast-paced or grueling. May imply you feel you are running a marathon or that you are feeling overwhelmed by your feelings or by a situation in your waking life. If you actually run marathons, dreaming of one may reflect your strength, endurance and stamina, or that you need more of these qualities.

Olympics

Implies you are in top shape or form, and at the peak of your abilities, or perhaps that your competitive nature is in the forefront. Do you feel at the top of your class or at your peak performance? Are you striving to be your best, do your best or accomplish great feats? May say your physical fitness is at an all-time high, or that you feel in control (emotionally and mentally). Suggests that you feel strong, action-oriented, powerful and exceptional. May be a pun on the "game you play" or "are you game?"

Puzzles

Could say you are puzzling over, pondering or considering something. May imply you feel confused, confounded or flustered about something. Is there a mystery or enigma you are currently involved in?

Perhaps you are trying to fit in or figure out how you fit in. A jigsaw puzzle may symbolize the totality of your being, so note if there are any pieces missing or if you are trying to make a piece fit. Pencil puzzles (for example, crossword puzzles) often reflect the intellect, analytical thinking or any mental activity you may be currently involved in. Dream feelings should help clarify the meaning of this symbol.

Running

Implies endurance, strength and stamina. May say you are in top shape or may point out the need for more exercise. Are you running from something, perhaps something you can't face? Perhaps you feel you are running late, on the run or rushing about all the time.

Skating

May represent your ability to glide through life or through a current challenge. May symbolize that you have good balance presently, or that you need more balance in your life. If you have never skated, it may suggest that you are trying something new, or perhaps that you are facing a challenge that will require patience and practice to perfect. Because this involves frozen water, it may represent frozen emotions (any emotions you have trouble feeling

or expressing). See also the entry for Ice in the *Water* section of this dictionary.

Skiing

Implies control, daring, power and manoeuvrability. Because it is done on snow, this may imply frozen emotions such as fear, powerlessness or any blocked feeling. If the dream feelings are positive, may symbolize an uplifting, smooth-flowing experience. May represent freedom, choice, vacation and relaxation, depending on your personal views about skiing. See also the *Water* section of this dictionary and the entry for Snow in the *Weather* section.

Soccer

May suggest you are kicking around a new or old idea, depending on dream feelings. Could reflect how well (or not) you feel you are doing with respect to some situation. Are you a team player or are you trying to hog the ball (do it on your own)? Could suggest you are playing the field or looking in broader directions.

Surfing

Represents freedom, choice, carefree lifestyle, rest or relaxation, depending on your views on surfing. May also represent the need for balance or suggest that you are in balance, depending on how well you are managing on the surfboard. Could denote a challenging situation or encounter. May speak of your swelling emotions or that you are riding high on positive feelings. May be a pun on surfing the net or riding the waves (of your emotions). See also the *Water* section of this dictionary.

Swimming

Because it is done in water, swimming reflects emotions and the feminine. Swimming in a pool often represents your spiritual nature. Clear water in the pool symbolizes a clear connection to Spirit; cloudy water suggests you can't see clearly (or don't have insight into something) at this time. Note how deep the pool is — the depth reflects the depth of your spiritual connection. If you are swimming in another body of water, note how smooth or rough it is. This helps you understand if your emotional life is choppy, overwhelming (big waves or tidal wave), or calm and clear. Could say your head is swimming or that you are reeling from something. You may be in over your head, feel like you are drowning (in your emotions), or need a life line. May imply that you either sink or swim, or that you need to take the plunge or dive right in. See also Feminine in the *People* section,

the *Water* section, and Swimming Pool in the *Backgrounds and Settings* section of this dictionary.

Tennis

This often symbolizes how you bounce ideas around in your head — going over something repeatedly or back and forth with your thinking or decision-making processes. May be about a mental match you are having with another person or competitive thinking. Could reflect how well you feel you are playing the game of life, or perhaps you think you have met your match. May be a pun on "the ball's in your court," meaning you need to make a decision regarding something. Because you play tennis with a racquet, the dream may be a pun about a current con game or con job you are involved in. Could also reflect a noisy racket going on in your thought realm, or that you are surrounded by too much confusion (noise/racket). Notice the dream feelings to help you discern what this symbolizes at this time in your life. Could be a pun on "love."

Volleyball

Because the ball goes back and forth over a net, this often reflects how you bounce ideas around in your head — going over something repeatedly or back and forth with your thinking or decision-making processes. It is usually associated with group behaviour, how well you work within a group, or whether you are a team player. May reflect how well you think you are handling your current affairs, relationships or any endeavour in which you are currently striving. Note the dream feelings to help pinpoint what this symbolizes. See also Tennis, since these games have some terminology in common.

Water Skiing

Because this involves water, it probably reflects your emotional life in some way. How are you currently handling your feelings? Are you just skimming over the surface of your emotions? Do you feel in control? Notice how you manoeuvre while water skiing and how it feels for greater insight.

.

Streets, Roads and Paths

In general, streets and roads represent the path you have chosen to follow, the direction you are going in, and the goals you are striving toward. Take note of the condition of the road in your dream. Is it under construction? Is your life under construction? Is the street a dead end, poorly lit or in poor repair? All these represent aspects of your self and the condition you are in. If you are having trouble manoeuvring down the road, this symbolizes that you are having trouble manoeuvring through your life at this time. A new road may indicate that you have recently made a decision, created a new pattern in some area or your life, or set new goals. Turning right on a street is often seen as making a right decision, whereas as a left turn may denote a wrong decision or that you are headed in the wrong direction.

Remember: These symbolic meanings are just suggestions. If these suggested meanings do not resonate with you, ring a bell, give you an "ah-ha" moment or otherwise feel right, search through your own experience or beliefs about the symbol to find what makes sense for you.

Alley

Often denotes a dark, lonely place accompanied by feelings of hopelessness. Is your dream alley dark and forbidding? Is it a dead end, narrow or confining? Do you feel as though you have reached some sort of impasse in your life, or have your viewpoints be too narrow-minded? Noting the similarities between your dream alley and your current life situation will help you understand how your dream symbolizes your current path or direction. Dreaming of an alley may represent that you feel limited or restricted in some way.

Amber Light – See Yellow Light

Asking Directions

Denotes that you are seeking help or advice about your current direction, choices or goals. May symbolize that you feel lost and in need of guidance. May be telling you to ask for help or get instruction. Remember that you must ask for help before it can be given (even by your guides, teachers, angels and guardians) — "Ask and you will receive."

Back Street

May say that you are not taking the most direct course of action in your life. Perhaps you are trying to stay out of the limelight or avoid being the focus of attention. May also indicate you are taking a longer route toward your goals than need be.

Bridge

Often seen as a way to get from one thing to another. A bridge may denote that you have made a connection, grasped an insight or connected with some aspect of your self in a new way. Have you bridged any gaps in your recent relationships, job or endeavours? Is the bridge complete and accessible? If not, it indicates that connections cannot be made at this time. Are you crossing the bridge in the dream or just considering crossing? May refer to crossing over to the other side or leaving an old lifestyle for a new one.

Bumpy Road

Indicates that your life path is feeling bumpy, uneven or rough. Could also say life is feeling stormy, choppy and turbulent. How big are the bumps in your road? How much trouble is it to manoeuvre around or over them? Note dream feelings to help you connect with what this bumpy road symbolizes for you.

City Streets

Could indicate well-used and well-travelled patterns of behaviour. May say that you are moving along at a fast pace or caught in congestion, depending on what the traffic is like in your dream. May say you are going along with the crowd or group consciousness. May indicate confusion, distractions or disruptions happening in your life. City streets tend to be busy, so they may say that your current undertakings are excessive and cluttered, or vigorous and dynamic.

Country Road

May symbolize that you are taking your time, not hurrying, being patient, or at peace. Perhaps you have fewer distractions and are more at ease in your current endeavours. Or, it could represent that you are a long way from reaching your goals or ideals, depending on how the journey feels in the dream.

Crossing a Road

Indicates choice to move to another viewpoint or desire to get to a new destination. Perhaps you have changed sides in a recent situation or have made decisions that were opposite to previous ones. Perhaps you see the other side of another person's story, or maybe you need to "cross over" and look at things from a new perspective.

Crossroads

Symbolizes that you are at a place of indecision about some situation — you need to choose a path. This is about choices and decisions that must be made now in order to move forward.

Crosswalk

May indicate a need to be cautious or on the alert. May represent a slight delay in some dealings or the need to slow down. Either way, caution on some level is indicated.

Curb

Represents a small step or a step up. Could also be a small obstacle in your path or a pun on "curb your enthusiasm," "curb your appetite" or any type of minor restraint.

Dead End

Represents that in your current life you are not headed in the right direction. In fact, there is no path to follow — it has simply ended. Is there is a situation, issue or relationship in your life in which you are not making any progress? Realize that you need to find and take another path. You have come to the end of something in your current endeavours or undertakings. Could be a pun on a dead-end job or that you are dead ended.

Deserted Road

Suggests that you feel alone or abandoned with respect to some situation, relationship or recent event. May symbolize rejection, feelings of defeat and/or feelings of betrayal. Perhaps you have forsaken yourself or have recently been left stranded. The feelings in the dream will help you discern what current life situation the deserted road symbolizes.

Detour

Conveys that you are not taking the easiest or most direct route toward your goals and endeavours. Could be that you have been re-routed in some current undertakings or that you need to detour from your present course of action. Could imply you cannot get to your destination (your goals) from your current point of view or stance. You may need to take a different path or change your attitudes or beliefs in order to correct your direction. This could also be a pun on being sidetracked from some current situation.

Dirt Road

Implies the path you are taking is either well travelled and proven, or that you have not formed a solid enough foundation (which would be symbolized by a paved road) beneath you. May say your path needs improvements and maintenance or that you are on a rough road at present.

Do Not Enter Sign

A warning that you should not go in a particular direction at this time. Look to your current relationships and undertakings to discern what situation is not right for you. Try to relate the dream feelings to your waking-time feelings for further clues as to meaning.

Downhill

Symbolizes that you are moving in a negative or unflattering direction. Is some project or current endeavour going downhill in your waking life? May imply a poor choice you've made or reflect that things are sliding out of your control. Conversely, it may represent that you are taking the easiest and least stressful route, or that things are going smoothly and rapidly in your current undertakings. Look to the feelings in the dream to help you discern whether this is a positive or negative downhill experience.

Driveway

May imply that you are parked and not moving forward in your life at this time. Could suggest you are "home" or at home in some current undertaking. May indicate a time to rest, or symbolize that you feel secure.

Fast Lane

Are you moving too quickly in some current undertaking? A pun on being in the fast lane of life, this indicates a need to slow down or change your ways. Could be a positive thing that you are fast tracking or taking the most rapid route toward your goals and endeavours.

Gravel Road

Represents a rough road and not a solid foundation for your current undertakings and journey. May indicate the need to be mindful of your "footing" in your current endeavours or relationships. Either way, it implies your path is not smooth, completed or realized.

Green Light

Means "go." Positive sign indicating that you can proceed with your current endeavours with favourable outcome. You are on the right track and should move forward at this time.

Guard Rail

Represents that there are some barriers or boundaries in your current undertakings or the path you are on. May be a pun on the need to be guarded on your journey or to boundary someone or something. May imply that you need to recognize some limits to where you can go.

High Road

May be a pun on "I'll take the high road" and symbolize the path that aspires to higher levels (i.e., higher levels of learning, insight and knowledge). On the high road you have a better perspective or view. Perhaps you have gained more insight on something recently.

Highway

May represent that you are moving smoothly and rapidly on your path toward your goals. Congestion or heavy traffic indicates that you are mired in some situation and not moving along well or at the pace you expected. May indicate you are going along with the crowd or group consciousness. May depict that you are flowing well and without interference, and that you are making good progress.

Hilly Road

May indicate a path that is characterized by obstacles or delays, depending on how well you are manoeuvring on the hilly road. If the dream journey is difficult and fraught with tension, so is the path you are on in your waking life. On the other hand, a smooth and effortless ride indicates you are moving well and happily along in your journey. Could suggest that there are many ups and downs in your life currently.

Intersection

Represents the point of making a decision about something upon your path or route. Which way do you need to turn, or what direction (decisions) do you need to go in? A right turn could indicate a right decision for you; a left turn may indicate the wrong direction or decision.

Main Street

Symbolizes you are taking the most direct route at present or the one that's most travelled. Could be you are following group thinking or group consciousness. Since main streets are usually busy and at the centre of activity, dreaming of a main street represents that you are on a busy or active path at present.

Mountain Road

Indicates that you are striving for high ideals, seeking God, or attempting to get closer to your God. How difficult is it to travel your dream mountain road? This will be a good indicator of whether for you it portends many ups and downs in life or an attempt to reach higher goals.

Muddy Road

Represents that you are currently mired in your own emotions. A strong warning not to let your emotions take over your sense of direction or deter you from your goals. Deep mud that is hard to slog through indicates that your emotions could stop you. Speaks of the need to work on emotions and attitudes that bog you down.

Narrow Road

Symbolizes a narrow mind or limited way of seeing something. Speaks to the need to broaden your thinking and beliefs. Could also say you are limiting your choices lately, or be a pun on "the straight and narrow." May indicate that you feel you don't have enough freedom or leeway in some relationship, endeavour or situation.

No Road

Represents that you feel you have no choice in the direction you are headed. Do you feel that there is no path to follow or that you need to create your own new path? Look to the feelings of the dream to help you understand if this is a challenge to be creative or a complete lack of faith in your ability to forge ahead.

One-Way Street

May indicate that you are looking at some situation in your waking life from only one angle or in one way, and the dream is trying to show you that you aren't seeing things from both sides. May say that you feel you have no alternatives or choices in some endeavour — there is only one path or direction to take. Do you feel that your choices are limited or that you have less freedom than you expected? May have a positive connotation, i.e., that the choices you made are correct and in the right direction, or that only one answer or outcome is possible. Going the wrong way down a one-way street is a strong warning that you are heading in the wrong direction and may need to back out of some situation.

Path

Symbolizes the track, route or direction you are currently taking in life. How well can you manoeuvre on your dream path? This will help you understand whether the direction you are heading in is the smoothest way. If the path winds through a nature scene, it may indicate you feel relaxed about your current undertakings or that you need to relax and take one step at a time. A nature path also indicates that you feel closer to your God. See also the introduction to this section.

Private Road

Reflects that you are currently undertaking something that should remain private, or perhaps you feel it is just right for you alone. May indicate a need to be alone with your thoughts or a need for peace and quiet. Are you comfortable or uncomfortable travelling the dream private road? Perhaps something is none of your business or you need to retreat from someone else's personal affairs.

Public Road

May indicate that you are in the flow or following group behaviour and consciousness — you are not thinking for yourself. May also indicate that something is out in the open and everyone can see it clearly.

Railroad Crossing

A temporary barrier or boundary in your way currently, or the need to set up some barriers or boundaries. Your path may even be temporarily blocked while you process some thoughts. Trains often indicate a train of thinking, so be aware of any trains are in your dream. May warn that you need to be more aware and to stop, look and listen. May be a pun on someone "crossing" or betraying you.

Red Light

Means "stop, look and listen." A warning to be mindful about some current undertaking. Indicates that you need to slow down and revise your thinking, actions, or words. May say do not move forward in some endeavour.

Road

Symbolizes the current path you are following and how well your life is going. Is it a rough road or a highway? Is it a peaceful road or full of hustle and bustle? See the entries for specific types of roads in this section, as well as this section's introduction.

Roadblock

A warning that something is blocking your current endeavours or undertakings. Could say you are energetically blocked at a chakra or that you have emotional and mental blocks. Look to the feelings in the dream to help you uncover the emotions behind the blockage. Look to any of your beliefs or thinking that may be holding you back and ask yourself why you are unable to move forward in certain areas of your life.

Road Map

Often symbolizes that you know the way at a deeper level of your being and that help is close at hand. It says that your path is clearly defined and you just have to keep your eyes open for signs and clues to the correct direction for you. May say that you already have a plan or know what actions will produce results. This is a positive symbol that you are receiving guidance and will reach your goals.

Ruts in Road

Symbolizes that you feel your path is not easy at this time. May indicate a rut in your thinking or feelings. This is often a metaphor for current feelings of being stuck in a rut or experiencing a one-track mind. This signals a need to look at your current behaviours, thoughts, attitudes and beliefs to see where you are stuck in a pattern.

Shortcut

Refers to the need to make a shortcut in some plans, or that you are unwisely taking a shortcut in some endeavour. Look to the dream feelings to help you understand if your dream shortcut is wisdom or folly.

Sidewalk

A dream about driving on the sidewalk is a warning that you are on the wrong track or path, and a strong indication that you need to take corrective action before something negative befalls you. Walking on a sidewalk often refers to taking a well-travelled route or participating in group thinking and behaviours. Is this a leisurely activity for you, or a hectic path such as a downtown city sidewalk? Could be a pun on being side-tracked or indicate that you are side-stepping an issue.

Smooth Road

Indicates you are feeling positive about your current undertakings, which are relatively easy and stress free. May be telling you it is the path of least resistance or the right path to take. Certainly the outlook is positive — smooth sailing is indicated.

Stop Sign

You need to stop some project, endeavour, pattern of thinking or negative belief. It's time to re-think something or take a closer look at your current undertakings. This symbol may also be a warning to proceed with caution and think before you move on. Perhaps you are moving in the wrong direction or need to make a turn (change directions). Driving through a stop sign in your dream may mean you are ignoring your own inner laws or codes of behaviour. This symbol is a strong indication that you need to consider your actions and their consequences. May refer to the need to create healthier boundaries in your life; that is, you may need to stop giving yourself away or over-extending yourself to others.

Street – *See the introduction to this section of the dictionary.*

Tunnel

May indicate that you have tunnel vision about something, or that you feel you are in the dark. May imply the need to go through the darkness in order to see the light (gain clarity). Tunnels are also about passing from one place to another, and therefore indicate that you may be working your way through to new ideas and goals. You will likely see the light at the end of the tunnel if you proceed with your

undertakings. Tunnels lead somewhere — where does your dream tunnel take you? Are the feelings associated with the destination positive or negative?

Under Construction

Symbolizes that you are making changes in the way you either see the world or live in it. Could be you are altering, modifying or transforming some aspect of your self, such as your beliefs, attitudes or the way you feel about something. Depending on how the construction scene feels in your dream, it may indicate a rough road ahead or the need to make adjustments in your current endeavours. Could also point toward new growth and new patterns. Perhaps you are improving old ways or making way for the new. Are there obstacles on your construction site or is everything going according to plan? Often a positive sign that you are doing something constructive or creative in your life.

Uphill

Could indicate you are having a tough time with some current undertaking, feeling or situation, depending on how easily you are able to make your way up the dream hill. Is it easy going or tough slogging? This will help you understand whether this is something you are struggling with or need to "get on top of." May be a positive pun on "its all uphill from here."

U-Turn

This is a warning that you are heading in the wrong direction and need to turn around and go back in the direction you just came from. It may indicate that there is no turning back or point to the fact that you can't change something. Conversely, it may be positive indication that you have turned some aspect of your self or your life around completely.

Winding Road

May represent a long process or long route you are taking. Perhaps you are circumventing the truth or do not wish to see something clearly. This symbol warns of challenges and the need to consider taking a different approach. If the feelings are pleasant and/or if the winding road is in nature, it may indicate that you feel at peace with yourself with respect to some aspect of your journey.

Wrong-Way Sign

A clear warning that you are heading in the wrong direction in some current undertaking, endeavour, belief, habit, relationship, pattern of thinking or feeling. Be aware of the decisions you are

trying to make in your waking life and be mindful of your attitudes.

Yellow Brick Road

May symbolize the path of fantasy or illusion. May also be symbolic of the third chakra, which is yellow. Could indicate you are headed toward a place of wisdom on your path, depending on how you feel taking the yellow brick road. See the entry for Third Chakra in the *Chakras* section for greater insight.

Yellow Light

Proceed with caution. This is a warning to slow down and be aware of the signs around you. You need to review, revise or change your way of thinking, speaking or acting.

Yield

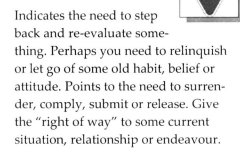

Indicates the need to step back and re-evaluate something. Perhaps you need to relinquish or let go of some old habit, belief or attitude. Points to the need to surrender, comply, submit or release. Give the "right of way" to some current situation, relationship or endeavour.

Tools and Weapons

Remember: These symbolic meanings are just suggestions. If these suggested meanings do not resonate with you, ring a bell, give you an "ah-ha" moment or otherwise feel right, search through your own experience or beliefs about the symbol to find what makes sense for you.

Tools

Tools are associated with building or construction, so they may indicate that you are creating something new and useful in your life. Conversely, they can be used for de-construction and destruction. How are your dream tools being used? Dream tools may represent that you feel you are an instrument or tool for achieving some task. They could also symbolize that you are "getting the work done" or that you need to work harder at building something in your life.

Tools can represent anything that you feel is a necessary ingredient to achieve any task or succeed in any endeavour you are currently involved with. For example, you may be a new parent and wish you had better tools (more knowledge and experience) to raise your child. Or you may be on a self-growth journey and recognize that you need certain tools to manoeuvre around a current obstacle on your path (in this case, the tools could represent more insight or even another person to guide you at this time). Your dream tools are whatever equipment or material would serve you best at this time.

Garden tools are also part of your creative processes. In part, they symbolize how you plant "seed" ideas and thoughts, and how you care for them while they grow and take shape in your life.

Hammer

May indicate that you are exhausting, belabouring or putting too much emphasis on something. Could symbolize how "hard headed" you are being or that you have been hammering a point of view home. Could indicate that you are constructing or creating something new and positive in your life. May feel as if you are labouring or working hard at your new creation.

Hoe

Used in gardening to prepare and tend the ground. A hoe in your dream may represent how you prepare yourself for something or how you tend to, or care for, yourself, some project, or some endeavour. May be a pun on "heave ho" — getting to work or getting a task done. For those familiar with Native American culture, the sound "ho" can be a greeting or mean "amen."

Ladder

If used for climbing up or down, a ladder indicates either your attempts to climb higher or that you feel you are coming down from a high. Do you aspire to climb the ladder of success? Could symbolize how you are aspiring to your goals and ideals. Negative connotation is that you have fallen off your aspiration ladder.

Level

May indicate higher levels of awareness or offer you a higher/different perspective on an old problem. May denote whether you are feeling balanced or level (equal). A level can also be about the intensity of a situation, so pay attention to the dream feelings. Perhaps you feel flattened, knocked down, deflated (levelled) or squashed in some way. Could denote the stage

(level) or rank you feel you have achieved recently. Could represent whether you feel level with (alongside) a peer, a work colleague, or another person. Notice whether the dream level is indicating balance or not to help you understand your current balance in some area of your life.

Nail

They hold things closed or shut. Is there any situation or issue you'd like to see temporarily closed or inaccessible to yourself or others? Have you recently felt like something or someone put a nail through your heart? Have you felt nailed to a cross, or that someone is nailing you or accusing you? Or are you or someone else being hard as nails? If your dream was about fingernails, see Hand in the *Body* section of this dictionary for more information.

Pitchfork

May represent your ability to take action and make things move or shift. May be a pun on how you "pitch in" on some community or group project.

Pliers

Often used to pull things apart or pry things open. Do you feel pried apart or pulled apart by something in your life currently? Also used to grip or hold things, so they may symbolize your stance on a situation or that you are holding on too tightly. Note the dream feelings to determine whether this attitude is helpful or harmful to you at this time.

Rake

May imply that you are pulling something into your life or shifting things. Note the dream feelings to help you understand if this is a useful endeavour or heavy work (a burden). Could be a pun on raking in the dough or feeling prosperous.

Rope

Used for fastening, attaching, securing, binding and towing. It may connect you with another person or with something. May be the ties that bind or suggest you need to tie things up. Do you feel tied up or bound in some way? May suggest you need help or a life line. Ropes can also be used for escaping or for rescuing. Note how your dream rope is being used and your feelings for greater understanding.

Sandpaper

May indicate your need to refine, polish or perfect something. May say that something is irritating you and it needs smoothing or ironing out. A dream about sandpaper may indicate that you are being too "rough" with yourself or another, and that you need to create a more peaceful space.

Saw

Used for cutting, this may be a pun on your thoughts, words or actions being cutting or hurtful to yourself or another. Could indicate the need to cut the ties that are (or were in the past) binding you. Could be a pun on something you observed or saw. May indicate the need to cut something out, whether it be an old behaviour, a habit or a current action.

Screw

Used to tighten, fasten, secure or hold two things together. May say you feel the need for more security or that you are holding on to something too tightly. May be a pun on screwing around, screwed up or feeling screwed.

Screwdriver

Since screwdrivers are used for making things tighter or looser, may indicate your own feelings of being wound too tight or be a pun on using loose words. May be a pun on feeling screwed or in a tight situation. Perhaps a play on words for screwing around or for feeling that you have screwed up in some way.

Shovel

Used to move things (especially earth), so may represent your ability to move or take action with respect to a current relationship, situation or endeavour. May imply hard work or the need to get a move on. Could be a pun on digging yourself out a situation. Or perhaps you have been shovelling the shit, bragging, or speaking arrogantly.

Tape Measure

May represent that you are planning, preparing or sizing up a situation or endeavour. May symbolize that you are appraising, evaluating or gauging something. May be a measure of your worth or how you measure up.

Vise

A tool used for clamping, bracing and clenching. Have you been holding on to something too tightly? Or are you bracing for the worst? Have you been clamping your jaws shut and not speaking your truth? Is it time to let something go and stop hanging on? Do you have a tight grip on a situation, or do you need to get a better grip on something?

Wheelbarrow

Used to transport heavy loads, this may represent some heavy load (or burden) you are currently experiencing. Is using the dream wheelbarrow easy work or hard? Or does it sit empty, representing your inability to move or take action at this time?

Wrench

Used for tightening or loosening things, this may represent your own "tight mind" or that you have been speaking "loosely" and without thought. May be a pun on throwing a wrench into the works or fouling things up. Could be you are warping or distorting something, or that you are straining or pulling too hard.

Weapons

Axe or Hatchet

May suggest you feel threatened in some way, or warn of an impending negative action or reaction (when the axe falls). Could be a pun on a job done poorly or that things are feeling out of control. You may feel hacked or beaten in some situation. Are you experiencing emotional trauma, or are you being mentally abused by yourself or someone else?

Bomb

An unexploded bomb may represent repressed or unexpressed feelings, or even an impending explosive situation. An exploded bomb likely symbolizes your own explosive feelings or a recent explosive situation, event or relationship. Bombs of any nature are a warning of feeling threatened, overwhelmed or fearful in general. Note the dream feelings to help you pinpoint what may have triggered this dream bomb. May be a pun on feeling that you have bombed (failed), or feeling like a washout.

Cannon

If exploding, this is a warning — something is booming out for your attention. Do you need to defend yourself in your waking life? Or do you need to get out the heavy artillery? Has there been a blow up in any area of your life or in your inner reality?

Club

A club that is used as a weapon may be a pun on feeling "clubbed," beaten or battered.

Gun

What do you feel you need to defend? Is there an issue, idea or belief at stake here? Are you defending or trying to justify a particular viewpoint of yours lately? Perhaps you have a desire to be rid of or kill off a part of self that is undesirable. See the section on *Death, Dying and Killing*. What do you feel is the cause of your recent problems and what would you like to be rid of. Guns are weapons or destruction and instant killing or wounding. Be aware of what you target in the dream is to help you determine what it is you may be trying to get rid of in your current life.

Knife

When used as an instrument of harm, knives often denote the mind and its ability to be cutting (in thought or in speech). Negative thoughts are as harmful to the target of those thoughts (either yourself or someone else) as speaking the actual words — energetically, they still "cut." Perhaps you want to cut something out of your life or out of yourself, such as a personality trait that you judge as being bad or wrong. Self-judgement is common in North America and our words and thoughts can be sharp and cutting. Have you been throwing daggers or do you need to sharpen your wits? Have you heard yourself saying "cut that out," "I need to cut down on this," or "it cuts like a knife"?

Noose or Garrote

Having a noose around a neck may suggest that you feel cut off at the throat — you haven't had a chance to speak up or speak out. Perhaps you have not spoken your truth or you have spoken non-truths (gossip or lies). Communication is often at the root of a noose or garrote dream, so search your memory for a recent faux pas or miscommunication on your part or that of another. Could also suggest you feel cut off from a current relationship, endeavour or group. May be a pun on feeling all choked up or feeling unable to express emotions or feelings. Hanging can be seen as a type of punishment. Have you been punishing yourself or feeling punished by others? Could suggest feeling hung up on a situation or that you have a hang up. See Fifth Chakra in the *Chakras* section for more insight.

Poison

May suggest you feel emotionally or mentally poisoned by another or are feeling surrounded by negativity. Do you feel infected, contaminated or diseased? May symbolize something in your life that feels tainted or corrupted. Perhaps you are poisoned by your own feelings, bitterness or anger. May suggest a toxic, threatening or overwhelming situation. May be associated with evil in general, or a feeling of being cursed.

Vehicles, Their Parts and Actions

Vehicles in general represent the way you are currently moving, steering or driving yourself. Since your body is a vehicle for your soul, vehicles can also represent your physical body and point out messages about the state of your health and overall condition.

Remember: These symbolic meanings are just suggestions. If these suggested meanings do not resonate with you, ring a bell, give you an "ah-ha" moment or otherwise feel right, search through your own experience or beliefs about the symbol to find what makes sense for you.

Types of Vehicles

Water Vehicles

Vehicles used in the water represent your emotional and spiritual life. Are you captain of your own ship and destiny? This is the ultimate goal, to be master of your own life and its path. Your spiritual progress can be depicted by the type of boat you are travelling in and how well it is navigating through the waters of your life. Are the waters you travelled in your dream charted or uncharted? Can you see clearly or is fog obscuring your sight? Boats are about your soul's journey and how you see the course of your life. Note the type of boat you are in and who is commanding it. A luxury liner or cruise ship may indicate the need for a vacation, more fun or adventure in life, or perhaps even the need to socialize more and get out in public. Note whether your dream boat is anchored — this will help you understand if you feel secure, stable or perhaps too fixed on something. Is your boat grounded and unable to steer the waters of your life? Sailing may represent the mood of your mind and thoughts and whether or not you have enough "wind in your sails." It may also say that things are flowing smoothly and you have a sense of freedom. A ship may be a pun on "when my ship comes in" or when your hopes, dreams and ideals come to fruition. See the entries for the individual types of boats and ships for further understanding. If your boat is leaking it implies an inability to deal with an emotional problem or spiritual crisis. You are feeling overwhelmed and under-prepared to deal with some issue, relationship or inner situation. If you are "passing a ship in the night" this would imply a missed spiritual opportunity or that something is passing you by. See also the *Water* section of this dictionary for greater insight.

Canoe

Represents a need for a balanced lifestyle or that you have accomplished a balance in some area of your life. Canoes may imply that a simpler lifestyle or a return to nature is required. Since you propel yourself in a canoe, it may say you are in control of or power your own course/path. You are going at your own speed and may be sharing some spiritual intimacy with another. How do you feel paddling your dream canoe? Are you up a stream without a paddle or is it an idyllic experience?

Cruise Ship/Luxury Liner

Often associated with vacations and therefore rest and relaxation, this may indicate the need to take a much-deserved break or the need to reflect on how rest and relaxation factors into your life at this time. Your personal associations and experiences with cruising will be of greatest value here. Perhaps you associate it with family members or specific friends who you have cruised with. Perhaps it means fun times and letting loose and, therefore, symbolizes something joyous you

are currently experiencing. This may also represent how you view your spiritual life and how you feel about it. For example, the well-known phrase, "when my ship comes in," suggests that you've got it all together or life is in great balance. Note how this dream ship may factor into your endeavours, ideals and goals at this time. In some cases, a cruise ship may represent your soul family or your spiritual family.

Fishing Boat

Is your fishing boat being used for relaxation purposes or work? This may represent the need to sit back and relax in your life, or it could symbolize that you feel you are working hard in your life. Note the dream feelings for greater insight. Ponder the need for more down time and the need to take a break from your daily routine. Are you feeling overworked and putting a lot of effort into your current endeavours?

Ocean Liner

These huge ships represent the ability to pull heavy spiritual or emotional loads or the need to pull your own weight. May say it's the time for using your own power or make a big crossing to something new. Implies spiritual leaps and moving in a spiritual way. See also Cruise Ship/Luxury Liner.

Paddle Boat

Represents doing things your way or under your own power or steam (especially if you are alone in the boat). May say you need to paddle harder or pick up the beat. For some people, a paddle boat may represent relaxation or pleasure. Note your personal associations with paddle boats for greater understanding.

Pleasure Boat

Represents a need for more pleasurable activity, thinking or action in your life, or that you are experiencing a peaceful and relaxing time, depending on the dream feelings.

Raft

May depict that you feel adrift in your life, without direction or control. Or may suggest you are going with the flow and not resisting what life is giving you. Do you feel a victim of circumstances or have a raft of problems? Look to the dream feelings for further understanding.

Rowboat

May suggest you feel under control or that you are plugging along at an arduous pace depending on the feelings in the dream. Is it a pleasant afternoon outing or a laborious journey? Either way, you are under your own steam and power. Is it a pun on the popular tune "Row, row, row your boat"? Are you having a row/quarrel with someone (or yourself)?

Sailboat

Denotes being under your own power or at the mercy of the winds (your mind, thoughts and beliefs). Could say things are smooth sailing or that you are in the flow. How well do you navigate your dream sailboat? Note your personal associations and experiences with sailing for greatest insight.

Speedboat

May suggest you are feeling in control or that you are moving through something (a recent encounter, issue, relationship, project) with great speed. Perhaps you need to slow down and review things; conversely, maybe you need to speed things up, depending on dream feelings. If the feelings are of haste or anxiety then it is likely that you are moving too quickly with something. If the dream feelings are exhilarating or pleasurable, this probably reflects that your current undertakings are also bringing you a sense of success and that you are managing something with confidence. Speedboats also suggest you may be feeling powerful or in charge about something in your life.

Submarine

Submarines represent being submerged in the feminine waters. Feminine here relates to feelings, emotions and intuition. Note how it feels to be in the submarine — is the experience pleasant or unpleasant? This will help you understand if the emotions are ones that you deem positive and allowed or negative and not allowed. A submarine may also represent a claustrophobic feeling for you, or a feeling of not having enough freedom to create and move in your life. If submarines are military vehicles to you, then this may denote defensive feelings or the need to protect yourself from someone or something. Note the dream feelings to help you understand this symbol further.

Sunken Ship or Treasure

Implies either a weighty spiritual burden, total immersion in something, or great abundance that has gone unrecognized until now. Look to the feelings of the dream and what type of boat or treasure is submerged for greater understanding.

Warship

May suggest you are feeling defensive in some way. Do you feel ready to wage war, or is there great conflict going on either inside of you or in a situation around you? A warship suggests you are prepared to do battle or meet a challenge head on. Note the dream feelings to help you understand if this is a healthy stance you are taking — a justly defended position — or a rigid viewpoint.

Yacht

May imply feelings of grandeur, wealth, abundance, prosperity and luxury. Conversely, it may say you feel unworthy of such splendour in your life, depending on the dream feelings.

Road Vehicles

Ambulance

Implies you feel you are in need of immediate physical, emotional, intellectual or spiritual attention. Are you already in the dream ambulance receiving attention, or are you lying injured or ill waiting for help? If another person is waiting for or in need of help, then discern what aspect of yourself they are playing or mirroring for further insight into which part of you is crying out for help/attention. If you are driving an ambulance, perhaps there is an urgent need for you to help someone else.

Antique Vehicle

Driving an old or antique car may suggest your goals and current path are out of date and need updating. On the other hand, if you feel that antique cars are precious and of great value, it could represent your sense of self as being worthy and that you are maintaining good care of yourself. May imply that your physical body is feeling old and in need of more care. Note how you feel about the antique vehicle for greater understanding.

Bus

A vehicle of mass transit, a bus indicates your flow of mass consciousness; that is, whether you are going along with the crowd or society's viewpoints and trends. Could reflect that you are not thinking originally or that you are following a beaten track. You may not be thinking for yourself or you may feel restricted in your freedom. A bus probably indicates that you have pre-conceived or prejudiced viewpoints. However, if the bus is your usual mode of transportation, it could have a similar meaning for you as a car. If you are driving the bus in your dream, it may say you feel you are in control or a group leader. If you miss the bus in your dream it may represent that you have missed an opportunity recently or that something is passing you by. A school bus could indicate group learning, group activities or freedom within a group.

Car

Represents your lifestyle or the way in which you drive yourself. What's driving you; what are your motivations; what goals or desires are pulling you forward? How is the car moving in your dream? Are you in the driver's seat or driving in the wrong direction? Do you feel as if you are in control in your life, or is something or someone else driving/pushing you? Is something driving you nuts or driving you to the brink? How are you "wheeling and dealing" in your life? The kind of car and the age of the car in your dream indicate something about your present lifestyle. For example, if it is a car you used to drive, this may represent that the way in which you move through life (drive) is out of date and no longer serves you well. A show car or trophy car may show that you externalize something beautiful, yet it is not the truth of who you are (i.e., your shiny outside is a facade). If it is a vehicle you once owned, it may indicate that you have reverted to behaviours or thinking from that time period. What direction are you heading in? May also represent your self-esteem and self-image. If your vehicle is dented or smashed it could point to an injury of your self-worth or that you are beating yourself up. Sometimes a car can represent your physical body, so take note of which part of the car is highlighted in the dream. For example, the headlights may indicate your eyes and the engine your power potential. See the specific car part later in this section for more information.

Convertible

May suggest your mind is open and receptive to new ideas. Convertibles are often associated with freedom, fun times, and the ability to be versatile.

Emergency Vehicle

A fire truck, ambulance or police car all suggest a cry for immediate attention or help from your body, mind, emotions or spirit. Where's the fire? What is urgent in your life? Telephoning 9-1-1 in a dream is a warning that at some level you are in crisis.

Fire Truck

May represent your urgent need for help from trained personal. Something is on fire in your life and is crying out for attention. Are you burned up about something or ready to explode? Is there a fire in your heart or do you have a burning desire? Do you need rescuing from a current situation, relationship or inner struggle? Are alarm bells sounding? Could also symbolize a brave part of yourself that is facing a harrowing or frightening situation.

Foreign Vehicle

Driving a foreign car or vehicle suggests that you are moving forward in your life in a unfamiliar or uncharacteristic way for you.

Garbage Truck

Represents your shadow aspects or that which you consider garbage, negative or not worth keeping. Do you feel like or treat yourself like trash? Perhaps you are being trashed or someone is trashing you. What heavy loads and burdens are you carrying around with you? Perhaps it is time to unload them and let them go for good.

Jeep

May refer to the need for fun and to be open-minded, depending on your feelings about jeeps. Could say that you have been having a rough ride or hardships. May represent that you are handling the rough roads in your life well and with confidence. Often associated with male drivers, this may represent your masculine energy and how it is driving you. Note your personal associations with jeeps for greatest insight. For example, if you associate jeeps with the army, you may see them as running roughshod over the countryside, not paying attention to who or what they run over or destroy. Has someone been treating you this way recently? Or have you been running roughshod over yourself or someone else?

Limousine

Could suggest you feel grand, big or important about something or about the way you are handling current affairs. May reflect your sense of materialism, wealth or over-inflated ego, depending on how you feel about limousines. Do you see them as a source of prestige or just for special occasions? Could suggest you have been showing off or acting like a big shot. Do you feel worthy to ride in the dream limousine?

Motorcycle

Often represents your ability to balance or how balanced you are. May suggest you need more balance in your life, depending on how you feel riding the motorbike. They are also about power and dexterity of movement. Do you own a motorcycle and is this your usual mode of transportation? Or is riding a motorcycle something you consider daring or adventurous? Could suggest you are doing things in your own style. Ask yourself whether taking risks drives or motivates you, and whether you associate motorcycles with risk taking.

Moving Van

Represents the need to move on or move forward, or that you are moving on and moving forward — look to the feelings to help you decide which of these applies to your life at this time. Perhaps a move is imminent on a different level of your being, a spiritual leap forward or a shift in consciousness and awareness. See Truck for further clarification. If you associate a moving van with a lot of hard work, this may symbolize something you are currently involved in that is challenging, overwhelming or burdensome to you.

Police Car

Represents authority, the
law, rules and regulations, and control.
May denote the need for help, attention
or the need for more discipline (inner
or external) in your life. May suggest
all black and white thinking, thoughts
or beliefs. Perhaps you feel you need
rescuing from some situation, or feel
the need for a stronger masculine
(action-oriented) side of self. If the sight
of a police car brings you a sense of
safety, then ask yourself if you are feeling vulnerable, insecure, or in need of
support at this time.

Scratched Vehicle

Represents a minor problem or irrita-
tion. Could say you have scratched
the surface of something. Requires
slight repairs or fixing at some level
of your being.

Sports Car

Suggests need for action, fun, enthusiasm or excitement in your life. If cars
are a hobby it may suggest that you are
at peace or fulfilled when in a sports
car. Could also say you have been
showing off or that you have a desire
to impress others. Perhaps you have a
need for recognition from within and
are looking for it externally.

Stolen Vehicle

A stolen dream vehicle likely represents feelings of loss. This could be a
loss of self-esteem, loss of clarity, loss
of face, or the loss of a job or goal. Note
the feelings in the dream and the type
of vehicle being stolen. If it is your vehicle, it symbolizes something current
and personal, whereas someone else's
vehicle being stolen could be a mirror
or reflection of some aspect of yourself
being lost (note the other person's
characteristics and traits to help you
understand what part of your self is
being represented). This type of dream
may denote feeling lost or that someone else has stolen something from
you, such as your identity, energy
or ideas.

SUV

If the SUV in your dream is your family car, it represents your family values,
morals or responsibilities. Or, you
could be using it to carry heavy loads,
either for work or pleasure (off-
roading). Note what purpose your
SUV is being used for in the dream
for further clarification. See also Car.

Taxi

Unless you use taxis exclusively as
your means of transport, then it denotes that you are being led, controlled

or perhaps even "taken for a ride." You may be following the crowd, group behaviour or the consciousness of the masses. It could also point to the fact that you need to allow others to help you with your goals or that you need to relax in some way. If it is a yellow cab it may be related to third chakra issues (see the *Chakras* section of this dictionary).

Trailer

Riding in a trailer (rather than driving it) may suggest you feel out of control or not at choice about something. Perhaps you feel that you are trailing behind in some current endeavour. May say you are going along for the ride or that you are following aimlessly. If the trailer is carrying a heavy load, this may symbolize that you feel you are carrying a heavy load or dragging something or someone along.

Truck

Usually used for carrying heavy loads, as work vehicles, and for doing big jobs. May represent a current undertaking or goal that feels like a heavy load or like a lot of work. Trucks are powerful and may represent your own power, endurance and toughness. This could denote how you feel about your responsibilities and how heavy they feel. Perhaps you are driving yourself hard, showing yourself little tenderness, or you are all work and not enough play. For further understanding, note the type of truck in your dream and what it is being used for. Is the truck loaded and heavy? Or is it empty and ready for action? May be a pun on "keep on trucking" or "a large haul."

Van

May represent family values, responsibility or ability to carry a load. Vans tend to be multi-purpose vehicles, so ask yourself how your dream van is being used. See also Car and SUV.

Vehicles That Fly

Airplane

Represents your ability to soar or take flight. Is the plane flying or grounded? Perhaps crashing? Flying often offers you a sense of freedom, a new perspective on things and a sense of control. Have you recently felt "high," in control, or that the sky's the limit? Have you taken a new viewpoint on something? If your dream plane was crashing, ask yourself if something is failing or falling apart in your life. If the plane is flying backward, ask yourself what is currently moving in the wrong direction for you. Because planes are often depicted in the air, this could then represent the mental plane or your thoughts, ideas and attitudes. For some people, airplanes represent their fear of flying — be aware of what airplanes mean to you on a personal level. They can represent your high ideals or goals and how well they are flying for you. Perhaps you feel you have risen above a certain situation, feeling or crisis. Are you landing or taking off in the dream? This will help you understand if something has returned to you or if you are about to take off in some new endeavour, relationship or plan. Perhaps nothing has taken off for you lately, you feel grounded in some way, or something has not gotten off the ground for you. If your plane has crashed, ask yourself what has "crashed" around you or within you recently. Have you been prepared or do you need to be more prepared for unpredictable events in your life?

Glider

May represent your need to glide or sail through something gracefully, or that you are currently doing that. May represent feelings of success or soaring, depending on the dream feelings. May also suggest that you feel powerless,

again depending on the feelings in the dream. May symbolize that you are "coasting" or not giving something your all, or suggest that you are accomplishing something with ease.

Helicopter

Flying vehicle that has more control, versatility and options than an airplane. May suggest you are able to move in many different directions. Suggests freedom, high ideals, thinking big and manoeuvrability. May represent that you are flying high, the sky's the limit, or you have whirly-bird (scattered) thinking. See Airplane for further clarification.

Hot Air Balloon

Associated with movement on air currents and therefore reflects the mental plane or your thoughts and thinking. May say you are full of hot air or that your ego is overinflated. Have you been boasting, bragging or otherwise inflating your own status? Conversely, you have a better perspective from the air and it may suggest you are seeing the whole picture or experiencing a different point of view on some matter. It may also represent some new endeavour, thrill ride or adventurous feelings.

UFO or Space Vehicle

Riding in a UFO or space vehicle could represent your desires to be far away from your life, problems or the planet in general. Or you may find this a great adventure, enjoyable and exciting. Look to the feelings to help you discern the meaning in greater depth. May be a pun on being spacey, being a space cadet or having flighty thinking. May suggest you are ungrounded or not fully present in your life and its challenges. Could mean that something feels totally foreign or alien to you. Suggests mystery, the unknown, the untried, or new worlds yet to conquer. Could be associated with a memory of when you experienced a different reality and plane of existence.

Other Vehicles

Armoured Vehicle

Suggests you feel the need for great protection or that you have been on the defensive lately. What do you keep locked inside of you? What do you need to keep secret or locked in the vault?

Bicycle

Suggests you are in balance and handling things well, or speaks to the need for more balance in your life. How does it feel to ride the bike in the dream? How well are you riding the bike? Is there a sense of being in control or does it feel shaky and difficult to manoeuvre? If your bike has training wheels, it may suggest you are preparing for something or require a bit of extra support and help in a current undertaking. May say you are playing it safe or symbolize dependence.

Bulldozer

Represents the need to push something (usually heavy) away from you. May be a burden you carry, such as guilt, or a heavy load of any sort. This implies you feel a lot of work and effort needs to go into something or that you need to make a major shift in some area of your life or inner reality. Are you sorting your way through things or breaking new ground? Bulldozing creates new avenues and can represent making a new path for yourself.

Camper

May suggest you are in need of a little rest and relaxation, if that is your personal take on going camping. Look to the feelings in the dream to help determine whether fun and vacation are impending or hard work, which can be associated with camping.

411

Dump Truck

Symbolizes that you are carrying a heavy load or that you need to unburden yourself of a heavy load. Perhaps you feel someone is dumping on you or that you have been dumping on others.

Farm Equipment and Machinery

Note the particular machine or what the machine is being use for to help you understand if this represents growth, sowing new seeds or reaping the benefits of your labours. Watch for plays-on-words such as "combining," "harvesting" and "cultivating," and how these relate to your current actions, words or thoughts.

Model Car

A miniaturized version of the real thing. Have you been feeling small or diminished about the way you are moving through your life? Perhaps it represents how you have been a model citizen or how your ideals are being displayed. You may be setting an example (model) for yourself or those around you.

Roller Coaster

Represents how your mind or feelings are on a roller coaster or a fast upward and downward trend. You may feel dramatic highs and lows and feel out of control, fearful or panicky. Note the feelings in the dream to help you discern if this is an exciting time in your life, full of surprise and enthusiasm, or a disconcerting endeavour or project you are embarking on. Because a roller coaster runs on a track, this could represent your thinking, thought and beliefs and how they adhere to prescribed ways or patterns of being.

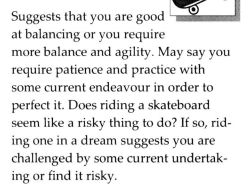

Skateboard

Suggests that you are good at balancing or you require more balance and agility. May say you require patience and practice with some current endeavour in order to perfect it. Does riding a skateboard seem like a risky thing to do? If so, riding one in a dream suggests you are challenged by some current undertaking or find it risky.

Sled

Suggests that you are gliding through some situation with ease, or that you are riding your fears (since snow often represents frozen emotions or fear). Could also say you need to do something playful or child-like. Note how you feel riding the dream sled for further understanding of the meaning.

Streetcar

Represents group thinking and group consciousness. May indicate you are following the crowd in your belief systems and the way you think. May symbolize that your values and actions are supported by society and there is little room for original thinking. Because streetcars run on tracks, they may represent your flow of thinking and suggest that you are either stuck in a pattern of thinking (a rut), or that your thinking is rigid and follows only one line. See also Bus.

Subway

An underground subway denotes the unconscious and the subconscious — what is below the level of your waking-time awareness. Subways are a reflection of your automatic (as opposed to deliberate) thoughts, feelings and actions — what you create in your life involuntarily, reflexively or without thinking. Similar to tunnels, subways may suggest you are coming out of the darkness, connecting to some new path or penetrating to new levels. Note how it feels to be on the subway for greater understanding.

Tank

An armoured military vehicle, a tank represents a serious defensive position or stance you are currently taking or a severe need for protection. Perhaps you are adamantly defending a point of view, belief or idea. Military-related issues are about power, authority figures, dominance, hierarchy, control, rigid rules and codes of behaviour. This may warn that you need to defend yourself more or that you sense a need for safety and self-preservation. Perhaps you feel the need to plough or push your way through something in a strong, powerful way.

Tractor

Represents that you are now ready to prepare new ground, plant new seeds and begin growth in some area of your life. Conversely, driving the tractor in the dream may feel like you are working hard or feeling burdened by responsibilities. Do you feel like a work horse or that you have a lot of work ahead of you? Note your personal associations or experiences with tractors for greatest insight.

Train

Represents your train of thinking in general and therefore the mental realm of thoughts, ideas, opinions and beliefs. You may be going down a particular train of thinking that is rigid and set in its way. The track is pre-ordained with little room for flexibility or original thinking. May include going along with the crowd and fixed ideas of society. Are you taking the path of least resistance or are your thoughts following the same avenues over and over? May be a pun on the need to train yourself, practice, discipline or rehearse for something. A derailed train would indicate derailed thinking or that you have lost your track of thinking. Perhaps you have been side-tracked or disheartened about something. A freight train denotes a long, heavy load you feel you are committed to. Trains can pull heavy loads for great distances, so a train in your dream may symbolize your ability to do this and commit for the long haul. May tell you your mind is pulling a heavy load or that you have trouble stopping or controlling your thoughts and thinking.

Unicycle

Suggests you have great balance and dexterity at this time, unless you are repeatedly falling off the unicycle. Suggests you are alone in your endeavours and may need more support. May represent a challenge that is demanding and/or complicated to handle. May symbolize that something requires a lot of practice before you can perfect it.

Wagon

May represent pioneering something new, blazing a trail, or any new undertaking. Could also represent your ability to carry heavy loads or that you feel burdened with responsibility, depending on how the wagon is being used in your dream. A child's wagon may represent a childish point of view or the potential to pull your own weight/load. Children's wagons are about play and irresponsibility — how does this fit in with your current undertakings? A covered wagon of old may represent old outgrown goals, attitudes, beliefs or behaviours.

Wheelchair

Implies you feel paralyzed, debilitated or unable to move forward under your own power. Your emotions may be numb or deadened, or you may feel lifeless, unenthused, powerless or hopeless. Denotes a crippling or impairing situation or event in your life — something has shocked and immobilized you. Perhaps you just feel too exhausted to move forward at this time, without strength, energy, stamina or vigour. You likely require better support systems from yourself (in your inner reality) or from external sources (friends, family, etc.).

Parts of Vehicles

Air Conditioning

May represent your lungs and ability or inability to breathe fresh air. Could also be a pun on the condition of your self or your lungs. Is the air conditioner working in the dream? Perhaps you need to cool down or chill out with respect to some situation that is driving you at this time.

Air Filtration

Could represent your bodily filtration systems, including your nose and lungs. Your liver, spleen, kidneys and skin are also considered filtration systems. Note whether the air filtration system is clean or dirty and in need of changing. May be warning that your own filters are in need of attention.

Back Seat

Being in the back seat of a vehicle is a warning that you are taking a back seat in your own life. It means that you do not feel in control, that you are allowing others command over you, or that you are leaving something to chance. It warns that you are not exercising your right to choice or that you are not exerting your power. Could be a pun on back seat driver, in which case you may be getting in your own way or cannot see your way clearly.

Battery

Symbolizes how much "juice" you have — your power or energy. Is the vehicle battery dead or in need of a boost? Could represent your heart or how much energy you have in reserve. A dead battery may suggest you lack motivation or staying power in some current situation. You may feel dead on some level or be dead tired.

Brakes

Represent the ability to stop or apply the brakes in a situation. Ask yourself what you feel you need to stop doing, saying or thinking at present. What patterns, behaviours or beliefs are no longer serving you? Perhaps your brakes have failed and you feel out of control and unable to manage yourself or another. Breaks can also represent your sense of discipline and control in life.

Bumper

Represents your ability to buffer, guard or protect yourself at this time. May represent the boundaries you put out or how you feel the impact of things. A bumper may also represent your buttocks or whatever part of your body you think is a buffer zone or absorbs things.

Dent

Symbolizes that you may feel dented or hurt by someone else's comments or actions. May imply scars, bumps or feeling knocked around recently. This could be an indication that your physical body hurts in the region that the dented car part represents. Read the entry for the applicable car part for further clarification.

Electrical System

Represents your nervous system and its condition. Note if there is a flaw or short in the dream vehicle's electrical system and where it is located (for example, a short in the engine may denote your chest or heart area). Could be a pun on how you are wired or that you feel hay wire or wired up.

Engine

Represents the chest area in general and the heart more specifically. How well is your dream engine running? Does it need a tune up, suggesting you get a medical checkup? Your engine gives you the power to go, to do and to be in the world. It is about your vitality, energy and motivation. If the engine is not working, it is warning that your

own vital life force is being lost to something (such as fear, attitudes, insecurities, other people, negative thinking, negative feelings, etc.).

Fender

Could suggest you are fending off something or that you are being defensive. Perhaps you need to defend yourself in a current situation.

Front Seat

Driving the vehicle symbolizes that you are in choice or in control of your own actions. If you are in the passenger seat, you may be feel that others are manipulating or controlling you. Note who is driving the car, for this may represent who is driving you. It may well be that someone is driving you nuts or driving you up the wall.

Fuel Pump

A broken fuel pump suggests that your ability to fuel yourself is in jeopardy. May suggest you have run out of energy to accomplish something or you are unable to motivate yourself in some endeavour. Could represent your cardiovascular system — your veins and arteries.

Gas Tank

A full tank suggests you have plenty of fuel to accomplish the tasks at hand; an empty one suggests you do not have the energy, motivation or drive to achieve your current goals. May represent your stomach or intestinal system. Could say you feel out of gas and lack energy, drive or enthusiasm. Perhaps you feel cut off from your source. A gas tank may also be a pun on intestinal gas or on what a gas (something funny or humorous).

Headlight

Represents your eyes and their condition. Also symbolizes how well you can see your way through life at this time. How well are the vehicle headlights working in your dream? May suggest you need an eye checkup or some insight/clarity on a situation. Dim headlights may suggest you are unclear about something, and no headlights suggest you have no insight, vision or clarity on something. In fact, no headlights suggest you are blind to something occurring within or around you. Fog in your headlights symbolizes your ability to either cut through the fog and see something, or that you are in confusion.

Horn

Blowing the vehicle horn in your dream may imply you are blowing your own horn or bragging about something. Could be your ego is a little over-inflated or that you have been exaggerating about something. Horns are also used as a warning to others, or to vent frustration and aggression aimed at others.

Ignition

Your ability to start something (a project, new habit, new belief, new communication or new relationship) is being represented here. How well does the vehicle start? If it does not start, it suggests you do not have the motivation or drive to start something new. If it fires right up, this symbolizes your vitality and energy to do something new. It may be a pun on how well you ignite yourself or others, or whether you are a self-starter.

License Plate

Identifies your vehicle and authorization to drive. This suggests you feel justified about your current undertakings and the way you choose to drive yourself. Do your plates have a specific number or name written on them? For further clues, see the dictionary sections on *Numbers* and the section on *Names* in Chapter 5.

Muffler

Since mufflers are designed to decrease the sound of your vehicle, note what condition your dream muffler is in to help you understand what it is representing. For example, absence of a muffler may suggest you are either making a lot of unnecessary noise (voicing your opinions or generally venting) or that you could be using your voice in a more useful way (expression). Do you need to make more sound in your life or express yourself more loudly? Perhaps you feel muffled, silenced or barely audible in the context of some relationship or situation. Note the dream feelings to help you understand more clearly whether this muffler dream represents a healthy expression of your self or an overly expressive (talkative, opinionated) aspect.

Rear-View Mirror

Suggests you can see what has happened behind you or in the past. May suggest hindsight on a recent situation, and may reflect the past or what you have left behind. Note feelings and what you see in the mirror for further clarification.

Seat Belt

Suggests your sense of security and how safe you feel in your current undertakings, depending on your views about seat belts. Are you wearing the seat belt in the dream and do you wear one in your waking time? May be a pun on feeling strapped in or limited in some way.

Steering Wheel

Symbolizes how you steer, conduct, navigate, manoeuvre and guide yourself in life. Are you in control of the steering wheel in the dream or is someone else? This will help you understand whether you are at choice or feel you are being manipulated at some level by someone else. If it is difficult or impossible to steer, it suggests you feel out of control or locked into some situation.

Tire

Represents whether you are able to move smoothly through life. Are you rolling along well or do you have a flat tire that needs attention? Tires can also represent your feet and therefore your understanding in some current situation. Wheels are also full of air and may represent your ego and whether it is overinflated. May be a pun on your wheeling and dealing or that you feel like a "big wheel." Being unable to move your vehicle due to a flat tire represents your inability to move forward at this time. Could be that something has gone flat — some project, relationship or endeavour. Dream tires that are wearing thin may suggest you are wearing thin and/or losing your patience about something. If you are spinning your wheels in the dream it indicates that you are spinning your wheels, using lots of energy and getting nowhere fast in some current undertaking or situation.

Training Wheels

Imply a need for support while you work something out or learn something new. Also suggest the need for balance, stability and security. Could say you

are in training for something or learning a new discipline.

Trunk

Being in the trunk is a serious warning that you are not in control and that you cannot see where you are going. Perhaps you feel like a prisoner in your own life and the way you manoeuvre through it. Could represent a body part such as your nose (elephant trunk) or your torso and chest area (trunk of the body). Also used for storage, to keep things private and out of sight.

Wheel – See Tire

Actions Related to Vehicles

Accident

Colliding with another vehicle may denote that you are on a collision course with another or that a crisis is occurring in your inner reality. May indicate a warning of impending emergency or a coming painful encounter. Have you recently injured your pride or your ego? Does some part of you feel wounded or do you feel you have failed at something? Perhaps your beliefs, opinions or ideas have collided with another's? Accidents are often wake-up calls for people. Be aware of what you are creating with the way you drive yourself. See Accident, page 439.

Backing Up

Implies you need to back up or take a step back and review something. May be a need to rethink your current goals or plans. May be a pun on backing out of a situation or having your back up. You may even need to go back over something in your mind. May imply you are heading in the wrong direction about something.

Buying

May imply you are buying into something or that you are creating a whole new lifestyle for yourself. You may have "purchased" new goals, ideals, beliefs or attitudes. A new vehicle represents a new expression of yourself, and could also say you have upgraded your thinking and goals. May also represent your physical body and how it has been upgraded or revitalized. Note what details about the new car appeal to you most or what its most outstanding features are for further clues about the new car's meaning.

Driving

Driving the vehicle is a positive sign that you feel you are in charge of your life, in control or at choice. If someone else is driving, it may indicate that that person is driving you in some situation or current relationship. It could also represent an aspect of your self that is driving you, either positively or negatively.

Driving Backward

A warning that you are headed in the wrong direction, you can't see what's in front of you clearly, or you are backing out of something. Implies that you are doing something backwards in your current thinking, goals, endeavours or understandings.

Driving Uphill

May denote an uphill challenge you are currently facing or something that requires effort. Note how well your vehicle manoeuvres up the hill for further understanding of how this climb is affecting you. Positive feelings indicate that you find your current challenges easy to overcome and that you have enough power to accomplish your goals.

Drunk Driving

May indicate that you are allowing addictions to motivate your actions at this time, or that you feel impaired (perhaps unprepared or ill-prepared) with respect to some current undertaking.

Hitting a Person or an Animal

Unless you hit someone or an animal deliberately in the dream, this likely reflects that you feel you have made a huge mistake, accident or error in some area of your life. It may indicate that your intent to accomplish something has backfired or is not working out according to your plan. You may feel blind-sided or totally taken by surprise by something or feel out of control or not in choice. If you have killed someone or an animal in a dream, it may symbolize that you have accidentally done harm to yourself or someone else, or that something has died (either within you or around you, such as a project). Note the dream feelings to help you understand what this reflects in your life.

Leaking Boat

Implies an inability to deal with an emotional problem or spiritual crisis. You are feeling overwhelmed and underprepared to deal with some issue, relationship or inner situation.

Lost Vehicle

Being unable to find your vehicle indicates that you feel lost in some regard. It may be an emotional loss, loss of self-esteem, or a loss of face. Or it could simply imply confusion about your current direction in life. Loss at some level is indicated and without your vehicle you will not be able to continue in the same way, so insight and change will be necessary.

Parking

Parking can either denote the need to take a rest and stop all activity, or that you are not moving (forward) in some area of your life (relationship, career or any situation). Note the dream feelings to help you understand whether this is a useful stop or whether your fears have perhaps gotten the better of you and stopped you from moving on with something. Do you feel immobilized, paralyzed or otherwise "parked" about something in your life currently?

Racing

Symbolizes a racing mind or a fast-paced lifestyle. Could mean you are in a great hurry, have been experiencing adrenaline rushes, or feel part of the rat race. Perhaps you are racing against time or have been pushing yourself too hard. If you find racing exhilarating, it may say you feel rejuvenated, stimulated or enlivened by something. Could also imply you are going around in circles, not accomplishing anything or getting anywhere.

Repairing

If the dream vehicle is in need of repair, note what part in particular is the focus of trouble and be mindful that it may represent a part of your body in need of attention. See individual car parts for greater insight. May also say your actual car needs maintenance, so bear this in mind. Otherwise it suggests that some aspect of your self or your life needs repair, or that you need to patch or mend something.

Riding

Riding in someone else's car may be saying that they are taking you for a ride or that you are going along for the ride. Indicates need to gain control over how you move through life.

Selling

Implies you are "selling yourself" or that you are letting go of old ways, habits or thinking. How do you feel about selling the vehicle? If it is hard, this suggests that surrendering the old is a difficult task for you. Selling with joy suggests that it is a positive move and allows for new and better things to come.

Sliding or Skidding

Implies you are somewhat out of control in your current expressions, lifestyle or behaviours. You may need to slow down and get more clarity on a situation. Perhaps you have put the brakes on too hard and are now skidding out of control.

Speeding

Represents that you are going too fast in some area of your life. May be a warning that your thoughts, words or actions are headed toward trouble if you don't slow down. A definite sign that you need not push yourself so hard in some regard. A speeding ticket is a warning that it is imperative for you to slow down.

Stalled

Symbolizes that you are currently stalled, delayed or otherwise not able to move forward with something at this time. May imply that you or your vehicle needs a checkup or maintenance. Pushing a stalled car may say that you are trying too hard, or pushing too hard, to accomplish your goals or current undertakings.

Stuck

Represents how you feel stuck or unable to move forward at this time. You may feel emotionally stuck and unable to access or express your self, or you may be stuck in a rut of thinking, doing or being. Either way, you are not making progress and need to re-evaluate some area of your life. What is blocking you and how can you manoeuvre around it? Also note the feelings in the dream for further clarification. Being stuck in mud is an indication that you are mired in your own emotions. Stuck in an icy situation denotes being stuck or frozen by fears.

Tune-Up

Does your dream vehicle need a tune-up? If so, this indicates that either your physical body or your car needs a checkup or maintenance. Get on top of this minor problem before it turns into a major one.

Turning

Turning or turns are about the choices you are making. Can indicate a turning point or a turnaround in thinking or ideas. Right turns may indicate a right decision you are making, whereas a left turn may be saying you are headed in the wrong direction about something or some choice. If you are turning out of fear, it may be pointing to a false direction or going back to where you started or in a manner that does not help your growth. Perhaps you need to turn around or have turned prematurely.

Washing

Implies a need to cleanse something about yourself (such as feelings, attitudes, old habits). Perhaps you need to clean up your act or clean out your ears. You may be in need of clearing up old attitudes and ways of moving through life. Does washing a car make you feel proud or accomplished? Perhaps shiny or sparkling to others?

Waxing and Polishing

Shows that you are taking care of your physical body and your life in general. Perhaps you need to polish up your act or brighten up on some level. May say you need to nurture and care for yourself at this time. May be a pun on the need for refinement, sophistication or education.

Water

In general, water represents feelings, emotions and intuition, depending on the type of water and its characteristics. It is also about your creativity, sexuality, passion, new dimensions, and forces.

Water is considered the source of all life and is a great conductor of energy. It symbolizes the unconscious part of self, the spiritual parts of self, and your spiritual depths. Note how clear or unclear the water is to understand if this is emotional mud or crystal-clear insight. Note the depth or shallowness of your dream water to help you understand if you are just scratching the surface of some feeling or reaching to the depths of your soul. For greater understanding, see the following entries on different types of water.

Because water flows, note how well your dream water is flowing, if at all. If it is dammed up or sluggish, it could reflect an emotional blockage or dulled feelings. Frozen water usually represents frozen emotions — often fear, but it could symbolize any emotion that renders you incapable of moving, expressing yourself or acting on the feeling.

We all label certain emotions as good or bad, right or wrong, acceptable or unacceptable. Let your water dreams help you discern how you categorize your feelings. No emotions are really wrong or bad — they are merely judged and unwanted or unloved parts of self. Dream feelings associated with water dreams will also be helpful in understanding which emotions are being symbolized by the water.

It is wise to remember that your emotions are a type of guidance system for you. Emotions are given to us in order to point us in the right direction. Your God knows what will help you to heal, and emotions are one way in which Creator communicates to us. Many people assume they are in choice about what they feel. You are not. You cannot control what you feel (nor should you try), but you are responsible for how you handle your feelings, how you react or respond to them, and how you relate to them. Allowing your emotions to have a voice without judgement is the most useful and beneficial way to create inner peace and a healthy relationship with yourself.

Remember: These symbolic meanings are just suggestions. If these suggested meanings do not resonate with you, ring a bell, give you an "ah-ha" moment or otherwise feel right, search through your own experience or beliefs about the symbol to find what makes sense for you.

Blocked Flow

Could be represented by a blocked drain, sink, toilet or sewage outlet. Anything that is blocking the flow of water likely represents how you are emotionally blocked. It symbolizes that you are unable to feel, access, understand, allow or express one — or many — of your current feelings. But it could represent any type of blockage in your life. You may feel out of control in a project, relationship or any situation. You may feel hopeless, helpless or like a victim when there is blockage.

Clear Water

Represents clear emotions, feelings or spiritual life. You can see your energies with clarity and understanding; nothing is hidden and all feelings are out in the open. Your spiritual flow is positive and unblocked. Note the dream feelings for greater understanding. If you are drinking clear sparkling water, this may symbolize spiritual refreshment or that you feel fulfilled on a spiritual level. Swimming in clear water indicates spiritual freedom and clarity, and may indicate spiritual mastery. Clear

water means you are feeling, seeing, experiencing or expressing your recent emotional states well.

Cloudy Water

Symbol of cloudy, unclear or indistinct feelings, emotions or spiritual life. Something or someone is clouding your vision and your emotions are somewhat disturbed. You need some clarity and understanding to clear matters up.

Dammed Water

Represents emotions, feelings or spiritual life that is dammed-up or stopped completely. This is a warning that unless you access your true feeling and express them, things may get worse or explode. Have you felt "damned," criticized or attacked?

Dirty or Polluted Water

Indicates you feel dirty or polluted on some level, usually emotionally or spiritually. This feeling may arise from the way in which you treat yourself (on the inside), or it may have been triggered by someone else. Either way, this symbolizes the need for clarity and cleansing of uncomfortable feelings. This can be accomplished by being aware of, accepting, and expressing the emotions you feel are creating the problem. Remember, you are not able to control what you feel, but you are responsible for how you respond and react to your own feelings. Be aware of your judgements about your own emotional states.

Dry Bed

Symbolizes that you are cut off from Source or there is no flow in your life (i.e., that you are not in touch with your feelings, emotions or spiritual self). May be pun on feeling drained, or could say you feel dried up and spent energetically.

Flood

Great emotional overwhelm is indicated with a flood. Feelings are out of control, overflowing and pouring out of you. Have you been carried away by your emotions lately, or do you need to dam the flow and get a handle on things? A flood of emotions is a warning to stop and look within to find the root of these feelings of being overwhelmed. Accepting these overwhelming feelings can be challenging and there is a great need for inner acceptance, support and expression while you undergo the sorting-out process.

Fountain

A flowing fountain suggests that you are in the flow (aware of and expressing your emotions well), whereas a dry fountain may suggest you are emotionally closed down or shut off (cut off from feelings). Fountains can represent prosperity and abundance on any level of your being and good flow in general. Note the dream feelings to help you understand if this is a positive representation of flow in your life or a negative association. May also represent the fountain of youth or wishful thinking (i.e., when you toss a coin into a fountain).

Ice

Frozen water represents frozen, numbed, obstructed or paralyzed feelings. Fear is often at the root of an icy dream. If you are gliding easily over the ice in the dream, it means that you are handling your feelings well or that you are ignoring them altogether. Melting ice symbolizes that you are beginning to deal with the previously inaccessible feelings, or that a forgiveness process has begun. Could be a pun on your being as cold as ice or an ice queen (unavailable emotionally).

Lake

Symbolizes the state of your emotions or spiritual life. If calm and tranquil, this reflects your inner reality as being a place of tranquility, stillness and peace. Waves crashing onto shore indicate stirred-up emotions that are trying to get your attention. Of course you cannot stop the flow of large waves, but it is useful to be aware of their patterns and effect on you. Note the dream feelings about the lake for greatest understanding of its representation. May indicate the need to rest and go still inside (meditate).

Leaking Water

If water is leaking in your house, this indicates an emotional overwhelm or excess trying to catch your attention. Note if leaking is excessive or a steady drip, and note the dream feelings. Water leaking through a ceiling suggests that thoughts are negative and influencing you in an adverse way. Leaking water suggests the need to release pent up emotions and feelings — you may need to forgive, grieve or let go of something from past.

Muddy Water

Indicates muddied emotions or unclear feelings. Some feelings may be unacceptable to you and therefore judged. This dream foretells of emotional upset and inability to access these shadow feelings. There is a need to accept these emotions as valid, and you need to express them in order to clear the waters. If you are totally immersed in muddy water, it could symbolize that you are in over your head or overcome by emotions.

Ocean

Represents a large portion of your emotional or spiritual life. Can be about the depths of your soul and your spiritual journey. Note the condition of the ocean and the dream feelings for greatest understanding. If the dream ocean is fairly calm and glassy, this may indicate the condition of your inner reality as one of peacefulness and tranquility. A stormy sea represents inner turmoil, conflict, or emotional highs and lows. Some sort of storm may be brewing — a big emotional upset and upheavals in your life. May represent cosmic consciousness or the Void from which all life, including all of us, sprung. An ocean dream can represent both the expansiveness and depth of your self and the All or Source from which we spring. Ocean dreams usually follow some great insight or epiphany — suddenly you can see the whole of a situation (not just the sum of its parts), or you've touched a deep place within your self, or you've touched on the truth. Or, it could simply mean that you've been expansive or deep in your thinking or actions recently.

Overflowing Water

Symbolizes emotional excess, confusion and overwhelm. Feelings have burst through your ability to handle them and a crisis may be on the horizon. Note if the water is clear or cloudy and what its source is. If the water is overflowing from a toilet, it may suggest emotional blockage or a back-up of feelings. Clear water could be a positive sign of spiritual renewal or refreshment; unclear water suggests an inability to deal with some highly emotional situation. Whatever emotion is being symbolized, you can bet you are feeling it in the extreme, or you are experiencing an emotional high or low. Dream feelings should help clarify.

Polluted – See Dirty or Polluted Water

Puddle

Represents a small portion of your emotional or spiritual life. If the puddle is dirty or muddy, it may say there is a small misunderstanding or that you need to get some clarity on your unclear feeling. Often left after a rainfall, a puddle may indicate that a spiritual cleansing has taken place, and therefore may be proof that you have cleansed and worked hard at clearing

issues. Look to the dream feelings for greater understanding.

Rain

Often indicates an emotional clearing or spiritual cleansing. Note the dream feelings for greater understanding. Rain washes away the muddied waters of our emotions and brings freshness, clarity and understanding to situations. Is someone or something raining on your parade? See Rain on page 435.

Rapids

May suggest you are having trouble dealing with certain feelings or that you are challenged by the way you have felt recently. Note if you are shooting the rapids (actively involved in facing emotional challenges) or just observing them (perhaps not dealing with them, but aware of the disturbance). Could be a pun on something in your life moving too rapidly. Perhaps you feel out of control about a situation, relationship, or anything else that's currently happening in your life.

River

Symbolizes the flow of your emotions, feelings and spiritual life. A river that is flowing smoothly and unobstructedly reflects that your inner reality as flowing peacefully and harmoniously. A river that is muddied, obstructed or overflowing indicates the state of your emotional life — unclear, feelings of being stuck, and overwhelmed. Note the dream feelings for greater understanding. Do you feel in the flow? Have your emotions and spiritual life been trickling along? Rivers spring from a source, which can represent God or Source and therefore the source all life and energy.

Sea

May also be a pun on "see" and represent the need to see something more clearly — behold, take note of, or observe a situation, a relationship or yourself! See also Lake and Ocean.

Steam

Water that has been transformed from one form to another may represent that you have been transforming something related to your emotions or your spiritual life. Could say you are involved in a steamy affair or are all steamed up.

Stream

Similar to a river but on a smaller scale. A babbling brook may be a pun on you babbling or being overly talkative and not listening to your self. See River for greater understanding.

Swimming Pool – *See the Backgrounds and Settings section of this dictionary*

Tidal Wave

Indicates a huge, overwhelming emotional upset and upheaval. May warn that such an upheaval is impending, depending on whether the tidal wave has already come ashore in the dream. Fear is often behind this type of extreme emotional upset. There is an urgent need to look at what has created this situation before further damage is done. A tidal wave may also represent any emotion that you consider to be unsafe or frightening to experience, which, of course, varies from person to person. See also Tsunami in the *Weather* section of this dictionary.

Undertow

Represents feeling weighed down or being pulled under by an emotional situation or overwhelming feelings. Could be a spiritual crisis or heaviness. Either way, it is an uncomfortable time and you may feel over-burdened emotionally. Perhaps you feel you are being sucked in or sucked under by someone or something. You may feel caught, trapped and not in control.

Wading in Water

Symbolizes you getting your feet wet or starting some new undertaking. Perhaps you are testing the waters, or new adventures are about to begin. Feet are about understanding and the beliefs upon which you stand. Note how this factors into you putting your feet in the water (which represents emotions or spiritual life). May say you have achieved greater clarity and understanding of things.

Walking on Water

Indicates you feel you have accomplished some great feat or miracle in your life. May say your ego is over-inflated or that you have been bragging lately. Could indicate you feel in great control over your emotional or spiritual life. May say you are walking in faith or that you are on top of things.

Waterfall

Symbol of great emotional or spiritual energy. Often refreshing, clear, unspoiled and directly from Source. May indicate your personal connection to Source/God or your higher self. Represents strong, unlimited resources are at hand. Note dream feelings for greater understanding.

Weather

In general, weather is an external expression of our inner realities. This includes our thoughts, feelings and spiritual expressions. Air is related to the mental plane, whereas water sources are considered emotional or spiritual in nature. Fire has to do with spirit, passion and creative energies (see the Miscellaneous section of this dictionary); earth is associated more with physical reality. Weather can be a prediction of things to come based on your current thoughts, words and actions. It expresses your emotional "atmosphere" and moods.

Remember: These symbolic meanings are just suggestions. If these suggested meanings do not resonate with you, ring a bell, give you an "ah-ha" moment or otherwise feel right, search through your own experience or beliefs about the symbol to find what makes sense for you.

Air

Usually an expression of the mental plane, including thoughts, beliefs, attitudes, opinions, prayers and ideas. All that you think is expressed through the medium of air. Therefore, the wind is an aspect of the mind and represents the general flow of your thinking. Big gusts of wind may suggest your ego is working overtime or that you have been bragging lately. Could say you are a wind bag and over-talkative. May suggest the "fury of your mind" or represent angry, frustrated thinking. A calm wind or day suggests peace of mind. Have you felt blown off course or blown away? Perhaps you are full of hot air or you need to air your thoughts and opinions. Note the feelings in the dream for greater clarification.

Clouds

Represent the clouds in your mind or what you are thinking. Suggests that your thoughts are taking form and shape in the material plane (you are manifesting what you are thinking). Dark, threatening clouds suggest negative thinking, fear and/or frustration — a storm of emotion is likely gathering when dark clouds gather. Puffy white clouds may indicate pure and positive thoughts. White clouds may also indicate that your prayers are being answered or your thoughts are manifesting on the physical plane. May be a pun on your thinking or your vision being clouded. Note the dream feelings and the shape of the clouds for greater understanding. For example, if you dream of a cloud shaped like a horse, I suggest that you look up that symbol as well for greater insight. If the dream feelings are fearful, this suggests that your mind is fearful about something.

Earthquake

Symbolizes an earth-moving or earth-shaking situation or event that has recently happened or is about to happen. When the earth moves, people take notice. What upheaval has recently happened in your life? Note that a dream earthquake is trying to get your attention big time. If the earthquake in your life is emotional in nature, there is a strong need for you to express the feelings; if it is mental in nature, there is a strong need for you to change your attitudes or thinking. Could be a pun on quaking in fear or that you need a shake. Since earth represents the physical plane, an earthquake suggests that whatever this is about has already manifested in the physical reality. Could be the wake-up call you need to move on with something. Since the earth is beneath your feet it suggests that the beliefs upon which you stand (or your understand-

ing) are at focus here. Note the dream feelings for greater insight. May suggest you are on shaky ground (or something is unstable) with respect to a relationship, endeavour or some current situation.

Fog

Often denotes not seeing clearly or not thinking clearly. Maybe your emotions are foggy and hard to grasp. Your mind may be clouded with negative thinking or unformed ideas. Indicates that you are not clear about your opinions, ideas or attitudes. Perhaps you feel as if you are in a fog, bewildered or confused. Are you in a muddle, perplexed or dazed?

Hail

Indicates frozen or fearful emotions raining down on you in an overwhelming way. It represents your need for emotional clarity and expression. Do you feel emotionally hardened or bitter? Suggests emotional deluge or excess that you don't have the ability to express at this time.

Hurricane

Symbolizes that a big storm is brewing emotionally. Suggests an impending upheaval, crisis and overwhelm of feelings. Could also say that your thoughts are blowing in a very unbalanced and destructive way. Be aware of negative thinking and attitudes that no longer serve you well. Indicates the need to prepare your self for emotional storms and gives you a chance to put your energies into constructive, rather than destructive, channels.

Lightning

Represents a lightning-quick mind or illumination. Have you had some great insight or wake-up call? May represent your nervous or neurological systems, depending on how the lightning is represented in the dream. Is it a quick flash (of insight that brings light to a situation)? Or does it touch your body in an electrocuting manner, suggesting you need a jolt to wake you up to something? Has something shocking recently been revealed or do you need a shock to get yourself moving in a new direction? Lightning represents power and can indicate a need to use your creative powers more, or that you have been using your power decisively. Seeing something struck by lightning may be a metaphor for you being struck by something, such as something or someone making a huge impression on you or a thought or idea striking you forcefully. Lightning can be destructive, so note whether your dream lightening does harm or just helps illuminate the scene.

Rain

Often indicates an emotional clearing or spiritual cleansing. Note the dream feelings for greater understanding. For example, feelings of peace within the dream may suggest this is a useful cleansing happening, whereas feelings of anguish may symbolize that your current emotional state is not clear to you — in fact, something may be dampening your ability to recognize your feelings. Rain can wash away the muddied waters of our emotions and brings freshness, clarity and understanding to situations. Heavy rain suggests a deluge of feelings; a soft rain indicates spiritual renewal, peace or forgiveness. Rain is often seen as God's blessings. Freezing rain denotes hardened, fearful or negative feelings in general that are being blocked from expression. Frozen emotions need to be realized and released in order to avert the damage caused by emotions being held in.

Snow

May represent frozen or cold emotions, depending on the amount of snowfall, the consistency of the snow, and the dream feelings. Heavy snow indicates heavy or burdensome emotions that you are trying to deal with. Soft fluffy snowflakes may indicate God's blessings coming down on you.

A snowstorm may represent an emotional overwhelm, usually one based in fear. May suggest you feel snowed under by emotional burdens or unable to cope with feelings. May be a pun on "snow job" or feelings that someone has put one over on you. Perhaps you feel blinded or unable to make your way clearly. Snow suggests a need for thawing out and letting go (release and surrender).

Storm

Storms of any kind suggest impending emotional crisis, upheaval or overwhelm. If the storm has not already hit, you need to be prepared for some uncomfortable feelings on the horizon. There is a strong need to be aware of these feelings and to allow them full expression without judgement. The storm will pass and it is wise not to let the pent-up feelings stay inside yourself, which can cause harm to the body and mind and create further emotional crisis. A storm also indicates the need for clarity in your thinking. Negative thinking is gathering and building the storm, and it requires your attention in order not to cause greater chaos within. You are out of balance when a storm is present in the dream time. Perhaps fury is building within you and needs release. Note the intensity of the storm for greater clarity and understanding. Remember that storms clear the air and

have a positive effect in this way. A storm can also represent a stormy relationship or any event, situation or encounter that feels overwhelming or threatening at the present time.

Thunder

An attention getter. Do you need a wake-up call or a "clap" to get yourself motivated? Thunder may represent your thunderous thoughts or God's hand in a situation. May warn of approaching storms or upheaval on the mental or emotional plane. Do you need to roar, scream or otherwise express your thunder?

Tornado

Symbolizes that a big emotional upset, upheaval and crisis are impending. Suggests negative and destructive forces are at play in your feeling and thinking. Have you felt blown away or sucked in by someone or something? Fear and/or the need to vent your frustrations in a positive way is likely the underlying factor. Tornados also represent vortexes of energy such as the chakra system, so look to the feelings to help clarify whether this is a warning or a positive insight (see the *Chakras* section for greater insight). Vortexes also open doors to other dimensions and realities — other levels of awareness and being — and they could say you are opening to such.

Tsunami

Represents a big wave of emotion, usually an overwhelming emotion that is happening or about to happen in your life. May indicate you are feeling in crisis or about to drown in your own emotions. Note dream feelings to help you connect with what may be causing this big wave of emotion in your life. For example, if the feeling is one of fear, try to connect that with an event, situation, relationship, or other aspect of your life that currently makes you feel overwhelming fear. This will help you to understand what the dream tsunami symbolizes. See also Tidal Wave in the *Water* section of this dictionary

Volcanic Eruption

Represents great passion, anger or fury coming to the surface. Note the dream feelings to understand if this is a positive expression of your creativity and passion or a negative expression of your anger. May be lust, obsession, spiritual hunger or a great need for emotional expression. May foretell that an emotional outburst is impending or that you have erupted already. Either way, you need to be in touch with this emotion and allow its full expression without judgement. May be a healthy expression that your first chakra is working well. See the section on *Chakras* for greater insight.

Wind – *See Air (in this section)*

Miscellaneous A to Z

Remember: These symbolic meanings are just suggestions. If these suggested meanings do not resonate with you, ring a bell, give you an "ah-ha" moment or otherwise feel right, search through your own experience or beliefs about the symbol to find what makes sense for you.

A

Accident

May be a warning that an accident or crisis is impending, or reflect that you feel you have failed at something recently. Do you feel that some misfortune has recently occurred, or do you feel you have "accidentally" acted in the wrong way? If the accident is a collision with another vehicle, it may say that you feel you have had a run-in with another person. Perhaps you have injured your pride or experienced some painful situation. You may be on a collision course or express that you are driving yourself in a non-beneficial way. Accidents of any kind warn of imbalance and inconsistency. See also Accident in the *Vehicles, Their Parts and Actions* section of this dictionary.

Ankh

A powerful symbol of mastery, enlightenment, and the ability to transform and transmute. To the ancient Egyptians, the ankh represented great potential within the self and was a symbol of immortality.

Ark of the Covenant

This has long been a symbol of mystery. It is actually a very powerful vortex of energy that creates a doorway for Spirit (higher energies) to enter the Earth plane. What do you need to open yourself to or allow into your current life?

Art

Represents your skill, cunning, creativity and expression in general. Depending on how you feel about the art in your dream, it may represent a beautiful, creative aspect of your self or a poor self-image. Art is about your talent, finesse, mastery and dexterity. Note what art is being depicted and how you feel about it for further insight.

Autograph

Represents your "mark," "signature" or personal identity. Note whose autograph it is and consider how this person's characteristics and traits mirror your own. May say you resemble this person or that you would like to take after them. If someone is seeking your autograph in the dream, this symbolizes your need for recognition or distinction.

B

Bag

Represents a container or a womb-like space. Maybe you are feeling too contained or restricted by something. Could denote a receptive state of being. It could also be a pun on expressions such as "in the bag," "bag of tricks" or "wind bag." May also denote baggage or attitudes, beliefs and ideas that you carry around with you.

Baggage – See Suitcase

Bait

Something that is alluring, enticing or otherwise tantalizing to you. Could be a pun on the fact that you have recently been baited or taken in. Have you taken the bait? Do you think someone is a good catch? Has someone been goading, harassing or teasing you?

Ball

May represent round things, such as the Earth, oneness or wholeness. Do you need to run with the ball, have a good cry (bawl), play ball or be on the ball? May also be a pun on "keep your eye on the ball." A (dance) ball may refer to your need to be in harmony (dance) with someone or some aspect of your self. Could be a pun on feeling like the belle of the ball, or point to a need for recognition and distinction.

Balloon

Filled with air, balloons denote the mind and its faculties, as well as your thoughts, attitudes and opinions. How is the balloon portrayed in the dream? Whether it is being tossed about, floating gently or deflated is a symbolic representation of your mind. A balloon may say your ego is over-inflated or that you are full of hot air. Could say you are going with the flow of consciousness or that you have been blown off course or blown away. Since balloons are often used for celebrations, it may reflect a current accomplishment or celebratory feelings. May also indicate that you feel light as air or positive about some current undertaking. See also Hot Air Balloon in the *Vehicles, Their Parts and Actions* section.

Basket

May represent your need to contain something or your need to get it all together. Baskets are fairly open containers for putting together ideas or thoughts. Are you feeling like a basket case? Are you putting all your eggs in one basket?

Bell

Are they warning bells trying to alert you to something going on in your life that needs your attention? Or are they celebratory bells (such as at a wedding)? Bells are also a symbol of peace, freedom and harmony within the self or in any current undertaking. Puns on this word are common, such as saved by the bell, clear as a bell and for whom the bell tolls. Do any of these puns resonate (ring a bell for you) with any current situation? May be associated with church and/or religion, depending on your personal associations of bells.

Bible

The holy book may denote whether you are feeling "holy" or "whole" about something. Perhaps you are feeling guilty about something or in need of some spiritual support? What importance does the Bible hold in your life? Does it remind you of how to live your life in a sacred or devoted way? Perhaps it is telling you to "turn to the book" more often, or that you have lost sight of (or are out of alignment with) your spiritual beliefs. If the Bible represents the truth to you personally, then it may reflect your beliefs about some truth you are adhering to at this time. How is your dream Bible being used? See if you can relate this to a current life situation, relationship or event.

Binoculars

Represent your ability to focus or to see things up close and clearly. Perhaps you see something as larger than life, or you may need to enhance some perspective. Do you require more focus? Do you need to tune in more closely to something? May speak of the need to be more fully present in the now; that is, more focussed in the present moment.

Birth – *See Pregnancy*

Birth Control

Symbolizes the need for protection or safety at some level. May say you fear getting pregnant or symbolically fear creating something new in your life. Could say you feel controlled or dominated (especially in your creative potential).

Blood

Symbolizes your vital life force, energy and flow. If you are bleeding, this suggests a loss at some level. You may be losing your vitality or energy to an unhealthy situation or relationship. Is someone or something bleeding you to death? Are you losing your energy to a "vampire" (someone who makes you feel drained)? Bleeding internally may suggest that you have inner pain or that you are losing energy to a dominating part of your self. Are you emotionally drained or losing energy to a particular feeling, such as fear, anxiety or any emotion you deem bad, wrong, or otherwise improper? Because blood is red, it probably reflects your first chakra and how it is functioning. See First Chakra in the *Chakras* section for greater insight.

Book

Represents knowledge, information, wisdom, awareness, intelligence, learning, perceptions or education. May symbolize a need for any of these, depending on how the book is portrayed and how you feel about the book. If the book is old its contents may be out of date or it may symbolize ancient wisdom. A book could also represent fixed ideas, because it is already in print or hard copy. Is the book fact or fiction? Is there some knowledge or information that you need to seek out? What type of a book is it — phone book, law book, reference book, comic book? This will help you pinpoint the meaning of your dream book. For example, a law book may point to rules and codes of behaviour that you are currently displaying. Are you being too rule driven and rigid in your thoughts or actions? Do you need to be more strict in some area of your life? A manual or how-to book could be signalling that you require directions or instructions in some area of your life and that you need to "do it yourself." A phone book may represent the need to contact someone or reach out and ask for help.

Bookkeeping

This symbol is related to accounting, facts, financial balance and figures. May say you need to account for your actions or justify your beliefs. A call for greater balance may be hinted at, or a need to account for yourself. May be related to your current financial experiences and a "statement of your accounts." May suggest a need for more orderliness or for keeping some facts straight.

Border

Represents your boundaries or lack of them. Do you limit or restrict yourself in some way? Or do you feel restricted, limited and confined? If the border crossing is patrolled, it may symbolize that a controlling, dominating, or authoritative part of your self is taking over or running the show in your internal reality. A border also divides two places — do you feel divided or torn between two things or choices?

Box

May imply limited thinking, thoughts and opinions. Or, may symbolize a place to store ideas or a framework for your thinking. May say you have boxed in feelings or a closed mind. Boxes are restrictive structures and therefore reflect something restrictive about your personality. But the square shape of a box can also represent solid structure and security, so note the dream feelings for greater insight. See Container for more clues.

Briefcase

Symbolizes work and the business mind. A place where you store ideas, thoughts, opinions, judgements and things to do with the rational mind.

May suggest that you are being analytical or that there is a need for more analysis. Could be a pun on "keeping things brief" or the need to be aware of the temporary state of a situation.

C

Cage

Anything in a cage represents lack of freedom or sense of loss. Do you feel caged in, cagey or restricted in any way? Do you feel imprisoned in your own mind or in some situation? Does the dream cage feel safe, or does it give you a feeling of confinement? Note what is in the cage and how it feels for greater understanding. For example, a bird in the cage may symbolize your feelings of lack of freedom (hopelessness, helplessness), or that you aren't following your instincts.

Calculator

Has your mind been calculating and analyzing anything of late? Perhaps you are scheming or making plans. Do you need to calculate the outcome of a project, idea or thought in a more organized way? What do you need to figure out, discover or ascertain in your life currently?

443

Camera

Since cameras take pictures and preserve or immortalize a moment, it could indicate the need to see this situation clearly and hold it dearly or close to you. The object of the dream's intent (whatever the camera is focussed upon) will help direct you to the emphasis of the dream theme or content. Perhaps something is out of focus or needs to be brought into focus. What is your dream focussing on or bringing into view? How do you perceive or see your current life challenges and situations? Are you overly focussed on an issue and out of balance? Do you need more balance and focus in an area of your life? Let your dream camera lens show you the area of emphasis. Cameras are a type of eye on the moment, so see Eye in the *Body* section to help further clarify the meaning.

Candle

Since candles provide light, ask yourself whether you require a little light in some area of your life. Is there anything you are not seeing clearly or need more clarity on? Since candles also provide a sense of warmth, ask yourself if you need a little warmth, fondness, affection or love in your life currently. "Doesn't hold a candle" is a popular saying and may denote that some rela-

tionship or situation is not appropriate or adequate for you at this time.

Cannon

If exploding, this is a warning — something is "booming" out for your attention. Do you need to defend yourself in your waking life? Or do you need to get out the heavy artillery? Has there been a blow up in any area of your life or in your inner reality? Since cannons are usually associated with war, it may be helpful to read the War entry in this section of the dictionary.

Cartoon

Represents falsity or not feeling real. If you dream of a cartoon character, perhaps you are acting in a way similar to the character's traits. May suggest you need some humour or funniness in your life.

Cash – *See Money*

Catalogue

Represents an index or inventory, possibly of your life. May be wishful thinking or your wish list. A catalogue could also symbolize that you have lots of variety or choice available. Note how you feel about the catalogue and its content for greater insight.

Change – *See Coin and Money*

Cheque

Represents money and therefore energy. May be a pun on the need to check things out before you continue with certain endeavours. It may symbolize money coming to you for services rendered. A blank cheque may suggest unlimited supply or potential.

Circle

Round things suggest wholeness, completion and oneness in sacred geometry. Could also suggest you are going in circles, or that something in your life has no beginning and no end. Or, perhaps you are getting familiar with some project, relationship or endeavour before you take action, the way an animal circles its prey or territory before it acts.

Clay

Symbolizes your ability to shape or create in any way you wish. Could say you are being moulded for something or allowing yourself to be formed by someone else's actions, thoughts or words.

Club

A nightclub may represent being part of the crowd, group consciousness, or the

need to be accepted. Note your personal associations with nightclubs to help you understand if this represents partying, and good times feelings or your distaste, dislike or repulsion of something. A club that is used as a weapon may be a pun on feeling clubbed, beaten or battered. See the entry in the *Tools and Weapons* section of this dictionary for greater insight.

Coin

Finding coins may indicate fortunate events on a small scale. Often this is a pun on change (usually small) occurring in your life. May indicate you feel you have insufficient funds at this time or not much "purchasing power."

Collision – *See Accident in the Vehicles, Their Parts and Actions section*

Compass

Represents the need for direction. May symbolize that you feel lost, directionless or confused. Conversely, you may have just found your way and this is a positive affirmation of guidance received.

Container

Represents a receptacle, holding area or womb-like area. What would you like to contain in your life? The feelings in the dream will help you understand whether this container holds something healthy or something you'd rather not contain or hold on to. Is there something that you need to let go of or release? Do you feel hemmed in, trapped or otherwise contained? Perhaps you are holding in (containing) your feelings, and dreaming of a container could suggest the need to let them out (voice them or express them in some way).

Cover

Covering something up may indicate the need for protection or safety. May also suggest you are hiding from something or concealing something.

Crafts

Symbolize creativity and either the need for more creation on your part or a positive affirmation that you have been co-creating well. May be a pun on being crafty or sly. Note your personal associations with craft-making and the dream feelings for greater insight.

Cross

Often a symbol of Christianity or the four elements (wind, water, earth and fire). The horizontal arm of the cross represents the plane of physical matter and the vertical post represents Spirit descending and penetrating the physical plane. May be a pun such as "the cross you must bear" or being at a crossroads. Relate this to your religious beliefs to clarify the meaning this symbol has for you. How do you feel about Christianity, and what role has it played in your life? May also be a pun on being cross or angry with someone or about some situation. May suggest you feel crossed or betrayed. Note the dream feelings for greater insight.

D

Dam

Suggests a blockage of emotions or feelings. Could be a restriction or controlled flow of emotions. Note the dream feelings to help you understand what emotions you may be holding on to or damming up. Could say you feel attacked, criticized or hindered in some way.

Dawn

Suggests new beginnings, a fresh start or the unfolding of something new. Something is emerging and perhaps dawning on you. What are you creating in your life right now? What are you about to give birth to?

Doll

May represent childish ways or attitudes, depending on how you feel about playing with dolls. May be a sense of security or old needful patterns emerging. May suggest you feel small, false or fake. May be a pun on how you would feel (either flattered or offended) if someone called you a doll.

Drain

May symbolize the need to let go of or release something. May be a pun on feeling drained or exhausted. May say you feel everything is going down the drain. Could represent loss of any kind.

Driver's License

Represents your permit or authorization to drive. Indicates whether you feel you are capable of running your own life at this time. If you cannot find your driver's license in your dream, it suggests you feel you have lost control of your abilities to steer yourself.

E

Electrical Equipment

May represent your feelings of power or powerlessness, depending on how well the equipment in the dream is running. May represent your body's nervous system. May suggest you are being very efficient and doing things at a good speed. See also Nervous System in the *Body* section of this dictionary.

Enlarged

Any person, animal or object that is enlarged in your dream is trying to get your attention. Something in your life is out of character or out of proportion. Emphasis is being placed on this item, which may symbolize a trait, habit, belief, thought pattern or feeling. Something is out of harmony and requires rebalancing and restoration. For example, if your feet in your dream are four times their normal size, it may imply that you are not being true to the beliefs upon which you stand, or that your "understanding" of something is out of proportion.

Eraser

Represents the ability to cancel out, delete or otherwise get rid of something. May say you need to eliminate something from your life or lifestyle.

Exhaustion

Reflects that you feel exhausted, spent or otherwise fatigued. May say you have exhausted a certain avenue, way of thinking or way of being. Do you feel tired and in need of rest?

Explosion

Speaks of buried, unexpressed emotions coming to the surface and exploding out of you. Often these are feelings that you have judged as bad, wrong or unacceptable. Could suggest you have an explosive personality or explosive thoughts. Either way, it is a warning that trouble is brewing if you do not shed some light on the situation.

Eye Glasses

These help you see, restore your sight or improve your perspective on things. Note whether the dream glasses bring things into focus for you or distort things; this is a good clue about whether your current way of viewing something is helpful or not. Seeing goes beyond what your physical eyes detect and speaks of seeing things below the surface or seeing the truth of a situation. Is relates to the third eye (the sixth chakra) and your insights, intuition and ability to visualize. See Eye in the *Body* section and Sixth Chakra in the *Chakras* section for more insight.

F

Fabric

Symbolizes the material from which you create and co-create. May suggest you need to stretch yourself or create more. Could be a pun on the fabric of your life or foundation of your life. Note type and colour of the fabric and how it is being used for greater understanding.

Fear

Experiencing fear in the dream time is a direct reflection of your fearful feelings in the waking time. Can you pinpoint what area of your life is generating these fears? The dream clues, such as background setting or characters, may be useful in identifying the source of your fear. For example, if the fear dream takes place in the kitchen, this often denotes the realm of the mind, thoughts, analytical thinking and opinions. Try to connect your fearful feelings with one of these symbolic meanings. Perhaps you have been overly analytical of yourself or in some situation, or someone may be using harsh words or opinions that raise fear in you. If a particular dream character is related to the fearful feelings, what three characteristics or traits describe the person (even if it's a stranger you can usually get a sense of their demeanour or character)? These traits often reflect your inner reality or parts of your inner self. Use these mirrored characteristics as a tool for self-reflection and self-growth.

It's also useful to try to relate your fear to the action taking place in the dream.

For example, being afraid of flying in a dream may indicate a fear of freedom or of losing control in some area of your life. Fear of open spaces in a dream may indicate overwhelming feelings of vulnerability and fear of being judged by yourself and others (because things are "out in the open").

Fear creates a type of static in your energy field, making clarity and "clear seeing" difficult. It also creates a tremendous loss of energy as you try not to feel the fear. See the discussion on nightmares in Chapter 3 for greater insight. Identifying what you fear in the dream (and what you fear in your waking life) will help you reclaim lost energy.

Feather

Associated with birds and therefore can represent freedom, soaring to new heights, spiritual forces and going with the flow. Also associated with the flow of air and therefore the flow of your thoughts and the mental realm in general. Indicates a lightness or floating quality. Perhaps you feel light as a feather and free from burdens and worries. A feather is sometimes a message from Great Spirit (represented by an eagle). Feathers are also used for healing and may symbolize a healing experience. May be a pun on "knock me over with a feather" and denote some recent surprise or event that shocked

you. If you know the type of bird the feather has come from, look up that species in the *Birds* section of this dictionary.

Fence

Symbolizes the need for protection, privacy or safety. May also say you are being defensive or feeling divided. Could represent healthy boundaries you are establishing or a block to further advancement or communication. You may be putting up barriers or setting yourself apart from others. Note the dream feelings for greater understanding.

Fire

Often representative of cleansing and purification on some level. Fire is destructive, and yet out of the ashes rises the phoenix or new life. How do you feel about your dream fire? Feeling calm and collected indicates a positive cleansing occurring. It may be a pun on being all fired up or symbolize rage that has not been expressed. Does some situation or person burn you or make you angry? Look to the feelings in the dream to help clarify. Fire transforms and can therefore be about your transformation and spiritual awakening. May denote your passion in life and is also representative of the first chakra. Note the characteristics of your fire for insight into how well your first chakra is functioning. For example, a weak or diminished fire would suggest a dampened first chakra energy. See the *Chakras* section for greater insight. See also Flame in this section.

Flag

The flag of a country represents the cultural beliefs of that country. May reflect your patriotism or lack of it. May be a flag of truce or a fun and colourful expression of yourself. Or does the dream flag act as a signal, warning or guidepost? Remember that "flag" can also mean to fail or waste away.

Flame

May represent your spark, fervour or passion. Could be a pun on your lover, sweetheart or someone you admire. May suggest that your awareness or consciousness has been sparked by something, or represent warmth and enlightenment. Could represent your first chakra and its functioning, so see the *Chakras* section and/or Fire in this section.

Flashlight

Symbolizes the ability to see more clearly, especially in darkness. May reveal hidden things or things that have been below your waking-time awareness (i.e., unconscious). Says that there is illumination, insight or understanding. May represent enlightenment or your ability to bring light into a situation by choice.

Foreign

Denotes that something you are doing, thinking, feeling or experiencing feels unfamiliar, new or alien to you. You may be out of character, or acting (or feeling) strange or in an outlandish way.

G

Garbage

Represents ideas, beliefs or attitudes that need to be thrown out or discarded. That which no longer serves you in your life can be considered refuse. Perhaps you feel as though you are wasting your life or that life stinks at the moment. Do you feel buried in debris, nonsense or stuff in general? What smells rotten or bad to you? What do you need to unload, discard or get rid of? Do you feel like trash or have you been treated like trash? What do you consider to be the garbage, trash or rubbish in your life?

Gate

Could represent a barrier, the need for protection, or defensiveness. On the other hand, it could be an opening — a gateway — or opportunity, depending on whether the gate is open or closed. May be the gateway to your future or a portal to another dimension. May be a pun on your gait; i.e., your walking pace or the way you walk.

Glue

May symbolize your ability to bond, feel secure or stick something out. Perhaps you need to get it together or are experiencing a sticky situation. You may be too stuck on someone or something, or perhaps you feel you are coming unglued.

Grail

These cups are receptacles, indicating feminine energies, containers, receptivity or emotions. The grail or holy grail was created from harmonic laws and measures or proportions in order to bring forth orientation in the midst of a sea of chaos and change. The grail in you represents your sense of measure and proportions, whereby your soul is a receptacle for infinite light and spiritual mysteries. Your grail is your pool of clear and virtuous soul qualities. Your blood is vital light and your body is a temple within the grail. That centre of your being (your grail) is lit not by the sun and moon, but your blood light (the luminescence of your soul).

Gravel

Denotes that you lack a sturdy foundation, basis or framework for something. May say your thoughts are not organized or you lack firm support for yourself and your endeavours. This may be a more challenging path you are pursuing, or it could represent loose footings. See also Pebbles.

H

Handle

Symbolizes the ability to grasp, control, manoeuvre or steer yourself in life. May suggest you need to get a handle on some situation or inner conflict. Note the dream feelings, which could also indicate that you have recently got a handle on something or that you are handling some situation or relationship well. Have you flown off the handle lately or lost control? Do you need to get a grip or is something hard to handle? Or perhaps you need to handle something with kid gloves?

Hole

Represents an opening, gulf or void. Falling into a hole denotes loss on some level or says you have really missed the mark. Being in a hole may symbolize that you are in over your head. May be a pun on hole as a type of hovel, sty or shack. May be a pun on a hole in your thinking, a hole in one, or a loophole. Note the dream feelings to determine whether this is a positive opening or opportunity for you or an indication of loss.

Hook

Since hooks are used to fasten, hold and latch things, they can be about issues of safety and security. Also used to enmesh, entangle and anchor, so it may suggest that you feel entangled in a situation or relationship. Note the dream feelings for greater understanding. May suggest you are being reeled in or hooked in. Could be a pun on being hooked or addicted to something.

Horns

Usually associated with the head and therefore "hardened" thoughts, thinking and judgements. May also be associated with the devil and therefore represent negative or nasty thinking. Could suggest you are hard headed, horny or locking horns with another. On a deeper level, horns can also represent an extension of your positive thinking and of the thoughts that link you to the Creator or to your higher self.

Hose

May represent a channel for your emotions and feelings to flow through, especially if there is water flowing through the hose. If the water is clean, it indicates clear running feelings. May also serve as an indicator that you are a clear channel for accessing your higher self and spirit guides. May serve as a conduit for bringing life-giving sustenance to your being. A blocked hose or one that can't deliver the water may suggest you are blocked emotionally about something or are unable to access (feel) your emotions.

Illegal Activity – *See Breaking the Law in the Actions section*

Insurance

May represent the need for protection and security. Perhaps you are looking for a guarantee or assurance. Do you feel you need a reward, benefit or support?

Jury

Could say you feel judged or that you are being judgemental. Do you feel as though you are on trial or that you need to plead your case? Perhaps you feel you should be accountable for something or that you have been placed in a responsible or decision-making role. Judgement is often internal, so begin to realize if you are being hard on yourself or punishing yourself from within.

K

Key

Not having a key to start your vehicle suggests you have no idea how or where to begin something. You cannot even start you new endeavour, and therefore you will need some insight and clarity in order to proceed. May be a pun on the key to success or the key to the situation.

Kite

Associated with the wind and therefore the mind, a kite flying often represents the state of your thinking and thoughts. Are your thoughts blowing about and out of control? Or are you enjoying the control and manoeuvrability of your kite? May say you have high ideals or the sky is the limit. May represent freedom, choice or playfulness.

Knots

Do you feel all twisted up in knots? Are you entangled or snarled up in a situation in your waking life? Could be

a kink or cramp in your style. May be a pun on not, as in do not, have not, will not or cannot.

L

Label

Suggests you are branding, marking or categorizing something — perhaps yourself. Note the dream feelings to see if this is a positive label or negative judgements you are pursuing.

Lace

Symbolizes something delicate, fragile or feminine. Could be a pun on to spike, mix or infuse (as in a drink). May represent an adornment, decoration or netting.

Lease

Represents an agreement of some sort. May be a burden, a commitment or a celebration, depending on the dream feelings. May suggest that you have a new lease on life, you need it in writing, or something needs to be legalized.

Letter

Receiving a letter indicates that someone is trying to relay some kind of message to you. How do you feel about receiving the letter? You could be unconsciously blocking the flow of information out of fear. A dream about a letter may indicate good news is on the way or that you need to do more writing/journal work. Do you open the dream letter — are you open to receiving information? An unopened letter may indicate that you have not heard or accepted messages or recent communications. Writing a letter symbolizes an expression of your ideas, attitudes and opinions, or the need for them to be expressed.

Life Jacket

Indicates you are in need of help, support or bolstering. Because life jackets are associated with water, look at your emotions to see if you are feeling overwhelmed, in chaos or confused. May suggest you need security or that you are feeling unsafe, especially about emotions. May reflect your need for a life line or connection with someone you deem as supportive.

Line

Do you need to draw the line with someone or something? Is there a line, value or creed that you will not cross? Where do you draw the line? Do your words line up with your truth? Or perhaps this is a guideline.

Line-up

Being in a line-up could represent the need to wait something out or foretell the need for more patience. It may suggest you are bored, anxious or in for a long wait. Are you awaiting, expecting or anticipating something? May be a pun on having something (such as a job) lined up. A dream about being in a criminal line-up may symbolize guilt feelings or feelings of victimization.

Lock

Represents safety, security and protection. Do you require any of these, or are you looking to break free of something or feeling locked out?

Lost

Suggests you are lost at some level of your being. This can be hard to see, but it indicates you are confused, bewildered or far away from your heart's desires and goals. Can also suggest absentmindedness, distraction and preoccupation. Can you relate to loss at any level of your being? Do you feel defeated, deprived or bereaved? Have you lost something recently? This can include loss of respect, loss of self-esteem, loss of love or just about anything, depending on your current situation. Perhaps you have lost your way home, suggesting you have lost connection with your higher self and your God. Note the dream feelings to help you understand the depth of your loss or how being lost has affected you.

Lubricant

Represents the ability to move with grace and ease. Have you stiffened up in your attitudes or feelings? Do you need to stop being so serious and lighten up? Note what needs lubricating in the dream and how it feels (positive or negative) for greater understanding. See also Oil.

M

Magic

Represents mysticism, enchantment and the ability to create something out of thin air. Do you need a little more magic, fun or excitement in your life? Have you been bored, hopeless or depressed? Maybe you need to add a little spark to your life and recreate in a new way. May represent the unseen such as your guides, angels and guardians. Could say you are already creating well in your life or that you are charismatic and have the attention of others.

Map

Represents a clear and practical way of doing or achieving something. Suggests you have a plan of action in mind. Implies you have a guide, framework or blueprint for your goals and ideals. Conversely, a map may suggest you feel lost and in need of guidance. Look to the dream feelings to help you understand further.

Mask

Symbolizes a cover-up, or that you are masking, disguising or misrepresenting yourself at this time. Could be a false face you are putting forward. We all wear different masks throughout the day. Who is wearing the dream mask and how does it feel? If someone else is wearing the mask in your dream, look to the traits and characteristics of the person wearing it. These will offer important clues about which aspect of yourself is being reflected. This could also be a warning that someone near to you is wearing a false mask. Note if you have been hiding your truth from yourself or others.

Merry-Go-Round

Represents going in circles, going along for the ride or not achieving what you set out to do. May also say

455

that you are having a fun time, are amused or have no cares. Note the dream feelings for greater understanding.

Mind

Symbolizes the home of the intellect, ego, thinking, thoughts, beliefs and attitudes. The mind "lives" in the third chakra and is masculine in energy at this level. At another level the higher mind connects you with your higher self, knowing and wisdom and is associated with the seventh chakra (crown chakra) and the feminine. See also Third Chakra and Seventh Chakra in the *Chakras* section and Masculine/ Feminine in the *People* section.

Money

Symbolic of energy and indicates the amount of energy you have within you, around you and coming to you. Also represents your sense of worth and power. Do money issues drain you or empower you? Acquiring money in a dream indicates an influx of energy into your life, which could be an abundance of feeling or anything that you consider positive. Losing money in a dream symbolizes feelings of loss on some level or that you are losing out on something. Look to the dream feelings for further clarification.

N

Naked – See Nudity

Needle

Because they are sharp and pointy, needles may represent a sharp mind or that you need to get the point about something. Ask yourself if someone or something is goading you, needling you or otherwise pestering and provoking you? Do you need a shot in the arm or a wake-up call? Perhaps you feel punctured or deflated. Do needles provoke fear in you? Could represent arts and crafts to some, and therefore be about your creativity. See Vaccine in the *Death, Illness and Medical Treatment Section.*

Newspaper

May indicate that something has been exposed and is in print, or that something of value needs expression. May symbolize group consciousness, thinking and doing, or be about the latest gossip. May represent mass media or public opinion. Note your own associations with newspapers for greatest meaning. For example, if you read the newspaper every day, this may represent a habit or ritual of yours. Or it could represent knowledge and insight. Could also be a pun on being well read.

Nudity

Indicates feeling exposed or caught unaware. Look to the feelings in the dream to help you understand if this feels good and empowering or embarrassing and humiliating. Sometimes nakedness can indicate a sense of freedom or overcoming an obstacle — taking a chance or stance and being free from restrictions. But feelings of discomfort are often dominant; they point to something you have done and don't want revealed. Do you feel unprepared, guilty or even naive? May say you have an inappropriate attitude, outlook or opinion about something or someone. May be a pun on getting down to the bare facts or getting to the bottom of things.

O

Oil

A greasy substance that allows for less friction and more harmony. Oil makes things run smoothly, so it may speak of your need for more smoothness in life or say "everything is running smoothly." Perhaps you need more grace and ease in your approach to things. See also Lubricant.

Old-fashioned

Suggests you are doing things according to old patterns of behaviour. You may be out of date, not up to speed or behind the times. Suggests that you need to update your ways of thinking, speaking or doing in the world. May say you are disappointed, discouraged or disillusioned with your life (or part of it). May be a past-life recall, depending on the dream content and feelings.

Olive Branch

Usually symbolizes a peace offering. May suggest you are branching out with respect to your ability to love (yourself or others).

Oversized – *See Enlarged*

P

Package

Similar to container and box, this may represent how you package and store your thinking and thoughts in a rigid way — you may be limiting your thinking or storing away good ideas. Perhaps you are holding on too tightly, unyielding or uncompromising in the mental realm. May be a pun on wrapping things up or a packaged deal. Could represent a burden you carry like a pack horse, or suggest the unknown if a packaged is delivered to you. Sometimes good things come in packages, so this may symbolize an opportunity for you.

Papers – See Letter

Pebbles

Similar to gravel, this suggests that the foundations upon which you stand are loose or insecure. This may symbolize that your root or core beliefs no longer serve or support you well. Because these are also small rocks, they could represent a minor aggravation or a hard step you are taking (because walking on pebbles is painful).

Pen

Symbolizes communication, creativity and the expression of your self. Writing often connects you directly to the unconscious or subconscious levels of your self. Note what is being written for clues to the dream's message. A leaking pen suggests you have lost the ability to communicate clearly. Also note the colour of the ink, and look this up in the *Colours* section for greater understanding.

Pole

Represents a staff, rod, crutch or fixed pillar. May be something you can lean on or hold on to, or something that supports you in some way. May symbolize safety, security, stability or strength. May also be a pun on poll (a census),

and therefore suggest that you are counting or tallying something in order to make a decision. Note what type of pole is in the dream and how it is being used for greater understanding.

Poor, Poverty, Impoverished

Indicates a lack of something on any level of your being. It may be a material lack, but more likely it indicates a sense of lacking on the emotional, intellectual or spiritual level. Be aware of your thoughts and how they may be creating lack and loss at an unconscious level. May be a pun on "poor me" or the need to recognize unworthy feelings and aspects of your self. May also indicate the need to care for yourself in a more loving, tender and compassionate way.

Presents

Represent gifts, rewards or accomplishments. Your dream may be showing your gifts, talents and attributes so that can own them. May be a pun on presence and symbolize a stance you are taking in your waking life. Could suggest you need to be more present and in the here and now. May imply how you present or display yourself, especially in front of others. This could also be a pun on the gifts you give and represent your generosity.

Price Tag

Symbolizes the price you pay for the words you speak and the consequences of your actions. Or you may be weighing your options (the price you will pay). Note if the price is high or low in the dream for greater understanding. Note what the price tag is attached to, the feelings associated with this object in the dream, and whether you can afford it.

Puppet

Do you feel like a pawn or instrument of someone else's design? Or are you being a fool and allowing yourself to be manipulated or controlled by others? Who is pulling your strings and how do you feel like a puppet in your own life? Puppets can also reflect playfulness and a creative imagination.

Q

Question Mark

Indicates that you are questioning yourself at some level. May symbolize that some of your actions, words, beliefs, attitudes or opinions are questionable. Have you been questioning some aspect of your life?

R

Robbed

Represents feeling cheated or deprived, or feeling that you have lost something. You could be robbed of your faith, your worth, your senses or your rights. Perhaps your self-esteem, pride or self-respect has been devalued or attacked. Do you feel victimized, assaulted or depleted? Being robbed is a warning to take stock of what you value and deem worthy.

Rock

Represents part of the earth element and therefore your foundation, basis and sense of home. May also be challenges you are currently facing or bumps in the road. May suggest things are rock solid or that you are on rocky ground. Could symbolize that you've hit rock bottom, or could be a pun on rocking or swaying (being unsteady or tottering). Could also suggest your feelings are rock hard and that you have lost your ability to be soft, feminine and/or receptive. Could also reflect your current thinking or beliefs that are unbending, immovable or unstoppable.

Ruler

Symbolizes a measuring device or a way to see if you measure up. Do you feel you are taking the right measures or the right steps? May be a pun on "ruler" as in leader, king or commander, in which case you should consider whether you feel dominated or in control. Do you feel you rule the roost or rule the domain, or are you being ruled or dominated by someone or something?

S

Siren

Usually heard in emergency situations, this may be telling you that a crisis is impending. In most cases, the crisis is an inner conflict that you haven't expressed or perhaps aren't very aware of. A siren denotes an alarm or signal to get help. Be aware of this attention-getting symbol.

Skull and Crossbones

This symbol may indicate piracy, feelings of being invaded or robbed, or loss of some sort. May also represent death on any level of your being, or suggest that you feel poisoned or corrupted. Sometimes seen as a symbol or warning of impending danger. The skull could suggest empty thoughts,

empty thinking or that you are a "dead head."

Smog

Associated with air and therefore with the mind, smog symbolizes that your mind is not clear — your thinking and judgement are clouded and/or you are confused. Could say you are in a haze or in a fog. Emotions may be obscured or hard to understand. May say you feel polluted, defiled, corrupted or unclean in some way.

Smoke

Often represents a smoke screen or the inability to see something clearly. When "smoke gets in your eyes" you cannot see well or with clarity or comprehension. Have any of your plans gone up in smoke? May suggest something is smoldering or on fire. May represent pent-up feelings such as anger or rage, or say that you are "fuming" mad. Note what is creating the smoke and what feelings are associated with the dream.

Spiral

Symbolizes the sacred dance of life, a vortex or the spin of the chakras. Spirals connect us with other dimensions and energies. May link you to your guide, guardians, angels or

God. May also suggest your mind or emotions are in a whirlwind or out of control. Spirals are powerful and may denote feelings of self-empowerment or powerlessness. Note the dream feelings for greater clarity.

Square

Represents strength, power or stability. Can be a fortress (four walls) and therefore represent a blockage, defensiveness or the need for safety and security. May also symbolize the materialistic, basic or practical. A square suggests limited thinking, inflexibility and barriers or obstructions. May be a pun on being square or dumb.

Stamp

May represent a brand, characterization or mark. May denote crushing, trampling or smashing something. May indicate a coin, mint or label. May be a seal or stamp of approval, or a sign of validation.

Stone

Implies hardness, connection to Mother Earth and rough surfaces. May say the going is not smooth or your foundations are loose (similar to Gravel). Could say you are like "stone,"

unbending, unmovable or unstoppable. On the other hand, you may be dependable, durable and solid as rock. See also Rock.

T

Tall

Implies "tall thinking," elevated thoughts or lofty thinking. Are you thinking big or is there a tall tale or something unbelievable happening? May suggest you are standing tall or standing up for your rights. Have your ideas or goals been far-fetched or outlandish recently?

Target

Symbolizes your mark, intent or purpose. What goals are you currently aiming for? Do you feel like a victim or a scapegoat? Do you feel that you are the target of someone's affection or the target of their anger?

Tarot Cards

Associated with mysticism, the future and the unknown. Represents "a reading" or communication from guides and Spirit. Do you need some insight into the choices you are currently making and how they will affect your future? Tarot cards are a tool for increasing your self-knowledge and self-awareness and enhancing your intuitive perceptions. Note the number or character on the tarot cards and the dream feelings for greater understanding. May suggest you require insight, input or guidance from another source.

Thorn

Represents something sharp, prickling and piercing. Have you been involved in any sticky situations or been the barb of a joke? May be associated with roses, which are a sign of growth and enlightenment. Note the dream feelings to be clear whether this symbolizes a thorn in your side or an opportunity to branch out.

Ticket

Suggests you have decided to go somewhere or travel, or that you have obtained permission to do something. Can also represent a label, tag or mark. May be a voucher or proof that you have accomplished something. If you dream of a lottery ticket, you may wish to purchase one or realize that you have an opportunity awaiting you around the corner. A speeding or parking ticket is a warning to slow down or get moving.

Trap

May suggest you feel cornered, blocked, overwhelmed or imprisoned.

Have you been misled or have you tried to fool another? Do you feel you have been framed, ensnared or set up? Have you set a trap or been caught in a trap? Could be a pun on "shut your trap."

Treasure

Represents your gifts, skills, talents and the beauty within you. Is the treasure buried and not visible to you or the world? Or is it some aspect of your self that you have recently brought out in the open and declared or discovered? Is it an old artifact, representing old patterns or old talents resurfacing? May symbolize something or someone you cherish, appreciate or esteem. What do you prize, value or hold in high regard? Have you been savouring or hoarding something? Note the dream feelings for greater understanding.

Triangle

Denotes trinity, great strength and stability. Also represents the merging of opposites into unity. Trinities can include mind, body, spirit, id; ego, superego; father, son, holy ghost; subconscious, conscious, superconscious; physical, non-physical, metaphysical; energy, matter, antimatter; and past, present, future. Could be a pun on a love triangle.

U

Underwear – See the Clothing section

W

Wallet

Have you lost your identity or found it? Has the dream wallet been stolen or found? Are you currently experiencing financial stress and fear losing a handle on your financial affairs? May indicate your purchasing power, security or "credibility." Since money reflects energy, this may indicate a loss of energy or a reward of energy. May also reflect power issues and your sense of power to do and be. See also Money.

War

Suggests an inner or external struggle, turmoil and conflict. Have you been berating yourself or is something killing you? Have you been raging (inside or externally) or are you taking a particularly harsh stance on something? Perhaps you will not surrender a point of view or will go to extremes (wage war) because of some dearly held belief. See the *Death, Dying and Killing* section of this dictionary for greater insight.

Wings

Associated with flying and flight, and therefore denote freedom, rising above a situation and a different perspective. If your dream wings remind you of the angelic realm, they symbolize a message from higher planes. May say you now have "your wings" and are ready to proceed with something. Perhaps you need to be uplifted or enlightened. May be a pun on "a wing and a prayer" or represent that it's time to take flight.

X

X

Represents your mark or signature. Can also denote deletion, striking out or the unknown. X also "marks the spot" or stands for a variable.

Landscapes and the Plant World

Landscapes are reflections of parts of yourself that tell you about your growth at all levels of your being. They help you understand the support you are receiving, or not receiving, from within yourself and from your external environment (family, friends, workplace, community). Landscapes reveal how you feel and think about yourself, your current life situations, conditions, and the world around you. They show you how your divine nature is presenting and expressing itself in your life.

The condition of the landscape reveals much about your health, be it physical, emotional, mental or spiritual. Landscapes describe your energy systems, your patterns and your overall development. They reflect current life circumstances and how you view them and yourself. What grows (or does not grow) in the landscape tells you about your own level of growth as you see it and from the perspective of your spirit and your soul's agenda. The plant world is a living, thriving ecosystem, just as you are, and it reflects and mirrors this about yourself. Plants, trees and flowers are all about things that grow, bloom, transition, wither and die.

How you care for the plants in your environment reflects much about how you care for yourself. If you are planting new seeds (ideas, beliefs, projects, relationships), the plant life reflects whether you are nurturing these things in a healthy and balanced way, and whether growth is actually happening or not. Plants require the elements (fire/sun, water, air and earth) in order to grow and flourish — just as you do. Noticing what elements the plant life is lacking or overwhelmed by will help you understand your own relationships to the elements and what your requirements may be. Note that the elements are synonymous as your physical body (earth element), your emotional life (water element), your intellectual side (air element) and your spiritual nature (fire element). In this way the plant world and its relationship to the elements can help you understand where you may be out of balance in your own quaternity (the four parts of self that make up the whole of Who You Are).

Earth/Ground/Land

Earth is one of the four elements that comprise Who You Are (earth, water, air and fire, or your physical, emotional, mental and spiritual subtle bodies, respectively). Earth is akin to the physical plane or body and therefore reflects your physical body, its health, and the balance between the four aspects that comprise Who You Are. Your physical body is made up of the atoms of Mother Earth and your spirit energy. This is what comprises your physical body and supports you and gives you life on the planet. What type of earth do you see and stand upon? Is it rock solid and supportive, or in a state of decay and death? This will help you understand if you currently feel supported, or if you feel that you are in a state of crumble, decay or perhaps falling apart. If the earth/ground is rock solid and rigid, could this indicate a stubborn or inflexible stance you are holding? Is there excavating and digging of a new foundation? This could indicate that you are in the process of building new foundations for yourself in a relationship, career, new belief system or any aspect of your life. Is the earth being moved by a shovel, plough or bulldozer? If so, how much effort is required to move it? How much effort do you feel you are putting into your current endeavours to make changes in your life or your physical world?

The amount of earth or soil may indicate an imbalance in the four elements of your being. For example, too much earth may indicate too much focus on the physical, whereas not enough earth may represent that you have not placed enough emphasis or focus on your physical body or the actions in your daily life. Since earth also symbolizes the place of manifestation and materialism, the amount of earth may indicate that you need to finish a project or manifest something. Alternatively, it may reflect that you have placed too much emphasis on materialism or not enough on generosity. Your feelings will help you determine whether you need to manifest something in your life (feelings of emptiness, boredom or unfulfillment), or whether you are placing too much emphasis on materialism (feelings of greed, guilt, or pride).

Is the land familiar to you? Does it bring you comfort? These will also help indicate if your current path is favourable to your desires and goals. If you are on unfamiliar ground, this may mirror your waking time feelings of being in unfamiliar and possibly uncomfortable activities, relationships, feelings or undertakings.

Landscapes

Desert

Often deserts are dry, barren landscapes that may indicate your own lack of water element (emotions, spiritual flow) or be akin to "thirsting at the well" (feeling empty, numb, void or dry inside). Does the desert bring you a sense of peace and fulfillment, or loneliness and foreboding? How do you relate to desert energy and what feelings does it create within you? Deserts may indicate the need to use the resources available at this time, or that there is hardiness in your struggles. Deserts are environments of extreme conditions, which may mirror your own life and your feelings that conditions are extreme, harsh, demanding or overwhelming at this time. Deserts may indicate that you need to learn to adapt in some unique ways at this time to survive. A desert could remind you that you can find beauty and success in your life even under the harshest of conditions, and that this can strengthen you. Deserts are also seen as places of survival and where vision quests have been undertaken (an opportunity to open and invite spiritual revelations to occur).

Forest

A forest reflects your inner and outer world (environments). Forests are places of birth (creation), growth, and death. Your forest may indicate how well you are thriving, depending on the type and health of the vegetation. If the forest is thick with tangle and there is no easy path to be found, this may indicate your sense of frustration at current challenges or roadblocks, or that you cannot see you way (path, direction) clearly at this time. A forest may indicate your current creative state. If you fear forests for any reason, this may indicate current fears about anything, but especially about expression and creativity. A forest may also represent the expression "you can't see the forest for the trees," meaning that you may be overwhelmed by something (the bigger picture) and unable to see the individual steps or beauty in the current situation.

A deciduous forest (trees that drop their leaves in fall) may be a reminder to pay attention to the rhythm; flow and natural order of things in your life and don't fight them at this time. A coniferous forest (trees that retain their leaves/needles all year) may indicate how best to protect yourself as you grow and strive on your journey, regardless of the current conditions in your life. A rainforest may indicate undiscovered aspects of self, new or mysterious growth (patterns that are new), or hidden wonders about yourself that you are about to unfold. If you think forests are full of monsters, darkness and the unknown, this may reflect fears about your own darkness (unknown parts of self), about others in your life feeling like monsters, or about unbearable relationships that are taking place. Of course your feelings about the forest (friendly or fearful) will be the best indicator of what the forest is trying to tell you about your life at this time.

Marsh/Bog/Swamp

Because they involve water, marshes and bogs often reflect emotional or spiritual states of being. Marshes and bogs are often stagnant, which may reflect not only your stagnant emotions, but also how you feel about your life in general. Do you feel bogged down by any relationship, situation or activity? Do you feel sluggish, inactive, and dull? Perhaps you aren't moving along smoothly or swiftly. Are you bored, lacklustre or feeling weary? All these could be what your marsh or bog indicates about your life.

Bogs, marshes and wetlands are also places of transition — life, death and rebirth. Examine your life to see what needs to die, crumble or decompose in order for something new to take its

place and grow within or around you. In order for new life to spring anew in you, something must be let go of, broken down or torn down first. These are transitional phases and reflect what is currently shifting and changing in your life. Some people associate swamps with a place of fear, danger or mystery. Be aware of what feelings or experiences you associate with swamps to better understand what it is reflecting about you or something going on in your life.

Meadow/Field

Meadows and fields are open spaces that may indicate a sense of freedom, choice and openness to new ideas and seeing far. Or do open spaces and choices make you uncomfortable or anxious? How you feel about open spaces is the best indicator of how this field or meadow relates to your current journey and activities in life. Meadows and fields can be about abundance, nourishment and fertility, depending on what is growing in your field (or is it barren?). A meadow can be a place of relaxation, silence and soft growth. It can reflect the need for replenishment and hope, or indicate joy and fun. It all depends on how you feel when you see or experience a meadow or field in your dream or waking-time encounter.

Mountain

As a landscape, mountains can be about discovering your own spiritual powers because they reach so far towards the heavens. Mountains (especially if climbed) may indicate current obstacles in your life or challenges. How big is the mountain and how challenging is the climb? This will help you understand the enormity of your current life challenges and how well you feel you are managing them. Mountains may reflect your loftiness or feelings of superiority; conversely, they may indicate a healthy feeling of empowerment and closeness to spirit (or to Your Creator). Mountains can be reminders that spiritual attainment or enlightenment can be yours if you have the courage to overcome the obstacles and challenges before you. A mountain may lift your spirits or give you a new perspective on things going on in your life (a higher perspective). It can also indicate that your intuition is heightening and that your creativity is at a peak, or that you have reached your peak in regard to any current endeavour or undertaking. What has been your personal experience with mountains and how did you feel when in the presence of one or when you saw one? This too will help you understand the meaning of your mountain as a reflection of self.

Sandy Soil/Beach

Beaches are sandy and usually not supportive when walked on. Do you lack support in any area of your life? Do you feel like you are sinking, or that your current foundations are shifting and moving in unexpected ways? Perhaps you find the beach a place of great comfort, joy, relaxation and play. If so, this mirrors what you are currently experiencing in your life. Because beaches are associated with water and water has healing qualities, your beach scene may indicate the need for healing and balancing, and/or the need to bring more of the water (emotional) element into your life. A beach can offer you the opportunity to find creative (water element) and unique approaches to any current challenges in your life. Or, it may simply indicate the need to rest, relax, rejuvenate and have some fun time or down time from the stresses or burdens in your life. The feeling you have about the sandy soil or beach will be the best indicator of whether you feel healthy and supported, or unsupported, unsafe or insecure.

Steep Landscape

Is the land steep and difficult to climb (indicating your path or journey seems awkward or difficult to manage)? Does it feel like a challenge you are up to, or one that takes too much energy to climb or overcome? The feelings associated with the steep landscape will help you understand what currently lies before you. You may be trying to achieve or create something in a relationship, work endeavour, or any aspect of your life by climbing a steep landscape.

Valley

Some may see valleys as places of security and safety (depending on your personal experiences of valleys). But because they are often sheltered areas that offer protection, they may reflect a need for safety, security, protection or sheltering, or that you are currently experiencing these feelings. Valleys can be places of great fertility or desolation, and thus can reflect growth and great creative expression depending on what is growing (or not) in your valley. This reflects what your feelings and inner reality are like at this time. We often see our lives in a series of highs and lows, or peaks and valleys. Do you associate valleys with a low period of your life, or a time when your energy is low or your emotions are not deemed favourable? If so, is the low period due to boredom, inactivity, lack of creativity, lack of movement, or apathy about something or some situation in your current life? What has been your personal experience of being in a valley? How did it feel? This should offer clues as to how your valley reflects something about your life at this time.

Gardens and Plants

Flower

Flowers are the blooming of the plant, shrub or tree. They are the cumulation or expression of beauty in your life. Something is blooming, flourishing, thriving, expressing or growing in your life. Is it a relationship, a new idea, a new belief, an endeavour, or a goal finally coming into bloom? Have you just finished a project or started a new pattern of behaviour that has become a positive habit or personality trait? Look inside yourself and think about what is going on in your life — what is flowering or filling you up? Have you hit a pinnacle, high point or peak in regards to something in your life? What is expressing itself in the most beautiful, colourful and bountiful of ways?

Flowers are colourful, and the colour may indicate a feeling, such as tickled pink, or a chakra and its overall state of function at this time (see sections on colours and/or chakra in this dictionary

470

for further clarification). Flowers often have fragrances and may indicate a heightened sense (intuitive or otherwise) or remind you of a person, place or event depending on your memories of the flower and its fragrance.

Each variety of flower has its own message and meaning. If you want to know more, there are entire books to help you understand the teachings of each variety. Understanding your personal associations will be of greatest benefit. For example, it is often believed that a red rose is a sign of love, whereas lilies are often used at the time of death (place in the dead person's hands) and therefore indicate the end or transition of something in your life. It is up to you to search your personal date bank (memories) for your associations with the flower to help you understand what it is reflecting in your life at this time. Flowers are also used for healing, such as herbs or as flower essences. Sometimes you will dream or see a flower or herb because you require it (or its essence) at this time in your life. Consider this and read about it in a book on herbs or flower essences to see if it lines up with what you require in your life at this time for your health and healing. The number of petals on a flower can also be of great significance, so if the number of petals stands out for you it may be a numerological associa-

tion you are required to read about (see section on numbers in this dictionary for further clarification).

Garden

A garden is something you design, create, plant (seeds of ideas), grow, nurture and develop according to your own tastes. A garden reflects your inner reality and how well it is thriving. It tells you whether you are caring well for yourself, whether you have planned ahead (for beautiful things to grow in your life), or whether you are neglecting yourself (dying, withering or weed-filled gardens). Gardens are the ability to take life goals, ideas and ideals and put them into action in your life. Gardens grow and produce, bearing fruits and edibles (nutrition). This corresponds with the growth in your life at this time. Something specific growing in your garden, such as a vegetable, may indicate the need to incorporate that into your diet at this time. Caring for your garden indicates your willingness to care for yourself (physically, emotionally, mentally and spiritually). Are you willing to plant, explore, and see what grows? Or do you allow your garden to accumulate waste, garbage or other non-essential items to build up and block the growth of your garden?

Plants/Shrubs

Plants, like trees and flowers, indicate your level of growth or your overall state of growth. They show lack of growth or the fecundity (richness) of your development, depending on the overall condition of the plant/shrub. Healthy growth is evidence that your divine nature is present and expressing itself. Plants (like your energetic self) have roots and (like your self) rely on the elements (water, air, earth and sun) to thrive and grow. So plants also indicate how well rooted (grounded) you are. They tell you if you are in bloom or wilting, taking care of yourself or in need of care, thriving or dying, and bearing fruit or undernourished. They also indicate the health of your overall growth and energy systems, for the plant realm is symbolic of your chi or energy system in general. If your plant is healthy, sturdy and thriving, this reflects your own state of well-being. A plant in poor condition, wilted or dying, also reflects your current life situation —whether it is about a relationship, a belief, a work situation, an endeavour, or any event unfolding in your life. You must make the connection between the plant's state of overall development and health and your own. Shrubs tend to grow laterally rather than vertically (such as trees do) and may indicate a stretching of your awareness (or becoming more aware of your subtle bodies or auric field).

Soil/Dirt

What is the condition of the earth or soil? Do you associate dirt with feeling dirty, bad, or as if you are doing or feeling something wrong in your life? Is the ground beneath your feet solid and bearing your weight well? Is the earth under your feet supporting you, or is it sandy, shifting, or allowing you to sink? This will help you understand whether your current endeavours, activities, relationships, thoughts, attitudes, beliefs and feelings are supportive. Is the soil rich and ready to plant seeds in? Or is it lying fallow and/or barren, unused and perhaps waiting for you to use it for growing or planting new seeds (ideas) for the future? Is the land rich with growth or dry with neglect? All indicate the state of your well-being, how you view your journey at this time, and whether you think you are in poor condition or able begin a new endeavour (grow something new). See Earth/Ground/Land for more info.

Weeds/Overgrown Garden

An overgrown garden may indicate that things or situations feel out of control or are overwhelming you in your life currently. It may further indicate that you are unable to manage or cope with a relationship, workload, situation or events occurring in your life. Gardens are places where you get to choose and control your environment, growth and willingness to take responsibility for your own life journey. Weeds (depending on what you consider to be a weed, herb or plant) may indicate that you have not been caring for yourself well, or that you have been weeding out what no longer serves you well. Weeds are often considered

nuisances, so they may indicate that someone or something is a nuisance, irritant, annoyance or hindrance to your overall growth at this time. How well is your garden cared for? Is it flourishing? This will tell you how well you are looking after yourself and in what areas you need to take better care of yourself.

Trees

Trees are living creatures and symbolic of your energy systems (chakra system). The Tree of Life is a Qabalistic symbol and metaphor for understanding your life, and it shows you a system or method for achieving enlightenment. The Tree of Life is your chakra system as seen through the eyes of Jewish mysticism. It teaches you about taking ideas from your spirit (crown of tree) and how to manifest these ideas in your life (the roots). Each part of the tree helps you to understand some part of your chakra system and the current health of your physical body, emotions, mind and spirit. Because trees bridge heaven (crown) and earth (roots), a tree is also about your level of consciousness and growth. Trees are considered the Tree of Knowledge and can help you understand just how much you know about yourself and the world around you. Buddha found enlightenment while sitting under a tree, and therefore trees are considered ancient symbols of power and illumination. Every tree has its own energy and symbolism. Every tree is a source of energy, healing and creativity in its own unique way. There are entire books devoted to understanding the messages that each tree brings to the human realm. To investigate your type of tree more thoroughly, it is suggested that you research using one of these books. But you can also begin the process of understanding the type of tree by asking yourself what personal associations you have with it.

Apple Tree

Because they bear fruit, apple trees are often associated with something coming to fruition or cumulation in your life. In the Christian tradition, apple trees have been associated with forbid-

den fruit and desires. Some people believe that "an apple a day keeps the doctor away," and therefore that apple trees are indicators of a strong and healthy body and energy system. What are you personal associations with apple trees? This will be the most helpful indicator of what your apple tree represents in your life at this time.

Branches

The branches of a tree can reflect your siblings or friends (because they are branches of your being), but they can also be about how much growth you feel you have achieved. For example, no branches may indicate you feel you have accomplished nothing. Prickly branches (such as those of a pine tree) could indicate a prickly nature, a need to defend or protect yourself, or that you require sharper and clearer boundaries. A tree full of healthy growing branches may indicate you feel you have achieved or acquired much, met goals or are aspiring (reaching out) toward greater targets. Perhaps you feel you have branched out in a new direction, grown or extended yourself in some new way.

Cactus

A prickly cactus may represent the need for stronger boundaries, or that you have a prickly attitude. But a cactus also has the ability to thrive and survive in harsh conditions, so it may represent your ability to adapt and/or find and express your beauty and strength in all conditions. What are your personal thoughts about cacti? This will be the most powerful indica-

tor of what a cactus is trying to show you about yourself at this time.

Cutting Down a Tree

Felling a tree may symbolize that you are cutting yourself off from your growth or your energy systems. It may also indicate you are not willing to see something about your divine nature, family tree (family members) or current growth. You may be ending a relationship or an endeavour, or cutting yourself off from a situation that you find unbearable or that you're not willing to participate in. It can also reflect an unhealthy conscious (or unconscious) decision to cut yourself off from life or life-challenging situations. It could also symbolize cutting yourself up (that is, demeaning or belittling yourself). Perhaps it is an end of something. Or, it may indicate the need to end something that no longer serves you well, especially if the tree being cut down is dead or in poor health. Note the feelings you have about cutting down the tree to help you further understand how this reflects what is going on in your life.

Fruit in a Tree

A tree that has fruit in it may indicate that something in your life has come to fruition, completion, or cumulation, or that you are bearing fruit with some current endeavour, situation, relationship or goal.

Knots or Holes in a Tree

Often blockages and congestions in chakras are indicated by knots or holes in a tree, whereas thickness or thinness may show you how much flow or activity an individual chakra currently has. Note at which level of the tree there is a knot or hole (lower, middle or upper section of trunk). This will help you understand at which chakra level there may be a blockage or congestion. A knot could suggest a hole in your thinking, or that you are missing some important fact or not seeing the whole picture. Perhaps you feel tied up in knots inside (emotionally) or unable to move forward or grow in a some area of your life.

Leaves on a Tree

The canopy, crown or leaves of the tree are indicative of your crown or seventh chakra. Thus, they show you how connected you feel to your higher self, soul, spirit, intuition and the world of your guides. Lots of leaves and a thick canopy can convey a message that you feel you have a crowning glory or success currently occurring in your life. Deciduous trees drop their leaves in the fall, so they

may indicate a need to pay attention to the unique rhythm at play within your life currently and work with it. Remember that there are times to germinate, blossom, shed and harvest. Pay attention to the stage or level of growth of your tree. An evergreen (coniferous) tree may indicate a need for adaptation and persistence at this time in your life in order to be successful. Ask yourself whether you are using what is available to you, whether you are being too sensitive (prickly or sharp like a pine needle), or whether you are remaining strong and persistent. Note the health of the leaves to further help you understand how they reflect your health and growth. Also, note the colour of the leaves, since they may represent your emotions.

Oak Tree

Often associated with majesty and calm strength (the mighty oak tree). An oak tree may indicate your own strength and endurance at this time. Because it has acorns, you may find that this indicates a fertile time for you or a time of great creativity or fruition. Think of how a single acorn holds the pattern and ability to grow into a magnificent and strong tree. An oak tree also indicates something about you and your stage of growth and strength at this time.

475

Planting a Tree

May indicate you are re-establishing your connection to nature, your energy system or show your willingness to begin a new growth pattern or habit. It may show you are awakening to new states of understanding or perception, or that you are blossoming new and stronger inner potentials. Planting trees are an act of affirmation and willingness. It may represent that you are willing to plant (begin) something new in your life and are willing to nurture it. What goals or desires are you wishing to begin or fulfill in your life at this time?

Roots of a Tree

The roots of a tree reflect your first chakra or root chakra. Roots may indicate your family roots, family tree, or the amount of support you feel you get from your family (friends and community as well). Roots indicate the health of your first chakra. Are they unhealthy, withering, dying, or absent?

The state of the roots will help you understand how rooted or grounded you feel, and how safe and secure you feel in your current life situations (and within yourself).

Trunk of a Tree

The trunk of a tree reflects your physical body (trunk) as well as your chakras 2 through 6, depending on what level of the tree catches your attention the most. If it is the base of the tree, then it is likely reflecting a lower chakra (second or third). The middle of the tree may indicate your third or fourth chakra, and higher up on the tree may represent your fifth or sixth chakra. Watch for indicators such as knots, holes, thickness or thinness of the trunk to help you understand the health of the chakra being reflected. For example, a thick, sturdy trunk may represent your own strength, durability or hardiness. Conversely, a thin trunk may represent that you feel disempowered or unable to stand up for yourself as well as you would like.

Appendix A – Your Personal Symbol Dictionary

As you work with the symbols that appear in your dreams, write down how each symbol relates to your life experiences. Over time, you will develop your own, personalized dictionary of dream symbols.

Symbol	Meaning for Me

Appendix B – Worksheet for Seer's Path Method of Interpretation

Feelings	Background or Setting	Theme
Most Significant Symbol	**Meaning of Symbols**	**Dream's Meaning**

Title:

Summary:

Decision and Application

Appendix C – Worksheet for Magical Path Method of Interpretation

Most Significant Feeling	Most Significant Symbol
Meaning of Symbol	**Waking-Hour Connection**

Appendix D – People Who Appear in Your Dreams

Dream Character	Relationship	Characteristics, Traits or Meaning

Bibliography

Adam. *DreamHealer*. Dreamhealer.com, 2003.

Andrews, Ted. *Animal-Speak*. Woodbury, MN: Llewellyn, 2002.

Bach, Richard. *Illusions: The Adventures of a Reluctant Messiah*. New York: Delacorte, 1977.

Baker, Ron. *Revelations for a Healing World: A Personal Process for Resurrecting the Soul*. New York: Children of Light, 2001.

Barasch, Marc Ian. *Healing Dreams*. New York: Riverhead, 2000.

Bear, Sun, Wabun Wind, and Shawndoese. *Dreaming with the Wheel*. New York: Fireside, 1994.

Brennan, Barbara. *Hands of Light*. New York: Bantam, 1988.

Bruyere, Rosalyn. *Wheels of Light*. New York: Fireside, 1994.

Cameron, Julia. *The Artist's Way*. New York: Tarcher/Putnam, 1992.

Castaneda, Carlos. *The Art of Dreaming*. New York: Harper Collins, 1994

Chopra, Deepak. *Ageless Body Timeless Mind*. New York: Three Rivers, 1993.

———. *The Seven Spiritual Laws of Success*. San Rafael, CA: Amber-Allen, 1995.

Diamond, H. and M. Diamond. *Fit for Life*. New York: Warner, 1987.

Eadie, Betty J. *Embraced by the Light*. Placerville, CA: Golden Leaf, 1992.

Foundation for Inner Peace. *A Course in Miracles*. New York: Viking, 1996.

Freud, Sigmund. *The Interpretation of Dreams*, 1938.

Gawain, Shakti, *Creative Visualization*. Novato, CA: Nataraj, 2002.

Gerber, Richard. *Vibrational Medicine*. Rochester, VT: Bear & Company, 2001.

Hay, Louise. *Heal Your Body*. Carson, CA: Hay House, 1998.

———. *Love Your Body*. Carson, CA: Hay House, 1989.

Hurtak, J.J. *The Book of Knowledge: The Keys of Enoch*. Los Gatos, CA: Academy for Future Science, 1982.

Jung, C.G. *Memories, Dreams, Reflections*. New York: Vintage, 1961.

Magdalena, Flo Aeveia. *I Remember Union: The Story of Mary Magdelena*. New Britain, CT: All Worlds, 2004.

Mayne, John and Coleman Barks (trans.). *Open Secrets: Versions of Rumi*. Boston: Shambhala, 1984.

Myss, Carolyn. *Anatomy of the Spirit*. New York: Three Rivers, 1996.

Newton, Michael. *Journey of Souls*. Woodbury, MN: Llewellyn, 2002.

———. *Destiny of Souls*. Woodbury, MN: Llewellyn, 2000.

Pike, Diane Kennedy. *Life as a Waking Dream*. New York: Riverhead, 1997.

Siegel, Bernie. *Love, Medicine and Miracles*. New York: Harper Collins, 1986.

Sugrue, Thomas. *There Is a River: The Story of Edgar Cayce*. New York: Dell, 1967.

Tachi-ren, Tashira. *What Is Lightbody?* Lithia Springs, GA: New Leaf Distributing, 1999.

Talbot, Michael. *The Holographic Universe*. New York: Harper Collins, 1991.

Tanner, Wilda B. *The Mystical Magical Marvelous World of Dreams*. Tahlequah, OK: Sparrow Hawk, 2004.

Thurston, Mark A. *How to Interpret Your Dreams.* Virginia Beach, VA: A.R.E. Press, 1978.

Walsch, Neale Donald. *Conversations with God: Book 1.* Charlottesville, VA: Hampton Roads, 1995.

———. *Conversations with God: Book 2.* Charlottesville, VA: Hampton Roads, 1997.

———. *Conversations with God: Book 3.* Charlottesville, VA: Hampton Roads, 1998.

———. *The Little Soul and the Sun.* Charlottesville, VA: Hampton Roads, 1998.

Weil, Andrew. *8 Weeks to Optimum Health.* New York: Ballantine, 1997.

Yogananda Paramahansa. *Autobiography of a Yogi.* Los Angeles: Self-Realization Fellowship, 1979.

Zukav, Gary. *The Dancing Wu Li Masters.* New York: Morrow, 1979.

———. *The Seat of the Soul.* New York: Fireside, 1989.

Index

Fence, 449
Fender, 416
Fever, 301
Fibroid, 229
Fiddle, 344
Field, 204
Fifteen, 351
Filing cabinet, 322
Finger, 229, 337
Fire, 151, 271, 449–50
    firefighter, 362
    fireplace, 251
    fire truck, 406
    fireworks, 264
Fish, 179–80, 314
Fishing boat, 402
Five, 349
Flag, 450
Flame, 151, 271, 449, 450
Flashlight, 450
Flood, 427
Floor, 252
Flower, 470
Flowing, 155
Flu, *see* Cold
Flute, 344
Flying, 155–56
Flying saucer, 411
Fog, 434
Foot, 229–30
Football, 379
Forefinger, 229
Foreign, 450
    place, 204
    vehicle, 406
Foreigners, 204
    see also Strangers
Forest, 205, 467
Forgetting, 156
Fork, 331
Foundation, 252

Fountain, 427
Four, 349
Fourteen, 351
Fox, 180
Freezer, 326
Fridge, 327–28
Frog, 180
Front seat, 416
Fruit, 314
Fruit in a tree, 474
Fuel pump, 416
Funeral, 293–94
Furnace, 326–27

Gadgets, 335
Gallbladder, 230, 272
Gambling, 379
Games, 375–83
Garage, 245
Garbage, 450
Garbage truck, 406
Garden, 205, 471
Gardener, 363
Garrotte, 400
Gas station, 245
Gas tank, 417
Gate, 451
Gemini, 192, 373
Ghost, 363
Giant, 363
Gifts, 458
Giraffe, 180
Glass, drinking, 331
Glider, 410
Glove, 279
Glue, 451
Goat, 180, 192
Gold, 286, 340
Golf, 379–80
Goose, 180, 216
Gopher, 181

Acknowledgements

Thank you to Linda Jenkins, my editor and friend, who has masterfully polished my book for publication with her remarkable talents and incredible mind. Thank you to Mary Hunter for her keenness and skills with the graphic design and production. For my friend Gerald Thomas, who undertook cover design of the first edition with enthusiasm and proficiency, my gratitude. You came back into my life with perfect timing!

For my mother Norleen, and my step-father Gordon Banks, I thank you for your support to get this book published especially with the initial twists and turns it took (a.k.a Kirkland Lake incident). Special thanks for my aunt Judy who went out of her way to help me when I moved to Ottawa.

Thanks to so many of my great friends who have lovingly supported all my efforts to pursue not only dream work but all my endeavours. Thanks to Jackie Cave, Anna Elmberg Wright, Paul and Marisa Gay, Marjory and Bruce MacMartin, Johanne Mercier, Tina Pane, Donald Paul, Dorothy Reno, Samantha Reynolds, Margaret Quigley, Janice Ryan Whitton, Debra Wright and Ann Tudor.

I am hugely grateful to all the students and clients I have had over the years. Know that you have been my teachers and educated me more than any book or classroom ever could. There are too many to list; you know who you are.

And for some of the wonderful people who have affected my life in a myriad of ways: Grant Banks, Peggy Brigham, Joanne DeGasperis, Lauren Dobrowolski, Anne Dranitsaris, Michelle Garieri, Lynda Goldson, Gord Grobelney, Ric Micucci, Sergio and Brittany Micucci, Susan Moore, Olga Nikolajev, Allaine Nordine, Doug Palframan, David Palframan, Richard Palframan and Linda Price.

To Sara Simpson who heard my signal for more funds to get this book published and readily offered a donation. Thank you, Sara.

And finally to Vera Lawrence, my first spiritual teacher and healer, who lovingly opened the doors to my remembering and made this book possible — my eternal gratitude.

About the Author

Kerry Palframan began delving into the power of the seen and unseen to help her overcome life-threatening illnesses. A registered nurse by profession, Kerry is a gifted teacher, healer, intuitive and spiritual medium who offers the wisdom of the esoteric and Ancient Mystery School teachings in a powerful series of workshops. She also gives individual intuitive readings and has produced a guided meditation CD.

Kerry describes herself as an Indigo Dreamer — an intuitive (Indigo) guide to the spirit world (Dreamer) who helps individuals find and hold a vision of their potential to fulfil their soul's journey. She assists her clients and readers in creating peace within themselves, their family, and their community, and on the planet. She gently and expertly leads others toward personal enlightenment, clarity, direction, insight, validation and vision.

Kerry currently resides in Ottawa, Canada and offers workshops at colleges, universities, school boards and from her home. She travels to teach and speak upon request. She spends part of the winter in Florida.

Email Kerry at info@indigodreamer.com.

www.indigodreamer.com

CPSIA information can be obtained at www.ICGtesting.com
225044LV00003B/3/P